Bandit Mentality captures Lindsay 'Kiwi' O'Brien's Bush War service from 1976-1980 at the coalface of the Rhodesian conflict. Starting in the BSA Police Support Unit – the police force's professional anti-terrorist battalion – he served across the country as a section leader and a troop commander before joining the UANC's political armies as a trainer and advisor.

Much has been written about the army's elite units, but Support Unit's war record was mainly unknown during the conflict and has faded into obscurity afterwards. Support Unit started poorly supplied and equipped, but the caliber of the men – mostly African – was second to none. Support Unit specialized in the 'grunt' work inside Rhodesia, with none of the flamboyant helicopter or cross-border raids carried out by the army. O'Brien's war was primarily within selected tribal lands – seeking out and destroying terrorist units in brisk, close-range battles with little to no support.

O'Brien moved from the police to working with the initial UANC deployment in the Zambezi Valley, where the poorly trained recruits were delivered into the terrorist lair; they had to learn fast or die. His account is a foreign-born perspective from a junior commander uninterested in promotion and the wrangling of Upper Command. O'Brien was decorated and wounded three times.

The author was born and raised in New Zealand – joining the NZ Army at 16 in order to run away from home. Afterwards, he roamed around Queensland, Australia on construction sites before heading off to London via Johannesburg. In South Africa, he stopped over and hitchhiked around before heading up to Rhodesia, where he eventually found work managing a tobacco farm. The farm lay inside the war zone – and two years later, after several incidents, he joined the BSA Police, where he was involved in the fighting between the government forces and nationalist insurgents until the ceasefire in December 1979. He was awarded the highest police gallantry award.

Subsequently, he has mined in Tasmania; rose to senior management in a retail chain in Queensland and Victoria; and has been running his own businesses for the past 20 years. Currently, he is writing and running a small business in Queensland.

BANDIT MENTALITY

HUNTING INSURGENTS IN THE RHODESIAN BUSH WAR, A MEMOIR

Lindsay O'Brien

Helion & Company

Helion & Company Limited
26 Willow Road
Solihull
West Midlands
B91 1UE
England
Tel. 0121 705 3393
Fax 0121 711 4075
Email: info@helion.co.uk
Website: www.helion.co.uk
Twitter: @helionbooks
Visit our blog at http://blog.helion.co.uk/

Published by Helion & Company 2017
Designed and typeset by Farr out Publications, Wokingham, Berkshire
Cover designed by Paul Hewitt, Battlefield Design (www.battlefield-design.co.uk)
Printed by Hobbs The Printers Ltd, Totton, Hampshire

ISBN 978-1-911512-02-8

British Library Cataloguing-in-Publication Data.
A catalogue record for this book is available from the British Library.

For details of other military history titles published by Helion & Company Limited, contact the above address, or visit our website: http://www.helion.co.uk

We always welcome receiving book proposals from prospective authors.

To my dear Sandra,
1950-2014

Contents

List of illustrations

List of terms and abbreviations

2IC	Second in Command.
A73	Police-issued backpack VHF radio.
Acorn	Radio callsign for Police Special Branch.
Aerial *spoor*	Trampled vegetation, broken brush and bloodstains on the ground.
AK	Kalashnikov range of assault rifle, including the AK-47 and AKM.
Alouette III	French-designed helicopter carrying a payload of four soldiers and crew of two.
Alpha bomb	Rhodesian-made bouncing anti-personnel bomb dropped by bombers.
Ambi cream	Skin lightener used by the fashionable African.
AP	Anti-Personnel.
APA	African Purchase Area.
Badger	CO Support Unit.
Badza	A blunt agricultural hoe.
Beaten zone	Ground where machine gun bullets strike – forming a cone.
Biltong	Strips of dried meat – known as 'jerky' to Americans.
Bivie	Overnight camping position.
'Black Boots'	Nickname for Support Unit. The police wore black boots and leather belts.
'Bludge'	Lazy, avoiding work (slang).
Braai	Barbecue (Afrikaans).
'Brothers'	An endearing term for the terrorists.
'Brown Boots'	General-duty police (slang).
BSAP	British South Africa Police: the Rhodesian civil police.
Bundu	Largely uninhabited wild region far from towns.
Canberra	1950s English Electric Canberra bomber.
Casevac	Casualty evacuation.
Charlie Tango	Phonetic alphabet for CT.
Chimurenga	Rebellion (Shona).
Chitupa	Identity document (Shona).

CID	Criminal Investigation Department (BSAP).
Clicks	One-thousand meters.
CMED	Central Mechanical Equipment Department, which repaired police vehicles.
CO	Commanding Officer.
CT	Communist Terrorist.
CV	Collective Village.
Cyclone One	Hawker Hunter jet.
Cyclone Seven	Helicopter.
DA	District Assistant, employed by the Department of Internal Affairs.
Dagga	Mud.
DC	District Commissioner.
'Doppies'	Expended shell cases (slang).
Fireforce	A helicopter force used to vertically envelop an army unit on the enemy.
'Floppies'	CT: they 'flop' when they're shot (slang).
FNLA	National Liberation Front of Angola.
Foxtrot Foxtrot	Phonetic for Fireforce.
'Freddy'	Slang for FRELIMO.
FRELIMO	Mozambique Liberation Front.
G-Car	Troop-carrying helicopter – general duties – armed with a twin MG.
Gandanga / Macandanga	Terrorist (Shona).
GC	Ground Coverage: police seconded to intelligence gathering.
Gomo	Hill (Shona).
Gooks	Slang for terrorists (taken from the Americans, but origins in Korea).
Grid	Lines on a survey map to enable the speedy pinpointing of positions.
Hawker Hunter	Supersonic fighter used for air-to-ground missions.
HDF	High-Density Force.
HE	High Explosive.
HQ	Headquarters.
Hyena	Armored troop carrier designed in South Africa.

Impi	A body of armed Zulu warriors involved in urban or rural conflict.
Intaf	Department of Internal Affairs.
'Ivory Tower'	Police General Headquarters in Salisbury (slang).
'Jam Stealers'	Base personnel (slang).
JOC	Joint Operational Command.
K-Car	Fireforce helicopter gunship armed with a 20mm cannon.
Kaya	An African house.
'Keeps'	Protected Village (slang).
Kopje	A rocky hill: rock slabs piled on top of each other.
Kraal	Name adopted from the Portuguese *curral*, which means 'African village'.
Ks	Kilometers.
'Lemons'	Operations that fizzled out to nothing.
LO	Liaison Officer.
Locstat	Exact map location (usually a six-grid reference number).
LSO	Lance Section Officer (temporary rank).
Lynx	Reims-Cessna F337 aircraft converted for military use.
'Ma-Sojer'	Soldier (slang).
Mantle	Support Unit radio callsign.
Mealie-meal	Flour derived from crushed maize kernels.
Mera	Stop (Shona).
MG	Machine Gun.
Mujiba	African youngster who scouted and worked closely with the terrorists.
NCO	Non-Commissioned Officer.
NSPO	National Service Patrol Officer.
OP	Observation Post.
OP 'Thrasher'	Operational area on the eastern border that commenced in 1976.
PATU	Police Anti-Terrorist Unit.
PF	Patriotic Front: the ZANU party in the 1980 elections.
PO	Patrol Officer: entry level for white police.
POU	Psychological Operations Unit (Psyops).
Povo	'The People' (Portuguese).
PR	Police Reserve: ex-police and other older civilian Reservists.
PT	Physical Training.

Puma	Armor-plated, landmine-protected truck.
PV	Protected Village.
R&R	Rest and Recuperation.
RAR	Rhodesian African Rifles: African infantry with white officers.
Rhino	Landmine-protected vehicle built on a Land Rover chassis.
RIC	Rhodesian Intelligence Corps: the army intelligence arm.
RLI	Rhodesian Light Infantry: battalion of white infantry.
RPD	Soviet-made, belt-fed light machine gun.
RPG	Soviet-made, shoulder-fired anti-tank rocket.
RPK	Soviet-made magazine or drum-fed light machine gun.
RR	Rhodesia Regiment: eight battalions of white Territorial soldiers.
SAS	'C' Squadron, Special Air Service: mostly deployed outside the country.
SB	Special Branch (BSAP).
'Sell-out'	CT term for traitors.
Selous Scouts	Multi-racial Special Forces unit.
SF	Security Forces: collective for army, police, air force and Internal Affairs.
SFA	Security Force Auxiliaries.
SFHQ	Special Forces headquarters.
Shackle code	Code replacing numbers with random letters for map references.
Sitrep	Situation report.
SKS	Soviet-made semi-automatic rifle.
'Skull Bash'	Assault, a beating.
SNEB	68mm air-to-ground missile.
'Snotty'	Gunfire (slang).
SO	Section Officer: a police rank equivalent to sergeant.
Sparrows	Tracker team.
Spoor	Tracks (Afrikaans).
Starlight scope	KKV night scope that is used on an FN rifle.
'Sunray'	Boss.
Superpro	Brand of canvas basketball boots popular with both sides in the war.
Terrorist	The government's label for the guerrilla forces.

Tour	Time a troop is deployed on operational duties (usually six weeks).
TTL	Tribal Trust Land.
UANC	United African National Council.
Veldskoens	Bush shoe.
Veldt	Open, uncultivated country or grassland.
WP	White Phosphorus.
Z42	Fragmentation rifle grenade fired off the muzzle of an FN rifle.
ZANLA	Zimbabwe African National Liberation Army.
ZANU	Zimbabwe African National Union.
ZAPU	Zimbabwe African People's Union.
ZIPRA	Zimbabwe Independent People's Revolutionary Army.

Preface

This is a memoir. This book is written from memory and cobbled notes jotted a couple of years after departing Rhodesia, but diaries were never kept at the time. It is not meant to be historically accurate, but simply a narrative of what I recall to the best of my knowledge. Not every incident or clash with the enemy is recorded, but simply enough to give a flavor of Rhodesian ground combat. This account is from my viewpoint only, as combat actions are often obscured; other witnesses may interpret history differently. Some names have been changed to respect their privacy and, while I may voice a skewed view, I try to be fair.

The British South Africa Police was the Rhodesian civil police that grew from the pioneering column of 1889 directly raised by Cecil Rhodes' British South Africa Company. The originals were employed by the company as paramilitary mounted infantry. In 1896, the force operated independently of the company, but retained the name 'British South Africa Police'. Whilst the force kept the core role of law enforcement, it also performed military functions throughout its history to 1980. During the 1966–1979 Bush War, the BSA Police provided the intelligence function and direct military encounters with part-time Police Anti-Terrorist Units (PATU) and Police Reserve (PR). The police also maintained a sizeable professional anti-terrorist component called 'BSA Police Support Unit'.

The BSA Police Support Unit initially honed its skills in the 1960s in anti-riot tactics, as well as providing a ceremonial piece for the governor's residence, border patrols and guards for political prison camps. When the terrorist war expanded in 1973, it swelled into a full-time, anti-terrorist police battalion of 31 troops (more than 1,200 men). Africans made up more than 90 percent and the remaining balance comprised European police. The light infantry, battalion-sized formation owned none of the specialist elements embodied in an army battalion like mortars, anti-tank, sustained fire machine guns, assault pioneers etc. The Support Unit specialized in the 'grunt' work inside Rhodesia, with none of the flamboyant helicopter or cross-border raids carried out by the army.

This account is a celebration of the African warrior – vividly remembered in the long, grinding marches, the dribbling sweat and brain-numbing boredom, the incessant flies and the constant dust under the blistering sun. Their stoic nature and patience are burnt in my memory – waiting through long hours and days in ambush and observation stints. The African police will be remembered for their gourmet meals of *sadza* and greens, laughing at hardship, operating uncomplaining in the cold and the rain, and the acceptance that combat equalled wounds and death. Without them, the police and Support Unit would have been impotent.

Acknowledgments

The author is grateful to the following people for permission to use their photographs:

Kiaran Allen
Ron Rink
Fiona Smith
Skip Dolega
Dave and Eileen Hughes

Map of operational areas

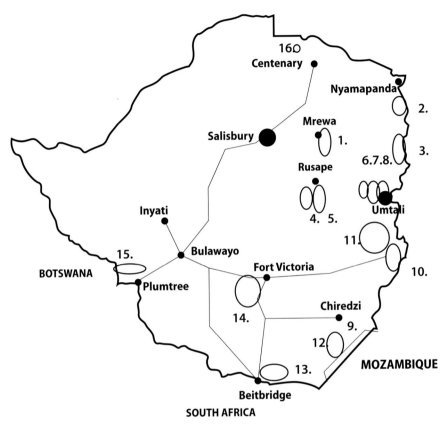

Map drawn by the author using a Rhodesia land tenure map from 1974 as a reference, which can be accessed at www.rhodesia.me.uk.

Key – TTLs operating within Support Unit and Special Forces:

1. Mangwende
2. Mudzi
3. Inyanga North
4. Wedza
5. Chiduku
6. Makoni
7. Manyika
8. Mutasa South
9. Gona re Zhou National Park
10. Mutumbara
11. Maranke
12. Matibi II
13. Diti
14. Chibi
15. Mpimbila
16. Gutsa
17. Centenary: Farming employment
18. Inyati: Uniform police work

1
Feeling the War: August 1976

By mid-1976, the Bush War had spluttered for 10 years. Clumps of nationalist fighters infiltrated the country from bordering African nations to challenge the white government, its laws and dominance. After years of start-stop infiltrations – each utterly destroyed by the Rhodesian Security Forces – by 1973, ZANLA finally managed a strong grip in the remote north-east. Like the American Wild West, African fighters attacked isolated white farms and government infrastructure – murdering some whites, but many more African residents. Despite major setbacks, they refined their strategy and skills so that by 1976, they were a permanent fixture inside the country – marching in from secure training bases inside Botswana, Zambia and Mozambique. It's at this point, I entered the conflict.

I slipped out of the Land Rover's vinyl seat to stretch and yawn. Whatever the good points about Land Rover seats, comfort wasn't one. Ian Jack (the driver) and I had just completed training and arrived at the Support Unit base, which was located on a commercial farm adjacent to the main road, 15 kilometers out of Rusape. Delta Troop, my posting, was already there; Ian was assigned command of Oscar Troop, also ensconced at this base. From the vehicle park, the headquarters – a simple farm manager's house – was the only visible building. An abundantly trodden volleyball court, which doubled as a parade ground, lapped up to the front verandah. Beyond the house, drab four-men tents – enough to house two troops, or about 60 men – were pegged out in straight rows, military style. From where I stood, these tents blocked the view of the perimeter.

Ian stalked off to the HQ to pick up the strings of command, while I stared at the drab sandbagged complex for a minute before an African constable approached. He was a strapping young lad dressed in a camouflage shirt, green shorts and black canvas runners, which were open, with laces undone; no socks or headgear.

"You Delta?" he smiled.

I nodded.

"I'll give you a hand."

The constable grabbed the handle of my black metal trunk that housed everything for a six-week deployment and helped to hoist it off the back of the Land Rover. Together, we lugged the heavy box across the flattened grass to a corner tent and dropped it inside the open flap. In the dapple light, I saw two other cots and trunks. The constable vanished before I could say thanks.

I stood back and surveyed my new home. The heavy canvas tent was old and worn from years of folding and unfolding, packing and unpacking, bleached by a roasting sun. Inside the tent, the men lived as comfortably as their ingenious minds permitted. A camp stretcher and a metal trunk were the only chattels. Personal knick-knacks dotted the sleeping area: paperback books, a travel alarm clock, crumpled comics, damp towels, safety razors and loose socks. Both ends of the tent opened and flaps were tied up (one end for the entrance and the other for the emergency exit), which provided fresh air. Four paces from the exit, a slit trench – hand-dug into the loamy soil – neatly converted into a small, muddy swimming pool in the summer rains. The trench faced surprisingly lovely countryside – lush grass paddocks in which white-faced Hereford cattle lazily fed.

Beyond the crumbling trench, the usual defensive fashion accessories were conspicuously absent. There were no trip flares, anti-personnel minefields, concertina barbed wire, elaborate pathways and ball bearing-stacked Claymore mines set to blast. Inside the lines, the typical defense gadgets were not available; no starlight intensifier scopes, infra-red glasses, fixed mortars, fixed line machine guns, recoilless rifles, stout bunkers, tall watch towers, or anything generally associated with an operational military base. A barbed wire cattle fence and personal weapons were the only defense. This was war on a shoestring.

I sorted out an empty space in the tent and opened the metal trunk. Inside, two thirds of the space stored food. The police paid cash – a travel and subsistence allowance – instead of issuing ration packs. Each man, armed with cash, bought and packed his own food. There was no cause to moan about tins of baked beans that frequently popped out of army ration packs, but whatever the individual tastes, rations had to be suitable for eating in the field – both portable and small enough for humping inside a backpack. Salisbury supermarkets were shopped for dry food. Trolleys were piled with tins of Spam and corned beef, soup packets, coffee satchels, condensed milk tubes, white sugar, tea bags, breakfast cereal, curry powder, white rice, mealie-meal, onions, fresh tomatoes, *biltong*, dark chocolate bars and cordial. Fresh food would be purchased in a town close to the operations base to supplement the dry rations.

Most police ate *sadza*, flavored with a relish. *Sadza* is a thick maize porridge, the staple African diet, similar to grits in the USA. To cook, boil water in a mess tin over a blue gas flame and gradually add white maize flour whilst vigorously stirring. Once the porridge reaches the consistency of thick dough – stodgy enough for a spoon to stand rigidly upright unsupported – the meal is removed from the heat. The diner used his fingers to eat – tearing off a manageable lump and dipping it into a separate vegetable relish of cooked tomatoes, sliced onions or fresh pumpkin leaves. *Sadza* filled the stomach in one meal. Those people who disliked *sadza* resorted to classical curry bully beef and rice, or other concoctions. During this bush tour, I learnt not to deprive the African of their basic diet. On one short patrol, I ordered all cooking to cease and supplied Pro-Nutro (a commercial breakfast cereal) eaten cold with powdered milk and sugar. After three days, deprived of their traditional diet, the constables became extremely irritable and sullen. Lesson learnt!

The rest of my trunk stored bits of replacement kit, clothes and footwear, and toiletries. Besides the issued kit, I carried four survival necessities: paperback novels, a dessert spoon, a can opener and rolls of decent toilet paper. I read popular authors like Wilbur Smith, Leon Uris and Michener. When not engaged on boring sentry duty or catching forty winks, reading killed the long, hot days. I visited Kingston's bookstore on R&R and stowed at least four books per deployment. A dessert spoon became another vital comfort tool. Used for slicing, dicing, eating, stirring and, if necessary, digging, a dessert spoon superseded the entrenching tool because the compact shovels were not available! A can opener, the tiny camping model, hung from the neck cord that retained my identity tags – necessary to open dinner. Toilet paper was the final, important consideration. Hard men wiped their arses on leaves and rocks and natural things, but I figured there were too many thorns, prickles or velvet hair (like buffalo beans) out there to assault my soft backside. I didn't need to reach for some prickly, thorny, poisonous leaf in haste and wear the pain for hours or days.

As there was no formal kitchen, or trained cooks or hot meals on demand, individuals were responsible for their own food preparation. The unit simply supplied the kitchen tools. In camp, a four-burner gas stove and a gas-operated chest freezer – compliments of a welfare fund – equipped the kitchen. In the field, a primus gas stove provided the heat. The men who returned from the field were left to their own devices. Police couldn't count on even an urn of weak hot tea. If the patrol walked in wet, knackered, or hot and famished, they still had to consider their own menu options and prepare their meal accordingly. With no steaming bain-marie chocked full of hot food – manned by sarcastic cooks poised ready to spoon it on an empty plate – men took shortcuts. In camp, hungry men teamed together to throw in their cans of goodies into a potluck stew, which was supplemented by fresh bread bought locally and spread with lashings of butter and strawberry jam. Sadly, the lack of greens in the diet burst out in red boils on the skin.

The base offered absolutely no facilities for the personnel. There was no social center with television, no canteen of any description, no air conditioning, no mess tent, no gym and no light entertainment such as movies, and no distractions apart from volleyball, transistor radios, thumbed Zane Grey books and 'Batman' comics. A rare steak and chilled beer at the Crocodile Motel in Rusape itself sufficed.

"All settled in?" asked Inspector Brian Gibbs when I reported to the headquarters building. He stood in the empty lounge room and sipped coffee from an enamel cup and smoked. I nodded. With origins in the Police Dog Section, he cut a figure of confidence and reassurance. In his late thirties, with a red face and chunky body, Brian reveled in the 'glamour' associated with counterinsurgency warfare. Under his stewardship, Delta Troop garnered a notable combat record and the Commissioner's commendations had just been awarded to the men after a successful engagement in the Honde Valley mid-1976. Gordon Kaye-Eddie, a section commander, and three constables had distinguished themselves in running battles. From the lounge, Brian guided me to a separate room. A constable, seated in a canvas director's chair, looked up from the radio transmitter, nodded and drew in on his cigarette. Brian sipped his coffee as he steered me to the map wall. I slipped my notebook out of my pocket and poised with pen in hand.

"At the moment, Oscar and Delta are reacting in this general area," he said, his arm sweeping widely across the maps. "There are police posts here in Rugoyi, but essentially, apart from Internal Affairs, there are no other Security Force callsigns."

Shit. Chiduku, Makoni, Manyika and Mutasa South TTL: an area measured in hundreds of square kilometers, with only 60 Support Unit men to call upon. I squinted closer … The 1:50,000 scale maps interlocked and pinned on the wall hinted at large clumps of hilly country. The closely knitted, brown swirly contour lines over painted light green denoted timbered hill country, which spelled seriously hard walking. The hills were bordered by flat pans, savannah and scores and scores of kilometers of open, level plains. Black caps, spread out like a linear rash, indicated long lines of African villages. There was only one road in and the same road out. How were we going to police that?

Later, I learnt that Makoni had been the center of rebellion against the settlers in 1896 and that the tribesmen and their traditional leaders were pronationalist, with a history agitating against the white government. Over many years, they had taken High Court action against government administration decisions and maintained a constant, low-key resistance to interference. The chiefs leaned heavily towards the nationalists.

"We are concentrating on southern Chiduku at the moment and just reacting to incidents in the other area," Brian smiled, as his enthusiasm bubbled. "We intend to protect the Dorowa Road by maintaining a presence right through the southern areas. We have patrols in there currently. Their callsigns are pegged there." He pointed to large white pins – each with the section's radio callsign penned on the flat top. His finger moved to smaller-colored pins dotted on the map. "These colored pins represent CT incidents. There are plenty of those both sides of the road. Update yourself by reading the incident log."

I gazed at the colored pins. Each color represented a separate incident type: red for a shooting contact, green for a CT sighting, blue for a landmine etc. The pins, dotted like multi-color acne, perfectly captured the fact that a sprawling, creeping, terror cancer that began here in early 1976, with one or two isolated incidents, had now escalated to several incidents a day.

"What about the terrorists?" I asked.

"They're a slippery bunch, about 30 to 40 strong in each TTL. They have the usual light weapons, are fairly mobile, reasonably ruthless and hard to find. That's your job."

I raised my eyebrows. Brian ignored my expression and went on to explain that Delta operated under the auspices of sub-JOC Rusape: the Joint Operations Command. The sub-JOC reported to JOC Umtali (OP 'Thrasher'), who reported to the National JOC in Salisbury. Each JOC was commanded by a committee, which was manned by representatives of the police, army, air force, Internal Affairs and Special Branch, and chaired by one of the members. Whilst Rhodesians continuously quoted the British Malayan campaign as a model of successful counterinsurgency warfare, they only plucked off parts of the strategy that appealed to them. The central reason why the Commonwealth won in Malaya was that a supreme commander was handed total responsibility – and the authority and the money – to get the job done.

Brian swept through the operational radio channels, the administration matters and base security. One section, of seven to nine men, always remained in base to provide the transport and radio backup. This was reinforced by personnel with minor injuries and the ever-present malingerer. If luck threw a hand in, one or two middle-aged police Reservists – male civilians on call-up from Salisbury – were available for truck driving and tedious radio operations. The base tasks rotated through each section so the men caught some useful sleep and maintained their equipment. As fragile as the base appeared to be in fortification and manning levels, there were no tales of a base being overrun and razed. ZANLA contented itself by standing well back – taking potshots and lobbing the odd mortar bomb.

There was no point asking about support arms; there were none. I noticed their absence when I farmed in Centenary. Trained in an army that operated within the range of artillery, I didn't see one piece in the Centenary area. The Rusape region mirrored the same. There was no artillery whatsoever to blast the enemy if they pinned down sections. There were no 81mm mortars to pepper shrapnel over the battlefield, no armor to screech in to save the day and no Engineers to lift the landmines. The only backup was a thinly dispersed airborne helicopter strike force, or a rare air bombing and rocket support from a much-stretched air force; however, it almost took parliamentary approval for an air strike. I remember a notice in one JOC that read something like: 'Why call in a $40,000 air strike when a $4 recce will do'.

The briefing was sketchy – a complete absence of information about enemy locations or intentions. The only facts were history colored with assumptions. I looked down at my notebook. I had written very little, as there was nothing of value to jot down. Later, I read the incident log … sheets and sheets of typed history. The lack of relevant, up-to-date information set the style of future briefings.

"There are three other section leaders," Brian mentioned offhandedly, "Gordon, Barry and Sergeant Zowah. You'll meet them in due course – they're in the scrub at the moment – and Paddy Allen, who's on leave."

After the 10-minute thumbnail briefing, Brian led the way out of the building and down the cement steps. Keen to get back to whatever he was immersed into, Brian lopped over to the tent lines. Spotting a tall sergeant, he called out and the lean man wandered to intersect us.

"Sergeant Barka," he greeted the man, "PO O'Brien."

Barka silently shook my extended hand and nodded curtly, his eyes curious, but unreadable. The sergeant stood over six feet tall, with a rangy, toned body, and his walk flowed easily in extended strides. With a long, haughty face and a matching prominent nose, he saw the world through piercing eyes that lacked humor and his facial expressions ranged from nothing to proud indifference.

"Introduce O'Brien to your men; he's the new section leader."

Brian turned about and stalked back to the HQ building.

Laughter drifted as we entered the tent line, where six constables lazed around an open tent flap. Two were playfully jostling and one stopped and hissed. Two others looked up from their checkerboard game and silently eyed me. One lay shirtless, sleeping in the sun, and opened his eyes. Another sat next to the groundsheet, which was covered with bits of a stripped MAG machine gun (the *Mitrailleuse d'Appui General* general-purpose machine gun) – the individual parts laid out as he lovingly applied rifle oil. Sergeant Barka stonily introduced me; then he pointed to each constable: Sibanda, Hove, Ruzawi, Chipanza, Mhiripiri and Elias. They surveyed me blankly. I read the message in their eyes … Jesus, another section commander! Easy come, easy go. I learnt later that they were from various tribal sub-groups – five with relatives in the police force – and that their service extended from one to eight years. The police force offered attractions for the African who spoke English and had learnt passable writing skills of regular pay, free medical, free housing, free uniforms, job stability and career direction: a chance to succeed and grow. Their skill mix was good. Among the seven were formidable trackers, fluent radio operators, MAG artists, a competent medic, average map readers and general roustabouts. Their only unspoken dilemma was the unknown, six feet plus, foreign-born section leader thrust upon them.

At 24 years of age, I had served in the New Zealand Army from 16 to 20 years old and departed after making a complete shambles of the career. I had held an idealized view of what a soldier should be and became unmanageable when I realized the wide gap between my ideal and the reality. The army shepherded too many non-thinkers, shielded by the 'Rule Book'. I was not an enthusiastic wind-up soldier, but more of a ratbag, stirrer, drinker and opinionated loudmouth, which easily upset career men. I acknowledged that men in senior positions viewed my anti-social antics and open questioning of the nonsensical rules with frustration, but I was never seeking a career. I loved the outdoor life and the smell of the bush, weapons handling and minor tactics, but hated the petty bullshit and politics that permeated the 'Army Machine': the grinding foot drill in the searing sun, dress-up parades for a visiting VIP, white-glove barrack inspections and autocratic authority invested in people with a petty and malicious axe to grind. While I loved the outdoors and tactical maneuvers, I still rankled at being the cog in the 'Machine' that directed the fighting. The 'Machine' took for granted that the higher the rank, the more gifted the individual. The top people's actions were rarely scrutinized. A senior commander may cause serious blunders and receive less condemnation than the lowest rank turning up on parade with dirty boots. The 'Machine' sanitized its own blunders, fended off criticism, rarely challenged its own methods and promoted corporate types. I flouted the rules with anti-social behavior.

I was particularly naïve on organizational politics. I believed in what other people call 'nonsense', such as a man being measured solely by his actions. I expended little energy to grease the wheels, to ingratiate myself, to curry favor. I didn't understand the fundamental need to cultivate relationships with men pulling the strings as essential to promotion and success. I walked my own path regardless of the fury of the organization. Looking back, while I produced good results, my behavior required a high degree of maintenance. Constantly stepping on people's toes did not endear future prospects. On the other side of the same coin, seriously unsuitable people rose through the ranks based purely on their political savvy – but I *was* hooked on the outdoor life.

I stood and chatted briefly with the crew. They smiled and laughed at a couple of tasteless jokes I tossed in, but an awkward silence followed each bout of conversation. Besides the experience gap – the canyon between veterans and newcomers – there was a definite cultural divergence. While I had worked shoulder to shoulder with African farm laborers and rural police, there was always a manager-worker relationship. I considered myself cheeky and flippant, characteristics I cautioned myself against around Africans in case I inadvertently insulted them. The tobacco fields taught the pitfalls of a second language. The African police spoke English as a second language and thus mentally translated words into Shona or Ndebele in their heads before speaking, which can lead to misunderstandings – particularly when English is laced with subtleties, irony and sarcasm. My concept of their world and their own intricate social designs were severely limited. I excused myself and wandered back to my tent to ensure my kit was ready for action.

The next morning, Brian spat out my very first mission: a cattle-dip sabotage. He presented the mission: "Take a tracking team, meet up with Special Branch outside Vengere Township and investigate. Track *spoor* if you find any and call base for support if required."

Just a couple of simple sentences, without the lengthy agonizing with staff officers over the conduct of the mission, he delivered a plain statement and pretty much told us to get on with it. The army lived with a systematic orders process: a warning order from above to prepare, initial briefing by commanders, a detailed intelligence examination from all sources, a minute examination of the ground on the maps and a briefing to the section handed the task. The police didn't deliver the same detailed briefings because the mission execution lay entirely in the hands of the section leader. A large amount of autonomy and judgment was handed to very junior leaders to get the job done. The police retained faith that junior ranks who investigated and documented the prosecution case at police stations, without obsessive hand-holding, were also capable of using their shrewdness to deliver a result in counterinsurgency. On my way out, I collected the relevant map and a shackle code, briefed Sergeant Barka to prepare three constables to be ready in 10 minutes for a quick tracking deployment and then walked smartly back to my tent.

Barka rounded up Mhiripiri, Ruzawi and Chipanza and split them between the transport: two South African Austral Hyena armored troop carriers – all tooled up to counter-punch. Each section member carried an FN R1 rifle (*Fabrique Nationale*) – manufactured under license in South Africa. The rifle, or variations, became the staple weapon for most Commonwealth countries and some European and South American armies. Stripped of the sling swivels and carrying handle, weighing 5kg loaded, with the stock and fore piece created from molded black plastic with a Zulu grenade sight attached to the gas plug, the FN was a formidable rifle. The only shortcoming: the plastic skin shone a black gloss, but that was eliminated later. The FN fired a 7.62mm NATO bullet, which packed an enormous punch. It was an elephant gun compared to the light munitions carried by current soldiers, so when the bullet hit, the man stayed hit. The bullet easily penetrated a small tree and killed the poor sod hiding behind it. Loaded with one 20-round box magazine, each man carried a minimum of four spare in pouches on the webbing belt and a further five boxes of ammunition stashed inside the backpack: 200 rounds of punching power. Unlike the army, the police FN only offered a semi-automatic; however, an amateur could file down the sear and convert the weapon to automatic. I didn't alter my rifle, as the FN performed poorly on automatic; it was hard to control and a waste of ammunition.

One man in each section carried the machine gun. As the police hierarchy strongly resisted the introduction of machine guns, Support Unit in 1976 owned a motley collection. Delta carried the famous magazine-fed Bren gun, converted to 7.62mm, and a heavy-barrel FN with a flimsy bipod and a 30-round magazine. My section had one of two MAG belt-fed machine guns. Designed in Belgium, this machine gun was devastating in the right hands. Nicknamed *Nata* (literally, 'drink much without pause') by the terrorists due to its firepower, the awesome rate of fire made or broke a skirmish. Robust, reliable, but worn, the 11kg machine gun was worth its weight in gold. The gunner lugged the MAG without a sling: 300 rounds in 50-round linked belts and another 500 rounds in linked ammunition spread among the riflemen.

We hurriedly departed the base – driving towards Rusape. The constables warily watched, anxious to gauge what sort of leader had been tipped on them, while I kept my eyes fixed on the countryside racing past. Meeting Special Branch on the outskirts of Vengere Township (an African satellite town on the outskirts of Rusape), we tailed their Land Rover into the Chiduku TTL. The Hyena rocked as it traveled on the dirt road, the V-shaped hull poised high over the chassis, designed to disperse the explosive force of a landmine. Inside, four men were belted in on a steel bench covered with a thin green carpet for the smallest comfort, designed to minimize spinal compression in the event of a landmine detonation. We sat with our backs to the outside, facing inwards. I watched the parched countryside flick past through the bulletproof glass opposite. I felt no fear, just curiosity and light aggression. Soon, the three-vehicle convoy arrived at the deserted cattle dip. The vehicles parked in a dust bowl and we jumped from the steel carrier. Nothing looked out of place. The cattle race, two six-foot parallel rock walls, shimmered. From the outside, the walls appeared untouched. What's the problem then, I wondered; however, once we confronted the entrance, we sighted large boulders piled up, blocking the race. The strenuous effort had to be a labor of love. To manhandle large, pumpkin-sized boulders for a hundred meters from the riverbed, across the flat open ground and heap them up inside the cattle race required determination and commitment. Scores of granite rocks stacked up waist high completely filled and jammed the cattle race. I wandered around the solid stone wall like a tourist – crossing the hardened clay pan cut to powdered dust by hundreds of cattle hooves. Barka sniffed the air and walked independently across the same dirt and paused to chat to Ruzawi, pointed to the ground and then wandered my way.

"*Mujibas*," he said.

"What?"

"Local boys," he added – pointing to the barefoot imprints in the soft dust next to the wall.

He eyed me like a voracious reader talking to an illiterate at a book convention. The ground told him the sabotage was the work of local youths, not armed terrorists. The typical terrorist wore shoes, whereas the civilians were mostly barefoot. This type of juvenile crime ran rampant throughout the tribal lands. Directed by terrorists, the youngsters dipped into sabotage, arson, break-and-enter, trenches dug across dirt roads, landmines and so on, and notched right up to murder. Cattle dips were an easy political target and, consequently, were vandalized. The terrorists ordered the peasants to stop using the dip. It was a white man's tool, they stridently insisted, and they didn't need it. They stressed that villagers herded cattle without dips before the appearance of the white man, so they concluded the program was a government plot to weaken their wealth. By 1978, most dips across the country had been closed and estimates of 250,000 head of African-owned cattle died in that year alone from disease that the dips were designed to control. The Special Branch duo wandered to the dip race, casually eying off the rock mass. One lit a cigarette and then both ambled back to their Land Rover. They were experienced detectives – sporting unruly hair and dressed in civilian clothes – and toting AKM rifles: the symbol of their murky intelligence profession.

"What now?" I asked the Special Branch driver, as he settled into the driver's seat and closed the door.

He shrugged, drew in on his cigarette, exhaled a white cloud and started the engine. I guessed that signaled the response. They skipped this job and, as the trackers couldn't find a set of shoe prints to follow, the hype deflated and we departed.

As the vehicles drove back to base, I observed the rolling countryside dotted with granite *kopjes*, thick wooded hills and over-grazed lowlands painted in Africa's harsh browns and drab green. In there, somewhere, roamed the enemy: invisible, crafty and wary. They wore fashionable 1970s denim trousers, with a variety of footwear which included platform shoes (all the rage at the time), at least two sets of shirts (one to shed if spotted) and headwear ranging from baseball caps or berets to slouch hats. Armed by the Chinese/Soviets, they carried a full range of weaponry from the SKS, AK range, to RPD and RPK and PKM machine guns, 60mm mortars and the RPG rockets. Hidden in bush caches, they stored 82mm mortars, 75mm recoilless rifles, 12.7mm machine guns and a variety of anti-tank landmines. The average ZANLA section was better armed than the police.

ZANLA recruits trained in military-structured camps inside Mozambique, and then walked into Rhodesia via scores of infiltration trails. Described as 'communist terrorists' by the government, as they were trained and armed by Communist China and the Soviet Union, they were more nationalist than communist. ZANLA set up operations in a tribal area, horribly murdered anyone likely to inform the police and, when the populace was under the thumb, the next ZANLA crew leapfrogged to the adjoining TTL and introduced the same pattern. Once inside the country, they're a motley crew acting more as bandits, looting and robbing. They were not the local population, not the classic 'farmers by day and fighters by night'; they were full-time combatants sponging off the poor rural people. They robbed buses at gunpoint, traumatized the passengers, busted into rural stores for cash, food and clothing, and robbed vendor vans, white-owned farms and unsuspecting villages – anything that was easy. Most people quickly handed over their cash or goods if an AK barrel was rammed up their nose. They also brutally murdered people suspected of being government spies, government workers or tribal leaders – anyone who got up their nose, as well as all whites that crossed their gun sights. Their killings sent a blunt message: cross us and we will sadistically torture and laugh at your excruciating screams; then butcher you in the most appalling and lingering way possible – calculated terror used as a tool to enforce their will.

While the government Security Forces pummeled the ZANLA forces in open combat, the guerillas were, essentially, underestimated by the Rhodesian Military Command. The underrated flaw was consistent with formally trained officers from West Point, St Cyr or Gwelo; if the opposing forces did not mirror their own professionalism, they were automatically deemed inferior. While ZANLA martial skills were imperfect – and there were plenty of marvelous examples of ineptitude that were laughable – they sat on an enormous, untapped reservoir of recruits. This huge manpower pool consisted of fatalists who had been brought up in unending poverty and grinding hardship, and who were mostly illiterate with no expectations in life, but they were extremely fit, psychologically hardened, were able to handle adversity and, over time, thwart the SF technological advantage. No matter how high their casualty rate soared, the survivors learnt new skills and baffled the forces pitted against them.

The terrorists' comfort zone lay in the tribal lands. In simple terms, the government divided the total land into a patchwork of white commercial farms, national parks and African reserves called Tribal Trust Lands. Each zone interweaved into the other, where commercial farms bordered tribal lands and either bordered national parks. For administration, the government divided the country into 54 districts, with each overseen by a European District Commissioner (DC). The DC and his white and African staff were the eyes and ears of the government in the tribal lands, where they conducted courts, supervised tax collection and gave advice to the chiefs and *kraal* heads on a wide range of subjects from cropping to education. The Tribal Trust Lands were set aside exclusively for Africans with no European settlements or business.

The Tribal Trust Lands equaled the Iron Age squatting in the 20th century. A single, rutted dirt road traversed from one end to the other, from which thousands of kilometers of dirt footpaths networked the villages. Electricity had not been introduced and there was no plumbing of any sort, none of the First World conveniences. The economy was, primarily, hand-to-mouth agriculture using cattle-drawn ploughs and hand tools, with some livestock such as cattle and goats. Industry did not exist. Time stood still.

Everywhere, there was an appearance of tranquility: long lines of basic houses – neat, patched, swept and orderly. The thatched grass conical roof and pole-and-*dagga* round wall construction – perfect for the climate, with nearby cattle pens constructed with cut logs and surrounded by plots of pumpkins, watermelons, peanuts and mango trees – looked serene. There was no outward sign of the swirling war and forceful political persuasion being mounted.

The average African farmer worked just to maintain life on an average of two hectares or less. The war brought constant demand for food from terrorists that sucked the poor dry. The older people had everything to lose and were reluctant supporters. They had their life's work sewn up in meager possessions and livestock. The war plundered what little they owned with no compensation. The educated class of nurses, teachers and storeowners supported ZANLA. Politicized and savvy, they played out their game on the edge of the war – tempted by its alluring danger without fully immersing themselves. The younger people, with nothing to lose, were enthusiastic about ZANLA and the excitement they created. Over the grueling years ahead, the adult population shifted slowly from passive to reactive. The Tribal Trust Lands became the primary battleground.

By mid-1976, the war flared from a bit piece played on obscure north-eastern border regions into a free-flowing conflict right across the north and eastern regions, with pinpricks in the west. In hindsight, 1976 marked the beginning of the end, but at that time, the war seemed eminently winnable.

2
Chiduku, Makoni and Manyika Trifecta: August 1976

The bus sank down on the dirt road at the edge of a business center – south of Matsika School, Chiduku – like a slain animal. The fierce flames licked off the thin metal skin – exposing the charred steel framework, which protruded like the ribs on a rotting carcass. The intense heat wiped off the bus company name painted on the side. A black scroll, with destination names, burst out of its glass enclosure above the driver's window and unraveled on the road. Tires metamorphosed into rubber bubbles – sinking the bus onto blackened rims. The surrounding bare road was coated in fine, black soot.

"They did a good job of that," Barka said offhandedly. He gave the blackened bus a cursory once-over; then turned his attention to the soot-coated road. The terrorists' shoe prints were conspicuous in the black dust.

"Where'd the passengers go?" I asked no one in particular. They had vanished.

I stared down the business center's deserted street. As the commercial hub, the business center was best described as a clump of retail shops – replicating the sun-baked Mexican town in American B-grade Western movies. Old and faded Coca-Cola, Colgate or Ambi cream advertising signs were tacked to the crumbling brickwork. Clint Eastwood riding on horseback in a 'Spaghetti Western' wouldn't have looked out of place.

Across the road from the destroyed bus, an African Council office stood gutted. A Peugeot station wagon parked outside felt the touch of arson. The searing flames wrote off the car. The African Council, an advisory board of local headmen tied into the Department of Internal Affairs (therefore tarred with white government influence), had again become a logical and easy target. The terrorists forcibly shut down all African Council offices within weeks of infiltrating a new area. A frail old man emerged from the shadows outside the burnt-out building, holding his battered hat in his hands, completely bewildered. He was the only visible person. The Ken Milne Special Branch team walked up to the plain brick and plaster building, scarred black with soot, and began their investigation.

Barka called out from the open field on the outskirts. I missed the words.

"Got *spoor*, Sarge?" I called back, as Barka shook out his three-man tracker team.

He nodded, grunted and, without waiting for me, commenced to track the dozen insurgents cutting across a furrowed field leading away from the burnt center. I radioed a quick report through to Brian. After a few snatched words describing the incident, I asked the escort team to wait with the Hyenas and bolted after the vanishing trackers.

Tracking was a core occupation in the Security Forces. Training emphasized tracking, and those personnel showing natural skills were whisked off to a tracking course to sharpen and expand the art. In some ways, the Security Forces were too heavily dependent on tracking; the tiny core of professional soldiers and the low ratio of soldiers to guerrillas forced the Security Forces to respond to incidents rather than cut them off at the pass. The African police displayed a mixture of tracking experience. A few spent their childhoods herding the family cattle and thus developed natural skills. Others were urban – born and raised – and couldn't track an elephant through snow. Barka possessed extraordinary expertise and appeared to be completely disinterested as he sauntered along, barely looking at the ground, his eyes scanning the countryside ahead. There were many men – blacks and whites – classified as trackers who had completed a formal tracking course and had the certificate as proof, but Sergeant Barka was the authentic, natural-born model.

The culprits headed south, along one of the maze of dirt paths that criss-crossed the TTL. Early in the hunt, the *spoor* was so sharp that even a mediocre tracker could follow. Their shoe imprints were clearly stamped in the dust like an advertising poster. They wore popular shoe brands such as Superpro basketball boots that branded whirls in the dust, the chocolate-slab Mars-pattern military boot and the soft, wavy smudges of Bata *veldskoens*. The imagination painted a picture of the wearers: they were will-o'-the-wisp, difficult to pin and scarcely seen – the ghosts who left hints and teasers of their passing.

The late-morning white sun scorched the open countryside. The air vibrated in the heat and tasted faintly dusty, and warped the middle distant. Sweat beads ran freely down our faces and poured from every pore. The shirt soaked up the perspiration and the cotton darkened. White salt crystallized on the fabric – accentuating the sweat migration. The shorts' crotch, soaked in sweat/salt, caused friction that rubbed the inner thighs. From time to time, the ghosts departed the grainy track, the *spoor* vanished and Sergeant Barka orchestrated his team to pick them up again, using minimum fuss. If I queried his skill, he simply looked haughtily over his hawk nose, pointed to a scuffmark and said nothing. On that 10-kilometer romp, I shut my mouth and deferred to his judgment.

The tracker team worked harmoniously, not a word spoken. Chipanza and Mhiripiri walked in front, each on one flank, guided by the experienced tracker, Barka himself. The flanker's job made certain the *spoor* didn't veer off to the left or right, and if they did, they signaled that fact to Barka. They also stayed ahead of the number one tracker to offer a tiny bit of protection against an ambush. Barka worked the aerial *spoor*, searched and assessed the broken ground ahead for the probable direction of the runners, and didn't constantly refer to the ground *spoor*. To the casual observer, he looked completely disinterested, on a Sunday afternoon stroll. Constable Hove remained behind the sergeant, carrying the radio pack. I sort of toddled along in the background.

The populace had disappeared. No one anywhere – not in the fields, not walking the tracks, nor in the villages. The landscape was completely emptied of people – a mass vanishing act that left an eerie *ambiance* hanging in the quiet rural panorama. The team remained dogged on the tracks till the *spoor* dispersed at the banks of the sluggish Macheke River. At the riverbank, we stood under the shady trees and surveyed the other side. Barka pointed to the holes in the coarse sand on the opposite bank created by the walkers. The *spoor*, plainly imprinted in the thick sand, stood out like flaming beacons. Clearly, the terrorists simply crossed the shallow water and strode straight up the opposite bank. They made no attempt to throw off pursuit by walking up or downstream in the river to disguise their exit point. Their straightforward exodus surprised me.

After tactically crossing the knee-deep water in pairs, we jogged uphill on a long gradient leading away from the river, across open cattle country. Surveying the terrain ahead, we still couldn't see people, just kilometers of brown *veldt*. The population simply evaporated, swept off the face of the earth. After jogging-walking the baking-hot kilometers, unexpectedly, the trackers lost *spoor*. The shoe prints led straight into granite sheets that did not capture sole marks. These slabs burst through the soil eons ago and blanketed the flat surface. While the trackers scrutinized the ground, I studied the map and plotted our position. We stood about a kilometer from St Crispen School. The three trackers conferred for the first time.

Barka walked over to me: "They have bomb-shelled!" he stated flatly, walking off to join the other three. 'Bomb-shelled': the standard terrorist ploy to throw off close pursuit.

With their base hidden somewhere, the CTs would agree on a rendezvous point: a prominent feature kilometers away. They'd split up and individually head there, staying on rocky ground, which made tracking extremely difficult, but Barka refused to give up. He joined his trackers and began a 360° search. In a three-sixty search, the trackers paced in a large circle out from where they lost *spoor* in an attempt to relocate it. The circle hopefully intersected with the straight line of walkers and we could start the tracking again. Barka patiently studied the ground under his feet, pausing to closely examine possible evidence. He extended the circle twice to no avail. He found useful signs – a crushed leaf here, a kicked stone there – but nothing solid. The trackers' circle widened further and further out. They were unable to recover tracks. Hours of work under the blazing sun for naught and, as I would later experience, this empty result was reality for a large percentage of tracking missions. Disappointed, we slogged back to the business center empty-handed.

Two days later, with the full section, we investigated a crime scene where terrorists had hijacked another bus, ordered the passengers off and then rammed it into a second bus heading in the opposite direction. Both vehicles smashed and littered the roadside not far from the burnt bus. The CTs had a strange fixation on buses. They warned the residents not to use white man's machines and to walk everywhere, like their forefathers. We wandered through the Chiduku *kraals* looking for evidence of the culprits. The population slowly ebbed back and edged into their daily tasks. We talked to a cluster of anxious farmers, who acknowledged the incidents, but obstinately stated they didn't know the perpetrators. Their shifty eyes and body language didn't match their strident words. In the middle of a strained conversation, a squawky radio call from Delta Base broke through. Brian advised that terrorists had been located and more troops were urgently required. Alouettes were on the way.

"Get to open ground – NOW! Switch to channel five, out."

Finding a rugby pitch-sized field, I switched radio channels and spoke to the helicopter pilot. After confirming our location, I quietly reminded the men of their helicopter drills. We crouched down, removed our caps and unloaded and reversed the weapons so that the approach to the helicopter was butt first. We shrugged off the backpack and gripped it in the other hand. Two choppers soon materialized into view … starting from small specks in the pale-blue sky, they emerged quickly. I popped blue smoke. They spotted the billowing blue cloud, confirmed the color on the radio and sunk to the earth – scattering dust clouds and dry maize stalks into the air. These French-made machines shrilly whined, not the whop-whop of the Iroquois famous in the movies. I held my breath and wondered how the boarding would go. We split into two parties of four men. This was a bit different to training. At depot, we ran across an asphalt parade ground to six casual chairs parked in a seating configuration.

There were no hiccups. The constables boarded like veterans. The pair of helicopters lifted off and the ground raced away underneath as the aircraft gained height. This was a way to fight! The ground, so painstakingly trod for two days, dropped away to a checkerboard of browns and greens; only the odd farmer bothered to look up. I squinted at the tribal lands that stretched out and shimmered in the scorching sun. The matte-brown and green merged into the bluish heatwaves that distorted the horizon. Within minutes, we flew over hours of hard walking. The men excitedly pointed out ground features.

The pilot interrupted my sightseeing and briefed me on the bare bones: PATU had trapped a ZANLA team and more men were required to seal in the enemy. RLI had already been dropped into blocking positions. That simple. Fuck. My stomach fluttered and my heart throbbed. I fiddled with my rifle fore piece. Mhiripiri, Ruzawi and Elias stared out the open side, their expressions now flat and devoid of emotion. The wind draft fluttered their cheeks. The helicopter technician, strictly business, gripped his twin machine gun in expectation of action.

No sooner than we reached a cruising ceiling, the chopper descended rapidly and the Dorowa Road flashed underneath. The exhilaration of flying into battle tweaked all my senses. The body tingled in anticipation. Within seconds of crossing the road, the helicopter hovered meters above the ground and then lowered itself like a self-conscious squat before the wheels kissed the dirt in a ploughed field in the shadow of the monolith landmark, Weya. As the helicopter rocked momentarily, all four leapt out onto the crumbly soil and sprinted across the open ground. Barka led three men from the second helicopter and then both aircraft lifted off in a scream of jet turbines and the stench of paraffin. They joined two other helicopters that circled the granite mountain like giant hawks studying the ground below for mice.

As we scurried across a dead maize field, a scruffy, bearded farmer appeared from the bush screen 20 meters ahead and signaled to us. His arm jerked with impatience, as if we had held up his little parade. Scooting over the brittle maize stalks, the section stopped right next to him. I still had no idea where we stood in relation to friendly forces or the enemy. While the men waited, wide-eyed and alert, the farmer offered a thumbnail sketch of the situation: his unit had tracked eight CTs from a horrific murder in a *kraal* and now had them pinpointed here at Weya.

"I need you guys to strengthen my sweep line," he announced, as we milled around, uncertain of the facts. "They're pinned down in there," pointing into the eight-foot-high scrub that decorated the granite base, "an' we need to flush 'em out."

"Who else is here?" I asked quickly.

"Army is in block groups on escape routes," he snapped, and strode off without looking back, impatient to give the enemy a flogging.

Chasing the snappy, bearded one, we linked with three other PATU farmers who stood silently in the scrub; then shook out in a semblance of a straight line. The grizzled farmer jerked his head left and then right to assure himself we had formed in a line, spat a gob into the dirt and stepped forward. Immediately, the section line lurched off – pushing aside light scrub and dancing around large boulders. The white sun radiated sickly heat and the choppers circled overhead, their shadow raced over us. Sweat trickled down alert faces, stomachs contracted into a heavy globe and heart rates accelerated as leafy branches scraped past to expose ourselves to enemy fire. Suddenly, six CTs – unseen by the ground force – bolted like startled gazelles straight up the bald granite side of Weya. Why did they choose that route? Six armed men silhouetted against an unadorned rock.

"K-Car, Black Two, have six Charlie Tangoes visual!" the flat voice of the G-Car pilot barked.

A twin .303 machine gun thundered and bright-red tracer balls ricocheted ferociously off the gray rock in all directions, including ours. Fuck! Huge, cricket ball-sized things, or so they seemed … bouncing off rock and flying uncontrolled everywhere! We paused and instinctively ducked. The rectum tweaked. Fancy being nailed by one of your own bastards! Abruptly, the MG stopped. The solid rat-a-tat-tat echoed off the hills and died.

"K-Car, Black Two … the fuckin' gun's jammed! See those bastards? Got maybe three, the others are gapping it along that crack, over."

"Black Two, K-Car, negative, can't see anything yet."

Fuck. How'd they miss some? Fuckin' ducks in a line. Keep down an' wait

...

"K-Car, Black Two, one's gapping it out in the open ... "

A long burst of a twin .303 MG erupted from a second helicopter; dazzling red tracer bullets rocketed down as the aircraft rolled around the impressive rock. The fiery balls lit up a fraction before the bullets disappeared into the drab green brushwood. A sharp ripping burst shot back from within the scrub and blistering green tracer sizzled past the hunting aircraft. Another long machine gun burst whizzed from the helicopter.

"K-Car, Black Two, got 'im."

"Well done!"

I learnt later that a lone CT had seized the moment to break out of the scrub that tangled the Weya base. He dashed headlong from the tree line into a fallow field, which was just a jumble of decaying maize stalks that afforded absolutely no cover from aerial view. Why did he choose that route? A circling helicopter easily sighted him scrambling, trapped between the daunting Weya monolith and the main Dorowa Road. Before he found a hideout, the G-Car swooped down like a hawk on a chicken. In desperation, the terrorist engaged the helicopter with his RPD machine gun until he was killed by the air gunner.

Inside the tree line, we waited anxiously until the gunfire ceased. For us, the clash had been machine gun fire from the air. Lots of noise, red blaze dots zapping downwards and a cascade of brass bullet cases, but nothing dangerous. The snappy farmer stood up, hissed to get my attention and waved the line forward. We carefully picked our way, walking stealthily through scrubby trees – dense enough to limit the vision, but thinly spread to easily brush aside. The butterflies fluttered in our stomachs and our hearts pounded louder as our eyes scanned the mottled leaves and branches. The crunch of rubber soles on brittle leaves amplified in the parched air. I hoped the helicopters recognized friendlies. I didn't fancy a MG bullet in the back! Abruptly, the line stumbled into a small grass pocket shaded by a three-tree canopy. A Sanyo transistor radio sat alone on a rock, playing soft music, and two crates of warm Castle beer waited for the owner. It looked like a juvenile gang's rest place for parties and mischief. We paused long enough to sink a bottle each.

"You push out over the road," ordered Mr Snappy Farmer, as he washed out his parched mouth with warm lager, "an' we'll mop up 'ere."

I smiled. Maybe there was more undiscovered beer.

"One's bleedin'," Barka called from somewhere in the scrub.

"Then let's go!" I called back and left our snappy farmer to the spoils.

We traced the bleeder over the deserted Dorowa Road and through the heavily wooded hillsides and deserted *kraals*. All the people living within earshot of the tiny battle had absconded. The villages stood silent and empty, their doors wired shut. The fields were equally deserted. The sudden crisis had swept them into hiding. The blood *spoor* soon dispersed and faded but, with Barka's infinite patience, was found again. The blood dots finally joined two sets of *spoor*. The sergeant tracker was performing at his best. The visible enemy footprints headed north, towards the Macheke River. They walked parallel to the same path we had tracked after the bus-burning, but headed in the opposite direction. This on again, off again tracking consumed most of the daylight hours.

"That guy's still trackin' us," said Mhiripiri flatly, as the section crossed the lazy Macheke River at dusk, "followin' us most o' the time since the contact."

"The same guy?"

"Yeah. He disappears from time to time, but he's back."

I noticed a shadow tailing us. A couple of hours ago, Mhiripiri commented about a man who trailed us at long range. We ignored the sighting and I just asked him to keep tabs on the mystery man. I'd been intent on the tracking and not concerned with someone trailing us, but Mhiripiri's constant eyes had not missed the shadow.

Once we sloshed across the river, I whispered to Sibanda: "Give me the gun."

Sibanda reluctantly surrendered his beloved MAG for my FN. The section dispersed into the dark trees on the embankment. I remained on the embankment and lay on the loose gravel, the heavy wooden butt locked into my shoulder, and flicked the linked ammunition straight. The shadow slinked about a hundred meters out.

"Tell him to stop," I hissed to Sibanda.

"*Mera! Mera!*" Sibanda bellowed, standing behind me in the open.

The shadow spun, ducked and fled – taking long strides up the grassy slope. I pointed the barrel roughly in his direction, tightened my grip and fired an ear-smashing 10-round burst. I didn't expect to hit, rather to scare the shit out of him. Sizzling red tracer tangled around him and he dropped out of sight …

"AHHHHHH!" The frightened animal squeal hit smack in the stomach. Fuck. He's hit! Springing to my feet, I snatched the MAG and sprinted into the cool water.

"I didn't mean to hit him," I cursed, "just wanted to frighten the fucker."

Sibanda and I splashed across the darkening river and sprinted up the opposite bank.

"What have I done?" I asked myself, a little worried.

We galloped out of the water together, across the open countryside, searching desperately in the murky light … a shadow, half sat up in a shallow gully … a teenage male, his face contorted in fright and pain, stared round at our aggressive approach, guns ready.

"Get everyone across here," I whispered to Sibanda, as we swapped weapons.

He departed, fondly hugging the MAG, as I tore off my shell dressing and walked to the rigid youth. Placing the gauze pad firmly over the bleeding hole in his calf muscle, I pulled the bandage tight. The bone had not been smashed, but the calf muscle had been mangled and shredded. The youngster moaned softly – biting his bottom lip to stifle noise. Sibanda led the section across the river and Barka spread them out. Ruzawi, the section medic, elbowed me away. He dropped his medic bag beside the tearful youth and opened the flap, extracted another field dressing and slapped it on the exit wound to stem the bleeding.

"Get some branches," he called to anyone, "about as long as your rifle."

He tied off the dressing and then scrambled through the medications to find a morphine sachet. Finding our one and only, he stabbed the morphine into his upper thigh and the boy laid back – and we'd used our only morphine. I hoped we didn't suffer a casualty. Mhiripiri and Chipanza stumbled back with an armload of chopped branches. Ruzawi sorted out suitable ones and tossed the others aside; then the medic stabilized the leg, tying off the green branches. I tried to talk with Delta Base, but the radio earpiece returned static. Either the A73 radio was faulty, or the communication was blocked by the rugged country. The mush turned to full static hiss. The dusk deepened into night.

Ruzawi worked furiously and compassionately to stem the bleeding. Inwardly, I churned at making that shot. I didn't expect to hit this man, just to stop him trailing and spying, but not to substantially hurt him – but what was done could not be undone. All we could was to expedite him to hospital.

"We need to get him outta here," Barka said, stating the obvious.

Using a woollen blanket, solid tree poles and nylon cord, the men knocked together a rough stretcher and heaved it up to their shoulders. It looked like a hammock, with the wounded man lolling in the blanket, and reminded me of hauling a deer carcass out of the Ruahine Ranges. The unstable stretcher sapped the energy during the cross-country hike to St Crispen School. At the school, the tired men gladly lowered the stretcher to the ground, whilst Chipanza and I knocked on house doors on the outskirts of the school ground. On the third, the door opened.

"Are you a teacher?" I asked the man.

"Yes."

"I have an injured man for hospital. You have a car?"

"Yes." (One of the very few who does.)

"I want you to take him into Rusape hospital."

"Now?"

"He's bleeding badly."

The man looked doubtful and then stated: "My car is here, but I need compensation."

"What?"

"I need money."

I flashed out my wrinkled leather wallet and pulled out a ten-dollar bill. Before I even offered the note, he swept it from my fingers into his hot palm and the note vanished into his shirt pocket. Satisfied with the payment, he grumpily led the stretcher to his car, which was parked neatly behind his house. We gently assisted the injured man into the rear passenger seat of the Ford Zodiac workhorse and closed the door. The driver climbed in behind the steering wheel, started the engine and we silently watched the vehicle depart. The red taillights vanished around a corner. The driver still had a bumpy journey ahead on the rutted road before swinging on the Inyazura Road. One consolation: there were no Security Forces nearby who might stop and harass the driver if they discovered a wounded young man. I recorded my first and last cash-and-carry casevac. Unfortunately, the *spoor* was lost the next day.

Later, the next afternoon, we traipsed back to the contact scene. Apart from the small camp, where the booze had now vanished, we saw no evidence that a firefight took place. The hour of frantic 'search and destroy' looked like normal rural countryside. The landscape lapsed to a peaceful bush scene, overshadowed by the massive granite. None of the combat debris was found. Loose bandages, abandoned rucksacks and shell casing litter was lost in the scrub. We hadn't even sighted the dead terrorists. They were immediately extracted straight after the firefight and flown back to Rusape for identification and intelligence purposes.

My first Support Unit action was summed up as an overhead rattle of helicopter machine guns, squelchy radio calls, uncertainty, pushing aside scrub branches, being poised for the first bullets to break the tension and then the sudden dilution of adrenalin when I realized the battle had been bypassed. Afterwards, Security Force politics came into play: RLI, who had provided Stop Groups further out from Weya and saw no action at all, claimed the kills – and so did the PATU farmer and Brian Gibbs, even though my section had not fired a shot. The air force said nothing.

After a day's stopover in camp, Brian borrowed Ian Jack's Oscar Troop Land Rover and handed it to Gordon Kaye-Eddie to deploy my section into Manyika TTL. We were to drop off just inside the TTL and patrol north. Brian asserted unconfirmed sightings – get out there and check it out. With Kaye-Eddie driving, I filled the passenger seat. The rest of the section scattered across the convoy of one Hyena and one RL Bedford truck. Three Oscar Troop men clambered on board to escort the vehicles on the homeward-bound journey … Standard Operating Procedure.

As the new section leader on the block, I hadn't met Gordon and had missed him each time I deployed. He was either in camp or away on patrol. He struck me as an earnest man, a bit reserved. Caught up in the compulsory National Service for young men, he probably eagerly counted down the days to his exit. The police accepted National Servicemen with O- or A-Level education, and while some ended up in police stations, more and more filled Support Unit section commander gaps. As conscripts, they tested the police instructors' patience by insisting on explanations to all the pettiness, something just taken for granted by volunteers. Gordon had just been awarded the Commissioner's Bronze Baton for Bravery – displaying outstanding leadership in clashes with ZANLA in the Honde Valley. This day, he drove the lead vehicle to chauffeur my section to a drop-off point and then scarper back to base. We happily scooted through Makoni in the shadow of the hills, chatting to get the measure of each other. Still fascinated with tribal areas, I absorbed the centuries-old, unchanged life pattern: the bullock and wooden plough in the dry fields, skittish people walking the donkey cart and rows of thatched African housing standing in acres of thorny scrub and brown grassland. We drove the full length of Makoni before the convoy crossed a dry streambed into Manyika TTL.

From the moment the vehicles trundled across, signs of life mysteriously vanished. Peering through the roadside scrub, the rough, ploughed fields shimmered unattended. Ahead, through the dusty windscreen, the deserted straight road – a sandy ribbon that sliced through the fields – distorted under the roasting sun. Normally, pedestrians or donkey carts might be seen. That day, there's not a solitary walking person – an unhealthy sign. I tightened my grip on the FN rifle. Gordon steered the Land Rover up the guts of the sandy road. Unexpectedly, abruptly, the Land Rover detonated a landmine. A huge explosion shattered the driver's side front wheel. I didn't hear it. One second, I registered the road ahead; then a dull red flash lit the windscreen and, within a split-second, a blanket of black dirt obscured everything. A sharp flash; then a split-second – total blackout! My eardrums cringed under the turbulent shockwave's enormous pressure. The Land Rover shuddered to a ferocious halt like a spastic horse. Fine, gritty sand hovered in the chaotic air and encased the stricken vehicle. Sharpened metal, dirt clods, rubber chunks and magnified heat all danced together, mixed in the shockwave. Falling lumps banged on the thin metal roof like hail. The air tasted of burnt explosive, fried rubber and fine dust. I instinctively unclipped the seatbelt and lurched out. The rest of the convoy braked hard and the men bailed off like burglars who had set off a shrieking alarm. Chipanza later described the event: from the truck tray looking ahead, he saw the Land Rover in front suddenly collide with a black column of dirt that spouted up from the road, like an unexpected blast from a small volcano. The Land Rover appeared to be sucked into the black earth explosion, and then BANG – the shockwave fiercely belted him around the ears.

Shaken and disorientated, I reeled around the front of the Land Rover and vaguely noted that the bonnet had been axed off. The engine compartment had transformed into a mash of steel bits and the right-side wheel had dissolved. A sizable crater had formed in the baked road, where the anti-tank landmine had evaporated the entire wheel and suspension. The dirt inside the cavity was laced with bits of burnt rubber. The bonnet had been blasted off and later was found 50 meters down the road – landing heavily on the stark ground. I'm OK, but Gordon's eardrums were damaged and he staggered out and sat down, disorientated.

The Land Rover had a mine protection package built in. A slab of steel behind the four-cylinder engine and a steel reinforcement under the cab floor deflected the blast away from the occupants. The upward explosion wrecked the engine compartment without touching the cab. Also, a mine conveyor belt was bolted over the rear cab window to slow slicing shrapnel from a rear wheel detonation. Finally, roll bars were fitted to assist survival if the vehicle flipped on its roof. If driven at less than 40 kilometers an hour and the occupants were belted in, there was a high chance they would survive the blast of a standard anti-tank mine. They'd be bruised and battered, but alive – but CTs sometimes won by boosting the standard landmine (usually a Soviet TM-46, or TMH) with additional slabs of TNT, or a cluster of 60mm mortar bombs, or a can of petrol, or two mines (one sitting on top of the other). If this occurred, the vehicle and its occupants were unlikely to survive unscathed.

In 1976, the Support Unit drove the RL and RM Bedford five-ton trucks that conducted the bulk of the troop haulage. The steel tray was reinforced with sandbags (steel protection-strengthened under the driver's seat) and tires were filled with water to dampen landmine blasts, but presented no protection from bullets. Whilst sandbagging the flat tray reduced casualties from a mine blast, basically they were standard trucks of light metal skin with the bullet-stopping capacity of cardboard. The Land Rover had been modified with the mine kit, but again, afforded no bullet protection. The South African Hyena armored carriers were the only vehicles fully armored and landmine-protected. A new generation of wheeled armor and landmine-protected vehicles were on the drawing board and not a reality until 1978. Anti-tank landmines were a certainty. CTs liberally deployed them to 'defend' their operational zones. Whenever a vehicle drove the dirt road, there was always a floating anticipation of exploding one. With no access to mine detectors of any sort, Support Unit suffered numerous casualties. The first existence of a landmine blast turned the world to shit in half a second: orange flash, black blanket, huge explosion and a shower of debris underscored a dawning hope of survival. The fear of the explosive device did not ratchet up terror of the roads. Most vehicles, driven correctly, absorbed the blast shock enough to minimize casualties. Some men took pride in the number of 'biscuit tins' they hit and survived. Survivors even formed a club. Once again, you paid your money and took your chances.

I radioed base to casevac Kaye-Eddie and waited. Ruzawi scrambled to his aid, kept him seated on the roadside and stabilized the sick feeling. Gordon felt nauseous and had difficulty retaining balance. I felt a little queasy myself, but determined to find the culprits. Medically, I didn't get away scot-free and lost 20 percent of my hearing – and I still have a permanent buzz inside the left ear. After a series of radio calls, a helicopter evacuated Gordon, along with the Land Rover radio transmitter and all portable gear. Delta, accompanied by the Oscar escort troops, embarked on an angry follow-up. Fresh *spoor* led away from the rubber-encrusted crater and we were hungry for a result. The mixed *spoor* of one shoe print and bare feet led straight into the nearest *kraal*

– and surprise, surprise, it was deserted! A five-house cluster stood sleepily, with the crude wooden plank doors wired shut, like the owners had suddenly disappeared on holiday. The shoe prints laughed back at us. Black hens pecked the solid baked ground.

"Sarge, the Oscar boys can remain 'ere. Take the section an' round up everyone in the area."

Barka called in his men and began a sweep of the *kraals* in the vicinity. On the radio, I asked Delta Base for permission to burn the offending *kraal*. I mean, why let them get away with it? They would've known about the landmine dug 30 meters from their front porch. They scattered into the bush when they heard our vehicles grind up the road, or maybe they sat perched in the foothills for a grandstand view of the show. I believed the occupants were accomplices. Brian stated that he would ask the JOC. I squatted on the rim of the village in the broiling sun – watching the chooks search for grubs under a primitive stand used for drying cooking pots – waiting impatiently for an answer. The radio remained mute ...

"Come on, come on. Make a bloody decision!"

Soon the radio responded with a lame answer: Brian had asked JOC permission, but they vacillated, saying yes and then no; then yes, but subject to removing the personal items from the huts, and then no again. It took over an hour – seated impatiently in the dirt, under the blazing sun – to end up with a negative response. Angered by armchair decisions, I burnt one hut anyway. I watched the flames ignite the dry thatch, which then threatencd to die, before rapidly accelerating into a fierce fireball as the orange flames sucked in the surrounding oxygen. I observed, fascinated like a junior arsonist, as the fireball roared like an engine, with turbulent air jetting into the center. The roof caved inwards with a tremendous shower of sparks. The mud walls blackened inside, but remained intact.

Meanwhile, Barka and the men herded all the people found within two kilometers of the *kraal* – a dozen tired-looking, dusty people who unenthusiastically squatted in the shade under Mhiripiri's eye. The real prize was three young men in their late teens. After extensive and fervent interrogation, two youths sulkily admitted they assisted in laying the landmine. Their story confirmed that the terrorists had supplied the explosive device; then instructed the youths on how to deploy it and had then left the operation up to them. One demonstrated by mime how he armed an imaginary landmine. Two lived in the occupied *kraal* – now reduced by one smoldering hut – waiting to join in the next ZANLA recruiting drive, and both were very unhappy. Our landmine boys were handed over to Special Branch, albeit slightly damaged. Back at base, one unhappy Ian Jack was told his Land Rover was laid up wrecked in Manyika.

On the next mission, the whole troop deployed to Makoni TTL on scanty information. The sections combed an area in the Shena Hills. Humping heavy packs and weighed down with ammunition, we scoured the hilly countryside – uphill, downhill and then up again. Barry's Delta Two, another Delta section, slogged up onto high ground to improve radio communications and, inadvertently, stumbled onto four CTs who were lounging in the open. The CTs were just as startled as Delta, and after a sharp exchange of fire, they sprinted away. The Delta section galloped after them – running hard across a low-slung hill – and engaged them again near a *kraal*, without success. Barry breathlessly radioed his request for Fireforce. By sheer luck, Fireforce was airborne – returning to Grand Reef airport from a 'lemon'. The four helicopters flew almost overhead when the call bounced from Barry's radio to Delta Base, from the base to JOC, from JOC to Grand Reef, and then to the helicopters. The Alouettes fractionally altered course and casually flew in the pastel-blue African sky. Below, the four CTs anxiously sprinted across open ground. Using the 20mm cannon, the K-Car killed all four. Shit luck for the CTs, who must have thought they were home and hosed; however, a clean sweep for Fireforce: the total elimination of the enemy unit – and without deploying one soldier on the ground.

Two days later, Barry's section walked into a nondescript *kraal* at early dusk in the same area for no particular reason and a tribal woman – seeing armed African troops in the fuzzy light – mistook them for CTs and excitedly told the perplexed scout that his 'friends' were eating behind the *kraal*. The section took full advantage of the invitation and walked around the back of the huts into eight CTs eating their evening *sadza*, but bad light and poor shooting – particularly the Bren gunner – resulted in only one CT killed and two weapons recovered.

The CTs struck back: a constable from Inyazura police station, on a bicycle patrol along the Dorowa Road, disappeared. Bicycle patrols were standard rural policing, where African constables rode bicycles to local areas for investigation purposes. This constable stopped in a business center on the Dorowa Road for a Coke and walked into a terrorist group, also shopping. They promptly murdered him. Unarmed, except for a hard rubber club, he didn't stand a chance. Didn't his boss know there was a war on? One of the murderers wore the police cap as a trophy for months to come.

At the same time, in the heart of Chiduku, an African prison officer on leave from Salisbury took it upon himself to poison CTs when they visited his *kraal* for a feed. He thoroughly seasoned the hot *sadza* with a toxic insecticide. Three terrorists later died in extreme agony. The enraged survivors returned, snatched the prison officer, callously tortured him with bayonets and then chopped him up (while still alive) with a *badza*.

Soon after, my first contact blasted off in southern Chiduku. Tediously following 20 CT tracks most of the day, the unseen enemy fired at our encroachment from the top of a small hill, which was about 200 meters away. At least 20 men pulled a trigger on automatic, which sent a flood of bullets our way.

The wall of bullets sharply crackled overhead. I shouted the magic words into the radio handset: "Mantle Delta Four, contact, contact, contact; wait, out!"

That's my first red pin on the wall map! The words alerted the base slackers, now poised, ready to play their part in the game. I stood and held my ground as the bullets crackled overhead, too high to be dangerous. The constables were startled and wisely scattered behind scrub, trying not to be seen.

"This is easy," I thought, and traded bullets with the invisible enemy. These were like the Centenary baddies. They couldn't hit a cow in the arse with a banjo – particularly at this range, shooting downhill.

I still vividly recall the questioning look on Barka's face, peering through a thicket. With only a couple of months left on his contract, he took all reasonable steps to ensure he'd walk upright when his term was done.

The drawn look on his face said: "What the fuck is this arsehole up to?"

Drawing fire onto the section! He was absolutely spot on – and I was having fun! Insane exhilaration! I shot the shit out of the ridgeline, traversing slowly from left to right. The aperture sight lined up the tree base on the ridgeline, I squeezed the trigger … the ball rounds smacking into something up there; then we heard the distinct sound: the launch of a mortar bomb.

"Mortars!!" bellowed Barka and everyone hit the dirt.

I reluctantly squatted behind a sizeable granite boulder and waited. The CTs still poured on the rifle and machine gun fire, albeit higher than they would have liked. A surge of bullets crackled above my rock shelter – winnowing branches on the tall trees. The seconds between hearing the ca-thunk as the mortar launched the bomb upwards, and then the actual resulting detonation, lengthened. The first bomb exploded well forward. I saw the brown explosive – a dirty cloud – and heard the CRUMP as the soundwave caught up. The next two exploded so far behind we didn't see the detonation. The final pair burst behind, a little closer. When the final two mortars exploded, the CTs ceased fire and pulled out, which they did at a hundred miles an hour! Hyped up, I thrilled in the experience – an early, easy firefight to whet the appetite. They wouldn't all be like this, but I was astonished at the extravagant use of bullets by our opponents. Given that they manhandled every single bullet from Mozambique, I assumed they would tend to be conservative. They certainly were not.

In base for a break – lounging about reading at 8:30 p.m. – Brian summoned the section and said to drive out to Inyazura, where the police were talking to someone who had just fled capture. A breathless RAR soldier reported to the Inyazura police station that he had just escaped seizure by CTs. He was adamant that the CTs were at his home – drunk and ripe for the picking. Arriving at the police station, we walked him into the car park, where he carefully explained his story again: sitting at home on leave, a villager told the CTs that the man was a soldier. They snatched him and held him prisoner, but as the night progressed, they drank heavily and he seized an opportunity to escape – a credible story, I thought. Once back in Chiduku TTL, close to midnight, his enthusiasm waned and he refused to lead the way back to the village. At first, he stated he couldn't remember where he lived! The constables were naturally flabbergasted. That's akin to someone born and bred and raised in a small town being lost on their main street! I quarreled with him, but he denied he'd been captured, and then played dumb.

Finally, after some arm-twisting, he half-heartedly agreed to lead … "Straight to the enemy," he mumbled.

Tramping over solid, bush-covered hill country through the night whittled my patience. He'd stop, argue, plea he was lost and then, suddenly, eagerly launch into a new direction, all for naught. By dawn, I was mightily pissed off. The villagers, questioned in the early morning, suggested they knew the man and that he willingly ran with the terrorists. They even implied that he carried arms of war; they described an SKS rifle. We handed him back to the police station with a couple of boot imprints on his pants.

The terrorist presence in Chiduku was only a few months old, unlike the three-year infiltration in the north-east zones. We slid into *kraal* after *kraal* and eyeballed people caught unawares. Women curtsied and clapped their hands in the traditional greeting according to custom, but remained edgy, probably because of the white man in the party. The males were generally helpful, happy to sit and chat, but tight-lipped on ZANLA, like someone hauled into a police station on a charge – trying not to displease, but being circumspect in what they said. The kids, fat-bellied and laughing, played naturally – giggling, pointing and running.

When we randomly stopped people, they were polite and not averse to chatting. We spoke of their cattle, their taxes, their kids, their schools, their crops, their maize stocks, the weather, the grain price, the beer drinks, the ox carts, the price of goods, the bus service, Salisbury, Rusape and anything else that touched their lives. They generously offered a food exchange: fresh eggs, peanuts and fruit for our rations. I closely monitored their expressions, facial gestures, voice tones and arm-waving to gauge their attitude. Pretty much all was well in the world, or least that's what they said. Apart from hiccups caused by the new boys on the block – the bus-burnings, cattle-dip sabotage and murder – they told us that not much had changed, but no one volunteered snippets about ZANLA or political developments.

The rest of the tour faded and fragmented into hasty chases after fleeting bites of intelligence. One report announced a murder of an African farming couple in the Ziyambe African Purchase Area. An APA consisted of a block of small, freehold farms – about 10 hectares – each owned by an African farmer. In theory, the APA gave African farmers freehold ownership that they could utilize to grow commercial crops, but a lack of credit facilities for modern machinery and land improvement – plus poor roads to markets – meant most farm earnings were marginally above subsistence level. We accompanied Special Branch and found the owner and his wife both dead. Machine-gunned at close range outside an empty shed, they had begun to bloat in the hot sun. His bloody shirt and her cotton dress were stretched to bursting point as the putrefying bodies expanded. The SB operatives doodled about picking up 'doppies' and anything thing else useful as evidence. ZANLA left a handwritten note pinned to the wooden door, saying these two enterprising Africans were 'sell-outs'. Special Branch claimed loudly they didn't know them, but that didn't mean the note wasn't true. Certainly, SB had no need to enlighten us. Intermittent rains washed away any *spoor*, but we swanned about down there for three days just in case. We found nothing.

Next, we spent three nights ambushing a small Chiduku medical clinic. SB sources claimed the CTs had visited to raid the medical supplies. An African nurse ran the government clinic and supplied basic medicines to local residents from rapidly depleting stocks. We squirmed outside for three long, dreary nights – watching the whitewashed walls, fending off blood-sucking mosquitoes and squinting at the luminous watch hands that moved excruciatingly slow. Before dawn, we retreated into scrub country and laid up – watching the villagers' daily lives play out. Nothing occurred and we walked out. JOC permanently closed the clinic weeks later.

The Rusape police rounded off the tour by requesting Brian and I attend the police station. A Chiduku resident complained that an SF section stopped a bus, pulled the complainant off, doused his personal luggage with petrol and set it alight. The complainant further claimed to have been seriously assaulted. As my section operated in the area, suspicion landed squarely on me. When I met the policeman, he assumed at once he'd caught the perpetrator. Brian asked him for the charges. The policeman formally read out the charges with a stony face, in a 'got you, you bastard' tone. His face reddened and his anger rose when I strenuously denied the accusation. That 'take it like a man' tone in his voice changed to a 'don't fuck me around' growl, but the case unraveled when the complainant described the assailants wearing berets, not combat caps. I left the station wondering why I would be wandering around the bush carrying a jerry can of petrol. Once the deployment finished, Brian publicly declared Delta Troop killed 14 CTs. I raised one eyebrow. The troop actually killed one CT and reported sightings that led to, or played on the fringes of, other SF units killing 13. Hmmm …

After the deployment, we crashed into 10 idle days of R&R. With six weeks' wages in a full wallet, we plundered the Salisbury city bars and nightclubs. Surviving each trip was a question of odds: the more bush tours, the more chance of being killed or wounded. The dangers were random, from the blindingly obvious – being shot by the enemy – to the other causes, such as road accidents, being shot by friendly forces or being dropped by disease. After six weeks in the wilder, rural outposts, we celebrated life, success and loss in a compressed social splurge. One drunken night was followed by another – 10-day booze binge until the money ran dry, or the hangover grew too oppressive.

Generally, the Rhodesian-born police filtered back home after a day or two of partying in Salisbury. For them, the fighting was not some foreign adventure. This was HOME: home of fussy grandmothers, primary school triumphs, first kisses, *braais* after cricket, Willard chips, camping at Kariba, coughing on the first Kingsgate behind the school toilets, scoring the first try, reading the raunchy bits of *Lady Chatterley's Lover*, failing the first driving test, smiling nannies, testy fathers, stealing the first chilled bottle of Lion beer, copping a feel at the bi-scope, Krest soft drinks, Supersonic transistor radios, swigging back Cane and Coke, falling asleep on Rhodesia Rail, counting the savings at Barclays Bank, caring mothers, Ranger bicycles, *'Rock and Roll All Nite'* by Kiss, shopping at Avondale, applying to join the police … HOME. There was no other place, no options, no anxious relatives waiting in Birmingham – everything was HERE.

Salisbury portrayed an island of tranquillity. Even with its ridiculous proximity to violent battles in the regional areas outside its leafy suburbs, there was a prevailing attitude of 'business as usual'. The Sally Donaldson RBC Forces radio show on Sunday afternoons reinforced the notion of 'boys on the border', and so the populace felt safe. At this stage, the city had not been touched by CT operators and the general feeling created a myth that the war was somewhere on the border, like a far-flung foreign land. The fact that the war had left the border and was steadily creeping towards the capital city had not been officially acknowledged.

I drank on the fringes with foreigners serving in the army. The foreigners found Salisbury placid. A city population of 463,000 (112,900 white, 1969 Census), it was a beautiful, regional-sized city – a slice of England transplanted into Africa. The avenues were planted with lines of purple jacaranda trees and the streets with orange flamboyant that burst spectacularly when in bloom. The place was akin to a large university city rather than a bustling capital. The city business district was compact and easily walked. Cecil Square, smack in the center, showed off the pride in Britain, with gardens laid out in a Union Jack. Among the medium, high-rise office buildings and government precinct, a smattering of restaurants and a Wimpy hamburger joint – and fashion shopping in First Street Mall – hid the bars and nightclubs. The army or police staked out one of the downtown hotel bars as a meeting place. The Meikles, Monomatapa, Park Lane, Terreskane got a flogging, and so did the nightclubs, such as Club Tomorrow and Le Coq Dor.

Salisbury did not host girlie bars, where scantily-clad lovelies offered a good time, and there were no brothels apart from real seedy stuff down the dark back alleys, no overt underworld operating with the accompaniment of sex, drugs and rock 'n' roll. This was not London, Berlin or Bangkok. Seriously edgy nightlife was missing. Only the periphery of white society played the game. The Queens and the Elizabeth Hotel welcomed a multi-racial clientele. I darkened the doors a couple of times, but found it wasn't my taste. The city's drinking establishments were well stocked with chilled amber fluid, so I rarely left their rowdy bars.

The citizens of the capital city couldn't believe the drunken antics of soldiers and police after operations. After six weeks of fear, boredom, frustration, violent contacts and, sometimes, witnessing gruesome death, servicemen were expected to arrive back in town, put their briefcase and lunchbox in the cupboard and quietly indulge in sport and social activities without upsetting sensitivities.

Apart from fistfights, all-in brawls, solid beatings, the odd glassing, or a pistol fired in a drunken stupor, there were booze games – games like 'Whales', where the roll of the dice promoted the highest scorer to 'captain' and the lowest to 'whale'. The game rules were simple: the 'whale' filled his mouth with beer and lay down on his belly on the bar floor, while the 'captain' stood high on a barstool. On a signal, the 'whale' 'swam' across the bar floor and, at an agreed point, rolled over and spurted the beer into the air.

"There she blows!" the rest of the delinquents shouted.

The 'whale' then bolted for the open door, while the 'captain' attempted to harpoon him with three darts. To be the 'whale', it paid to be pissed.

3

Eastern Border: September–October 1976

The Delta convoy drove in to the Nyamapanda police station – the last stop on the main road into Mozambique. The modern, red-brick building squatted among hastily constructed sandbagged trenches and bunkers built from railway sleepers. On 15 August 1976, terrorists launched a brutal bombardment of the police station using 122mm rockets, 75mm recoilless rifles and 82mm mortars. Patrol Officer Britland and two other policemen – including Constable Muduve from Support Unit – was killed.

A border fence ran just east of the station. Prior to 1974, Rhodesians casually motored through Nyamapanda on their way to balmy holidays on the beautiful Mozambique beaches. Sun baking on white sands and dining in the buzzing street cafés, they drank copious amounts of Portuguese red wine and ate through plates of prawns smothered in peri-peri, a hot Portuguese sauce. Portugal had since withdrawn from their colony. Now, due to escalating squabbles between the Rhodesian Government and a new African regime in Maputo, the border was shut by government proclamation and the traffic flow ceased. The customs post sat abandoned. The sweltering, flat, brown border countryside was the closest a Rhodesian could get to a Mozambique beach.

Standing near the border fence, I zoomed in the binoculars. Africans shuttled about, walking back and forth across the tarmac road – ordinary people wrapped up in their own lives. The roadside bush broke up what appeared to be a small town, logically their customs post. They didn't peer back at us, but simply got on with their work.

"See anything?" asked Paddy Allen, shuffling up beside me.

Paddy had already served over a year in Support Unit and had been on leave during the Rusape deployment. A tall, gangly lad with a sparkling, cheeky smile and a razor-sharp wit, he had a reputation for seeking out a good time no holds barred. The son of a serving police Assistant Commissioner, he initially worked for the Department of Internal Affairs before joining the police. One time, when pissed, he'd driven his motorbike through a plate-glass shop window – an early claim to fame. With his easy-going, reckless personality, we hit it off from the beginning.

"Nothing really," my sweeping binoculars strained to spot something exotic.

An enlightened Rhodesian, Paddy didn't think the sun shone out of the PM Ian Smith's backside. When we killed time, waiting for orders – waiting even longer for iron-clad decisions – he talked about his respect for Allan Savory, a visionary politician who deserted the Rhodesian Front and formed the Rhodesia Party. Savory recognized the need to create an African middle class – people with property rights, money in the bank and middle-management positions in the police, army, civil service and judiciary that would give them a real stake in the country. By expanding this small, middle-class elite, it offered a tiny chance to remedy the march to oblivion. While the vision appeared non-threatening, the Rhodesia Party aspirations had been badly savaged at the ballot box.

I soon learnt Paddy was an exceptional marksman. He scavenged a set of steel bipods, attached them to the barrel – flush with the fore piece – and patiently practiced his shooting. He only operated with open sights, never using optical enhancement. Later, during an operation in Inyanga North TTL, both sections occupied a heavily-wooded hill – overlooking the Ruenya River Valley. Unexpectedly, we sighted two CTs creeping out of the heavy scrub on the opposite bank. They were tiny figures; their status confirmed through binoculars. They sidled through the waist-high boulders to the river's edge and ducked down to the sparkling water, where they filled small bottles. Crouching, they suspiciously eyeballed the bush-speckled bank opposite. If we had attempted to close in and corner them, they'd be long gone. The thick scrub and boulder country was not conducive to swift movement, so Paddy elected to shoot from the hillside. One shot, one hit. The bullet velocity lifted the terrorist right off his feet; the other CT didn't wait his turn and vanished. A downhill shot over 400 meters was difficult to master. The shooter compensated not only for the height, but also for the long range, the wind drift, his breathing, the target movement and the refraction of light broken up by shimmering heatwaves. I thought the shot was incredible – particularly when I classed myself only fair to average.

Gordon Kaye-Eddie did not return to Delta after his brush with the landmine. Apart from Paddy, that left SO Barry, the other white section leader. Whilst I had been introduced to Barry on the last trip, I did not know him. We rarely spoke. When I rested in camp, he tramped the bush. Compared to the 'five-minute wonder', he outranked and had accumulated years of service. In a police station environment, there would be no doubt who was boss, but here – both as section leaders – the seniority and rank line blurred. A man of average height, with fair hair, a fair complexion and a serious demeanor, Barry was married and, naturally, disappeared into the bosom of the family back in Salisbury. He struck me as an aloof, professional policeman with a promising career that had been abruptly sidetracked into Support Unit. Dealt the 'Go to Jail' card, his baffled stance and awkward statements portrayed a man lost. A studious policeman by choice, he resented playing soldiers.

Delta had been saddled with border patrol operations – the bread and butter for a number of troops. The border operations were dreary and uninspiring. The primary duty required routine patrols of the border fences to examine for breaches. North of the police station, the border was contained by a fenced minefield sown with small anti-personnel mines, which were designed to injure by blasting off a leg or a foot. The 'experts' stated that a wounded man jolted the enemy more than a dead one. Apart from the psychological impact on survivors viewing his mangled foot and listening to his painful pleas for help, his injury tied up six or more mates trying to get him medical aid.

For any minefield to be effective, the deadly obstacle needed to be under constant surveillance and fire. That meant guard towers or blockhouses at every point where a geographical feature obscured the view from another. This required a mass of troops and equipment that the army et al simply did not have. To have slavishly adopted the 'Good Book' would have drastically drained manpower reserves, so instead, each morning, dummies like Support Unit drove their designated sector from Point A to Point B assessing the dirt road, the chainmail fence and the minefield itself for any incursion, breaches, shoe prints, exploded mines, body parts and cut wire and so on. Unfortunately, numerous wild animals were also trapped. They stumbled in, exploded the mines – crippling them – and then lingered in an agonizing death. Vultures were known to feed off the dead animals till they were so full that they needed a running take-off. Three or four paces and boom! They exploded into a shower of feathers.

The main danger on the 'drag' – the nickname for the motorized patrols – were anti-tank landmines laid on the minefield service road. A number of Support Unit vehicles were blasted while conducting the routine search. The anti-tank mines were heavy, and the lazier ZANLA sections – laden down with months of ammunition supplies – got rid of them early by laying them on the very first road they stepped upon inside Rhodesia.

On our first briefing, Brian announced that Delta had been assigned the responsibility of maintaining surveillance on the border fence running south of Nyamapanda, in the wilds of Mudzi TTL. Brian's pointer tapped the map. He stressed that the minefield had yet to be constructed there. Excitedly, he outlined his tactics: the sections would walk out every night, ambush a track in a specified grid box and, in the morning, walk east to the border road and check for signs of incursion. Each section was tasked with an individual stretch of the border road. Two sections walked their allotted portion and when they completed their checks, they were uplifted by vehicle. The section nominated for the closest grid walked home. If we discovered an incursion, orders stated emphatically not to follow, but to sit tight and radio the base. Brian would engage JOC on the merits of the report and subsequently relay orders. The JOC had three cards to play: either the section got off their arses and executed the follow-up, or the task was allotted to a Fireforce or a helicopter-borne sparrow team. If Fireforce or sparrows were activated, they endeavored to cut off the infiltrators by leapfrogging a tracker team or dogs by helicopter kilometers ahead of the crossing point. The pursuit team then cross-grained the ground till they picked up the enticing *spoor* and chased onwards. If the exercise worked, it would substantially cut the time required to close the gap and hopefully hit the CT while they were complacent. If we found nothing, we returned to base.

On my first deployment, we laid an ambush on one of scores of dirt tracks that criss-crossed the arid countryside. At first light, we abandoned the ambush position and backtracked to the border road. I was shocked to discover a rusty, four-strand cattle fence dividing the two nations. The fence hardly looked like an international border, more like a dilapidated barrier on a rundown farm. A dirt road graded parallel to the fence line cut a swath through the lean scrub and grass country. Convinced that the border fence should be something substantial, I rechecked my bearings and conferred with Barka. He agreed we were on the border. We patrolled to a pick-up zone, searching for telltale fresh shoe prints.

Once the early-morning 'drag' was completed, provided we had not stumbled on anything of interest, the section was uplifted by vehicles to base camp to carry out training. That consisted of whatever Brian dreamt up; then a couple of hours of volleyball and beauty sleep. The day may be interrupted to investigate some incident or other, but we counted on gross boredom.

"Look at this shit place," Paddy Allen grumbled, as we surveyed the blackened scrub west of the border road.

The whole countryside was burnt out, blackened, dry and bloody hot. I don't know who burnt off hundreds of acres of scrub, but the fire had substantially reduced the tree shade available to silly bastards wandering out in the midday sun. Along with the lack of decent shade, the shortage of water became acute. No streams ran through our area, so we either humped it in, or helped ourselves to the smoky water available in the PV.

"What's it like on the other side?" I nodded towards the wire fence.

"Mate, one hell o' a party," Paddy grinned, as he recalled his Mozambique ventures before the war. "Let's 'ave a look."

"Yeah," I agreed, and we crossed the cattle fence and strolled into Mozambique for about three kilometers.

We weren't out to prove anything, but rather acted as sightseers. I wanted to see whether the grass was greener on the other side. It wasn't. The bush was exactly the same: shitty, dust-stained, thorny scrub. The impoverished villagers appeared listless and curiously observed our progress, so after an hour, we decided to wander home before a runner alerted the closest Mozambique Army unit. We weren't concerned, though. We were confident in our immortality; we were invincible!

One afternoon, Brian shook me awake from my nap: "FRELIMO has crossed the border an' stolen 60 head of cattle," he said sharply, as he stuck his head in the tent flap, "so get after 'em!"

By the time I struggled into my kit, he added: "They are heading straight for Mozambique."

They must have a bloody barbecue ready to go. With the map coordinates in one hand, I rounded up Barka and the boys. The vehicles dropped us as close as practical to the last sighting. My section hit the ground and sprinted until we found the cattle trail. The dozens of sharp cattle hooves cut into the baked soil – making tracking ideal – so easy that even I could follow them. The men ran for kilometers, sweating and chafing under the scalding sun, closing in on the rustlers. I imagined shooting one steer for the pot ... T-bone steak on the hoof! Washed down with a chilled beer! But they beat us to the border. We discovered that a series of fence posts had been chopped at the base and the fence laid down flat for the cattle to scramble across. We had missed them by 20 minutes. Strict orders prevented the section from following after them. I radioed base for permission, knowing the answer would be a resounding NO.

We stood in the baking heat, knackered by the run, and cursed FRELIMO. I departed, wondering why the 'Machine' hadn't deployed a section straight down the border road to cut them off. Mine is not to reason why, blah, blah, blah.

Night after night, the section sneaked out to ambush likely infiltration routes. The actual path selection was scientifically based upon pot luck. With many routes in and few ambush parties, the odds were stacked in the terrorists' favor. We were not issued with any type of pyrotechnic illumination, no trip flares or parachute flares to light up an ambush zone. Claymore mines – the South African copy of the American anti-personnel weapon – were sited along the lonely footpaths and covered by the MAG machine gun. The Claymore packed 700 ball bearings and, if detonated, blasted with the force of a shotgun at close range. We only carried two per section, so banks of them were unrealistic. I set up an exotic grenade necklace – utilizing five old British Mills 36 grenades, a detonator cord, an electrical detonator and a hand-piece. These were hung from the scrub on the trail – 30 meters away from the ambush site – acting as a Stop Group. I never witnessed the effectiveness of five fragmentation grenades linked together at genital height, as whenever the time and the patience was available to erect the fireworks, no one used that particular foot track.

Once the ambush settled in, the nights were truly black. Far from artificial town lighting, even with a clear night sky, only the outlines of close objects were visible. On sentry, I'd sit back, mesmerized by the zillions of twinkling stars. An active imagination pondered on the probabilities of the universe staring back. The mind indulged in the 'what ifs' when confronted with a moving cosmos. The intellect acorn tossed around simple theories – calculating what life means. Still, on those endless nights, I never found the answer, at least not one outside a beer bottle.

The night that reduced visibility, amplified sound. We heard people half a kilometer away moving noisily along a path, but we were unable to leave the ambush for fear of bumbling into other friendly forces. Voices and scrapping sounds drifted in the quiet night. It was most frustrating! The next morning, if we were very lucky – and if the constables had correctly estimated the sound location – we pinpointed the *spoor* and we chased after them. Nine times out of 10, the tracks fizzled out.

Early one morning, after a night ambush, while we were walking back to a pick-up point – dreaming of fried eggs and Spam and hot instant coffee – Brian broke through on the radio.

"Delta four, move to the following grid … "

Oh, fuck, there goes breakfast!

He rattled off the new task: there had been an attack on a PV the night before.

"Get your arse there and follow up!"

Shit! Tired from a continuous series of night ambushes, we grumpily tramped across Mudzi to the grid reference. We humped kilometers cross-country through light scrub – stomping over the crumbly soil – before we finally sighted a sprawling, dusty township squatting under the boiling sun. The smudges of people sharpened as we walked closer.

This was my first sighting of a Protected Village. The PV had been built as part of a national strategy to remove the rural population from the terrorists' grip, to keep them safe. Once constructed, Internal Affairs trawled the scattered population from the surrounding countryside and unloaded them into one center bounded by a security fence. The theory espoused that settling the rural African population into guarded centers would cut off food supplies to the CTs was based on the 1950s Malaya Emergency experience, where the Chinese living on the jungle outskirts were rounded up and housed in a PV to cut them off from the Chinese terrorists; however, in Malaya, the rural Chinese were a minority. In Rhodesia, the rural African counted as the vast majority. The Rhodesian Government did not have anywhere near the same funds and resources that the Commonwealth threw into Malaya.

Once resettled, some Africans liked the PV because fresh water was on tap and facilities – such as a medical clinic, which were not always available in the traditional *kraal* areas – were on site. Others squatted in conditions they found distasteful: hastily constructed houses crammed together, unlike the open spaces of rural villages, and people living in close proximity to families with whom there had been long, simmering feuds. All the villagers endured the daily hassle of being searched going in and out, as well as the long, hot tramp across country to tend their fields and being forced to return before the dusk curfew.

Crime, virtually unknown in the rural villages, began to emerge. The CTs roasted the PV concept in its propaganda war and successfully described Protected Villages as 'concentration camps' – scoring lots of press with the gullible overseas publications.

We arrived tired and irritable. Only a few people were visible inside the wire. The nervy Internal Affairs guard on the main gate pointed out their

An Alouette helicopter arriving at a landmine scene; Nyamapanda, 1976. Note the Internal Affairs Lee Enfield .303 in the foreground. (Ron Rink)

living quarters. They lived in demountable buildings surrounded by a rammed earth wall – a strongpoint as high as the roof peaks. We strolled in to find the buildings deserted. Doors were open, but nobody home. Climbing to the top of the earth ramparts, we quickly spotted the shaken staff clustered like curious tourists around the terrorists' firing positions. A pile of expended bullet cartridges and a hole in the baked dirt, where the mortar operated, fingered the firing positions. Fortunately, they had not incurred casualties.

Sergeant Barka lost interest in the attack position and trailed the *spoor* back to the fence. There he found evidence of 10 CTs who had cut the diamond mesh fence using the AKM bayonet and scabbard (combined, they were an effective wire cutter), had slipped inside and then partook in a hot feed with the residents. Once fed, they thanked the Security Forces for providing the venue by firing small arms and mortars on the strongpoint. The Internal Affairs guardians squirmed for cover. Barka, in his usual business-like fashion, slipped through the hole in the fence, located the intruders' *spoor* outside the PV and called out to separate the curious constables from the skittish guards. We followed, slipping through the gaping hole. He pointed out the *spoor* for my benefit and, without waiting for instructions, began the tracking. I radioed Brian and told him that we were on *spoor* and took off after Barka. Within 10 minutes, JOC radioed with instructions to halt and wait for an RAR sparrow team. I started to argue. Why did we need a sparrow team? I had competent trackers, but they insisted (roll out the inter-force politics again), so we sat on our bums alongside the *spoor* and waited. Fifteen minutes later, a helicopter appeared and deposited the RAR trackers.

"Recognize that tall one there?" said Sergeant Barka nonchalantly, as the four-man sparrow team jogged our way.

"Should I?" I grumbled, pissed at the time wasted.

"He's the guy who refused to show us the *gandangas* in Chiduku," stated Barka, as he tossed a dry pebble into the scrub.

"So he is," I replied, very surprised. A small world indeed! What happened after we dumped him back in the police station? Did anyone investigate my report?

The RAR tracker suddenly recognized us, blanched and shied away. Their four-man team stood to one side and argued before a corporal stalked over to me.

"We're not going on without backup," he said adamantly.

"What about us?" I smiled.

"I need army."

"Come on, Sarge,' I turned to Barka, "we'll do it ourselves. They can sort out their own problems."

We left them engrossed in discussion and went alone. Once again, within 10 minutes, the radio crackled and I was ordered to stop and wait for the RAR trackers. Shit, what's going on? The four finally caught up and took over the tracking.

The tracking exercise was a time-waster. The sparrow team had good trackers, but when they lost *spoor*, they just simply sat down. I couldn't believe it. What the fuck got into their pants? When I asked them why they stopped, they simply shrugged. I ignored them and waited until my men rustled up the *spoor*; then we all got on with the job. The anxiety of the RAR 'gook' contributed to their hostile attitude. Barka grew increasingly antagonistic as his head tracker position was usurped. Each time the sparrows lost *spoor*, the problem dropped into his lap to clean up. He irritably snapped at the constables and completely ignored me.

The tracking was on and off all day across open ground, under the vindictive sun. *Spoor* was lost and found, lost and found, while we bathed in sweat and sunburn. The shoe prints finally led to a dry riverbed, where new diggings revealed a small ammunition cache – two metal cases of 7.62mm Intermediate ball, and a half-dozen Chinese 60mm mortar bombs buried in the gritty sand – and that was that. The RAR boys decided it was home time, so they huddled together, talked into the radio handset and soon an Alouette helicopter appeared in the sky and picked them up. I was glad to see them go and bemused why they were involved at all. They're competent trackers, but maybe our Chiduku 'friend' poisoned the relationship.

As a result of this incident, night ambushes switched from border paths to inside the PV wire. After uneventful nights, just before the red clouds of dawn, two CTs marched brashly up to the barbed wire fence and loudly called out to the residents. They ordered hot food and tea and demanded Nyamapanda Room Service for 20. A PATU stick welcomed them with a volley of rifle fire – killing one CT outright and wounding the other. The wounded CT stumbled away from the fence into a scrub-filled depression, stuck a Chinese stick grenade to his head, pulled the cord and the blast decapitated him. My section – ambushing another part of the same PV – backtracked the *spoor* of the two raiders, found the point where the main party of 15 had waited for breakfast and then chased them back to the border, where we had to stop.

On the Mozambique border, Paddy's section stumbled on a fresh line of shoe prints entering Rhodesia. Brian ordered him to stay and wait. JOC assigned a Territorial Army tracker team to take up the chase. They aggressively leapfrogged two four-man sticks, one ahead of the other. Using a single helicopter, the air force flew one team ahead of the ground hunters – dropping them kilometers in front to relocate the *spoor* – and returned to retrieve the first team to repeat the operation. The trackers speedily chased the CT trail for kilometers inland; then, astoundingly, they caught four CTs dozing on the lee side of a ridge. The terrorists, so confident they were ahead of any pursuit, hadn't bothered with sentries. The TF unit captured one and shot dead the other three.

A spate of minor operations interrupted sleep time. Booted out of the cot to assist a PR unit that reported fresh CT *spoor*, my section jogged for kilometers under the blazing sun – sweat draining from every pore, trying to close the time gap. When we finally linked up with PR (four middle-aged men from Salisbury), Barka deduced in seconds that the PR had been following Delta's own two-day-old boot prints!

After only two and a half weeks into this border tour, Delta Troop suddenly packed up its equipment and redeployed to Inyanga, due south of Nyamapanda, on the eastern border. Brian drove off with Barry and the advanced party – leaving Paddy and I to transport the bulk of the troop. Driving an inland route, Paddy and I decided to pop into the Mtoko Hotel for a quick beer. It was dark when we parked the convoy in the asphalt car park and, with promises of a beer for each constable seated on the two trucks, we entered the bar in good spirits. The taste of a cold beer was within reach. A few roughnecks straddled stools in the fine mist of cigarette smoke. Paddy ordered two Lions to whet the appetite and three dozen beers for the troops waiting in the car park.

The white, middle-aged proprietor shrugged his shoulders as he uncapped the two beers and stated: "Sorry boys, I don't serve kaffirs in this hotel."

I stood stunned.

"We aren't asking you to," Paddy smiled menacingly. "They'll have a beer on the back o' the truck, out in the car park. No one will know."

"Sorry, I can't do that," the proprietor stated emphatically.

The white locals drinking at the bar sat in silence – supporting neither the publican, nor us. "Mister, they'll be staying out there!" I interrupted, pissed off with the intransigent attitude that pervaded white conservatives. "They won't be drinking in the pub."

"Sorry," he said stubbornly.

"Fuckin' stick your beer," snarled Paddy. "Let's go."

These petty racial incidents cropped up from time to time. Two years on, I overheard a Member of Parliament discussing the construction of new barracks at Chikurubi with a senior police officer. The MP asked why the police were going to the expense of housing the African police component. Surely, they don't need proper houses?

Delta motored into Ruangwe, to a police station under construction in the Inyanga North TTL. Before Delta Troop arrived, the base had been home for 3 Independent Company – an army unit comprised of young National Servicemen completing their 18-month service. ZANLA had given them a touch-up one night: they bombarded the camp using a 75mm recoilless rifle, 82mm mortars, 60mm mortars and small arms; the company suffered 12 wounded.

Approaching on the road from Inyanga, the police post – sited on a ridgeline at the peak of an escarpment – was a perfect silhouette against the sky. The camp itself resembled a construction site where the builders had suddenly downed tools and walked off. They left behind completed demountable buildings, part-finished concrete formwork and basic foundations. The troop's vehicles halted inside the perimeter and the men scattered from the trucks to stretch and eyeball their new home. I curiously wandered to the highest point on the spine of the escarpment, where I surveyed the tribal lands sweltering below. As far as the eye could see, lush bush covered rolling hills, which merged into the heat haze – obscuring the Mozambique border. Viewed from the hillside, the terrain looked unpopulated. Valleys were hidden by the canopy of undulating timber country. Underneath the forest treetops cut clear, cold streams – a camper's wonderland. An SF bush operator felt a twinge, like being on a camping holiday. The thriving woodland and the close proximity to Mozambique, coupled with a lack of commercial farms, made an ideal ZANLA free-flow area. This TTL intersected with another TTL – allowing considerable freedom of movement for terrorist bands.

An hour of confusion reigned as Brian attempted to organize a camp. Police GC and army elements had snatched the prime empty buildings, so Brian stamped his authority and evicted unhappy people. The constables unshackled the baggage trailers to commence the setting up, with the NCOs snapping at their heels. Paddy and Barry mixed with a couple of hairy GC operators (police they knew from earlier in their service). The white population was small enough that police born and raised in Rhodesia knew someone who knew someone. The chances of meeting someone they recognized, either growing up or as adults, remained high no matter how remote the camp. They slapped backs – laughing and chortling.

Once the troop pitched the tents and sorted out the operational kit, Brian called the section leaders together for a briefing. He converted a demountable building into an ops room and hijacked a completed map board. A sergeant set up his radios as Brian stood impatiently in front of the maps, a pointer in his hand. Once we settled, he filled out the details of the topography. His pointer tapped the prominent land features, the rivers, the Mozambique border and our operational boundary. He spelled out the history of the local conflict.

The pointer stopped at the Avila Mission. He stated adamantly that the Avila Mission closely supported and assisted the enemy. As evidence, he cited Bishop Lamont – an Irish priest who promoted open support for ZANLA at Avila and now was facing trial in Salisbury. Gibbs went on to state that section leaders were not to enter the Mission under any circumstances; it was a no-go area, a legal minefield. His unambiguous instructions told us to stay away unless specifically ordered to enter. Paddy sniped with 'what if' questions, such as being within striking distance of the enemy in the Mission. All were overruled: "DON'T ENTER. FULL STOP."

Brian's briefing concentrated on the large numbers of reported ZANLA – groups up to one-hundred strong operating around Avila. Paddy looked at me and rolled his eyes. A seven-man patrol versus a hundred terrorists ... that would be fun!

He fielded the obvious question: "How does a section fight a company-strong enemy?"

Brian just stared at him.

"Shouldn't we operate in strength? Two sections together?"

Brian ignored him. There was no way Brian was going to double sections.

"What about another machine gun per section?" Paddy continued, baiting Brian – knowing machine guns were scarce as rocking horse shit.

Brian hurried his briefing along – brushing aside the question like we were awkward children. The best way to handle the problem was to ignore it! Paddy shrugged. Barry sat silent.

Straight after winding up the briefing, Brian wasted no time and deployed three Delta sections before we had time to settle in: Barry's, Paddy's and mine. Maps and shackle codes were handed out, and areas assigned. Sections were given a warning order to deploy. We loaded up our backpacks with our kit and briefed our men. Late afternoon, we humped our heavy packs down the gravel road and past the hastily erected tents. Intelligence Corps soldiers and elements of PR stuck out their heads and gave us a knowing smile. They didn't envy us. They were tucked up in a base. We struck northwards to be sucked into the wooded countryside.

Late on the second afternoon, towards dusk, Barry – Delta Two – came on the radio channel.

"Delta Base, this is Delta Two, over."

The base acknowledged the radio call. I lay back on the timbered hill, leafy floor occupied since mid-afternoon – my ears pricking up to grab every word. We tucked ourselves into patches of cooler shade – fending off mopane fly attacks and big black ants biting from within the dead leaf carpet. The mopane fly was a pinhead-sized bee that flew straight into open orifices – tickling with microscopic feet. They tunneled inside the nose, ears, eyes and mouth. Wherever body moisture existed, they descended in thick clouds. Even insect repellent, liberally slapped on the skin, did not deter them. If killed with a frustrated slap, the sickly, sweet odor emitted from the squashed body attracted more of the buggers – a definite no-win situation! They had been known to madden lazy cattle into raging stampedes and to cause some tired SF operators to abandon their post.

"Delta Base, Mantle Delta Two," the voice spoke quietly through the plastic earpiece, "we, um, we had a terr visual, over."

"Copied that," replied Brian, his voice booming over the airwaves. "Confirm you've had contact, over."

"This is Delta Two, ah negative," whispered the voice. "We had one visual, but before we could open fire, he disappeared. A sentry, I think. It's getting too dark for a follow-up now, over."

"Copied," grunted Brian excitedly. "You'd better base up there tonight, an' get on *spoor* at first light, over."

"Roger," replied Barry, unenthusiastically.

The night enveloped the land.

Early the next morning (20 October), a reluctant Delta Two lumbered up the suspect hill where the terrorist had been sighted. They stepped over the summit and tramped downhill. The scout spotted a *kraal* snuggled at the base. Barry paused to size up his options: he decided to split his section in two. Four men were sent straight into the village, while the other four scurried around the outskirts in a flanking movement. The flankers soon disappeared into the timber. With only one radio, the leader, who had lost sight of one stick of four, could not coordinate them. Meanwhile, my section sat on the dead leaf carpet, which was warming under the early morning sun – fending off a plague of mopane flies and contemplating a hot cuppa tea – when a solid roar of small arms fire rent the still air.

"Jesus, someone's in the shit," I muttered to Sergeant Barka, as I seized the radio handset. From a distance, the gunfire magnified and rebounded. I waited in wound-up suspense. The handset remained silent.

"Sarge, make sure everyone is packed up an' ready to leave. We may be needed."

The roar steadily amplified. The cacophony of small arms blurred NATO and communist weapons. The individual blasts moulded into one gunfire orchestra. From our hidden position, west of the contact, a small range of forested hills blocked the view. Standing up, we weren't able to discern even tracer bullet colors; then the rumble spluttered, faded and finally evaporated.

After at least a minute of complete silence, the radio squawked: "Delta Base, this is Delta Two, over."

"Delta Two, Base, read you threes, go ahead, over," sung Brian's chirpy first-thing-in-the-morning voice. Obviously from his tone, the sounds of battle had not drifted to the base camp.

"Delta Two," said the shaken voice, "we've had contact! I've lost half the section. Jesus! They were just waiting for us. They shot the shit outta us, over!"

"This is Delta Base," replied Brian, in a calming tone to suppress the evident panic, "say again slowly. Are you in contact now, over?"

"Ah, negative," he whispered.

"OK, copied," soothed Brian. "What's happenin' right now?"

"Ah, the firin' stopped an' half the section is missing. Jesus. What should I do?"

"Take it easy. What happened to the half section?"

"I split the section to sweep the *kraal*," Barry whispered in shock, "one half walked into an ambush. There must have been dozens of 'em."

"Delta Four," snapped Brian, now all business, "copied?"

"Delta Four, that's affirmative, over," I replied.

"Move in that direction. I'll move Delta Three, an' sort this out, over."

"Roger. We're on our way, over."

"Delta Four, Base, out to you … Delta Two … "

The men scrambled off the wooded hill, keen to assist. At this stage, there was no confirmation of enemy strength. I didn't care. I willed ZANLA to stay so we could kick some arse. Our speed was hindered by the ancient terraces that didn't promote fast foot movement. The knee-high stone walls are a pain in the arse. Laid out similar to the paddy fields common in Asia's hilly terrain, they had been long defunct and no one was too sure (in the 1970s) who had constructed them. The theories included a Shona tribe, Arab slave traders and very early Portuguese. Whoever assembled them back then managed to slow down our foot movement today. The hillsides throughout Inyanga North are littered with the rust-colored stone rubble of an older civilization.

I pushed the men hard. We tried to cut off possible escape routes north of Avila Mission by running for kilometers in the blistering heat. The sweat poured off and saturated our clothing. White salt crystallized around the armpits and the back of the shirt. The harness webbing chafed the hips red, the rucksack dragged down the sore shoulders and the ammunition belts weighed a ton. Elias abruptly collapsed. We quickly revived him by pouring precious water over his face and body, and then detoured to the Ruenya River and plunged him in. Elias' collapse was unexpected, as the Africans were fit and hard, with enormous reserves of stamina. Rarely did the elements affect them. Their tough upbringing also psychologically strengthened them. I peered at the others as Elias regained his strength. Sibanda, the MAG gunner, barely raised a sweat. He had massive thigh muscles, as if he sucked on steroids. He totted the 11kg machine gun and 300 rounds of ammunition, his webbing and backpack at the run, without a peep. A keen soccer player, who had represented the BSA Police, he dreamed of an elusive future in professional competition. The others looked haggard, but ready to push on. Once Elias surfaced, we slogged up the river – searching for potential crossing points. Crossing the river back and forth did not impress them. We nearly lost Mhiripiri over a waterfall. The swift water flowed over slippery boulders – a formidable obstacle for tired and heavily laden constables. Mhiripiri lost his footing, slid on the greasy rock and plunged into the fast-flowing water just above a three-meter waterfall. He dropped his rifle as he clung like a limpet to a rock. His pasty face attested to his fright. We stopped the patrol. Chipanza stripped off his equipment and boots to dive several times into the cold, fast-flowing river to recover the lost FN rifle.

We entered all *kraals* located between Avila Mission and the river – talking to scores of unlucky people. The day marked harsh interrogation and heavy-handedness. The African villagers sat sullen and uncooperative, and adamantly insisted there were no CTs living in the TTL. They stared defiantly – spitting out their answers. Hearing the constant emphatic denial all day, unsupported by the facts, chipped the edge off my patience. It was akin to listening to a child blurt outrageous lies over and over again. The more I listened to them defend the indefensible, the more abrupt I became. The information was frustratingly devoid of anything interesting. Having hit a blank wall, I took a long shot that the CTs had a base camp in some isolated spot. I eyed the heavy forest in Lawleys Concession and stomped through that unpopulated virgin timber country, but we found absolutely zilch. The terrorists had eluded detection, so we rested up and waited.

Later that afternoon, the word said four constables from Delta Two had walked straight into an ambush by 20 CTs. The section medic, Constable Isaac Chipara, was shot and killed. The men were pinned down by an extraordinary volume of small arms fire until the CTs slipped away. Barry, separated from the ambushed party – and without information or visual connection – froze. Fortunately, Chipara was the only fatality. It could have been much worse.

Paddy's Delta Three tracked a large swath of *spoor* from the ambush straight to Avila Mission. Outside, the shoe prints dissolved – kindly swept away by the staff and children with snapped-off tree branches. The staff's blatant actions announced they were exempt from any consequences. Even the used branches lay abandoned on the newly swept soil – mocking the section. Without permission to enter the Mission grounds, Paddy stood helplessly outside. He radioed base and argued heatedly with Brian, but No was NO.

Avila Mission sat like an untouchable sanctuary – a beacon of rest and recuperation for ZANLA boys. Irish Catholics – ZANLA supporters – headed the Mission staff. While some missionaries sat on the sidelines, Catholic missionaries throughout the country spread African nationalism and legitimized the terrorist campaign. There were continual sightings and small incidents involving ZANLA within spitting distance of Avila – evidence of the Mission's complicity – but the government kept its hands off. To us simple sons of bitches, we couldn't understand why these safe havens were allowed to operate with flagrant disregard. The government should just shut it down and be done with it; stop pussyfooting around.

We kept up the momentum around the Mission for 10 days after the loss of Chipara. Talking, patrolling, interrogating, ambushing and days of observation applied pressure on the region. We searched every hut, every grain storage bin, every cattle enclosure, all road traffic and every individual's luggage. We surged through the population like a dose of salts – and then, something happened … at 4:45 a.m. on 31 October, I was suddenly jabbed in my shoulder. What the hell? The gray zone between cranky tiredness and wide awake evaporated. I awoke immediately, with no fogginess inside the head; no loud yawning or stretching; no rapid blinking, but straight from a semi-sleep state to being utterly alert and sharp in a snap.

"*Gandangas!*" hissed Ruzawi.

My eyes peered apprehensively between the dry grass stalks and adjusted to the misty light. A movement caught my attention: dark figures, blurrily outlined, visible from their knees up, spread out three paces apart, walked by with a quick gait. Shit! My heart rate cranked up notches. They were less than 15 paces away. Three, seven, 10, how many more of them? The shadows strode along the weed-choked tsetse road and more were coming. Without forethought, little by little my arms and fingers worked the FN rifle through the stubby grass and propped the plastic butt into my shoulder. The dry blades rustled as they parted. The minute crackling boomed in my ears. Shit! Shit! My teeth gritted …

A tall shadow led. The outline of an Aussie-style slouch hat and a light machine gun carried in both hands contrasted against the drab bush backdrop. The washy dawn light still fought off vestiges of the black night rearguard hazing the walkers. Their outlines were shoddy, but definitely armed. My eyes flicked to the right, along the shadows that followed the tall man, and saw a distinctive AK-47 banana magazine dangled down the side of the fourth walker. As my eyes swiveled further right, my heart incurred a minor seizure. A backpack lay carelessly on top of our protective wall. What motherfucker left that there? Stupid, stupid bastard! But this was no time for recriminations – this was it!

The FN butt tucked into my right shoulder, the barrel leveled until the lead man's hazy body filled the aperture sight … there was no time to contemplate the merits of the killing act; shut out all useless thoughts and allow the training to override reason. I sucked in breath and fought off buck fever that threatened to spoil my aim. "Hold it" rattled in my head as the lead man ambled unknowingly across our hidden position. The scale of the landscape contracted as I concentrated on the man inside the gun sight. Within seconds, he'd be shielded by gloomy roadside bush. I sprang the ambush, with the forefinger curled against the trigger, and eased it back … Now! A thunderous roar rebounded off the granite hills. The tall man dropped sharply like a wooden puppet whose invisible strings were suddenly clipped. The constables fired – sending out a shockwave of bullets – accompanied by an ear-tingling thunderclap. The walkers immediately hit the deck. We were amazed at their reaction speed. One second, they casually walked; the next millisecond, before the sound of the first shot died, they vanished from view – melting into the scrappy cover.

Our weapons produced an awesome barrage – a thunderous racket and bullets smashing into everything. Seconds after the initial combined firepower, the shooting fragmented. From our camouflaged position, among the grass stalks growing on a thick contour ridge, smack in the center of a fallow field, we unleashed a curtain of bullets. Nothing moved. They lay rigid – attempting concealment in the shallow ditch on the opposite side of the dirt road. The air thickened with burnt cordite and fried rifle oil. We spotted the colored smidgens of clothing. Dazzling red tracer bullets zapped into the gray-green scrub. Bullets struck the dirt – churning up clouds of fine dust that obscured the tiny color splashes. The area, no bigger than a basketball court, teemed with bullets – snapping off green branches, stripping the leaf like a wild scythe, ploughing into the cracked soil, slicing dry grass stalks and thudding into exposed human flesh with a sick whack. After six quick shots, I snapped a glance at our own line. The men, snuggled as low as snake shit into the crackly dry grass, concentrated on their individual targets. Hot brass shells ejected violently from the rifles – flying through the cool air, or piling up together underneath the staunch MAG machine gun. Sibanda, his aim aided by the steel bipod, fired streams of bullets into the unprotected roadway. Further down the line, however, two constables – obscured by others and the longish grass – were, by the angle of their rifle barrels, apparently fending off an airborne attack! Arseholes! I made a mental note to kick arse later.

In the first minute, a number of terrorists – cowering under the scrub and grass shield in the shallow ditch – collected their wits and opened fire. Their bullet streams flew dangerously over our ambush line, with the sharp whip-crackle adding to the boom of our small arms fire. With the increased gush of adrenalin, I ignored the incoming bullets and concentrated on opportunities. The color splashes made excellent aiming points (those not completely obliterated in the dust curtain). I aimed and fired, aimed and fired and hoped the bullets were effective.

Lying in a close-quarter, fierce firefight is difficult to describe. It's the compressed excitement of a football final – wrapped up in surges of jubilation and tempered with streaks of fear and trepidation. It's not rational, not sane, almost hysterical; it's intoxicating madness and adrenalin-driven anxiety with overlapping exhilaration but, unlike a feverish football game, the final result is death and serious mutilation. With scores of frenzied bullets and jagged shrapnel indiscriminately zapping everywhere, this ramps up the chance of sudden death exponentially.

Under a hail of bullets, a single terrorist dramatically broke cover from the shallow gutter and, in a flash of movement and a smudge of blue, scooted desperately across a ploughed field on his hands and knees, with his arse pointed up as he frantically employed his arms and legs to propel his body. I had never seen anyone crawl that fast. He was absolutely motoring – clambering over the dry sods towards tree cover. I fired four times. Dirt sprayed next to and beyond him. At least one bullet hit him, judging by the involuntary jerk, but failed to slow his desperate lunge for freedom. He decamped behind a small boulder and a tree clump in the open field; then, in a flash, as sudden as the one-sided firefight had been sprung, events turned … a fearless terrorist, who had been walking at the back of the single file (and was, therefore, outside the ambush site), decided not to cut and run; instead, he sneaked – undetected – along a low ridge 30 meters further west of the overgrown road and positioned himself in thick scrub overlooking us. With an unobstructed view, he simply announced himself with a scary burst of automatic fire. Bullets splattered lumps of dry dirt in our faces. He delivered his business card. The distinctive, sharp rip of the RPD belt-fed machine gun tightened my arsehole. We sank lower in the spiky grass, watching for his next burst, in order to pinpoint his position. He squeezed off another 10 rounds, followed by another 10. The green tracer originated from a deep blue-green scrubby knoll. The bursts were unimpeded and solidly struck the walled contour ridge. We huddled down. We couldn't see his exact position, distracted by rifle fire from the ambushed group, but this boy had our range. I sensed we couldn't just hide against the earthworks and do nothing because he had secured a firing position slightly above ours and, in a short time, his aim would zero on target; then we would incur casualties. In the decision-making millisecond, I made an impulsive move: to get a better view, I suddenly knelt up from behind the wall and, exposed from the waist up, fired aimed shots. As the bullets thwacked into the bush screen, he instantly replied – and SMACK! A bullet struck my left shoulder. Later, we discovered the 7.62mm Intermediate had punctured the trapezius muscle on my shoulder blade (about an inch from the shoulder joint), had followed the bone along and exited just before the spine. Lucky, lucky, lucky!

I didn't need any more encouragement; I'd got the message! I swiftly ducked down behind the contour ridge and tested the arm. The shoulder throbbed, but my left arm still worked. I could still operate. The next burst danced over the ridge top and struck the sergeant's rucksack. (Barka sulked for days about the hole in his favorite spare shirt.) Now, forced to squat below the ridgeline, I retrieved a Z42 rifle grenade from my webbing pouch. Swiftly extracting the ballistite cartridge from the butt of the missile, I yanked out the safety pin and rammed the rifle grenade over the rifle muzzle. Unclipping the rifle magazine, I cocked the weapon to unload the bullet from the chamber and manually loaded a ballistite cartridge into the empty chamber; then I released the cocking handle, replaced the magazine, changed the gas plug around, popped up the Zulu sight and aimed. This was all in a speedy, but measured movement that bettered any time I'd fumbled through in training – amazing the powerful incentive to apply speed a sky full of bullets can produce. The RPD sprayed another burst just over the top of the ridge and I fired. The savage recoil booted into the web of my hand. The rocket-shaped missile jetted into the dawning sky like a black dot, high above the gunner's position, and then sharply dropped. It looked like the grenade would overshoot, but a steel-gray cloud marked the exact impact spot. CRUMP! On or near the target! The RPD shut up. The gunner did not fire again. The rifle grenade had dislodged him. We never discovered whether he'd been hit. The Z42 exploded – showering fine steel fragments and slivers – but it rarely killed.

The gunner had done his job well. By pinning us to the contour ridge, he enabled some shocked survivors to snivel away. They melted away like mercury on a flat board. Their rifle fire evaporated on his intervention and, once the RPD ripping ceased, a ringing silence hung in the air. The Z42 explosion had rang out like a full stop at the end of a long, noisy paragraph.

I lay in the grass as a warm slick expanded in my shoulder and ran down the back. There was little pain. After unloading the Z42 cartridge, my rifle re-cocked, we concentrated on the ambush zone – looking for tell-tale signs of life. Breathing slowly, I divided up the area in my head and scrutinized every meter. Nothing moved. The dust cloud thinned and settled. No groans or cries of pain lifted from the ambushed group. The acrid taste of cordite and cooked rifle oil fragranced the air.

After three or four minutes of clear stillness, the time had come to move. I didn't want to stay too long, or there could be a mortar bomb greeting.

"Reload!" I called and heard the metallic clang and clatter as fresh 20-round magazines were clipped to the rifle housing. The MAG slammed closed the top cover, which announced Sibanda was ready. The men jostled into their webbing belts, clipping and shuffling the canvas straps, but careful not to expose themselves.

"Sarge, you an' Sibanda cover us. The rest, follow me!"

Sibanda and Barka's facial expressions displayed relief as they tucked themselves against the dirt wall. I jumped to my feet, swiftly orientated and broke into a run. I ran behind the constables to call out each individual's name to make sure they knew I meant them. Their faces appeared strained and anxious but, like a rolling wave, the constables rose and sprinted behind the leader. We charged along the exposed contour wall, completely in the open, not a steric of cover, feeling like naked men running past watching villains! Now that was a rush! If I wanted a dizzy high, running exposed to enemy fire brought that on. We broke all national running records. The line galloped right to the end of the contour ridge and then plunged straight through the thick scrub's intertwined branches that lashed at exposed arms. Swallowed up by the scrub, I slowed, paused to judge my bearings and turned 90° left. After I counted the heads of the runners – and was satisfied we survived – we all embarked on a mad dash through the waist-high undergrowth and burst across the dirt road to outflank the enemy before they fled. After 30 seconds of the mad dash, once again I halted briefly, turned left again and assessed our location. We stood at right angles to the MAG, the crew visible. The machine gun barrel pointed like an accusing finger at the enemy. With hissing and cursing, the men juggled and formed a rough sweep line facing the enemy position – using the tsetse road as the axis of advance. We ducked down out of sight and swiftly caught our breath. A quick peek up and down the line showed blanched faces and nervous eyes.

"You've been hit!" whispered Ruzawi, as he drew past me and stopped to lower his medic pack.

"No time for that. Let's go," I murmured.

We stood up and strode briskly through the light scrub – using the old tsetse road as a guide. My heart whammed hard against my ribs, my stomach fluttered madly and my mouth was as dry as a sandpit. I glanced to the left and right and saw the men stamping forward in line. The six cautiously searched the scrubby ground ahead, attempting to see through the botchy leaves and criss-crossed branches, as well as remaining roughly in line with the person either side. As we ducked in and out of trees, the line contracted and expanded and the men apprehensively watched for the enemy.

Our line burst out of the scrub into the open field, where we suddenly spotted prone bodies. I clenched my rifle, the butt jammed in my shoulder, my finger stroking the trigger. "Shoot the armed ones!" I called, as we pressed in.

The men promptly appraised the strewn bodies and fired a single shot into armed men at point-blank as they passed. This was not cruelty; this was strictly OUR survival. With small numbers, no overhead aircraft, we couldn't afford to get into a bloody close-quarter battle in the midst of a sweep. The last thing we needed was the 'dead' to rise up after we scooted past and shoot someone in the back. The single shot, into the head, insured against a fight-to-the-death fanatic. Along the shallow gutter, the bundles were slumped like broken dolls and soaked in their own dark blood, with fine grit embedded into their skin where they had slammed hard into the grainy dust, their clothes worn askew and messy. The flies were already honing in.

The constables rounded up the survivors roughly. Death hovered, so we didn't have time to be considerate. Some unarmed people did a great job faking death, but a solid boot in the ribs soon put that right. We seized a fistful of clothing and hauled them to their feet. One girl pissed herself. We herded the survivors, propelled them into the open, punched them down before we strode into the mottled tree country 10 paces away and then crouched in the shade, waiting for a counter-attack. Insects hummed as the air warmed. We waited, with all senses tingling alive to foreign smells, noise and movement. Our eyes combed the scrub to detect signs, to strip away the leaf, to search for those lying just out of reach. Although no crying or screaming came from the skirmish field, Constable Ruzawi kept a keen eye on the huddle of captured left behind. Once I was satisfied the enemy had fled, we flitted back and began the task of searching the bodies.

Constable Mhiripiri jerked each of the captors upright. They sat dishevelled, wide-eyed with shock and with fawn dust clinging to their stunned faces. They looked like actors caught half-way through applying their make-up. All were young people of military age, slowly registering the overpowering event. One minute, a quiet walk through the park; the next, caught in a murderous flurry of bullets. They nervously looked around the dirt paddock at the loosely scattered dead, and at each other – a far cry to the recruiting overtures played out to them back home: the ZANLA call to arms. I stared at a captured youth and realized right then that I held the exclusive power to kill or spare. I could easily shoot him and be done with it: walk straight up, look into his round mortified eyes, lower my rifle barrel, squeeze the trigger and blast his life away, as easy as that! Unleash the monster within. Shoot and be damned. No remorse, no regret. No divine intervention. A good terrorist was a dead terrorist. He stared back, stunned and shell-shocked, unable to prevent or avoid any action taken. I shrugged and walked away.

"So, this was the enemy?" I mused, as I knelt by a dead terrorist.

This boy was the end product of the ground *spoor*, of the 'Dracula' propaganda and the blood-sucking evil murdering bastards as painted by the media. He now laid harmless, de-fanged, reeking of stale sweat and fresh coppery blood and ammonium piss – a lifeless statistic. Looking at the ordinary face, I recognized that physically, he was the same as my men. There were no evil-looking faces with horns! The same youth, but dressed different and not governed by police rules, ethics and social norms. He was young, invincible, cocky and given *carte blanche* to kill or harm – a young man pumped with propaganda, armed and unleashed on the population, with all the historic frustration and pent-up hatred until sudden death.

I stood up and gazed down the track. The tall terrorist lay crumpled where he fell when shot – an RPK light machine gun still clasped in his hands. The high-velocity bullet punched through his back and entered his chest cavity – tearing organs indiscriminately before it burst out the ribs, leaving a fist-sized hole. The coppery blood spread, interlocking with the cotton threads, and took on a dark and rusty look as it pooled in the dirt. The slouch hat, a trophy stolen from Internal Affairs, slid off to one side. Maybe he plucked it from a murdered district assistant. 'ZANU' was penned in black letters on the upturned rim. I turned away and idly watched Elias search the dead. He sat a body up to remove the weapons and webbing. I left him and wandered off across the open field in search of the frantically crawling terrorist from earlier in the firefight. In the crumbly soil, scuffmarks stood out like arrows right across the dirt. They attested to his crawling prowess right to the rock sanctuary. Behind the rock, the hardened ground revealed a dark blood pool rapidly soaked up by dry sods – a lost Chinese stick grenade, but no corpse. He'd vanished. I systemically surveyed the ploughed field right up to the wild scrub on the perimeter. He had staggered off – sunken shoe prints and splotchy blood left an easy trail. He's definitely wounded, probably lying inside the thick scrub? Do I look for him? Was he watching me? I decided not to press my luck. Lying hurt in the woods unseen, he'd be a cornered animal. I returned to the others.

From the flat ambush scene, radio communications with base were non-existent. Chipanza and I walked across the lumpy field where the crawler had disappeared and, being mindful of his existence, we cautiously climbed up a sharp granite ridge. I called Brian Gibbs and gave him the result like a football score. He promised reinforcements and casevac; then, on the spur of the moment, we cut across and scrambled up into the ridge where the RPD had been king. A straight, stiff climb over granite slabs, layered on each other like pancakes – and amply covered by umbrella shade trees – proved the enemy gunner to be a fit bastard. On the crest, Chipanza silently pointed to the mark where the Z42 had detonated. The explosion left a white circular smear on the gray granite – hardly impressive. Three paces away, a pile of expended machine gun shells denoted the RPD position. There was no evidence that the gunner had been hit.

Scrambling back to the kill zone, I organized the final sweep. Leaving Barka and his men behind, I rounded up Chipanza and Ruzawi to follow *spoor* and blood splatter. Whilst my shoulder gradually stiffened and ached, I thought we might catch a seriously wounded enemy. The tail end of the enemy outside the ambush had split and scattered like frightened gazelles into the heavily wooded hills. With bullets flying, these guys had had a real incentive to run. We estimated that there had been up to 30 people, in single file, ambling to the recruiting office in Mozambique. From the blood splash, we calculated at least two survivors of the four wounded, who fled with bleeding wounds into the harsh scrub, would die. The crawler was one, and another who had left large blood smear marks on the foliage. I wondered how many of the fleeing recruits would once again line up for the ZANLA recruitment, as a devastating ambush was not a good beginning for a terrorist career. From the road, we tracked a crisp set of shoe prints, but after three kilometers, the trail petered out. With the *spoor* gone, we slogged back along the weedy road and back to the ambush scene.

Confirmed kills: that was the name of the game; no pussy blood trails or 'intelligence estimate'. Only actual bodies of dead terrorists counted. The dead had to own a weapon of war, or at the very least, wear webbing with rifle magazines stowed inside. The bow was stretched on occasions on what constituted a proper kill: a young man wearing stolen shoes (couldn't possibly afford those); a man with a pair of binoculars (neighborhood watch?); a man wandering in three sets of clothing (professional shoplifter?). Civilian dead were not lumped with CT dead to increase the score rate – they were counted for what they were: civilians. The tallyman in JOC entered the dead into separate columns: 'Civilians', 'Baddies' and 'Goodies'. CT kills were accurately monitored to record the SF success, and so each unit bragged its score to measure its worth in the bush. The numbers were never a measure of the campaign's success, but just a statistic units bandied about to boast.

The ambush killed four terrorists outright, recovered six weapons and also killed four recruits and captured five. It was the best result for a Support Unit non-Claymore ambush inside the country to date. Thirteen killed or captured, and at least another four had been gravely wounded, judging by the blood spray.

Later, Special Branch revealed that the group had not been responsible for the ambush of Delta Two, but had walked from the Headlands area, kilometers to the south-east. They were on their way out of the country to collect an ammunition supply and to deliver 20 or so recruits. One of the captured female recruits claimed to be a serving policeman's wife. The war truly divided African families.

Paddy drove in after the follow-up burnt out: "Jesus, O'Brien, why aren't you dead, you ugly bastard?' he mocked, as he scrambled from the Land Rover. "You're worth much more dead than alive!"

As invincible warriors, we joked about insuring each other so that the survivor reaped the cash benefit of the other's death. Insurers offered products without the War Clause. We figured that if one was killed, the other should benefit. It was all talk. Even afterwards, we were too busy partying to action our smart idea.

Loading the dead and captured onto a truck – leaving Sergeant Barka and the crew to clean up the scene – Paddy and I drove in the convoy from the ambush spot and along the dirt road through Inyanga North TTL to Ruangwe, from where we departed alone to Umtali hospital, stopping at every drinking hole on the way. Ambushing was, after all, damn thirsty work. I had lost quite a bit of blood, so the alcohol hit the head quicker than usual. When we finally arrived at the hospital, the surgeons refused to operate because of my blood alcohol level. They cleaned up the wound and left me to sleep it off.

Wheeled into surgery the next morning, they opened and cleaned the wound, stitched it closed and then I relaxed. I slumbered in clean bed linen and ate good tucker. The hospital provided world-class surgery and post-op treatment; the wards were scrupulously clean, with trained staff and attentive nurses and doctors. While in hospital, ZANLA launched 122mm rockets at Umtali – fired from inside Mozambique – just for good measure. They missed the city and the missiles landed on the outlying areas. I didn't hear a thing. Delta copped another casualty. A Troop RL Bedford truck detonated a landmine and the driver suffered concussion and was evacuated to Umtali. I stayed a couple of days before returning to Delta Troop, neatly stitched and bandaged.

On my return, I stuck to base duties, radio schedules and driving vehicles to pick up sections. While I settled down to boring base routine, an army team arrived to demonstrate SF firepower to the cynical locals. The idea was to dazzle them with the technology at our fingertips. They herded the wary peasants up a grassy hillside, on the opposite side to our base, to give them a grandstand view over a *kraal* that had been custom-built for the exercise. Once the audience settled, the show began. Three Alouette helicopters flew in low from behind the audience and, without warning, opened fire at the grass roof huts with twin MGs and a 20mm Hispano cannon. The bullets showered the mock village; then they landed a section of RAR soldiers with plenty of MAGs, who ripped up the village with machine gun fire and rifle grenade explosions. The helicopters departed, circled overhead and, on cue, dived in and uplifted the RAR. I stood behind the villagers, watching with professional interest. Suddenly, two Hawker Hunter jets swooped and screamed low up a valley; then they strafed the wooden huts, using a combination of rockets and 30mm cannon, which blasted the structures to smithereens. The thunderous blasts of exploding warheads echoed off the hills. Dirt, timber and debris showered everywhere. The crowd instinctively ducked. The hut skeletons smouldered as the airplanes peeled off and vanished into the cloudy sky. The crowd emitted a groan of awe and amazement. After the exhilarating performance, which excited me more than the local people, I noticed a constable talking to an old man. With the considerable chatter and many hand gestures, I was curious.

"What's he chattering about?" I asked the constable.

"He said that if we are so powerful, why are there so many CTs in the bush?"

Good question.

The Rhodesian Intelligence Corps boys operated from Delta's base. They were part-time Territorial soldiers led by a blond captain. Keen to improve the intelligence collection – and using limited resources – they took risks. RIC had had little to no impact on intelligence gathering to date, as they didn't have the long-term sources to match Police Special Branch. They had started off well behind the eight ball, but still were determined to try.

Shortly after the firepower demonstration, they drove out of camp in one Land Rover. They only owned one Land Rover and continued to demand a Delta section escort, which was rarely available. Delta was already stretched just attempting to make a dent in ZANLA operations, without additional duties, so the RIC occasionally risked an ambush by traveling locally in one vehicle. Late one afternoon, their Land Rover ran over a TM46 landmine which was buried in the road at the base of the escarpment; however, the mine failed to detonate, even though the top of the mine was crushed by the weight of the vehicle. An Engineer team arrived hours later and lifted the anti-tank device. Underneath, they uncovered nine slabs of TNT. RIC were very, very lucky.

In the final days, Sergeant Barka became agitated over the talks between the US Special Envoy Henry Kissinger and PM Ian Smith. His contract ended at the completion of this tour and he had already formed a partnership in a taxi business. Stuck out in the wilderness, news fragments of a proposed peace deal floated in on transistor radios. He worried that we might be still fighting after a peace deal had been brokered. His uninterested eyes flickered in anger. Translated, he meant to serve out his last few days quietly, in peace, in camp. I didn't blame him. Delta handed Ruangwe over to Alpha Troop and scuttled back to Salisbury. On the journey back, Barka seemed jumpy and irritable, but once we drove through the outlying Salisbury suburbs, he breathed a huge sigh and, for the first time, I witnessed a beaming smile!

On R&R (also known as I&I: Intercourse and Intoxication), Paddy and I flew to Victoria Falls. He left his *fiancée* behind at Trout Beck and, needless to say, she was not amused. We stayed at the grand Victoria Falls Hotel – an excellent example of classic early 20th century architecture. Armed with an A-Z cocktail book, we made a determined effort to try each one. We found an African barman who knew how to mix all the exotic cocktails and settled down to a day/half the night drinking session. I read out the cocktail name, and the barman smiled and flamboyantly mixed the ingredients. An Alaskan Redeye was the only cocktail that stumped him.

Each morning, we rolled out of bed (worse for wear), ate a full breakfast on the deck overlooking the spray mist thrown up by the Victoria Falls and then adjourned to the bar, where we started again – drinking and laughing the day away – not bothered with the sights. One night, we entered the Elephant Hills Hotel to gamble at the in-house casino. Paddy brought a chunk of elephant's turd, salvaged on the outskirts of the golf course, and tossed it into the foyer 'to make it more authentic'. They chucked us out. On a Zambezi booze cruise, upon boarding, we handsomely tipped the waiters to exclusively serve us. Stuff the rest! The cruise guide soon received whining complaints from other passengers that the service had slackened, so he chewed out the waiters. We, in turn, harassed the waiters about their slowing service, so now they were caught in a sandwich, but they had accepted the early tip. When they hurried off to serve everyone else, I helped myself to a number of beers from the unattended bar. We slumped next to the rail and continued drinking from the Lion Ale line up – at least eight bottles ready to be swilled. The waiters were instructed not to serve us, as clearly, we were pissed. We were banned from further cruises.

We also heard Hollywood had arrived. A film crew was lodged at the

Victoria Falls Hotel to produce the adventure drama *'King Solomon's Treasure'*. The movie starred Britt Ekland, but she wasn't on location. They set up their film camera gear at the top end of the gigantic falls, so we wandered down from the bar to have a look. An athletic-looking stuntman exercised on the grassy bank, doing press-ups and sit-ups. A cluster of anxious men surveyed the river, arguing about the stunt. They chose a spot where the water ran swiftly – producing lots of white caps created by the protruding rocks. These waves ensured that any swim would appear extremely hazardous. On a word from the director, the stuntman walked into the boiling water and swam out parallel with the huge drop over the waterfall. Obviously a dangerous stunt, the swimmer wore a safety line held by a support team. On his swim back to shore – fighting the current and looking like he was on the verge of being swept down and over the falls – a local African nonchalantly walked into the river with a fishing net, within the camera shot, which neutralized the danger of the swimmer's stunt. The director swore and yelled at the puzzled wader. They had to film again. We were asked to leave the set after we applauded and clapped the astonished fisherman.

After the return to Salisbury, I reported to the Morris Depot hospital. The medical officer examined my shoulder wound and pulled out the stitches. It had healed beautifully. My shoulder still throbbed, but I wanted to deploy; I didn't need a clerk's job in headquarters. The Support Unit, critically short of section leaders, did not interfere.

After R&R, troops spent a week retraining. Fierce road runs, sharp foot drill, plenty of shooting and minor tactics were carried out to shake off the holiday. Midway through the re-training, a special guest had been organized. As we sat waiting, a captured terrorist – escorted by a Special Branch officer – walked in. He was colored (mixed race), shy, but arrogant. The men sized him up, chatting amongst themselves. I was intrigued, as he was the first live one to speak to us. He stood up on a rostrum, whispered to the Special Branch officer and then concisely outlined terrorist tactics. To round off his speech, he boldly stated that he was very unlucky to have been caught. The Security Forces, in his view, lacked street smarts. He pointed out, for example, that our black plastic rifles could be seen from afar. The plastic reflected light and the straight lines gave us away. The next day, the hierarchy relented and cans and cans of brown and green house paint arrived, and we were left to paint creative camouflage patterns on our weapons.

4

Inyanga, Chiduku Tango: December 1976

L aden with our kit, Delta's two RL Bedfords – hooked up to four-wheel trailers – arrived at Inyanga Township. Our two Hyenas and a Land Rover led the way and they all parked near the police station. Support Unit vehicles were painted a distinctive lime green, brighter than other police vehicles, with a swooping yellow eagle stenciled on the front fender, which was an ideal aiming point for a half-competent RPG artist. Brian slipped off to visit the JOC for intelligence and deployment briefing. The men lounged around the Bedford trucks smoking and chatting, pissing in the grass and stretching their limbs. Paddy and I decided to raid the single men's mess at the Inyanga police station, but as we crossed the lawn, Taffy – a chunky, Liverpool-born Special Branch officer – cut us off. Paddy and Taffy knew each other from way back and, after much handshaking and backslapping, Taffy led the way into the bar.

"You know, this bastard has the thickest service record in the force," Paddy laughed, as he opened the fridge, snatched three Lion beers and fished about for an opener. "What's it now, an encyclopaedia set?"

"Nah," Taffy grinned, "two ring binders."

"Two ring binders?" I stated in disbelief.

A record of service was generally a thin, buff manila folder with each year's assessment and other miscellaneous records – nothing even remotely approaching one ring binder, let alone two.

"Had a history of disagreements with the 'Ivory Tower'," said Paddy, with a grin from ear to ear. "What's happenin' lately?"

"Just had fuckin' assault charges dropped," mentioned Taffy offhandedly, as he uncapped his beer, "playin' poker when this fuckin' inspector tried to cheat. I took him to task, he got punchy, so I upped an' headbutted 'im. They tried to charge me, but the arsehole backed off when questions were asked about gambling on police property. Still, there's the ole rap over the knuckles."

I studied the stocky detective: a shock of black hair and a black moustache above an evil grin belied his record. I imagined a note pinned to the service record ring binder: 'Never ever promote' and 'to be left in operational areas only'.

We drank the chilled Lion like water and became progressively rowdy. Taffy chatted about some of his more non-policeman-like exploits. The local police superintendent – a haughty, distant man – did not head the popularity polls with the rank and file. Taffy played a little joke at the officer's expense. A superintendent's rank badge was stuck on a pet black pig that freely roamed the police camp, and all the lower ranks saluted it with great enthusiasm. ('Black Pig' became the officer's nickname.) Of course, Taffy had been implicated – another tick added to his reputation for hard drinking, even harder fighting and flagrant insubordination. Brian barged into the mess to shunt us out before the party got out of control.

Delta departed Inyanga – driving north back to Ruangwe once again. The tribal lands looked vacant as we drove, the grass expanse denuded of people and the Nyanga Mountain brooded in the background. We drove for two hours before arriving at the police station grounds, expecting to find Alpha Troop packed up and squared away, poised to depart. Although their transport lined the side road, Alpha personnel fluttered about, uncertain and agitated. Normally, a troop keen to get home waited anxiously for their relief. The newcomers were greeted by jeers and clapping – signaling the troop's final release. Old faces caught up and exchanged news. The new troop commander was almost frogmarched into the operations room and quickly briefed. The outgoing troop 2IC signed over camp assets and then everyone scrambled on their vehicles to return to Salisbury for a well-earned rest, but when Delta drove into Ruangwe that morning, the Alpha Troop commander did not burst forth to greet Brian. Gibbs, slightly peeved, parked and told us to wait on the trucks while he sought out the commander. We stood up on the back of the truck, stretched and questioned a passer-by. He said something unusual was happening, but couldn't enlighten us. Gibbs found the boss in the operations room intently engaged on the radio. An Alpha section had dropped into a spot of bother. They were pinned to the rocky bank of the Gairezi River, the border with Mozambique. The sergeant and his team wandered down the embankment to replenish water bottles and, lo and behold, FRELIMO trapped them using heavy MG fire from across the other side. The section couldn't move up or down the bank. Fortunately, they had not suffered casualties.

The Alpha boss requested Fireforce, but JOC Inyanga was extremely

Paddy Allen at Mukumbura, 1975. (Author's collection)

reluctant to deploy helicopters to any incident on the border. The presence of a 12.7mm heavy machine gun also concentrated the thinking. The loss of a precious helicopter would set back the cash-strapped nation, as it wasn't just a matter of going into the marketplace with a briefcase full of cash and purchasing a replacement. Rhodesian dollars were worth zilch in the world financial arena, and the United Nations had imposed sanctions that, naturally, included weapons of war. To buy a helicopter required months of subterfuge and wheeling and dealing.

Waiting by our trucks, shooting the shit, the gossip soon reached our ears: some Alpha section was pinned by a machine gun. Shit. Brian reappeared, florid-faced, and ordered Delta to remain on the vehicles – giving Paddy and me the evil eye ('that means YOU'), while he scooted back to find out how he could help. A short time later, he scampered back and, before we could scratch ourselves, he scrambled Delta Troop.

"Kiwi, you and Sergeant Zowah's sections will have to close down that machine gun. You'll be driven up to the drop-off, from where you separately head to the river, and then close in to shut it down."

"Meaning?"

He stared angrily at me, like I was an uncooperative kid; then flicked open a map, thrust it under my nose and ran his forefinger on a line.

"We'll drop you off at the end 'o this road, and patrol in there independently." His finger followed the contour lines to the river. "Alpha is at this loc." A blue dot marked the spot. He continued: "Zowah will follow the river an' link up with you to increase the firepower."

"Will he?" I asked. A rumor circulated that the good sergeant took shortcuts in the bush.

"I'll brief him personally. I want you guys to pin down Freddy so Alpha can get out."

Oh good.

Paddy laughed.

"You get your section ready to go," snorted Brian, as he shot Paddy 'The Look', "in case these guys need help."

Brian slipped me a spare map, plus the coordinates written on a slip of paper. He insisted both sections tramp to the river edge separately so that both callsigns wouldn't get hit together if the worst happened. Meanwhile, the four-wheel trailer full of kit was unceremoniously unhitched and the trucks redirected to face out of camp. The two nominated sections, plus escorts, scrambled aboard. After the skimpy briefing, Zowah and I joined our sections on the sandbagged tray. The two trucks departed the camp, headed down the escarpment and rushed north along the dirt road. What a fuckup I thought, as the front truck churned up the dust – obliterating the one following. The men gazed over the truck sides and watched the tangled bush zip past – another well-thought-out response. What will we do when we get there? How do we shut down a 12.7mm MG with light arms? Exactly where was the enemy? On our side of the river, or on the other side? No one knew. The information gleaned was hardly specific.

Somewhere south of the St Martin's Mission, the sections shunted off the vehicles. Sergeant Zowah and I compared notes and agreed on each route to the embattled Alpha section. We split up, as ordered, and proceeded to hike cross-country to locate a position overlooking the river. Sergeant Zowah led his section north and I cut north-east. On his bearing, he should hit the river first; then swing right and follow the Gairezi. My section hauled ass in a direct line across country till we linked up, or so said the plan. Wearing a basic webbing harness, full water bottles and carrying weapons, we ate up the kilometers – alternatively running and walking. My heart thumped with the anticipation of a firefight with FRELIMO. I didn't need the map to find them, as we honed in on the intermittent and booming bursts of automatic fire.

We walked and ran – finally (and breathlessly) stopping 50 meters back from the grassy slope above the sluggish Gairezi River. By the time we reached the riverbank, a Lynx airplane (a civilian Cessna that had been modified for military use) flew extremely high over the contact zone, out of harm's way, and relayed radio messages to the trapped section. We couldn't see the Alpha section because the embankment jutted out; however, the FRELIMO position across the river – a partly concealed stout bunker – was visible. The fort, dug into a thick scrub and rock position, heralded a superb view of the river. We ducked down and crept forward. The men lined up on the grassy slope and I observed the enemy position through binoculars. Running the glasses over the bunker, it became apparent the structure stood well out of range for the tinny Z42 rifle grenade, our only support weapon.

"Mantle Delta Two, this is Four, over," I radioed Zowah.

Silence.

"Mantle Delta Two, this is Delta Four, over."

Silence.

"Mantle Delta Two, this is Delta Four, over."

Where was Zowah? He had the shortest route. I seethed – scanning up the riverside with the binoculars. The mottled scrub and grassland swayed in the mild breeze. I couldn't see him. Switching, I contacted the Alpha section briefly to let the leader know we were in a position above him. He anxiously acknowledged and stated that he was still pinned and couldn't move. The good news: there were still no casualties.

We settled along the riverbank, like lying on a rifle range mound. I switched attention back to my section.

"Fire aimed shots at Freddy's position."

Six FN rifles and a MAG machine gun opened fire – concentrating on the dark fort. Leaves and small branches around the FRELIMO position collapsed from the cascade of bullets, but showed little other visible effect. The solid fortress slept impervious to the light weapons' fire. I lay prone and watched tracer bullets strike the enemy position. The red sizzling balls zapped across the river and disappeared into the deep green scrub. Puffs were visible where bullets struck earth. Would we neutralize the MG to allow Alpha to escape? I hardly thought so. I wondered what to do next, as bullets had no visible effect; we might as well use slingshots. The radio mush came alive.

"Mantle Delta Four, Delta Base," Brian's voice grated over the airwaves.

"Delta Base, Delta Four, read you threes, go ahead, over."

"Delta Four, Delta Base, roger, Cyclone One has been authorized to blast out Freddie. They should be overhead in figures 10, over."

"Delta Four, wonderful."

"OK guys, a coupla Hunters will come in to finish the job," I told the constables, "so don't fire unless you spot something."

I laid back and watched the Lynx drone monotonously above the wooded terrain. The pilot must have ordered the Hunter strike. Light weapons were of little use against dug-in positions. Apart from the Z42 rifle grenade, which was ineffective anyway, we didn't carry weapons capable of denting the enemy's pride. Support Unit was not issued with portable 60mm mortars or shoulder-fired rocket launchers, or 40mm grenade launchers or anything capable of a big bang. We lay impotent. Suddenly, the FRELIMO switched their fire from Alpha toward the Delta irritants and we hugged lower into the ridge. Their heavy MG bullets tore up the spiky grass like a manic gardener.

I called Zowah on the radio again. Silence. Ten minutes later, almost on the dot, FRELIMO's green scrub screen was suddenly saturated in gray clouds of exploding warheads. We cringed in alarm. Although we knew the air force was coming, the unexpected explosions without hearing the jets startled us. Red One and Red Two (two Hawker Hunter jets) streaked in low from the west – firing SNEB rockets and 30mm cannon on the first run; then, after banking sharply and gaining height, they dived in once again and dropped a bomb apiece, smack on target. Right on the button! Two huge spurts of black dirt, surging upwards – rapidly followed by shuddering detonations – obliterated the bunker. I felt like jumping up and cheering, but my shoulder wound reminded me of the consequences of elation. The air force jockeys nailed the target and FRELIMO disengaged. The jets circled round once and accelerated off inland. Gray smoke hazed the bunker. Silence lingered over the river. The Alpha section, embarrassed and shaken, extricated itself and rushed back to the waiting transport.

After that rude introduction, my section returned to the pick-up point.

Zowah sat comfortably in the shade, waiting.

"What happened to you, Sarge?"

"The radio didn't work properly," he grumbled, avoiding my stare.

"That didn't stop you from pressing on up the river."

"You might have shot at us if I couldn't talk," he said, unconvincingly. Discreet enquires later found he did not report a defective radio.

Several days later, the Signals Intelligence Section stated that intercepts had confirmed a number of serious FRELIMO casualties.

When I arrived back at Ruangwe, Paddy and a new man, John, were lazing on their cots in their tent. Paddy teased the shit out of me as I set up my cot.

"Why haven't you set up yet, you lazy bastard? Pull your finger out, O'Brien!"

We laughed and joked as I sorted out a space to spread out my camp stretcher. Barry had not returned – on annual leave, I was told – and never reappeared. John became the silent replacement. A serious, young National Serviceman with wavy fair hair and a smooth face, he joined Paddy's ribbing with awkward smiles. As I assembled my cot, Brian burst in and announced he had a job for me. I had hardly settled in.

In the ops shed, Brian tossed in red-hot intelligence, just off the press, that claimed the enemy definitely would use a 'known' infiltration route in the next five days. SB predicted a supply column, heavily laden with ammunition. Brian traced their route on an old road drawn on the map and suggested positions for an OP. He virtually radiated excitement.

"An absolute certainty," he stated firmly.

Really? Well, according to the Gospel of Special Branch … seven days should easily encompass the time zone. Blah, blah, blah.

A certainty. Hmmm. I packed my rucksack and then, at dusk, lined the men up to check their equipment. I learnt in the first trip to ensure we carried sufficient armaments, as lazier constables left behind ammunition and hand grenades in favor of more food. I checked each man's rifle ammunition, machine gun belts, grenades, pyrotechnics and radio batteries. Once I was satisfied, we departed base on foot. A night walk ensued – humping a heavy backpack laden with enough tinned food and water bottles for seven days. I heavily padded my left shoulder to absorb the weight without rubbing the wound. We walked in three-hour stages and rested for 30 minutes. The nightlight guided the team. The moon sliver shone enough to see the route. By the wee hours of the morning, the section finally ensconced themselves on a heavily wooded hill that overlooked a deserted vehicle road.

According to the briefing, the road was a former tsetse control route. Rhodesia falls smack in the tsetse fly belt and, where the fly exists, cattle and humans are susceptible to sleeping sickness. With the tsetse fly, large areas of suitable agricultural land could not be utilized. Tsetse control officers had worked hard in isolated areas on the eastern border to aid in the study – and the eradication of – the flying pest, but the terrorists had halted the major ongoing health project. By now, their work had ceased. Tsetse inspectors' Land Rovers had been wrecked by landmines and their lonely existence became precarious. They abandoned their work. Nature began to reclaim the road. The men settled in for a long session.

Once the lookout position was established, one person manned the OP, with one other assisting to confirm movement, while five lay behind, camouflaged. I plotted our position on the map and wrote the six-figure grid reference on the margin to aid an accurate Fireforce call. All day, Delta Four scanned the visible 100-meter length of the overgrown road. Sentries stared at the faded wheel marks until their eyes ached. The OP was not like city police watching a suspect's home. In the city, the cop drove close to the suspect location; then settled back in their car seat, listened to rugby on the radio, sent out for Chinese takeaway, chattered with their partner, wandered off to stretch the leg muscles and had a second crew relieve the OP when the first crew grew tired or bored. In the bush, the crew tramped for kilometers across rugged country, every bit of kit manhandled to the site. Once we chose the OP site, movement was curtailed to eliminate noise – particularly alien noises, like metal banging together, dropping mess tins or scraping a weapon. The isolated bush amplified sound and fingered a hidden OP group. The men squatted in one place, dozed, read or played checkers to fill the hours. The only movement allowed was to scramble off for a shit. The hours crept by. There were no sightings of anything human or animal. It was just mopane flies, stifling heat and tedious boredom.

On the third dreary day, the rain began. Steady afternoon rain swept onto the tree canopy and drip-dropped onto the dry leaf mat. The men slithered under granite outcrops, wherever the rain couldn't penetrate, and tried to stay as dry as possible. The dampness filtered the air and began to work on all the equipment. Canvas webbing swelled and became less pliable, tabs in ammunition pouches stiffened, metal begun to rust and a fine moisture coating settled on sleeping bags and woollen blankets. Inevitably, the men got caught in the steady rain and remain soaked for the days and nights ahead.

At night, the section tumbled down the hillside and set up a simple linear ambush. Once the men settled, the guard began, which was staggered from dark to pre-dawn, with two out of seven men awake. Those nights were deathly quiet; no light, sound, nothing. With cloud cover, it's amazing how dark the night grew; in fact, it was so dark that close landmarks, in spitting distance across the road, were indistinguishable. The objects displaying clear characteristics in the daylight, like tree stumps and prominent rocks, blurred and were, finally, obscured by darkness. If one watched where they should be, they shifted inside the imagination. Did something move? The eye tested the mind, watching the object obliquely. Well, did it? Awkward questions floated in the head, like: 'Is the rifle safety catch set to fire?'

On night sentry, ears tuned for alien sounds. The ever-present mosquitoes had a field day and resumed where the mopane left off. They deliberately buzzed within an inch of my ear, driving me crazy. Their presence droned shrilly all night, the persistent mongrels. Insect repellent was avoided, as the enemy easily smelt foreign aroma. The crackle of bodies turning on mushy leaf sounded louder than reality. Somewhere, far off, dogs yapped or trees rattled. Ignoring the nocturnal sounds, the mind took a holiday and journeyed through the better moments in life. Thoughts floated through the best bars, the best food eateries, fishing for kahawai in the Manawatu River, the crashing surf on a deserted Foxton beach, the state house where I grew up, sizing up and shaping the detail, my non-existent relationship with my father. Girls were catalogued: the where and when sex happened, the fragrance of their soap or perfume, what they wore – each mentally scrutinized and undressed in the night. Unremarkable life events extracted from the memory banks were analyzed and processed.

On sentry, time was not equal. It crept by sluggishly, slower than engaging in almost anything else. The luminous watch hour and minute hands ticked by at their leisure. I'd check the time and stubbornly attempt not to examine the watch again; then I'd try and guess the time, try and beat the clock. I'd sit staring into the blank darkness – processing random thoughts and surveying the dark lumps that slept each side. I'd even sing songs in my head and recall images of something mundane – processing it one frame at a time. After what seemed a good hour, I'd peer at the watch face again. Fifteen minutes had past. Shit! The watch stopped! The luminous spot on the tip of the second hand swept across the face and dispelled that thought. Two hours felt like two days. No sooner had the two hours crawled to a finish and I laid my head down, someone would wake me for the next stint. Before first light, we tiredly scrambled up the slope to reoccupy our day position and the game began all over again – and still nobody walked down the road. After seven days, the team walked back hollow, wet, tired, moody, hungry and sweaty.

On our return to base, Delta Troop had packed. Men hoisted their trunks onto a stationary trailer. Tents were flattened and folded. We were departing; so much for a decent sleep. Paddy had already packed and was squared away by the time I tramped into the tent. He laughed as I tried to pack my gear and fall asleep simultaneously, but as I had not completely unpacked, my gear sorted itself quickly. Delta withdrew from Inyanga. We drove to Rusape, where Constable Mhiripiri, who had been on leave, joined us. The troop returned to the farm base outside Rusape, which now had been expanded to accommodate three troops. It had become the new Mantle Base 151 Alpha – the latest Support Unit tactical organization which was designed to make better use of scarce resources and provide more boots on the ground. Until mid-1976, Support Unit sent out troops from Salisbury into the operational areas, with each operating individually under the JOC umbrella. This 'scattergun' approach was now consolidated into a Support Unit base (Mantle Base). Three or more troops were based together under a superintendent's command. While I didn't particularly enjoy operating from formal bases, they made sense from a command, control, logistics and supplies point of view. From the base, more could be achieved with less.

Superintendent Fred Mason helped pioneer the Mantle Base concept. I had met Inspector Mason in 1973 when, out of curiosity – and after reading in the *Rhodesia Herald* about a border war being fought in the north-east – I wandered along to both the army and police recruiting. Major Lamprecht sat in the army recruiting chair and made it abundantly clear that the army demanded a pound of flesh in brain-numbing foot drill and pedantic barrack inspections whether or not there was a war on. He conveyed the distinct impression that the war was all but won. He lost me! I walked into the Spanish-style Police General Headquarters to speak to Inspector Mason, who was a first-class salesman. I'm sure I didn't present ideal recruiting material – arriving dressed in a black cowboy hat and sporting long hair, a green army shirt and denim jeans, as well as being dripping wet from a summer rainstorm. I didn't have my army discharge papers, so I didn't pursue it further. Besides, I was only window-shopping and soon after, disappeared into the north-east farming.

Promoted to Superintendent and posted to Support Unit, Fred Mason was passionate, quick-witted and full of bubbling enthusiasm about stamping

Support Unit's mark on the war effort. In his late thirties, of average height and sporting a military-type regulation moustache, he exuded the confidence of a successful salesman. His easy manner and approachable style, coupled with his rank, enabled him to override red tape and improve the men's welfare. As a commissioned officer, he exerted more influence at the JOC. Politically astute, Mason networked to his advantage and acted like a man anointed for bigger things.

Within 24 hours of our arrival, my section was dispatched to Rusape to pick up a captured terrorist. The men remained on the trucks in the police station car park, while I entered the Special Branch realm in their first-floor office. After a superficial briefing by Ken Milne, an SB detective who walked the rarefied super-secret atmosphere, I joined an SB constable and collected a teenager dressed in a crackling new SF camouflage. Kitted out with webbing harness and backpack, he carried an FN rifle with the firing pin removed and no ammunition. The SF uniform allowed him to simply blend in and not to draw attention to himself. We walked him to the waiting vehicles.

"Look after him," I told Sergeant Ndoro, Sergeant Barka's replacement.

The grimy constables stared down at the hangdog youth standing awkwardly on the asphalt. The teenager cringed like a delinquent anticipating a smack around the ears. Hove sighed, leaned over the tailgate, gripped the shy man's wrist and hoisted him onto the tray. The boy sat down on the disintegrating sandbags, nervous and twitchy. Hove reached over and gently stroked his cheek. The capture flinched. The constables roared with delighted laughter. Hove had never seen a terrorist this close. He marvelled at how much the man was just like him: scared – nay, terrified – but the same as him.

"We should just kill you," stated Chipanza sullenly.

He had lost family members – murdered in a terrorist killing frenzy. He couldn't fathom why the white man kept them alive. It must be instant death to all these murderers. The constables burst out laughing, and the capture – understanding the laughter was not derision – smiled a crooked smile.

"Don't smile," scolded Hove lightly, "he means it."

The smile vanished.

The convoy drove out of Rusape to Makoni TTL in two Hyenas and an RM Bedford truck – carrying five days' supplies and an anxious capture. He's a lightweight – a young man captured near Chipinga escorting a wounded CT commander back to Mozambique for hospitalization. The little knowledge he retained about CT operations had been wrung out of him. He only spent three months in the country before being volunteered as a stretcher-bearer. After Special Branch had finished with him, they handed him over to us. Milne stated that the man knew three base camps in our operational area that CTs used time and again. Special Branch guided the section by plotting the first alleged base on the map as a starting point: it was just inside Manyika TTL.

On route to the first drop-off point, the convoy motored across a small river. The lead Hyena crossed without a hitch, but the second bogged in the shallow river crossing and the engine stalled.

"What's wrong?" I asked the driver, as he pressed the starter button.

"Dunno," he muttered.

The lead vehicle, driven by Bob Packer, drove on unaware of the bogged Hyena. He disappeared over the opposite side of a sloping riverbank and had to be summoned by radio to return. Bob was a popular policeman from Matebeleland, who had spent time in Highway Patrol chasing speeding motorists before being posted to the Support Unit. I once accompanied him on R&R to his Bulawayo stamping ground. On arrival, we entered a police bar that was crammed with chatting drinkers hidden in a veil of cigarette smoke. The crowd was three deep at the bar and we couldn't get service. To overcome this tiny problem, Bob strolled back to his car, opened the boot and retrieved a smoke grenade. He calmly wandered back into the bar and tossed the grenade into the crowd. The sharp crack, as the striker lever flew from the grenade body, echoed in the jam-packed bar and people scattered, panicked, thinking it was a real grenade. Through the colored smoke, Bob calmly sauntered to the deserted bar and ordered two beers. Lots of recriminations were angrily tossed about and one or two wore Bob's fist before we left. I don't remember a hell of a lot about that leave; too much booze.

Bob acknowledged the radio call and conducted a three-point turn on the loose dirt road – gunning the motor in the process and detonating a landmine. The roaring blast severed the front right-side wheel. The explosive shockwave traveled the path of least resistance, up the V-shaped hull and dispersed, but the force of the explosive lifted the armored vehicle as it circled – the center of gravity pitching slightly and the blast flipping it onto its side. The stricken vehicle, shielded by a hill slope, crashed out of sight. At that precise moment, exasperated with the whining starter motor, I unsnapped the seat harness and prepared to exit the stalled vehicle when the huge explosion rent the air. No one witnessed the blast. For a second, I envisaged an ambush and that an RPG rocket had blasted my armored carrier. We debussed that vehicle through the rear exit like cartoon characters off a cliff!

Landing knee-deep in cold water, I recovered, waded out and then ran up the dirt road and around the corner to find the lead Hyena lying on its side. Breathing sharply – and expecting a barrage of bullets – it suddenly snapped that a lone landmine had caused the enormous blast. Immediately, four of us scrambled to the resting vehicle. A constable rammed open the rear exit door and we saw the lads hanging – trapped in their seatbelts. Inside sat Mhiripiri, Chipanza, Elias and a constable from Mike Troop, who was riding as shotgun. Chipanza switched at the last minute from the Bedford to the Hyena in order to remove himself from the capture. The constables reported sore backs. Being strapped into the steel seats protected them from the blast, so I figured they were hurt by the vehicle side flip. We unfastened the canvas roof, reached inside and unbuckled the men's seatbelts. Once freed, we gently eased them out of the opening and lowered them onto the side of the road. Bob emerged unscathed. I used the radio to request a casevac.

"Oscar Alpha, Mantle Delta Four, over."

Oscar Alpha was a relay station somewhere in the high country, so I used that instrument because direct communications with Mantle Base was impossible from where I stood.

"Mantle Delta Four, Oscar Alpha, read you fours, go ahead, over."

"This is Delta Four," I reaffirmed, as I traced the grid lines on the map unfolded in front of me. "We have hit a Lima Mike at Victor Quebec 223 576. I have four, I say again, figures four casualties, require casevac, over."

The relay station read back the grid reference and the message, and told me to wait. As I squatted on the roadside, I noticed a small crowd of Africans assembled outside a lone general store 200 meters further down the dirt road. The faint breeze carried the muffled jeering and laughter.

"They're laughing at us!" spat Sibanda, as he knelt down on the road shoulder.

"The bastards," I seethed, and picked up his MAG, which sat next to him on the steel bipods. Raising the weapon to my shoulder, but aiming high and wide, I fired two 10-round bursts. The brilliant-red tracer pointed the fall of shot: wide, but still close enough to scare the shit out of them. The jeering ceased and the people scattered like startled deer.

"Mantle Delta Four, Oscar Alpha," called the relay station, as I lowered the warm machine gun, "a road casevac is under way and should be at your loc in six zero minutes, over."

"Oscar Alpha, Delta Four," I spat into the handset, miffed at the cheeky villagers' reaction to our dilemma and at the JOC's response, "the casualties have back injuries. A road trip will aggravate them further. I need a Cyclone Seven, over."

"Delta Four, Oscar Alpha," replied the patient voice, as if talking to a backward child, "we requested a Cyclone Seven, but it was turned down, over."

"This is Delta Four; you tell 'em to send Cyclone Seven and they can shove their trucks, over."

"We'll give it a go, out to you … "

The dirt roads throughout the TTL were slowly decaying. Rain, road traffic, wind and other factors had severely eroded the dirt top and the surface had disintegrated into a corrugated and pitted mess, with great chunks completely washed away. Each year, the Internal Affairs budget included the cost to upgrade and service the roads, but with the escalation of terrorism, they postponed the upgrade as roadwork equipment was diverted elsewhere. Road travel was not an option for back injuries.

The wait dragged on. I hated the moments when I had to request, beg, shout or rage to a relay station. The passion and emotion of an argument became completely lost in the repetition. What if the relay station didn't care? Didn't argue a case? Censored my message? The outcome was out of my control. A helpless feeling swam about me as I waited impatiently for the reply. The relay station came back on air and told me in clipped sentences that JOC had not changed its mind; trucks were on the way and that's all there is to it! Angry, I snatched the radio set and stormed across the flat *veldt* and climbed to the top of the nearest hill and radioed Fred Mason direct, who (through contacts in the 'Old Boys' Network') discovered a helicopter standing idle at Grand Reef and, by the grace of God, the crew agreed to fly out to the rescue. Less than 20 minutes later, the helicopter arrived and evacuated the four. Once the communications equipment was removed from the stricken Hyena, we motored back to the Rusape base. Fifty percent of my section was now out of action: Mhiripiri, Elias and Chipanza, along with a Mike Troop constable.

Brian met the vehicles as we rolled into base and immediately assigned Sergeant Zowah's section to me, plus John (the new lad) to get the job done. I left Sergeant Ndoro and the three unscathed section members behind to rest and took out the untried section. As a by-product of landmine blasts, although the Rhodesians pioneered many of the life-saving concepts in vehicle design, many serving people had ongoing back injuries both minor and major, which rendered them unfit for further active service. Of the four evacuated, Elias, Mhiripiri and Chipanza never returned to active duty.

We motored back to Manyika – a section of strangers. Sergeant Zowah, unhappy with this new arrangement, sulked and stared down at the sandbagged tray. He replied to comments with a non-committal grunt. Once inside Manyika, we were deposited on a roadside, off on a base camp discovery tour. The three camps, spread far apart, required a gruelling tramp to each. The section did not bond and an underlying awkwardness governed the team behavior. After two days of tramping – entering two nondescript base camps, with neither holding anything of interest – the young capture led us to a third CT base. We quietly approached the third base from the opposite side of a wide valley and hid up in the grassy hills to watch the *kraal* for a day. We didn't want to frighten off any occupants. The capture explained the base lay hidden in the trees behind the village, but nothing unusual occurred. People came and went as expected. We carefully scrutinized each individual person, and we quizzed the capture about them: some he recognized, but most he didn't. We hid on the hill overnight and studied the area the next morning. The *kraal* activity seemed normal. By mid-afternoon, I decided to move down from the OP and into the village to confront the people.

We entered the village and rounded up the old *kraal* head. At least 60 years old, with a thin, weather-beaten and wrinkled face and gnarled, crooked fingers, the elder was the heredity clan leader. He had lived hard and lean for decades – the toughness reflected in his rimy eyes and etched into the lined face. His calloused hands and feet attested to a life of harsh labor. Dressed in a worn, dirty gray suit jacket and torn gray flannel trousers, with sandals manufactured from car tires, he squatted down and intently scrutinized us. His watery-brown eyes initially flashed defiance, but then toned down. Sergeant Zowah tossed questions at him, but while the elder attempted to be friendly, to radiate warmth, he neatly deflected his answers. He emphatically denied knowledge about the CTs or the base sitting behind his village. Shaking his head, as if the questions were outrageous, he spoke slowly and deliberately. Tired of the denials, we gently escorted him 20 meters up into the trees behind the *kraal* and, surprise, surprise, we were standing on the indisputable evidence. Even standing right on the base, with old chicken bones and moldy cigarette butts lying about in the dry grass, he still vehemently denied the CTs were ever there. I introduced the captured terrorist to the stubborn headman. Confronted with the man, who confirmed his complicity, the elder still doggedly clung to his denials. We were much too soft with these people.

"You know that man?" I asked the capture.

"I have seen him. He looked after the 'Brothers'."

"When you were in this base, did his *kraal* feed you?"

"Yes … along with all the others along here."

"Did you force them to, or did they volunteer?"

"Sorry?"

"Were they happy to feed you?"

"Oh, yes, very happy."

"Including this village?"

"Sure. We only based in very secure areas."

"The rest of Manyika?"

"They're always happy to see the 'Brothers'."

The old *kraal* head stood placidly – eyeing us cautiously to gauge our attitude – and spoke only when spoken to. He was known as a contact person for transient gangs. He memorized every face of the genuine CTs to hinder the ability of Selous Scout pseudo teams infiltrating the area, who were disguised as terrorists. If the old man did not recognize the face, a game of deception began to be played, where the Scouts could be set up for the chop. He was a vital cog in the engine of terrorism.

"We don't base somewhere unless it is completely secure."

The words rang in my ears. Even faced with the physical evidence of the base – and a captured CT, who specifically identified him – the man continued to strongly deny. Whilst I understood his motives for the denials, because the man had to live here long after we had gone, his words fell on deaf ears.

"No one has been here for two months," stated the tracker, after he had surveyed the base site.

"Take him with us?" asked Zowah.

"What for? No. Leave him 'ere."

We walked off, but the urge to hurt the man or burn the *kraal* boiled inside me. His unshakeable denials and whining slithered under the skin, but apart from a quick hiding or arresting the man, there was little I could do. Neither was an option. We left him standing alone in the base area and felt his eyes as he keenly watched us depart. I decided to walk off the simmering anger.

We marched away from the *kraal*, downhill, through a small valley that followed the hill contours until it spilled onto a flat plain – and a small business center became visible in the distance. We hiked across to the business center, where we stopped and rested in the general store's shade. The men purchased warm Cokes and cooked dinner. As the dusk sky reddened and light faded, the section and its reluctant prisoner packed up, departed the business center and tramped away on a main dirt road. I had no particular mission in mind. The capture had pointed out three bases that had been long deserted, so I thought it might be productive to ambush the main road.

As darkness finally wrapped up the day – trekking up the road a kilometer from our dinner spot, with my mind in neutral – mortar and heavy MG fire suddenly erupted from outside of the business center. We instantly scattered into the shadowy, unplanted field and turned to face the colored bead show. Long strings of green and orange tracer criss-crossed the lonely buildings. The intricate green and orange stitchery fiercely lit up against the matte-black sky. The whine of an RPD on long bursts was accompanied by five loud mortar explosions; then, as suddenly and violently as the assault began, the gunfire stopped.

"OK, let's form up, spread out and sweep back," I called.

I urgently wanted to hit back – counter-attack while the CTs pulled back.

"No, we must not walk in the dark," called Sergeant Zowah stubbornly.

"What?"

"It's too dangerous to go out there," he growled.

To my anger and surprise, the section sergeant did not support the counter-strike. I recalled Zowah at the Gairezi River, where he had vanished. We didn't hear a peep from him, despite the fact that we were supposed to reinforce each other. My section constables grumbled that Zowah simply faded into the scrub, never to be heard until the mission was over.

"We must wait," the MAG gunner called from the darkness, "it is better in the day."

"Bullshit! Do it now!"

"It's too dangerous," Zowah blurted angrily.

"Fuck me!" I thought, as the men's attitude backed up the sergeant.

Do I insist? Is this the moment to shove some steel into their backbone? The section reacted as if they were scared of the dark, or petrified of a firefight. I stood still and surveyed the men. Those faces I saw remained sullen masks, eyes cast down. They were edgy, rebellious and uncertain. John, unsure, shrugged. I bit my lip in anger and decided to leave it to the morning. We dosed down right there.

I did not sleep. I lay awake – watching the star-filled sky and seething with rage. What happened? Would they shoot me? I wondered. Had I trod on enough toes to really piss them off? I hadn't heard of murder in the bush, but there's always a first time. A definite mutinous undercurrent undermined authority. The capture worried me. Is he part of this theater? Am I paranoid? How far do I test them? I instinctively knew this wasn't the right time. My FN stayed clasped in my hands all night.

Up before the morning sun, we shook off the driblets of moisture and got ready to move.

"Let's go," I ordered, and we rapidly walked back to the business center.

The resistance to action dissipated, as if nothing out of the ordinary occurred the night before. The shop buildings and attached living areas were completely deserted. The residents had fled in the night. A number of black hens scratched at the hardened dirt road, but otherwise nothing moved. From the silent locked buildings, the men slowly crossed into the adjoining fields and fanned out. Within minutes, the tracker found the firing positions behind a crumbling contour ridge. At least 12 CTs had participated in the sound and light show. Expended cartridges littered the embankment. The CTs must have thought we were kipping in the business center when they opened fire. Had they seen us enter? Followed us there? Or had someone tipped them off? I was keener than a razor-sharp knife to take the fight to them, but the more assertive I became, equally the more reluctant the men grew to push the pace. A strange resistance membrane formed amongst them – an intangible unease that held like glue. They sauntered hangdog about the firing positions. Ordinarily, finding the firing spot produced an electrified excitement of the hunt. There was not even a small spark that morning. They acted more like frightened spectators than revved-up players. I had to prod and snarl to induce any action. Finally, the tracker confirmed the line of flight, so off we trundled in a fighting formation, but even the tracking was tedious, with two or three constables arguing over the verification of the *spoor*, stopping far too often. They mucked about aimlessly when the *spoor* obliterated and their body language suggested that my constant urgings irritated them. I didn't know any of them personally; we were strangers thrown together for this exercise.

As we walked, the constables huddled up to the capture and whispered in Shona before shooting me fervent looks. Had they grown an affinity to him? I had to break up the small gatherings a number of times to get them to work at the *spoor*. Zowah distanced himself from the arguing constables and made no attempt to intervene. He stood to one side – separating himself from the bickering and flicking wary glances at me. Was he measuring my response? The capture appeared more comfortable in our midst.

"What's happening here?" I wondered.

The dynamics were askew. I shrugged off my unease and focused on the main game. John, new to the game, stood uncertain as to how to get involved. The constables offered little encouragement for his participation, so he must have felt like a lamb at an Easter festival of wolves. He lingered close to me and watched uncomfortably as the action unfolded – uneasy with the hostile attitudes and unspoken dilemma. As a conscript on his first deployment, he must have wondered what he had dropped into.

With verbal prodding, the shoe prints led the irritable section back up the same small valley we had walked down the previous afternoon and directly to the village of the aged *kraal* head. Naturally, the *kraal* was deserted and all the wooden doors were wired shut. The terrorist *spoor* drifted over the loose dirt particles and spilled out into the open, flat, grassy valley, where it receded to nothing. The constables were still edgy, but said nothing. The designated tracker roamed out while we waited, squatting in the grassy valley, keeping him under surveillance. He soon shambled back, disinterested, to state he couldn't find the *spoor*. I had watched his lackluster performance with building annoyance – certain that his tracking efforts were half-hearted. While he stood to one side, I launched out again, leading the way – vigilantly searching the gentle grassy slope – while the rest tagged behind like bored school kids. Whilst my tracking ability was third class, with a bit of patience, I figured I might do better than these guys. Irritated, I strode on the grassland – a second 360° search in a desperate attempt to pick up signs of *spoor*.

Abruptly, a deafening thunder of rifles exploded from the side of a small hill above us (about 50 meters away) and bullets crackled in the air and swept the grassy slope. Instantly, the African constables split and ran like hundred-meter sprinters – leaving John (the untested) and I to fight back. One second, the group milled in a line behind me; then a gigantic roar rent the air, and then the next second, the constables rocketed off. I simply hit the deck next to John, alongside a dirt track, with absolutely no cover. The tufts of reedy grass provided our only shield. We both instinctively returned fire – single shots into the bush screen. The MAG's dominant presence couldn't be heard. I swiveled my head in time to see Zowah and the gunner slither to a skidding halt and quickly drop in the dry grass, about 20 meters to my right. The MAG gunner, fortunately, regained his composure, slammed the butt into his shoulder and hammered the ambush position with tidy bursts of fire. Zowah lay tucked next to him. From the corner of my eye, I saw four African constables race – bunched together, in a headlong dash – down the gentle grass slope. The four tried vainly to outrun the bullets. Why people attempt that still puzzles me ... fear must blot out rational action – all the repetitive training down the toilet, as primeval instinct clamped hold. They ran upright, sprinting furiously, without attempting to zigzag or evade. Thunk! Thunk! Thunk! Thunk! I heard each metal rattle as the bomb dropped into the tube. ZANLA launched four 60mm mortar bombs, one after the other.

"Mortars! Take cover!" I shouted.

After a long, lingering pause, as bombs flew into the clear sky, I twitched – wondering where they would finally land. CRUMP! CRUMP! CRUMP! CRUMP! Two exploded to the left of the runners, one overshot and one landed smack on target. Two constables ran straight into the gray explosive cloud, which decked them.

"Jesus!" I swore out loud, as I switched my attention to the front.

The heavy automatic fire still rained down. Bullets swept the dirt road. There was no chance of racing to the felled constables. We flattened out lower and returned fire. Bullets snapped and crackled overhead, and some hit the road and splattered dry dirt into the air. Finding adequate cover was definitely an effort. With luck, one's molecules might merge into the dirt. A shallow depression in the ground would have been lovely, but there was no point in digging. Entrenching tools were not supplied. The only tool at hand was a dessert spoon, which was somewhere inside my backpack! No wonder the *kraal* head clamped up yesterday ... they were probably there, watching us!

I quickly expended one 20-round magazine. That helped to recharge my confidence. I slowed down the rate of fire – putting aimed shots into likely positions. Two shots here, two shots there, wherever there were likely hiding spots. There were shots to the left side of trees and rocks, on the premise the opponents were right-handed and, therefore, shot from the left side of cover. John kept up a controlled rate of fire and appeared cool and engaged. He lay exposed as I and exchanged bullets with those on the hillside – his shooting precise, as if he practiced on the rifle range. Externally, he looked calm and collected. Tiny green fireballs jetted overhead and burnt cordite and cooked rifle oil tickled our nostrils. Gunfire crackle echoed off the hills and the initial leaking fear was roped in and contained. Assistance fled from my fingertips – that option ran down the hill, with the A73 radio pack on his back – so unless the constable decided to do something, radio communications were out of the question. I consoled myself that we were in a valley, and that alone may hinder good communication anyway. Some consolation!

Time congealed into another dimension. After 10 minutes – elastic enough to seem very short one second and ultra-long the next, with a close-up view of intrepid ants walking across the dirt grains that constituted the road; of three empty rifle magazines lying in the dirt and puffs of dry dust; and hearing the sharp crackle of bullets snapping overhead – the momentum slowed. My heart rate smoothed out and my stomach settled down. The MAG kept up a solid rate of fire; the red tracer rocketed into the drab green scrub. With the men scattered, the choice of a counter-attack was ruled out. Our only option was to shoot our way out.

The ambushers unexpectedly disengaged – using fire and movement. I saw them for two or three seconds – a momentary flit of color and movement. One individual ran from a shed-sized rock to another – heading fast for the back of the grassy hill. Waiting for him to emerge from behind the giant square boulder to cover the gap to the next rock, I caught him as he darted forward once again. His dark figure crossed onto the rifle foresight – a blur of dark blue. I fired and he stumbled out of sight, but as a body was never recovered, I don't know the effectiveness of that shot.

As the terrorists ran, some remained and laid down a terrifying volume of bullets – particularly the belt-fed RPD. The captured CT, once under the guard of the constables, found himself separated. John and I lay pinned next to the dirt road at the top of the slope. Sergeant Zowah and the MAG gunner fought back from the spiky grass 20 meters away, and a further 20 meters, the lone prisoner sought cover. He lay flat, in the dry grass. Down the bottom of the grass slope, four frightened constables were flattened. As the firing petered out, the capture seized his chance. He suddenly bolted upright and sprinted along the grassy slope – away towards a small wooded hill. I noticed the impulsive movement. It was foolish, as he had 50 meters of open ground to cover. I rolled over and shot him. Once the capture flopped into the stumpy grass, John and I scrambled down the hill to assess the condition of the wounded: one constable crumpled in agony, with multiple shrapnel wounds from the shoulder to the ankle – all seeping blood – and the other escaped remarkably unscathed, with only three shrapnel wounds in the right leg. We rammed our field bandage cotton wadding into the larger wounds to stem the bleeding. John tied them off. I checked the two unscathed constables: they sat upright – shocked and speechless.

The medic's eyes bugged out from an ashen face, while the radio operator blinked – frozen in terror. I squatted and quietly talked to the medic. I needed him to assist. The medic blinked and stared, uncomprehending; then my words snapped his brain freeze. As if nothing had happened, he stood up and began to help John complete the minor bandaging. He stripped out the medical kit – finding extra bandages. A plasma line was set up. His training kicked in.

The radioman sat solid and unmoved, so I simply unhooked the radio set from his backpack and humped onto a nearby ridgeline to establish contact. I radioed base. Brian's voice boomed loud and clear. Even after explaining the shambles, Brian still urged me to pursue the ambushers. I couldn't believe his order. I refused point-blank to lead troops who had just run away.

"What's the point, when the bastards can't be trusted?"

I was furious, firstly, for the shits taking the gap, and secondly, for being suckered into the ambush. It won't happen again. Brian personally drove in three hours later with another Delta section and they took up the chase. The two casualties were eventually evacuated by helicopter.

I seethed at the section's performance and demanded that the runners be charged with cowardice. They had been in a mutinous mood from the start, Sergeant Zowah in particular. The powers that be hedged and hummed, and officially stated that the allegations would be investigated back in Salisbury, after emotions had died down. Unfortunately, under the Police Act, there is nothing that defined 'cowardice'. The closest would be 'failure to perform a duty'. A decision was taken not to proceed with any charges and the incident was squashed and silenced.

As a postscript, an SB NCO sidled up to the mutinous men to learn whether I had 'murdered' the capture. Were they anxious to pin something on me? Fortunately, the men stated firmly that the capture was shot fleeing. Firstly, I was surprised that SB queried the shooting in such an underhanded way, and that the constables supported the truth even after our clear differences – and I was more surprised that the same constables bothered to tell me about the SB questions. I returned to base older and wiser.

My section substantially wilted with the departure of Sergeant Barka. The one landmine had swept the core of the section aside. Constables Ruzawi (the medic), Sibanda (the gunner) and Hove were the last of the original section I inherited in August. Sergeant Ndoro, still new in the troop, was lean and muscular, with a savage countenance of someone who might proudly bite off an ear in a bar fight, but the craggy face contrasted with a quietly spoken man. He brought 12 years' service and no special skills, and had the tracking ability of a cow, but he was firm and fair with the constables. Brian plucked two constables from within the troop to make up the numbers. Constables Magama and Chikobvu linked into the section, steered clear of me and settled down.

Meanwhile, Paddy's section – operating clandestinely at night, inside Chiduku – reported automatic fire. They sighted tracer bullets zapping through the velvet sky like green dots. While the bullets were definitely not headed in his direction, Paddy radioed everyone to try and establish just who had shot at whom. No one reported taking fire. The next morning, he discovered a hastily evacuated CT base camp in the area of the shots. Subsequent questioning of the locals uncovered a story that alleged the CT detachment commander, pissed as a parrot from drinking brandy all night, had staggered home to the base and let fly at his own men with his RPD. Someone must have really upset him.

After a week skulking around Chiduku, Mantle Base directed the section back to the Rusape police station. Paddy's section had also been trucked in to link up. We were both told that the Support Unit commander, Jim Collins, would meet us. Milling aimlessly around the car park, we decided to cruise into the police bar for a quick chilled beer before our meeting. We raucously entered the premises, laughing and joking, with the taste of a chilled beer tempting the palate. As we stepped up to the bar, a seated army major immediately accosted us and wrinkled his nose as we ordered our drinks.

"You people can't come in 'ere dressed like that," he snapped sternly and swiveled on the barstool.

Our camouflage clothes and canvas shoes gave off the distinct, sharp ammonium body tang – a mix of dirt, piss and stale smoke – and neither of us had shaved for over a week. Our smelly uniform wore no rank or unit insignia.

"What's the matter with you, mate?" asked Paddy, with a smile on his dial as he downed the cold beer.

Incensed that he had been called 'mate' by some dirty scumbag, the major slipped off the bar stool and postured in his best military swagger. He was dressed impeccably, in his neatly ironed and lightly starched officer's uniform – the fawn shirt, with campaign and good conduct medal ribbons; the colored stable belt; the sharp fawn shorts and matching fawn socks, which were pulled up to the regulation 'three fingers below the knee'; and the spit-polished leather shoes. He puffed his chest out. It was quite a contrast to our tired, smelly, dirty attire – another base camp warrior.

"You can't enter the mess in that filthy outfit. There are dress standards, you know," thundered the major, repeating himself.

An awkward silence followed.

"Mate, this is a police bar," said Paddy, with a twinkle in his eyes, "so you can piss off if you don't like it."

"I beg your pardon?" stuttered the major, unused to being spoken to so brutally.

"You heard."

Blood rushed to the major's cheeks. Paddy turned his back on the man and we chatted as if he was not present. The rest of the bar reverted to a deathly silence. A captain from the Signals Corps sidled up to the major and whispered something in his ear. Meanwhile, I ordered the next round.

"Don't serve these men," snapped the major, as the African barman headed to the beer fridge, "both of you out! Now!"

"Don't listen to him," replied Paddy to the stunned barman, "two beers!"

Then, in the nick of time, Assistant Commissioner Collins walked into the mess, smelt trouble and gently led the major away – explaining softly that it is a police facility after all; then he exploded and gave us both a solid dressing down about military courtesy. As quick as his anger was provoked, Collins changed into a business tone and questioned us about how operations were progressing. Afterwards, Paddy was assigned a singularly important task: an Internal Affairs callsign had reported a single green flare in Makoni last night, and now they were hunkered down, waiting for trouble. Paddy found himself tasked to find the source – kicked straight back into the bush.

"Good luck, Paddy!"

I returned to Mantle Base with my ears still red from a good chewing out – words like 'bloody insolent' and 'won't be tolerated' bouncing in my head. Career men and I didn't mix well. Brian chuckled when he heard, but added nothing. Paddy was chasing Chiduku ghosts as punishment. I hit the sack and, the next morning, was summoned to the headquarters building.

"Your section will deploy in 60 minutes, O'Brien," ordered Fred Mason, and added: "Ken Milne will be 'ere with a bunch of junior police JOC officers to inspect a murder. Don't get mixed up with them. Find the *spoor* an' get after the killers."

Great! That's all I need – a bunch of career policemen in tow! 'Jam Stealers' out for a peek at the war … combat voyeurs. The section kitted out for five days and sat patiently in the motor pool for the Special Branch team. They arrived by Land Rover, followed by an RM Bedford, with a dozen police inspectors – all dressed in their pressed summer uniforms and polished leather, just oozing schoolboy enthusiasm. They were each armed with shiny new FN rifles, which they held distastefully. A tame government media contingent accompanied them. They were all warmly welcomed by Superintendent Mason, who offered the crew a cup of tea. We dozed while they hobnobbed.

Afterwards, we mounted an idling truck, joined the inspectors' convoy and departed. With SB leading, the convoy headed straight into Makoni TTL, which was down the main dusty road for several kilometers, and then we stopped in a business center. The four-store complex hummed in the midday heat. A quick examination confirmed the shop doors were padlocked. The place looked like a ghost town – a ball of tumbleweed rolling through wouldn't have raised eyebrows. The vehicles parked in the middle of the road, the team debussed onto the baked ground and then looked about. Although the street was empty and quiet, the dead were easily located. The sickly-sweet aroma of decaying bodies is unique and quite unforgettable.

"Around the back," said Ndoro, as he walked up the side of a store.

The constables followed the putrefaction scent. As Ndoro arrived at the back of the store, he sighted the source of the odor: in the shade, broken bloody corpses were sprawled in the dust. As we closed in on the massacre, the blowflies rose in a black cloud, buzzing angrily. I swept them aside as they zoomed around my face and studied the death scene. I counted six bodies, slumped in unnatural postures, with their dreary clothing askew and rumpled, salted in grainy dirt. They looked like lumps of sacking tossed from a moving van. The dead were all teenagers, three of each sex, with their faces contorted in an agony mask. Unrecognizable, even to their mothers, their faces were distorted and swollen from savage beatings, caked with dried blood and mixed in gritty dirt. The bodies began to swell. Already, neat white maggot egg clusters formed in the corner of one open mouth. Investigations later concluded all six were from Salisbury and had been visiting relatives in the TTL for the Christmas holiday period. The autopsies confirmed they had been brutally beaten with heavy poles – the type used for pounding maize grain into fine flour. The vicious, calculated beating fractured their young bones before they were either callously shot or gruesomely bayoneted to death. Once the flower of youth, they now began to swell and putrefy. I wondered what they did to deserve that

… maybe they refused the recruiting overtures.

After a quick glance at the murder scene, the men spread out to search for clues. Shoe prints were stamped all over the dusty ground around and among the jumbled bodies. The prints interlocked and headed back and forth out to the tilled field. The dozen inspectors edged near the dead with clean handkerchiefs pressed over their mouths – pointing and offering advice to Milne. I was happy to get away from the cluster of pen-pushers.

Hove, now the tracker, and Sergeant Ndoro circled out beyond the disgusting slaughter and quickly found enemy *spoor* in a ploughed field. With a loud hiss and urgent hand signals, Ndoro rounded up the men and Delta departed – leaving the ripening dead to the inquisitive sightseers. We chased the ingrained shoe prints for kilometers across flat country – loping beside the undisguised tracks. The murderers stuck to the beaten dirt footpath; they had at least a 15-hour head start. I thought we'd be bloody lucky to nail them, but there was nothing like a slaughter of innocents to get the blood boiling.

After five hours trotting on shoe prints, the real danger loomed. Announced by the subtle, moisture-tainted wind change, a steel-gray band of heavy rain swept across the dark-blue hills to the north-east. The rain engulfed the hills and raced furiously, cross-country, in our direction. Within a half-hour, the heavy downpour washed the *spoor* away and that was that. War's element of chance beat us. Luck rode with the murderers.

We remained in the general area – patrolling in persistent rain. If we persevered, I decided, luck might switch back to us on the slight chance that we bumped into the murderers. One chilly rainy night, following a wet sloppy foot trail, we found ourselves on a tenuous goat track. The slim path wound along a slippery rock cliff face. It was very hairy. Hugging the wet slimy rock and praying to a God I didn't believe in – hoping not to step off into black space – my fingers felt awkwardly along the rock face in the velvet darkness. Cliff climbing was never my forte, so cold fingers clamped onto every minute crevice – my heart beating so hard it used up its mileage allowance. The constables were not happy people – particularly Sibanda, who lugged the steel machine gun and three heavy ammunition belts, and clung for dear life. Soaked, cold, tired and very tense, we finally made the flat plateau area without losing anyone.

The section searched all the lonely *kraals* and surrounding country for kilometers for similar shoe patterns, but it was like the proverbial needle in the haystack. The conversations with locals stupid enough to hang around were monotonous.

"Where are all the young people?" Sergeant Ndoro would ask the locals in Shona.

"They all go."

"Where?"

"To the city to find jobs."

"All of them?"

"Some to South Africa in the goldmines."

"Any to the white farms?"

"Not many."

"To Mozambique for training?"

"Oh, no."

"You are so certain."

"Maybe ... I don't know."

"Who tends the fields?"

"The women."

"An' the cattle?"

"Those who go to school."

"The harvest last year ... grain bins full?"

"Not very good."

"No?"

"There's not enough if there is a poor crop this year."

"But good enough to feed the terrorists, eh?"

"No."

"Sure?"

"I don't know these people."

"What do you know?"

"Nothing."

"Have you heard about the terrorists?"

"No."

"Never? Not even on the radio?"

"Never."

"Fuckin' crap."

And so on and so on – round and round in circles.

One small comic interlude: a terrorist commander in Makoni carried a severed (vandalized) telephone receiver in his pack and, at meetings with local people, he pretended to ring the President of Tanzania for support.

"President Nyerere?" he stated theatrically into the dead mouthpiece of the Bakelite handpiece, "this is Comrade James in the Makoni area. Can we get tank support? That's great Mr President … "

The peasant farmers lapped it up.

After five days without a sniff of the enemy, the section humped cross-country to the main Rusape Road. While we sat on the roadside, on the main highway near Juliasdale – wet and tired – waiting for trucks, the boys had the distinct pleasure of motorists who stopped their cars and fed the constables Christmas cake, mince pies and Christmas cheer. God bless them.

In 1971, in Malaya, an old sorceress warned me that I would be lucky to survive 1976. She wasn't clear on what 'survive' meant, but painted a picture of a long life if I scraped through. After a landmine, a gunshot wound and constables absconding, I decided to wait till New Year. I'm not superstitious, but hey, why tempt fate!

In the first days of January 1977, Delta Four escorted the John Padbury Special Branch team to Makoni for a scheduled meeting with the villagers. The date had been pre-arranged through Internal Affairs; their field staff informed the villagers, so there was a good chance of an ambush or a landmine greeting. The convoy darted down the main road and onto a barely used offshoot. The minor road cut through waist-high scrub and wound around house-sized granite boulders. The bush snugly hugged the roadside – so close that an ambusher could reach out and touch the passing vehicles. This was the only road in or out, which was perfect for a premeditated ambush. As a precaution, John ordered the convoy to stop and asked my section to dismount and walk ahead of the Special Branch vehicles. Using the road as an axis, we spread out in an extended line and searched for signs of an ambush or landmines. Within minutes, I heard a voice.

"Mine!" hissed Hove anxiously.

The unit had no mine prodders or detectors, or even bayonets, so we relied on the scouts' sharp eyes.

"Where?" I asked and lunged through the spiky scrub.

I stopped on the road shoulder and looked at the tracker. Hove pointed. His hand indicated a patch on the road surface showing disturbed soil and mismatched dirt grains. If it had rained after the mine was laid, the downpour would have smoothed out the rough edges. That's what they were counting on.

"Dirt over here," called Ndoro from behind a shed-sized boulder.

The loose dirt sat in a single lump behind a granite rock on the roadside.

The excess dirt confirmed a mine hole. The sergeant emerged and nodded to affirm the deadly situation.

"Mark the mine," I said to Hove, "so we can come back to it."

Hove scavenged and dragged over a dead tree branch and laid it on the road to mark the spot, which pointed to the offending surface. I returned to the stationary Land Rover.

"Mine," I said to Padbury, who was sitting behind the steering wheel of the idling Land Rover.

"OK, we'll park here and walk,' he replied – pointing to a flattened grass area.

The drivers conducted a three-point turn and reverse parked – pointing the vehicles back down the road – and they stayed behind to mount guard. The rest legged it down the roadside to the meeting place, which was a primary school. The sand road emptied onto a soccer field that grew as much grass on the pitch as a supermarket car park. The goal frames at each end barely stood upright. On the far side of the soccer field, two simple, rectangular school buildings loomed – their white plaster walls glowing against the matte-brown *veldt*. My section spread out onto the soccer pitch – noting a crowd of Africans standing on one side, who were listless and sullen. We quickly formed a semi-circle on the field and faced out. Castle-like granite *kopjes* overlooked the flat ground, and I imagined a lookout posted on one – ready to range in the mortars.

The Special Branch representatives strolled over to the anxious flock of about 80 peasant farmers and their families. The villagers milled around like a crowd desperate to leave a football ground where their team had just lost. A senior African detective mingled in the crowd – pausing to shake hands and chatting like a local candidate in the next election – before he walked beyond the throng and settled the people down. He mounted a small anthill to elevate himself above the masses and launched into a speech – his voice changing inflection, as if impersonating a politician trying to soothe the mob of disbelievers. His rumbled voice carried well, with good timbre and tone. I ignored the speaker haranguing in Shona – concentrating on potential attack points instead. Seated in an open, featureless area surrounded by timber and granite boulders, the crowd was vulnerable to a surprise attack.

After the loud speech ended, I told Sergeant Ndoro – pointing out thatched roof peaks visible above the scrub – to round up villagers who lived in that *kraal*, or any close to the school, to dig up the mine. I worked on the theory that local people were informed about landmines in case they accidentally detonated them – and that some of the keener members actively assisted in laying them. Ndoro strolled into the crowd and began chatting with the men. Three were selected – all males over 40 years old. Special Branch chose a dozen people for questioning back at Rusape and we all marched to the waiting vehicles. As we left the school grounds, the crowd fractured and then scattered home. The soccer pitch was deserted within a couple of minutes. At the vehicles, SB sorted through their pick of the bunch – questioning and taking notes.

Our 'volunteers' were herded over to the mine marker. We had not told them what we suspected lay under the road, but as they drew closer, they became silent and edgy. Hove stared at the mine site.

"These guys have walked all over it," he stated – staring at the drivers leaning against their vehicles. Someone had tossed aside the mine marker and fresh boot prints littered the mine site, with the sole patterns treading every which way. The drivers, bored waiting, had walked around the device and someone had uncovered the top. The soil, swept aside, exposed the mine.

"My God," I thought, "what if there were anti-personnel mines laid accompanying the main bastard?"

That was thoughtless – stupid, stupid!

"We should get these buggers to dig it up," I said to Ndoro – indicating the three nervy villagers – "they probably laid it."

Ndoro simply smiled, knowingly.

I leaned over and peered into the hole. The mine looked like a rusted gallon tin squatting in a hole. I hadn't seen this type before and the mine didn't show up in examples displayed during training. An iron ring circle sat above the round body.

"A British Mark Five anti-tank mine," John Padbury said, as he ambled over and peered at the device, "compliments of our British cousins. I reckon about two kilograms of TNT."

"Where'd they get that?" I asked.

"The British probably left it behind with one of our neighbors after Federation and they handballed it to ZANLA."

I stood at the mine site, radioed JOC and requested the Engineers to remove the explosive device. They weren't sure one was available, so I withdrew my dessert spoon from a webbing pouch, sat on my haunches and gently dug around the outside of the body so it began to look like a miniature castle turret surrounded by a dry moat. The three villagers helped scrape away the loose dirt, wary as hell, touching the soil like it was contaminated.

"You know, if this thing explodes," I said to Ndoro, who watched, fascinated, "you an' I won't know; we'll evaporate like steam!"

He nodded grimly, knelt down and, with his hands, turned the loose soil away from the British device – advising the villagers to speed up. Get the job over quick! Within a few minutes, the mine sat in a small excavated crater.

Uncovering a mine was one thing, but removing it was quite another. Sophisticated anti-handling devices, from intricate mercury switches to a simple armed hand grenade underneath, detonated the mine with the tiniest movement. More advanced mines were fitted with a light sensor that exploded the mine once the soil was removed. Obviously, that did not apply. While we stood back, the villagers eased off to the roadside and huddled together.

"That'll do," I said, looking at my handiwork, and then turned to Ndoro: "Take 'em away."

Ndoro herded – then shepherded – the villagers behind the boulder, where they squatted, as he handed out tailor-made cigarettes. Soon, a helicopter arrived and an Engineer alighted. It was his baby now.

We returned to Mantle Base, where the troop packed up and launched back to Salisbury. Leaving the base didn't require dismantling the tents, nor waiting for a relief troop: simply jump on the trucks carting our personal kit and whistle back to civilization.

The bar room waltz began. The booze kicked off on Saturday morning at the Oasis Hotel, where the swimming pool area was jammed with scantily-dressed women and aggressive young men in T-shirts with printed slogans or army unit badges – all belting down Castles or Lions, or Cane and Coke, and smoking Madisons or Kingsgates. If someone walked in alone, they'd soon spot someone they knew. Inside the gloomy bar, seated on stools and swilling beer, bearded men shrouded in cigarette smoke bullshitted each other. "Who are you with again?"

"Can't tell yer, OK?"

Wink, wink.

The party raged on through the Copper Pot, the Police Club and the Prospectors' Bar and on to the Le Coq Dor – one day winding into the next.

Word filtered in that Phil Smith had been wounded. Smith, a UK lad, enjoyed the same police recruit course as I in 1975, where he scored top points on the course in the fitness challenge. A fresh complexion, with a beardless face, mischievous eyes and a cheeky smile – coupled to a sleek greyhound body and superb fitness – Phil loved a spontaneous party; he danced like John

Travolta and mimed David Bowie. He became an expert at slipping away from the barracks at night to immerse himself in the city's nightclubs, but then making sure he was always back before dawn. In recruit training, he had been implacably opposed to the bush. Phil swore black and blue 18 months ago that he would not be caught dead living in the scrub. He confirmed very early in police recruit training that city policing was the only game in town – sticking with all the city creature comforts. Directly after police training, Phil was posted to Salisbury Central, while I was banished to the Matabeleland scrub. Smith, the anti-bush, anti-warfare man, arrived for the same Support Unit training course that I had busted my arse to get into for 12 months. He said city policing bored him. Immersed in a Fireforce action near Mrewa, Phil stalked along a sandy streambed – chasing elusive terrorists spotted by the all-seeing helicopters. One frightened CT was sheltering in an alcove carved in the sandy bank – its entrance disguised by a thorny scrub. As Phil slowly crept past the hidden entrance, the man opened fire at point-blank range. One shot rang out. The bullet sliced through his leather boot and furrowed along the edge of the flesh, but with no serious damage. Phil swiveled and shot him, and then hopped away. Later, someone examined the AK-47 rifle and found that the weapon had jammed. The shooter slotted the change lever to automatic, instead of the expected automatic roar, and only one bullet fired – very, very unusual for the AK! Lady Luck held Phil's hand that day.

After R&R, when I returned to HQ, the CO accosted me outside the offices.

"Have you been to the hospital to see your wounded men?" Collins asked.

"No, Sir," I replied, thinking that Brian Gibbs would have done the honors, since the section technically belonged to Sergeant Zowah.

"Get yourself up there and see if they need anything!"

I drove to the Harare hospital to visit the two wounded constables. What could I say? They left us in the shit and fled. I could not get my mind past the fact they took flight – leaving everyone else to deal with the mess. When I visited the ward, they were extremely embarrassed. We danced around the small talk and spoke awkwardly about their needs. I penciled a list in my notebook and left. I arranged for Zowah to deliver their requirements. I didn't want to engage in the small talk dance again.

5
Mantle 151A: February 1977

Delta Troop ended back at Mantle Base 151A. With an established base, the men did not pitch the tents, nor set up the infrastructure. We merely moved into the tents vacated by the departing troop. With four other troops based here – a bigger command structure – this deployment felt less personal, just a cog in a bigger operation. As a section commander, I was one of 16 others. Brian Gibbs relinquished his tactical role and merged in with the other troop commanders and base commander in the token house – removed from Delta's day-to-day activities. The orders came from the house were directed at any one of the 16 section leaders.

The mottled gray skies hung over the region. Once again, Delta Four dropped into Chiduku TTL, close to Chiware school. Over the first two weeks, an accidental sighting sent the terrorists scuttling off – disappearing into the damp timber and lost before a chase began. The rain fell steadily. Soaked, we flitted from hill to hill. While squatting on an anonymous hill, dripping wet – thinking about a dry bed and a medium rare T-bone steak served by a scantily-clad wench – a voice broke through the daydream.

"*Gandangas* are there," Hove insisted, with certainty.

I didn't doubt him. He pointed to three young people who moved in and out of the bush at the hill base.

I radioed Mantle Base the location of a suspected enemy base and the current situation. They radioed back and asked for confirmation on men and weapons visual. I told them no; we only saw suspicious activity. Mistake Number One. After approximately an hour of to-and-fro on the radio, Mantle Base ended speculation and stated Fireforce was engaged elsewhere. Shit. What now? The lush bush below had swallowed up movement.

"See anything?"

"They're still there," said Hove, the rain dripping from his cap peak.

Magama nodded.

I knew other Delta sections were a half day's walk away. They were little help.

Mantle Base did not offer additional help. Without other callsigns within running distance, I decided to take up the boxing gloves. We scuttled behind the ridgeline and formed up directly above the suspect bush base. I outlined my basic plan: form an extended line on the ridge and sweep downhill. No one spoke. Their faces paled as they waited. I stood up first and stepped over the ridgeline; then down the hill. Looking downhill, tree trunks, shoulder-high scrub and gray boulders stood strewn amongst the dead foliage on the forest floor. The police line weaved among the solid tree trunks and knee-high boulders. Rifle butts were locked into shoulders, safety catches were switched to fire and tired eyes were straining to catch a glimpse of movement – a color, a shape or an outline out of place. The line flexed in and out, around the tree trunks. Our boots squelched the dead leaf matter louder than I wished. Water launched from lower branches as we brushed past, which added to our discomfort. My throat felt *biltong* dry and the heart played the tom-toms.

An FN's throaty roar boomed! A double tap from the left! I flicked my head to glimpse at the source, but a scaly tree trunk blocked my view. A sharp crackle of AK rifle replied.

"Fire! Fire! Fire!" I bellowed, and aimed my rifle – yanking the trigger and blasting the scrappy scrub below. "Follow me!"

I led the charge – ducking and weaving. The MAG thundered and raked the ground to the front, with medium branches, large raindrops and spotty leaves showering down. A thin tree toppled over in slow motion. The downhill rush combined a blur of movement, heightened anxiety and plucking branches. My eyes zipped from place to place to ensure the men stayed roughly in line. The romp exhilarated the brain and tested the vision. Thirty seconds later, the section swept inside the camouflaged base camp. The nerves stretched tight, like a drawn longbow. Where were they? My eyes flitted from tree to boulder to tree. We spotted no one. Not one person! Five brown and blue nylon sports packs sat abandoned in the crushed leaves, along with a brace of three RPG-2 rockets and boosters, which were tied together with tree bark, but the occupiers – along with the local fan club – had cleared out. I stood, chastened, while the constables began to search. While I was 90 percent sure that the CTs were down here, there floated a tiny element of doubt. I didn't want to open fire into the anonymous scrub and come up with a pile of dead civilians.

"Who fired?" I snapped at the constables.

No one answered.

"Who fuckin' well fired?"

"I did," murmured Chikobvu – a young, boyish-looking constable.

"What at?"

"I fired to the sentry. I saw one standing in the bush."

"Did you hit 'im?"

"No."

"Fuckin' good one, mate."

After the sarcasm inadvertently slipped out, I later wondered if Chikobvu thought he was being congratulated or condemned, but we missed them. We were unable to find the bastards. The shooting skills desperately needed to be upgraded.

The patrolling continued unrelentingly. One night, we set an ambush on an anonymous arterial track in the middle of nowhere. A sharp nudge in the shoulder woke me. Hove slid from sitting up onto his belly. I blinked to orientate and heard a whispered mutter filter out of the murky darkness. There was no need to ask why he woke me. I stared hard into the blackness. An overcast night blanketed the natural light. I heard feet scuffing the ground, but still couldn't see anything. My thumb touched the starlight scope's 'on' switch. The bulky scope was affixed to the rifle slide cover. The flick of the switch launched a hum noise. The purr sounded extraordinarily loud. My heart flipped. The scope had been issued during the pre-deployment training and I had experimented using it on a rifle range, surrounded by noisy, inquisitive people. The banter had subdued the electronic sound, but on this tranquil night, the hum rattled my ears. Within a couple of seconds, however, I realized the noise was barely audible – the level only magnified by imagination. On a quiet, inky night, any small sound amplified.

Out of the blackness, two shadowy figures emerged – walking fast. As they lopped closer, they merged into a single blob. I pressed my eye into the rubber eyepiece, opened the shutter and fixed the white circle – the aiming spot – on the front shadow. While the scope intensified the available star and moonlight, I still couldn't see whether or not these turkeys were armed. The overcast sky nulled the sharpness. The greenish light dramatically singled them out, but within seconds, they tramped close enough to step on us. I fired one round and dropped one. The MAG fired instantaneously and bowled over the second shadow.

There were no 'Written Rules of Engagement' to hamper the Security Forces. As long as the commander used reasonable choices when engaging a target, that sufficed. In the operational area, we diligently enforced a dusk to dawn curfew. The after-dark curfew had been slapped on every TTL after the terrorist incursions. Notices were pinned in all public places and all chiefs and *kraal* heads were personally notified of the new regime. Villagers could not claim ignorance. They had to be visiting from Mars to be unaware. Curfews enforced a restriction in terrorist movement. They all knew the rules: walk at night and you're a terrorist. Plain and simple! One dark night, a young National Serviceman in Support Unit stepped out from behind cover to arrest curfew breakers and was shot in the face by the CT who walked behind them. Here endeth the lesson.

The brief firing blitz ceased in five seconds. The last gunshot echo bounced off the distant hills and silence swallowed the land, except for distant village dogs yapping. The night enveloped the two bodies and transformed them into smudges, like two fuzzy blobs. We settled back to monitor events. Unexpectedly, a low whine rumbled from deep in the gut and then lifted its intensity – escalating to a choking stutter; then a shrill cry and, finally, a heart-wrenching shriek. The scream faded down the pain roller-coaster until it became a low, gurgling noise; then it petered out. Ruzawi, the medic, crawled from his position.

"We must help him," he pleaded.

"No one goes out there," I admonished him.

"They're not terrs … terrs don't cry, boss," Ruzawi whispered, "they crawl away and die."

"No one goes out," I repeated firmly.

The voice muttered and slowly faded.

We lay awake through the night. Finally, the morning twilight floated and the formless dark lumps sharpened into recognizable shapes: two African males. One was splayed out – hit once, straight through the heart – and the other had been mauled by a number of bullets, with half golf ball-sized lumps of flesh splattered across the parched grass. I stood up and surveyed the human wreckage. While I felt slight remorse, they all knew the game. Walking at night was a dangerous business – particularly kilometers away from villages. Later, one was identified as a schoolteacher; the other was unknown and the body was never claimed. The bodies were carried out to a pick-up point.

A curfew joke circulated: a patrol shot a curfew breaker at three in the afternoon. When the JOC questioned the patrol leader, they asked: 'How can you claim to shoot a curfew breaker mid-afternoon when the curfew begins at dusk?' The patrol commander answered: 'I knew where he lived and there was no way he would make it there by dark!'

Still patrolling, the scout spotted movement in rocky country and we headed there to investigate. An RPD machine gun fired from 300 meters. The sustained burst ripped and scattered the men as the bullets whiplashed, which were too high to cause casualties. We ducked and dived – sprinting forward between the solid granite boulders, but pausing to measure the danger. We couldn't exactly determine the gunner's location. The scary RPD whipped up another storm of bullets and they crackled overhead. We slowed our advance – urgently scanning the broken country for valid signs. An RPD light machine gun is belt-fed, with a high rate of fire, and the muzzle – supported on bipods – enables even a poor shooter to keep the rounds on a flat trajectory. It was a very dangerous weapon, even in the hands of amateurs. As such, I didn't underestimate our predicament. After closing the distance to 150 meters, Ndoro and two constables jetted over grass to a large boulder, while we focused on finding the attacker. They didn't fall for that trick.

A female voice cackled and shouted something in Shona. A long burst of fire underlined her voice and deadly bullets clipped splinters off the rock. They found our range. We shrank lower among the granite. Female laughter rolled after the bullet crackle. The same female then yelled out in a singsong manner. Another long burst punctuated her voice and the bullets slapped into the rock and whined hideously into the distance, followed by more raucous female laughter. We stayed put, glancing at each other. They had our measure. The voice called out again in Shona, followed by peals of hysterical laughter.

"What's she saying?" I asked Sibanda.

"They just want to kill the white man," Sibanda stated awkwardly.

I don't know if the female voice was the actual machine gunner or an accomplice, but we didn't find them. After a couple of long bursts, they broke off the attack and scattered into the green timber. I smiled, as I hadn't been 'pinned' by a woman in months!

The mission thereafter was reacting to terrorist sightings, CT incidents and Special Branch tips. The information required walking kilometers, chasing rumors and whispers, which came to naught. We trucked back from one hound-and-hare chase and disembarked at Mantle Base. Before I could scoot off to my tent, Brian told me to see Superintendent Mason.

"Why?" I asked.

Brian smirked, shrugged and walked on.

I saw little of Brian Gibbs that tour. Somehow, the bigger operation sucked him from the day-to-day troop involvement and I assumed he had sunk himself into the wider picture. Even Paddy and his section disappeared into the scrub when I returned to base, and we saw each other even less. The 'troop concept' began to unwind.

I found Mason in the operations room. He stated plainly that I was transferred to take command of India Troop. I was totally surprised. No one talked to me about command, but the decision appeared a *fait accompli*. The only problem: I didn't want to step back from the bush. Later, I spoke to Brian about the troop commander job.

"Up to you," he said, "but it'll give you more independence."

'The Machine' assumed I'd take the job. Support Unit expanded: fast and experienced commanders were in short supply. Wary that the commander's job required paper-shuffling administration and inter-unit politics, I pumped Brian for more details. He sat amused – outlining the duties the role entailed. Satisfied I still could play my own tune within the game rules, the troop leader opportunity presented a new challenge. Brian said that the transfer was effective immediately.

I shifted my gear over to the India tents and sought out the troop commander. I introduced myself to Inspector Baldwin. We had not met and I knew nothing about him. A smaller man, Baldwin wore a clipped military moustache and had intense eyes. Slim and fit, he was immaculately dressed, with the stare of someone who had 'seen the light'. He looked to me like a man with something to prove. I later heard, through the gossip mill, that in uniform police, he became overweight; however, with iron self-discipline, he had drilled himself into a high level of physical fitness. At the introduction, Baldwin smiled and shook hands, but I sensed he didn't like me; my rebellious behavior spelt trouble. I didn't hold any specific cause to dislike him, but I anticipated a collision of attitudes. We straddled different planets: the inspector – a corporate man who stamped on deviations from the Good Book – and I was a smartarse and improviser swimming against the tide.

India had messed up a night ambush two weeks previously. According to hearsay, a CT party walked through India's killing ground while the African sentry lay asleep. Paddy, woken by the terrorists talking, saved face by tossing a fragmentation grenade, which wounded one terrorist. I learnt later that a National Service patrol officer fled during a contact in Nyamapanda – sparking general panic that culminated in a loss of equipment. A discreet inquiry confirmed the facts, but no action was taken, as 'it could seriously affect morale'.

An India Troop (red and blue) lanyard and Support Unit shoulder flash.

"Great beginnings," I thought.

Someone slept on ambush and another leader fled a firefight.

On my first night with India Troop, Paddy Baldwin announced a quick patrol. We tramped over the timbered hills of southern Chiduku, south of Weya, before the boss admitted being lost. At daylight, he switched to a search of local stores on the Dorowa Road for ZANLA notes, based on a theory that storekeepers kept handwritten notes on the premises for goods requisitioned by terrorists – a sort of promissory note that claimed 'we'll pay in full after the war'. The stores had accumulated a mind-boggling array of merchandise that could excite any enthusiastic bargain hunter. Behind the sales counters were piled jumbles of crap, but nothing was found.

Once the week ended, Baldwin was promoted to Support Unit Chief Inspector – managing all the training programs. He developed a battle camp at Concession – a tiny farming community north-east of Salisbury – for training raw recruits and retraining troops prior to their deployment. The battle camp certainly took an enormous step forward in conditioning the men to the rigors of the campaign, but I didn't like its commander. By now, Baldwin and I didn't see eye to eye. He disliked unconventional commanders and we had crossed swords over training and minor tactics. He'd love to grind me into the deck in front of the India Troop constables, so I stayed away.

In Salisbury, I celebrated my promotion to Lance Section Officer by a heavy drinking session with Paddy Allen and some other pisspots, which ended in throwing a few things around in the Regimental Institute at Morris Depot. Chief Inspector Pearce of the Horses lay asleep in a drunken stupor against a table while this skylarking played out. The night frolicked, but nothing extraordinary occurred. The next day, the institute telephoned Support Unit – querying the loss of a prize exhibit. Assistant Commissioner Collins went ballistic! Headquarters frantically radioed. I was coaching shooting at the Chikurubi rifle range when the hullabaloo caught up.

"Get here now!" cried the radio.

"Do I bring the troop?"

"No! Just you! Now!"

I left the men under their section leaders on the rifle range and drove back. I couldn't fathom the 'please fuckin' explain' tone in the exasperated voice. I drove to HQ, parked and wandered down the footpath among the buildings. An African sergeant standing near the armory smiled as I wandered past the door and gave a low whistle – shaking his head sadly.

"You've done it this time," a white instructor smirked, as he marched past.

"Done what?"

"You're in deep!" he laughed, as he vanished around the corner.

What's going on? Everyone knew except me. Last night was tame. I didn't even sport a hangover. Arriving at the door to the office complex, Superintendent Mason glowered and then whisked me into Jim Collins' office.

"Where's the fuckin' medal?" demanded Jim Collins – red-faced in rage.

Collins, the unit boss, was an unorthodox Assistant Commissioner – an ex-World War RAF veteran. He didn't bother with preliminaries.

"I don't know what you're talking about, Sir," I replied – looking straight ahead to avoid the CO's wild eyes.

He blasted off in full throttle, with choice words, and then dismissed me.

"Get out of my office!" he yelled, "an' wait outside. I'll fuckin' have your balls, O'Brien!"

They thought I had stolen the Victoria Cross! A rare Victoria Cross awarded to a BSAP trooper in the 19th century Shona Uprising. I couldn't remember touching the wall plaque. I sat alone – stewing on a bench outside the office complex. The staff shuffled back and forth in silence and shunned the detainee as if I had leprosy. They weren't going to catch my disease. What the fuck is he on about? The night was a blur, but tame.

The minutes crept to an hour. At 10:30 a.m., the barman calmly turned up for work and retrieved the gallantry award. Concerned about our rowdy behavior, he had taken the VC off the wall and hid it.

I was marched back into Collins' office.

"I'm sick of your drunken behavior!" he shouted, as I slammed to a halt in front of his desk. "You're busted to Patrol Officer! Now get out!"

"OK, Sir," I said, before I moved, "but unless I am an LSO, I can't deploy with India Troop next week."

Collins glared at me. I was sure he wanted to punch me on the nose!

"Alright," he said, "keep the rank and deploy with India! But I don't want any more of this shit! You hear?"

Well, not really! Demotion had lasted less than two minutes. The Regimental Institute imposed a ban.

Collins decided to make his life easier by splitting up the unruly elements and ensuring that their R&R did not coincide. As 'unruly', we did not harm anyone, but just played boisterously and flamboyantly enough to upset sensibilities. The commissioned police lacked a sense of humor, so Paddy Allen, Phil Smith, Ron Rink, myself and others saw little of each other on future R&Rs.

I threw myself into troop training – leading gruelling road runs and minor tactics to gauge the level of commitment before India deployed. While I was non-regimental, I took this work seriously. Early each morning, 30 men ran Enterprise Road as residents walked their dogs or motored into the city, which kept the troop on its toes. To improve marksmanship, we spent a full day at the Chikurubi rifle range – firing sacks full of discolored ammunition that had spoiled in the operational area. Hundreds of bullets ploughed into the butts. I walked up and down the mound and corrected shooting techniques. The sections conducted battle drills through empty paddocks in Gun Hill, which were under the scrutiny of retired residents as they sipped pink gins on the balcony, and 'Advance to Contact' – up and down the grass paddocks from the Support Unit back gates to the RBC television studios – until the men had the drill hammered into them.

The critical personnel were scrutinized – and I was particularly interested in India's section leaders. The two white section commanders – Garry and Van – appeared hesitant. A new troop commander complicated life – especially in India, where my appointment was the third in six months. They just got the measure of a troop commander when a new posting arrived. Each new commander exuded their own personality: likes and dislikes, weaknesses and strengths, and their attitude towards the men and the war itself. By the time I arrived, they were probably wary of yet another boss.

Garry – fair-skinned, with freckles – only grew bum fluff around his jaw. Tall and skinny, he mirrored a tired high school lad, but he was willing to have a go and carried a cheeky, happy disposition. Van had a lean and hungry look about him. He was tanned, wiry and fit, but was untried when it came to mental hardness. He had acquired limited leadership skills and, in my opinion, would have been better suited as a private soldier in the army. I hoped that the repetitive refresher battle drills I conducted would assist in building his command confidence. Both, in my opinion, required more experience to confidently command a section – and experience, unfortunately, only came in the operational area. Pushed, both stepped up to the plate, but given a choice, they would rather not be there.

To be fair to them, the police provided superficial training for anti-terrorist bush work. Support Unit hosted a six-week training course, which was considerably less than army basic training. The white police were, automatically, section leaders after the training – leading seven veteran African police. If the white policeman harboured doubts about his abilities and life experience, the African policeman either reacted helpfully or shied away, depending on the section sergeant. It was a big step from high school to police training to Support Unit training and then to immediately leading men into sharp, vicious battles. Some white leaders sat naturally in the role and were excellent; others did just enough to get by.

Senior Sergeant Tambe – a grizzled veteran with close to 20 years' service – was the troop senior NCO. With a noticeable gut and a slight double chin, he typified a senior NCO identified in all armies and police – one where dreary peacetime years had whittled away his enthusiasm and had left him surly, cynical, bored and practiced at avoiding work. When I spoke to him, he stared under his half-closed eyelids and displayed difficulty suppressing a yawn. He'd heard it all before and I was just another troop commander to manipulate.

As I intended to be a bush bunny, I allocated myself a section. The section NCO, Sergeant Chewa, was a tall and toned man, with round, enquiring eyes. He gave the impression of a serious, dedicated professional. Thumbing through his service record, the typed pages spoke highly of his professional attitude;

of his ability and knowhow accumulated over 12 years. He looked the part, dressed the part and acted the part, but a hidden flaw exposed itself later.

My personal section of pirates consisted of Moyo, the tracker. He was a thin, strapping constable who recognized the humor in just about everything. As the section comic, he was always laughing and kept morale light-hearted. He was 'The Joker'; then there was Mandaza – a forceful, droll constable who dropped quips unexpectedly into conversations and remained unpredictable. He was 'Mr Give Me the Facts'; the MAG was lugged by Tutani – a squat, mischievous man, with a wry sense of humor and outrageous off-duty behavior. He was 'The Playboy'; Tsumba was a trained medic, with a serious demeanor to boot, who employed the brains of the section. He was 'The Thinker'; then there were two boys: Banda and Chipangora. Besides me, Banda was the other foreigner – born in Malawi – and was educated at a mining village school in Matabeleland. Both were young and inexperienced, and only months out of basic training. They were 'The Youngsters'.

As the boss, I could have avoided nights tramping through the bush by overseeing operations from camp. Among Support Unit troop leaders, there was a mix of action men and administrators. Most used the position as a tactical command and administration job – liaising with JOC and politically maneuvering amongst the Security Force's leaders to enhance their own career prospects. A proper troop commander should be a tactical administrator and a welfare man, but I was here to hunt. To me, a troop commander led from the front, as simple as that. He set the example and the pace, and took risks. To do this, he spent as much time in the field as his men – leading operations. The only direct orders required were 'Follow me!' I came for excitement and bravado, and there was none in the base; only bush operations provided the kind of exhilaration burst that sizzled through the body like electricity. I was hooked on the adrenalin rush and did not shirk the opportunity of a firefight. I may have been a better troop commander residing in the base – shuffling paper and inventory counts – but that held no appeal to me. I was certainly not there to build a career. As paperwork and politics were not my forte, I found it best to delegate.

After retraining, on the weekend before India Troop deployed, Paddy Allen and I were arrested in the city for causing an affray and being drunk and disorderly. The irate city police hauled us into Salisbury Central police station, where we told the exasperated inspector that we were Support Unit. Rather than toss us in the cells, he locked us in an office, while they attempted to find out what action to take. We sat on the desk – passing ribald commentary and writing comic remarks on paperwork in the 'IN' tray. Soon after, an indignant inspector burst into the room and released us. He almost booted us out the door. Apparently, the inspector had telephoned Collins at his home and woke him. He had his ears chewed off for his trouble. Needless to say, our ears were mercilessly chewed the next morning.

"See this gray hair?" Collins snapped ferociously the next morning, "You're responsible!"

Not only I. There were others that contributed to the gray hair, like the men who shimmied up traffic light camera poles to face the camera, as their mates deliberately drove back and forth on the red light enough to set the camera amok. The unimpressed Traffic Branch boss tossed the hard-copy evidence onto Collins' desk. There were plenty of pranks and un-policeman-like conduct on R&R to fill half a book! An angry Jim Collins was now more determined than ever to ensure none of the rebels were in Salisbury at the same time.

6

Mantle Base Again: Late February 1977

India Troop arrived in steady rain at Mantle 151 Alpha. The command element shifted from the farm a kilometer up the main road to a large, bald dome rock, with a concrete PTC telecommunications tower slap in the center. The command element – including the radio communications network – set up comfortably inside the tower. The rest of us remained on the farm – housed in four-man tents roped down in the slush, with the canvas stretched tight in the wet. I watched the water pour down, form puddles and slither under the tents. The constables, already wet from hours sitting on the back of the trucks, shuddered at the sight. The camp was hardly enticing. Looking around, I didn't like this place. For me, the scrub was the place to be.

I got my wish: quickly, the India sections were deployed back to the southern Chiduku area once again. It was like going home – in and around the hill country that bounded the Dorowa Road. There were sightings reported, but without results. Either Fireforce was not available, or the sighting was too brief to act upon. One or two short, sharp firefights amounted to nothing. Like an abstract war, we hardly ever saw the enemy. Lengthy patrols continued – winding among the *kraals* and through isolated bush country. The infantry's monotonous, grinding slog – carting kit on the shoulders, watching from hillsides until the eyes ached, lying in ambush for days, fighting off biting insects, sucking up cold tucker, always on the edge of hunger, drinking tea flavored with ants and small debris, digging shallow holes to defecate and a constant lack of decent sleep – jolted with short, sharp, heart-wrenching adrenalin rushes of bullets, rockets, mines and mortars.

The troop still spent large chunks of time sifting out intelligence, either by routine patrol or OP. Walking into a village, we cheerfully greeted the occupants and quickly settled down to the questioning routine. This is Africa Central: straw thatched, round pole-and-*dagga* houses, and the lingering scent of salt, smoke and sweat. There were zero amenities – no plumbing or gas, or electricity or telephone – just brutally austere villages of six to eight huts. The people owned very few modern conveniences – a battery-powered transistor radio or record player stretched the limit. Most pottery and implements were handmade; there wasn't much sign of plastic, store-bought stuff.

On our sudden entrance, the men greeted our abrupt arrival with traditional words – returned in kind by the patrol sergeant. Some were comfortable with our presence; others eased themselves back into open doorways to drop out of sight. Those caught unawares trembled minutely. Most were skittish, avoided casual conversation, answered in monosyllables and acted edgy, as if we were close to tripping over a cache of stolen goods. They were shiftless, jittery and fidgety, like parolees caught in the company of a known felon. They were uncertain what stance to take. One or two engaged the constables in small talk, but they eyed us nervously – particularly when the constables asked them to be seated.

The village women politely curtsied in the traditional manner at our trespassing and, when asked, sat on the hard-packed earth – their eyes curious and hesitant. They wore cotton dresses (usually one color – a plain and simple cut). Mothers slung babies on their backs using a colorful bath towel – tucking them in close. The younger ones ogled, as if a ghostly apparition had sneaked into their dreams – maybe the first white person they saw in their village? The kids, snot-nosed and dusty, were like kids anywhere: smiling, chatting; some shy, some cheeky.

The sergeant automatically separated males from the womenfolk. Except for the *kraal* head, older men were ignored, as they were downright stubborn. The old people were as tough as rubber soles – their faces heavily lined by life's hardships; their hair turning gray to white; their clothing a shabby mishmash. They knew everything that happened in their sphere of influence, but had little to say on any subject. They stayed on the edge of the nationalist wind – trying to judge which way to jump. Their red-rimmed, smoky eyes gave nothing away as they protested at our interference. They had the most to lose – a lifetime of hard, physical labor and the resultant retirement currency of cattle stood at risk. They were guarded even when engaged in innocent conversation about local events and the weather.

The *kraal* head, however, was considered a likely contact man for transit ZANLA gangs. He was the heredity community leader reporting to the chief. As a headman, he was either closely entangled with the ZANLA boys, or the walking dead; there was little middle ground. ZANLA brutally murdered, without compunction, any *kraal* head who appeared to lean towards the government. To survive, *kraal* heads became the ZANLA conduit in his area of influence. He memorized every face of the genuine CTs and he also ran the message system between ZANLA groups, where he walked with handwritten letters and deposited them in dead-drop letterboxes; organized young kids to scout for government forces; coordinated local intelligence; collected village taxes and policed the region for traitors. *Kraal* heads also immersed themselves in the coordination of ZANLA logistics – arranging hot food, cold booze, warm blankets and luxury goods. *Kraal* heads adamantly insisted they saw nothing, heard nothing and knew nothing.

The question and answer process kicked off. The patrol sergeant circulated among the seated villagers to examine the *chitupa* – a compulsory ID document that all African adults carried. (The *chitupa* was the African name for the blue, A5-sized paper registration certificate issued to every African adult. It had their name, tribe, chief, *kraal*, father, district and their physical description. The holder's details were typed on the appropriate line and the *pièce de résistance* was a smeared thumbprint at the bottom. Unfortunately, the written description fitted roughly 80 percent of African people and the thumbprint was worth jack-shit in the bush.) The grubby paper did not include a photograph of the holder, and thus became freely traded amongst CTs, but it was a starting point.

Once the sergeant completed the *chitupa* exercise, he split likely people from the seated groups one by one and shared them among the constables. The constables sat in pairs on the village outskirts – one constable talking to a villager and one alert and covering any entrance track. If we got lucky, we'd aim for military-age folk. Young people aged between 16-25 were at a premium in the tribal lands. Most fled either to find employment in the cities, join the Security Forces, join the terrorist forces or seek jobs in the underground mines in South Africa. Those left behind had little future and, with nothing to lose, they threw themselves enthusiastically behind ZANLA.

Once selected, each villager ambled over – attempting to look calm – and sat back on his heels. After squatting down, the villager stared at the baked ground – not knowing how to act. They listened guardedly to the questions and either replied in a monosyllabic manner, in clipped sentences, or in a lengthy diatribe, with arms animated and facial expressions changing with the tone of the dialogue. They were unable to be friendly.

ZANLA spies – prying eyes and counter-spies – logged unusual occurrences. They talked like they had a mad uncle watching from close by. The fingers of political terror hovered. Everyone was ultra-cautious – and we were not welcome. There was no benefit in them aiding us. There was no offer of food, possibly because they had so little themselves. The CTs were now permanently seated at their dinner table – and we caused an unwelcome ripple across their society.

Constables advanced a line of questioning about local activities, the weather, the crops and the cattle, which slowly led in a circuit to questions about CTs. It was traditional and polite to beat about the bush in conversation before going for the jugular, but the CTs were the 'elephant in the room'; everyone knew they were there, including us, but no one said so. The villagers never, ever volunteered a titbit of gossip. When we mentioned the CTs, the word provoked a steely, negative response. Like the *kraal* head, they heard nothing, saw nothing and knew nothing. Their mouths sealed closed like clams, but we endured the arduous process as, on the rare occasion, a detainee slipped up and led us off on another tangent.

I sat back against a tree trunk and brewed tea over the camp gas stove. What did I know about these people? Not much, but I held a smidgen of underlying admiration. The kids are kids everywhere, with some serious and some open, and some shy and some playful. Who couldn't smile at their antics? The adults, however, were gristly – seasoned and hardened by life. They were not complainers, although their precarious existence gave them plenty to complain about. Their fragile farming life rode on nature's whims and, with no property rights, they could not acquire a line of credit to carry them through the lean years. They could have handed us a long list of woes, such as why wasn't the government doing this or that to help them, but they didn't – not to my soldier-police intrusion. They were stoic, tough and resourceful – and they just wanted to be left alone.

Sure, I had spent a couple of years working the tobacco farms with a crew of foreign nationals – men from Mozambique and Malawi – but what did I know of their world? I had discovered farm workers were shrouded in mystery. They had an undercurrent dislike for the white boss garnished in manners and obedience. There was definitely a language barrier, but also different cultural perspectives. I couldn't put my finger on anything specific, except that the longer I worked with Africans, the less I knew. When I thought I'd grasped a subtle idea, a farmer would sneer with: "You've been 'ere five minutes an' you think you know them." They were bound up in ancestor spirits, unbelievable superstition and family totems; in tribal complexities and inter-family politics. They lived close to the soil and read the world through a different script. They tended to just agree to get along, whether they agreed or not. I closed the yawning gap with humor, but very marginally. They saw the world through the African lens, and I, through the white optics.

The operational tours were six weeks. What could be achieved in six weeks? We barely scratched the surface before withdrawing and being catapulted into another region. We were strangers looking in from the outside. We didn't grasp the complexities and nuances of tribal politics, nor understand the nationalist impact on the tribe's people. The convoluted inter-relationships between families and *kraals*; between *kraals* and the chief; and between the *kraals*, chief and the government were outside our remit. The associations wound up tightly in a many-stranded rope that required a wizard to untangle.

The seated village mob snatched sly glances at me – trying to gauge my reaction. I, in turn, observed them closely. They were peasant poor, with no coins to jingle in their pockets, and wearing threadbare clothes with large holes. They were not First World poor, with a menial job, TV and a tired old car parked on the street; they were dirt poor – no cash, television or consumer goods. Clothing was stitched and patched, and stitched and patched again. Some shirt holes were so large that I wondered why they bothered to wear them at all. Their calloused bare feet produced soles harder than Nike. While they were inquisitive, they avoided my eyes. When I snatched a glimpse of their doleful eyes, they betrayed nothing – no hate, no fear, just bewilderment. Their lives were topsy-turvy. As I stirred the sugar crystals into my tea, I knew it was impossible to comprehend their view of the world: here, in this simple, but practical village, their world radiated out about 10 kilometers. They stored future food in a small cubicle building. If the rains failed or the crop died, then it was tough shit! There was no social welfare and little government role in their lives. Their course was charted by family and tribal belief that delineated firm social roles and a socialist community aspect. Now, their lives were violently intersected between the clash of white and black culture. The Liberation War dropped straight into their laps and they began to be immersed in slogans and murders on one hand, and interference on the other. I wondered what they really thought about the events, out of their control, but slowly squeezing, like an unwelcome guest, into their lives.

Questioning continued *kraal* after *kraal*: round up, sit down, check the *chitupa* and filter them out one at a time – hours spent listening, rechecking stories and cross-checking answers. We gauged the level of resistance by the outcries of innocence. On rare occasions, direct force was used – especially where hard evidence of the CTs' presence was strongly denied (a CT boot print, tailor-made cigarette butts or a piece of CT military kit). Once, we stumbled upon denim jackets hanging out to dry – one with 'ZANLA' inked across the back. The emphatic denials resulted in a leather boot up the arse, a hefty punch in the ear, a swift pummelling of a cheeky delinquent, a bloody nose and feathers ruffled.

If a whole family were jointly implicated in assisting the CTs, but vehemently denied their complicity, I'd destroy one of the buildings. This reprisal act was carried out where hard evidence of their involvement was stamped out for everyone to see, but still emphatically denied. A random *kaya* was torched – the thatched roof ignited by the lighter flame. The family stared stubbornly at the sudden burst of flame, but still dug their heels in. Burning houses was not a tactic encouraged at JOC level, so it was rarely reported.

Counterinsurgency warfare success is premised on the notion that Security Forces protect the civilians from the insurgents. That pre-supposes that the African civilians supported the central government, which many certainly did not. In limited operational areas, the government spent heavily to collect the population into PVs in order to cut off easy access between the terrorists and the people; however, in most tribal areas, villages ranged across hundreds of kilometers of bush and savannah, with many isolated by poor logistics. To protect these villagers, huge SF numbers were necessary and the government simply didn't have the cash resources or manpower. The central government also lacked the cash and political resolve to substantially lift the peasants' living standards, so the SF hit a stalemate. Even with enormous largess and massive spending, the USA couldn't lift up the peasants' living standards in Vietnam, so the Rhodesian Government – with extremely limited spending power – had no hope. The best job kept a lid on the insurgency until the politicians came up with a solution.

During these drawn-out grillings, I loved the African view of time and distance. Unworried about the clock, they had no difficulties waiting hours – even days – to catch the local bus. In the white world, if public transport didn't arrive exactly on time, it ignited a considerable gnashing of teeth and boiling anger. In the tribal area, if the bus didn't arrive, the passengers slept, chatted, ate and generally mooched about until it did. I soon discovered their estimate of distance was flexible.

"How far is so-and-so?" I'd ask.

"Very close." (Means up to 10 kilometers.)

"Close." (Means 10-20 kilometers.)

"Ahahah." (Get a helicopter!)

If questioning didn't produce useful leads, we patrolled – searching for physical signs of CT shoe prints or base camps. The section advanced to contact and would then spread out in a shallow arrowhead formation to scour the land. Occasionally, we stumbled upon CT shoe prints scorched into the dust. Terrorist shoe prints stood out, as most villagers walked in bare feet or sandals crafted from discarded car tires, and only the upwardly mobile terrorists preferred pilfered running shoes, *veldskoens* or an issued Mars pattern military boot. A mixture of two or more of these sole prints, clumped together in the grainy dust, stood out like a neon sign shouting: 'Terrorists walked this way'.

On other occasions, the section traipsed through the wooded slopes, just above the *kraal* line, to search for base camps. Villages were generally built close to the foot of the high country to maximize the arable land. Terrorist bases were sited strategically behind a *kraal* in the trees, so that approach routes were kept under surveillance and, most importantly, their escape routes were hidden from view. A terrorist static position – referred by the SF loosely as a 'base camp' – described the turf they temporarily occupied. There was no structure or diggings. The 'base' encompassed a flat piece of ground undistinguished from the surrounding terrain. The giveaway signs included flattened grass, where CTs had sat or slept; worn paths, where they walked to their sleeping spot; dry chicken bones and tailor-made cigarette butts, plus loose cellophane wrappers, an empty Bols brandy bottle, a forgotten enamel plate and, occasionally, an AK magazine or RPG rocket booster that had been left behind.

When the terrorists based up for the night, or a few days, they chose to be close to people. The closer they were, the less hurdles in food, water and blankets supply, plus easier integration with the villagers for political lectures. Once inside their operational area, the terrorists did not live hard. Again, eight times out of 10, they lived within 10 kilometers of an active business center, a thriving beer hall or an operating primary school. They liked the good things in life, like cold beer, loud music, marijuana and tobacco cigarettes, willing girls and packaged foodstuffs. Many abandoned base camps produced evidence of beer and brandy consumption.

Our open-style patrolling also kept locals on their toes, but terrorist bands soon picked up ripples about our presence. If patrols were carried out consistently, they easily neutralized the enemy and they either departed, or shut down operations. While continuous patrolling was frustrating – the long, hot days walking through the sleepy *kraals* and quiet business centers, waving the flag – our presence pinned down terrorist activity and curtailed their freedom of movement. Occasionally, open patrols frustrated them into launching an attack. Unfortunately, the results of open patrolling were not measurable. Like a ship ploughing through the seas, the moment the SF sailed on, the terrorists moved back in. With an emphasis on kill rates – and low SF numbers to cover huge tracks of land – overt patrolling was only a small part of our armory.

Patrolling meant large stretches of time walking in silence, which was broken only by heavy breathing and the occasional grunt; the ssshhhh of rubber soles parting dry grass; the creak of canvas webbing; the odd sharp crack of footwear snapping twigs. Soon, the soldiers/police become grubby and sweaty and, as the days flipped by, the men tuned out the aches and abrasions. Even food options melted as the appetite faded – and a meal was simply habit, not hunger. To our footsloggers, the days could be arduous, tedious and uncomfortable, but it was the essence of soldiering.

Walking the TTLs could produce sharp excitement. Once, in Delta – crossing the Ruzawi River – Hove claimed he saw beady crocodile eyes brushing the water's surface. His face suddenly transformed to a pasty color as he stood in hip-deep water. When he blurted "Croc!" the section didn't stop for an explanation. We sprinted across – parting the water in our desperation to reach the bank. Huffing and puffing on dry land, I wondered if he saw a crocodile. No one else had; then again, we weren't about to argue with him midstream!

Out there, we lived with another enemy … 'Big Game' rarely roamed the tribal areas, but the microscopic game did. A number of exotic diseases lurked about for the unwary, with the usual suspects including tsetse flies, typhoid, malaria, tick bite fever, gut worms, cholera, tetanus and dysentery. Later in the war, rabies flared up and spread quickly – particularly among African dogs. Bilharzia is a waterborne parasite that lives in the static water of dams and along the edges of slow streams. As a newcomer, I was warned not to swim in still water, as that's where bilharzia struck; running water, such as streams and rivers, was OK. The parasite is a blood fluke picked up by snails living in the inert water. It messed up the stomach area, and one symptom is tiredness. Sometimes, tongue in cheek, I reckoned we all were afflicted!

Another charming insect, the putzi fly, laid eggs on washing drying on the clothesline. If the clothes were not ironed, the egg hatched and the maggot burrowed under the skin to begin its life. The larvae produced an ugly boil. To cure, the enflamed boil was coated in petroleum jelly and, starved of air, the larvae tunneled out! All clothes, including underwear, were ironed to prevent the attack.

There was also exotic plant life, such as Buffalo Beans. A flowering vine, the Buffalo Beans' seedpods were covered in a very fine hair. If a person brushed past, the hair fell onto the skin and produced an extremely irritating rash, which drove that victim mad with scratching. To cure, the afflicted had to coat the affected area in wet mud, allow the mud to dry and then peel the shell off. For one's enemies, coating toilet paper in the hair produced a nasty ordeal.

We returned cold and wet to Mantle Base for a cold shower and a pot of homemade stew. Van and Garry reported no sightings, and Tambe looked too refreshed to have worked hard. In the morning, Superintendent Tom Naude, the base commander – a formidable man, with little humor (particularly with transgressors) – planned a three-troop operation in southern Chiduku. He ordered the troop and section commanders to attend his briefing. Gathered around a wall map, Tom pointed out the route he plotted for India. I closely examined the course, which meant crossing the Macheke River at night. With days of heavy rain, the river had to be flooded.

"Ah, Sir," I stated – observing his finger resting on the blue squiggle that denoted a river, "the river is likely to be right up. I think that'll make it hard to cross."

Tom studied the blue line on the map and replied: "No it isn't."

Was he serious, or was he just firmly shutting down any objection? Superintendent Naude wasn't the type of officer to brook a challenge to his authority.

Lo and behold, the Macheke River raged. We heard the ominous churn before we reached the bank. With no bridges in our allotted zone, we had no alternative but to cross the invisible water. I chose the crossing point at the shallowest part, I remembered. The men hovered on the gravel river shoulder, close to the dark, rushing water, and were filled with considerable apprehension. The rapids sounded loud and wicked – shielded by the darkness and amplified by the imagination. We were not strong swimmers, so the thought of being swept away – laden with 20 kilos of operational equipment – bounced inside my head. I instructed the men to seize hold of the backpack tabs of the man in front. Lined up on the shore, one behind the other, I took the lead and stared at the cream-cap waves tumbling over rocks. Holding my breath, I stepped into the fast-moving water and immediately struggled against its force. To be waist high in cold, bubbling water in the drizzling black night – tentatively feeling the way ahead with rubber-soled shoes, sliding on unfamiliar rocks; with a rucksack weighing heavy, with five days' supplies on sore shoulders; with webbing, which weighed us down, along with our ammunition, and a rifle clamped in one hand – had its moments. With the water rushing above my crotch, I knew that shorter constables struggled in waist deep and higher. A foot slid too far and my heart double-flipped! The line edged across, with the constables supporting each other, looking like a bloated centipede. Fortunately, nothing catastrophic occurred and the line crossed to the opposite bank, soaking wet, but delighted.

On the fifth consecutive rainy night on the Inyazura River – a tributary of the Macheke River, just north of Dendsa – in an ambush on a prominent foot trail connecting one *kraal* line with another, Sergeant Chewa woke the sleepers. At the tap on the shoulder, I woke instantly: one second, semi-asleep; the next, wide awake.

"Someone's out there," whispered Chewa doubtfully.

I raised my head and gazed into the matte-black night – blinking to clear the brain, with my eyes adjusting minutely. The rain drizzled. The night was so dark that even the rock outline, which was two meters in front, remained invisible. Everything beyond that marker stood hidden behind a blank, black screen. Soaked, uncomfortably cold and with icy, clammy clothing, I shook off the last vestiges of disorientation and concentrated. Muffled chatting and suppressed laughter sifted through the dark blanket. The constables – snappy alert, with rifles tucked in their shoulders – left no doubt who the talkers might be.

A group of a dozen CTs stopped on the waterlogged trail to raid a mango orchard. Though not visible through the black veil, they made enough noise to rouse us without a sentry. The rifle butt climbed into my shoulder, with my cold forefinger stroking the trigger. The impenetrable blackness was still awash in falling rain. The CTs, still unseen, continued on their way – strung out in single file and walking fast along the slushy track. I switched on the starlight scope – the hum once again amplified by sensitive ears. My right eye sank into the rubber optical protector, which opened up the shutter. The world transformed into dark shades of green and light, like a two-dimensional photograph. The wait dragged on. Their spoken words drifted in, which were accompanied by the audible slosh-slosh of footwear hitting wet mud. Even the scope couldn't define the target with any certainty. The cloudy, raining night obliterated any nightlight. The slosh-slosh amplified; then a black blob loomed and a second merged behind the first. I lined up the second man. His shape appeared blotchy in the poor natural light. I centered the aim circle and, without mucking about, squeezed the trigger. The FN roared. White sparks shot from the muzzle deflector. The bullet definitely hit, and I swung onto the next blob and fired again. Possibly two hits!

The CTs retaliated instantly and fired back. Deadly streams of green tracer zapped over our soaked position – the glowing balls appearing larger than life against the blackboard background. We huddled into the cold muck. The MAG roared into play – reciprocating with bold, incandescent red tracer balls. Wild tracer soared back and forth; then the machine gun jammed and stopped! The rat-a-tat-tat strangled and ceased. The terrorists upped the tempo with remarkably heavy fire. The white sparks from their gas regulator twinkled through the murk. Without our dominant machine gun, the constables' rifle fire sounded ragged and pitiful. The firefight raged for three minutes, but it seemed like three hours at close quarters. While the riflemen switched to suppress the RPD machine gun, Tutani scrambled to strip off the MAG barrel. Fiddling with a hot barrel under steady rainfall – blindly prodding to clear the obstruction – took steely coolness. By the time he completed the task, the CTs disengaged. The retreating RPD gunner stitched up India's position and his tracer bullets pinged off the granite rock overhang protecting the MAG gunner. Credit to Tutani: he didn't miss a beat. Once the obstruction was cleared, he sent a long burst of machine gun fire down the track – the brilliant-red balls illuminating against the black background like giant meteors. The enemy fighters broke off and the rain stepped up its performance to bucket down like a final curtain. Steam rose from the MAG barrel.

"Anyone hit?" I called – the rain dripping off my cap peak.

No response.

"Everyone's OK?"

"Yes," Chewa murmured, from the gloom.

A stony silence hovered. Concussion resonated in my ears. The muzzle of one rifle was too close. My left ear sang a tune inside my head. Apart from my ear troubles, the abrupt stillness sounded unnatural. We waited – keyed up like a wound-up rubber band. As the minutes clicked past, and there was no further action, I breathed out slowly. Satisfied the enemy had escaped, I attempted radio communications with a squad of Support Unit trainees manning an OP on the dark hills over the other side of the river. Nothing. The line was dead. I wanted other sections to close in by the morning to attempt to leapfrog ahead of the enemy. Without communications, that had to wait. I learnt later that the trainees lay awake and watched the brilliant tracer criss-cross. Their role was to facilitate unfettered communications, but they had been mesmerized by the pretty-colored tracer bullets, because they didn't answer calls.

A half-hour later, a muffled explosion rent the night. Shit! Had the enemy just mortared us? The men cuddled the drenched ground tighter. My back tweaked, anticipating another bomb – a deep-seated fear of a mortar bomb landing smack on it. I didn't hear the launch, so fear fluttered unrestrained … one explosion, but where's the second? The damp, fine hair on the back of my neck stood up. My heart rate ramped up and my imagination caught a dozen bombs airborne. I held my breath, but still nothing happened. The quiet night accentuated. My heart settled down. Time crept by. I relaxed. We lay awake – miserably saturated – through the cold hours, which finally slinked into the first, muted morning rays. Cold rain, wet clothes and pumping adrenalin had sunk any thought of a catnap. It was a long, long night, with eyes and ears sharpened for enemy movement. The watery dawn illuminated the sodden foreground. Slowly, as the darkness lifted, we tentatively made a move.

"Let's go," I whispered to the tired, grumpy men.

Stiff, chilled and soaked, the men rose – gasping out loud as wet shirts clasped their warm bodies in an icy embrace. If any men slid back to sleep, the ice-cold slap across their skin rudely tore them awake.

"Sarge, you stay here with Tutani an' cover us," I said – and, with a wave of my hand, said to the others, "follow me."

I'm sure Chewa was delighted not to tiptoe into the murky scrub.

The men stalked forward under the MAG protection. In the flat killing ground, thick blood goblets clung stubbornly to grass blades, and four lonely hats – a cowboy type, two caps and a beret – lay where they fell. From the liberal blood splatter, I estimated that three were hit hard. The rain washed away lighter blood smears, apart from the thick goblets. Disgusted at not finding a body, I extended the sweep further out. Stamping through the waist-high wet scrub, the collected raindrops poised on the tiny leaves splattered soaked uniforms – further numbing the cold body. Angry that I had missed the fuzzy target, I plunged furiously through the waterlogged scrub – knowing the rain had wiped out any chance of tracking the survivors. The constables screwed up their faces at the flying droplets – wondering when I'd stop.

Shoving aside the thin branches, unexpectedly, I stumbled on a dead CT.

He was posed head down in the thick, wiry scrub, like a diver off a diving board, but frozen in mid-air. His soaked denim jacket was clearly visible. On closer inspection, a yawning bloody hole in the chest cavity revealed itself: it was black, with congealed blood and protruding ribs. He'd conveniently killed himself with a grenade by cuddling the explosive over his heart. His right hand had been blasted off – leaving a bloody, cauterized, mangled stump. This explained the single explosion heard last night. Standing there, I radioed the OP and the trainee operator instantly responded by excitedly interrupting and asking about the contact. Incensed by his stupid questions, I abused him for not relaying my calls. After a splutter of excuses, the instructor in charge snatched the radio handset and damned *me* for using colorful language on the airwaves. At least he had his priorities right! I reported the contact and the result: one CT dead, one AK-47 rifle, four magazines and a stick grenade recovered. I calculated two other CTs were badly wounded and on the run.

As we dragged the dead man back to a pick-up point, JOC relayed orders for India to wait for additional troops. Sodden wet, and not a dry piece of equipment, we simply appreciated more opportunity to sit in the cold rain! After five days and six nights, why not? Two hours later, police tracker dogs arrived by heavy vehicles on a muddy road with a wet handler team, who looked mighty incensed at being called out in the rain.

"What's the fuckin' point in gettin' us out 'ere in the fuckin' rain," the patrol officer moaned – tucking his green plastic raincoat tighter.

"Don't ask me, mate," I replied, in a shitty mood (the whiner had just got his feet wet and we'd been stuck in the crap weather for days), "I didn't ask for you."

He muttered on, but I didn't care.

Some tactician at JOC had ordered them in. The big black and tan Alsatian sniffed here and there, just going through the motions. Any scent trail had been long washed away. They are like tits on a bull in the steady rain.

I had used the night ambush technique with success. Rather than camp at night in a defensive formation, I elected instead to ambush a track, *kraal*, cattle dip, bridge or business center. It was purely speculative. The section spread in a straight line – facing the selected killing zone – within an arm's reach from each other. We didn't bother with Claymore mines or illuminating paraphernalia; it was a simple rifle and MAG affair. Once settled in, sentry duty began. Each man, myself included, conducted sentry duty while seated in their position. By insisting they sit up, I was able to glance throughout the night to ensure the sentry had not gone to sleep – at least, not while lying down! If they heard suspicious noises, they'd touch the man either side and so on till the whole section was awake and alert. It took seconds and entailed little movement.

Part of the success required walking up to 10 kilometers away from where the section had last been spotted. For me, the essence of anti-terrorist warfare was mobility, unpredictability and surprise. We hiked three hours through the night – avoiding *kraals* so as not to leave a trail of barking dogs in our wake. If possible, I identified the ambush position during the day and returned at night, or we walked and walked until I found one that met my criteria. I tried to ambush from the least likely position. The ambush in Inyanga North was on a grassy contour ridge running across an open ploughed field, slightly below the level of the road. The CTs looked to their right at the heavy scrub and rock country, and none surveyed the open fields on the left; catch them when they were least alert.

On our return to the base camp, with hardly any time to dry off, India Troop was suddenly flung into Weya TTL for a High-Density Force operation. A relatively tiny TTL – a mere teardrop encircled by Headland commercial farms – Weya remained a sharp thorn in the farmers' skin. The Weya Africans had been swept off land seized by whites for tobacco farming in the 1940s and had resettled. Since the resettlement, they had seethed with resentment, but they didn't take their forced removal lying down: they accumulated a history of dissident action well before the war marched in. The locals viewed both the white farmers and the government as the enemy – employing a number of active agitators – and had challenged the government intrusion through the High Court. In the 1960s, there were 56 white families living around Weya. With active tribal support, by 1977, there were very few white farmers left, as they had been either murdered or driven off.

Superintendent Naude briefed the police troops and outlined a simple plan to swamp the small tribal land in a good dose of police and soldiers. Two Support Unit troops, as well as elements of 2RAR and the Rhodesia Regiment, were thrown into the exercise. All the units deployed separately to the target TTL. India Troop trucked out at 2100 hours along the winding backroads that snaked through European farms. At the appointed spot, still in the farming country, the truck slowed right down to five kilometers per hour and the men flung themselves into the darkness – loaded with weapons, ammunition and heavy backpacks; that was always fun. The jump from a moving truck disguised the precise drop-off points. In theory, the jumper tossed his body into space – nose first, leaning forward – and landed on the balls of his feet, which allowed the truck's forward momentum to jerk him upright, but in practice, half the troop landed hard on their arse, not correctly compensating. They staggered off the roadside – bruised and aching.

Once the trucks vanished, only the blurred outline of the white road ribbon and tall trees in the immediate foreground were visible. Using a covered torch, I orientated the map to the ground. With limited visibility, Sergeant Chewa and I agreed on the rough location and the direction of the start line. I packed up the torch and map and we walked off the road in single file – reliant solely on the eyeball to walk in a straight line. Without a compass (one of the many basic tools we lacked), the journey was fraught with miscalculations. Leading the way, the troop plunged into the woods. We walked and walked and, two hours later, crossed a sandy road.

"What's this road?" I hissed to Sergeant Chewa, not recalling one on the map.

"It's the same one we deployed from," the sergeant stated glumly.

"Bullshit," I growled, as I surveyed the white ribbon of road.

"We jumped off about two Ks down there," Chewa said, as he pointed down the road.

Moyo nodded gloomily, agreeing with Chewa.

Fuck! I looked up and down the shadowy road; it looked like any other. If they were right, I had led the men in a wide circle back to the drop-off road. The map came out and the torch was switched on as we recalculated our position. How did I end up here? I must have stepped around tree obstacles on the right side and not sufficiently compensated, so a continuous (but minor) deflection to the right at every tree put the troop back to the road we started on. What a proper fuckup! I thought the bush country was thin enough to navigate by eyeball alone. During the trek, Sergeant Chewa had attempted to steer me, but I didn't listen. Shit, I know best! I wouldn't do that again. Sheepishly, I looked at the troop. Tambe leered at my failure. He wore the 'I'm too old for this shit' face and spat a large gob into the darkness.

"Stick that up your arse!" he seemed to say.

"Let's go!" I hissed and we jogged back through the terrain – this time, with Moyo leading – and made the start line before dawn.

At dawn, the SF units simultaneously embarked on a sweep from different directions. Before the sun rose, the four India sections swooped on the targeted *kraal* lines and many half-asleep residents shat themselves when we floated by. The SF was the devil incarnate to the sleepy peasant – staggering out the open house door for an early-morning pee. Our task involved clearing a long *kraal* line and the hills immediately behind them. Our briefing included facts about prolific cattle rustling. The people had no qualms about raiding cattle from the white-owned farms to slaughter for food. The troop was urged to locate stolen cattle. We tramped through the awaking villages and on the deserted slopes behind. Sweating in the expanding morning heat, we found nothing remotely resembling terrorist occupation, nor any evidence of stolen cattle. At 8:30 a.m., an RAR section reported a short, sharp contact and they recovered an AKM rifle and medic pack – otherwise, it was a long, boring and drawn-out day, followed by two more fruitless days.

Once the HDF formally wound up, the troop was plucked out and deposited back in Chiduku to engage in normal operations. I sat with the section leaders and doled out their new areas. Garry and Van feigned interest, while Tambe stared vacantly into the distance. With his face turned to the side, I was sorely tempted to smack his jaw hard. I bit back my anger – knowing he had no intention of aggressive patrolling and likely would hole up somewhere safe … he'd spend five days in the shade, eating and sleeping, radioing false locstats and sitreps. My turn would come! The four sections separated to get on with the job.

When not patrolling, OPs were established where practical. Many Support Unit sections conducted very successful OPs where, hidden from view, the men spotted the enemy and called in helicopter-borne army units to kill. To have a chance at success, the local population must not know of the OP party's existence. That required careful and calculated movement into the target hill – avoiding populated areas, dirt tracks and using anti-tracking techniques. Even the most casual eyeball recognized boot marks. Most marches were carried out at night, with the movement confined in scrub country and disused slabs of ground, which minimized the chance of being detected. The best OP operators walked in bare feet to copy the native walkers, but I did not subscribe to the native code.

Once on the hill feature, the OP selected was a position below the hillcrest, on an anonymous part – avoiding prominent trees and rocks. Sometimes, we stumbled into lazy OP positions, where other SF had holed up. Cigarettes were butted out and left in the dirt, and squashed baked bean tins were buried lazily under loose leaf or grass that had been trodden to death, which spelt the location. If we spotted the obvious, so did the villagers. The villagers saw the same hills every day and were exceptionally good at spotting anything abnormal, no matter how small. Where possible, an OP was sited from where the spies saw the exact area where the local women went for a shit. There are no toilets in villages and people wander off into the scrub to defecate – and no, it wasn't depraved voyeurism; we didn't see the action take place, only the bush tops where they chose to go, but women (being women) were unlikely to shit where they suspected males were watching them, so if they suddenly changed the location of their ablutions, we had good cause for believing the OP had been compromised.

Much of Support Unit's time was spent squatting on a featureless hill – baking in the sweltering sun, eating cold muck, sniveling away for a shit, sleeping fitfully, killing endless time and being hounded by tsetse flies, blow flies, mopane flies and ever-incessant mosquitoes while watching till the eyes ached. If the reader thinks an OP is a holiday, try staking out a local park for four days while remaining undetected, so that you can spy on the locals – and don't forget to carry in all your food and water for 20 kilometers undetected, plus you can't bring any of life's distractions. Water was the one factor that reduced the time on a hill: if we consumed too much, or we'd be stuck there too long, we would be eventually forced to leave to fetch some.

More often than not, the OP didn't catch a glimpse of the CTs, but interpreted signs that pointed to them living in the area. Indicators included young women walking into the scrub with aluminum buckets balanced on their heads, large amounts of *sadza* being prepared in a single village, a lot of activity in a confined area, people coming and going into a single patch of bush, people carting food ingredients from other *kraals*, people carrying in lots of firewood bundles and, finally, large outdoor cooking fires. The African was better placed to assess whether activity was classed as 'normal' or 'unusual'. Most constables originated from, or had families living in, the tribal areas, and so they had a sixth sense about normalcy. Convinced they had all the right signs, the OP would radio for a Fireforce callout.

Back in Chiduku, another OP ended in a farce. Adjacent to St Crispen School, very close to my first contact, Moyo observed eight CTs walking coolly (about 600 meters away) across the drab brown and green fields that stretched out before us. The binoculars certified they were the real McCoy. They skirted around the open fields – heading cross-country for densely forested hills. I radioed Mantle Base, requested Fireforce and was told subsequently they were on the way. If they arrived on time, these eight were dead meat. With nowhere to run, trapped by an aircraft, it would be like shooting at lame deer in a cage.

"Mantle India One, K-Car, over," the nasal voice drawled into my ear 20 minutes later.

"Go ahead, K-Car."

"Still have the gooks visual, over?"

"That's affirmative, over."

"Roger. Mantle India One, any weapons visual, over?"

"K-Car, Mantle India One, negative. They're about 600 meters off an' closing, but they're definitely Charlie Tango. They're all in the open, over."

"Ah, roger that. Mantle India One, I'm sorry, but we've been diverted to another scene. There are 30 gooks an' weapons visual, over."

"Copied. Confirm you're not, I say again, not coming here, over."

"Sorry, it's out of my hands. Good luck, over."

Well, thanks a million, you bastard! We watched the eight dark shapes drift further north and then we sharply radioed base for a section to be trucked in, but the attempt was futile. By the time a section kitted up, were briefed, had collected maps and radio codes, and filed onto trucks, the CTs would be in Disneyland. We helplessly observed as they finally reduced to dots and disappeared. Some days later, at Rusape JOC, I hunted for a record of the diversion on the daily sitreps. Not surprised, I read that the '30 gooks' were, in fact, locals and the 'weapons visual' were *badzas*. Someone had miscalculated, we had lost a definite result and Fireforce had added another 'lemon' to their score. The wet, frustrating and thankless tour ended and India Troop trucked back to Salisbury for R&R.

In the weeks on operations, the world bypassed us. World events occurred without our knowledge, and even national news headlines slipped by. There was no news of other Support Unit actions either. We were cocooned in a separate time zone, where matters that only directly impacted us were known. If someone got their hands on the *Rhodesia Herald*, the news was out of date. No news fostered wild speculation, and the void fed the rumor mill. In the NZ Army, I was thrown into a field exercise in 1969 when mankind's most historic journey took place – the landing on the moon – and we were not aware that the enormous step had happened!

Back at HQ, we were greeted by shock news! Tim Hewitt, commander of Echo Troop, had died as a result of wounds received in a vehicle ambush on 2 February in Wedza. Tim drove the Bedford truck – dropping off sections along a road – when the convoy was ambushed at close range. Although badly wounded, he returned fire with his shotgun – and afterwards, continued to organize the counter-attack. He was awarded the Police Decoration for Gallantry posthumously. Constable Mazarire, who was on the truck, was later decorated with the Police Cross for Conspicuous Gallantry for his astonishing bravery in the same action. Fighting off the ambushers at close range, he assisted Hewitt from the truck cab and exposed himself to the CTs' fire. Wounded five times, he lifted Hewitt down from the cab to a less exposed position. Tim was a popular troop commander and a policeman just short of his two-year Support Unit tour, with a posting back to Uniform Branch already approved. He was an acute loss.

While conducting routine duty at Tomlinson Depot, a senior policeman sharply reprimanded me for not wearing the Rhodesian General Service Medal (RGSM); I was in a state of undress without the campaign medal. I didn't bother to apply for one until I left the force. Everyone in uniform during the 'state of emergency' received the RGSM. Whether you parachuted into Mozambique with the SAS, or wrote out parking tickets in Baines Ave, all were equally entitled. Men who fought toe to toe with the enemy at the 'sharp end' for 10 years, or who had performed undercover Selous Scout operations, wore the same medal as the men in King George Barracks who had counted and filed the ammunition requisition forms for six months. I didn't get with the program. As usual, the drinking marathon began, day after day, till the R&R died.

7

Wedza Twice: April 1977

The government trumpeted a major change in military operations. Lieutenant General Peter Walls – the top army man in the war effort – headed a new Combined Operations Headquarters. Finally, after 15 years of committee leadership, the government appointed an El Supremo. Walls became the army celebrity on TV and in the newspapers – the face of the war. Finally, I thought, the government stepped up and a new commander would savagely cull ineffective leaders. We anticipated aggressive and meaningful change, where early retirement is thrust upon tired, old soldiers and police, and younger, bolder men with get-up-and-go were flung into critical positions. I figured: "Retire all army officers from colonel and above and replace them with uncompromising lieutenant colonels and majors, inspectors and superintendents, and squadron leaders and wing commanders," but unlike Malaya, where the top man had sweeping power to achieve that end, Walls could not act unilaterally to cull the deadwood from the police, army, air force and Intaf to revitalize the leadership. There seemed, from my level on the totem pole, no sense of urgency in the military campaign. All the old faces remained until retirement, and the replacements were selected on seniority, as if on a peacetime footing. The upper echelon did not let a mere war stand in the way of their careers, so the war rolled on – offering more of the same leadership.

India trucked down the main Wedza dirt road in light rain – surveying the timbered country to the west and flat grassland to the east. Tim Hewitt had been killed here in February, so we were acutely conscious of the risk. On the road south, the convoy slowed for 'Ambush Alley'. Here, the tight scrub tucked right up to the road and, in one section, the road wound around wooded spurs, where we sat at a definite disadvantage. All eyes combed the wood shadows. The men didn't need instructions to be fidgety alert. 'Ambush Alley' lived up to its name in the weeks ahead.

This was my first independent command (in other words, not subject to Mantle Base micro-management). The troop had been assigned a tour outside the Mantle Base orbit, but I wasn't flying solo. November Troop was ensconced in an Internal Affairs camp at the southern extreme of Wedza, where India would join them, but operate independently, within the shadow of a more experienced troop leader. The vehicles rumbled through the gate into the Internal Affairs camp and parked among other Support Unit vehicles. I climbed out of the Land Rover to survey a lovely timbered hideaway. It was a big, sprawling house, with toilet facilities and outside *braai* areas – an oasis backed into mature trees. The District Commissioner used the camp as an administration stopover. I imagined the Commissioner riding in on horseback, during the pre-World War era, after a hot day, ready to relax. Large trees sheltered the permanent buildings – lavishing the camp in deep, cool shade. It was a pleasant sanctuary.

The camp hugged the base of a timbered hill, which provided a scenic backdrop, but gave the enemy a decided advantage. ZANLA fired on the base with small arms and 60mm mortars before India arrived. The CTs attempted another night attack a week before the troop departed. Once again, they formed up on the hill directly behind the house, but, unbelievably, our sentry heard them arguing over who should fire first! The sentry opened fire and the terrorists fled. Once we parked, Sergeant Tambe rounded up the constables to pitch tents and erect other camping requirements. He slipped into his role – his gruff voice whipping slackers. Van and Garry scouted around the house to see if they knew anyone. Gray Barker, the November Troop commander – and also a veteran policeman – stepped out of the house to greet us. A bull of a man, with no neck, Gray emitted a no-nonsense aura. He displayed the demeanor of a blunt policeman, but I quickly discovered he had a great sense of humor. He guided me into the house for a cup of tea and introductions.

After refreshments, we adjourned to the operations room, where Barker presented a scanty run-down on Wedza on the operations map. The tribal land abutted the Chiduku stomping grounds and was hilly, rugged, folding, isolated wooded countryside that was ideal for guerrillas to hit and run. Apart from the usual *kraals*, schools and business centers, two Christian Missions popped up on the map: Mount St Mary's – a Catholic-owned Mission, with large schools and an equipped hospital in the north – and the more basic, Protestant St Anne's, which was south-east of St Mary's.

"St Mary's is a Charlie Tango sanctuary; they come and go as they please. St Anne's, well, we haven't heard much there an' Acorn thinks there's nothing happening. They get all they want at St Mary's," said Barker – squinting at the map. "The road running south here in this windy section is 'Ambush Alley'.

You'd driven through on the way here and experienced the tight corners an' heavy bush. The Charlie Tango had some success ambushing vehicles on that portion."

He continued: "Tim was killed here," pointing to a road to the north. 'He was ambushed during a deployment. The Charlie Tangoes are fairly aggressive and organized. There are at least three sections in Wedza and one in Ziyambe. Armed with the usual light weapons; no heavy ones reported yet. All the incidents are on the log, so run your eyes over that to familiarize yourself with the latest. We know the name of the ZANLA commander: Bob Killer."

He smiled. Bob Killer … now that's a real war name.

The briefing was cut short and sweet and contained zero actionable intelligence. For operational purposes, Gray sliced Wedza in two. India was to operate north and west of St Anne's Mission, and November would look after the south side. The update continued on administration and communications, Allied forces in the area and camp routines, but there was no intelligence on enemy intentions. I had already learnt that a troop had to ferret out its own.

Apart from colored pins denoting historical CT activity, and a typed log stating the bloody obvious, the maps were devoid of anything interesting. Police Special Branch secured the franchise on intelligence sources. From their office in the Wedza police station, in the far north of the TTL, they ran their secret operation – their fingers and eyes extending into the tribal lands. Special Branch theoretically distilled their reports into something JOC Rusape could act on. While they funneled intelligence direct to JOC, that didn't mean the information was handballed to Support Unit. There was any number of army units that also prized up-to-date data, whose skills were better matched to the facts supplied.

Thus far, I personally had little interaction with Special Branch. As a section leader, I sat at the bottom of the pecking order and unquestioningly followed up tips handed out. Now a troop leader, theoretically I would have some small say in the information war. To me, Special Branch resembled weather forecasters. They incorporated a detailed analysis of what actually occurred, plus weighed all the known facts to best guess the future. Like the weather, terrorist intentions can be whimsical. From my level on the food chain, little useful information filtered down. The crumbs that dropped into my lap were, at best, speculative long shots. To be blunt, we would have starved waiting to be fed by the intelligence people. In saying that, Special Branch – the backbone of the counterinsurgency effort – performed exceptionally during the conflict and provided timely intelligence for many successful actions. Much of their 'hot' information was flicked onto elite army units who were better trained and more flexible to deal with it. My troop sat somewhere down the bottom of the overall SF structure, and so intelligence gems were handpicked by other units. Consequently, we were generally fed rumors and unsubstantiated gossip. This is not a criticism; it's my personal experience. To be effective, we needed to know where the enemy was today and likely to be tomorrow, and therefore used our own police skills to source intelligence *kraal* by *kraal*.

So far in this Bush War, I deduced certain CT traits – and two weaknesses stood out: while they mingled with the population, they were, initially, strangers and slowly built up their local knowledge over time. That meant the CTs often employed guides in new areas and walked on well-trodden tracks. Hundreds of dirt tracks meandered through the tribal land – crossing and linking villages to fields, to villages and to the main road. Also, their logistical lines were extremely long, and they walked outside their operational zone back to Mozambique to fetch resupply – using the myriad of dirt trails. On return, they navigated by eyeballing large, prominent geographical features, but stuck largely to walking tracks. This reliance on footpaths left them open to ambush. Secondly, the CTs tended to base near a village complex, where food and blankets were sourced. They fed on the peasants' meager food stocks and borrowed blankets for overnight stays. From their base on the village outskirts, the CTs engaged in the political education of the masses. These selected *kraals* were usually within an easy walk to a business center, where soft drink, bottled beer, canned food and other necessities were close at hand. While they operated with a level of cleverness, they had two failings: walking tracks and consumer goods.

To add to tactical considerations, a ringing tone in the left ear reinforced the danger of landmines. The enemy loved the weapon and mined many roads. I decided to condition the men into walking everywhere, both to and from operations – humping everything with them. The use of road transport had to be minimized once we lodged in a tribal area. Vehicles endangered the men from landmines and easy ambushes.

My tactics boiled down to four parts:

1) Walk everywhere; keep driving on roads to an absolute minimum; avoid tracks and footpaths where possible; walk cross-country.

2) After dusk, walk at least two hours in the dark to slip out of the area we were last sighted.

3) Night ambush major footpaths.

4) Reappear in the morning at least five kilometers away.

I applied my tactical options. Studying the pattern of past CT incidents, I decided to concentrate on the mid-section of the tribal land west of St Anne's Mission, from the Chigondo business center to St Paul's School. I gathered the section leaders; Garry, Van and Lance Sergeant Nguruve – a young, energetic NCO who had joined India (and who showed promising leadership skills) – listened to my plan. I wanted a four-pronged sweep north through the parallel valleys. I emphasized a detailed forensic search and insisted on good intelligence. From the four prongs, I anticipated gathering enough information to concentrate on two areas only. Garry shot Van the 'do we have to camp out there in this shit rain?' look. Van shrugged, as he considered what to carry … less food, more clothes? I tasked Sergeant Tambe with finishing off the camp to bed down the troops, which delighted him. Duties included assisting with radio duties, sentry roster and organizing drivers if we required reinforcements. I didn't want him in the bush, hiding. I needed four sections to diligently carve up the zone for the enemy. After the briefing, he silently mocked the sections by standing outside with his arms outstretched – testing the falling rain and sneering at Nguruve.

The patrols walked out of base camp pre-dawn – the rain still steady and the ground drenched. The men squelched out in progressively heavier rain and a chilling breeze. Everything was wet: the grass, the dirt, the trees and us. On the combat cap, water dripped off the visor like rain falling off a roof without guttering. I banned the green poncho; in the rain, it gleamed, as water reflected obscure light. To a casual eye, it looked like what it was: men ambling in raincoats. I'd rather be soaked than a target. The cotton clothing soaked up the rain, but if we walked, we were warm enough. Soon, the rain seeped through the stitching on the backpacks onto sleeping bags, dry stored clothes, equipment and, eventually, the men's morale.

We sighted only a few villagers in the field (they had wisely elected to stay home and keep dry). The countryside displayed a checkerboard of empty, unproductive fields, coupled with tall, mature maize stands and rolling timbered hill country, with tidy *kraals* tucked on the hill base. It was similar to the Chiduku geography next door, just thicker wooded terrain glistening in the rain coating. Walking through the saturated terrain, the raindrops sat precariously on the branches and leaves, and sprayed everywhere as we pushed through. We had soaked boots, wet socks, saturated clothes and mud splattered everywhere.

The villagers appeared suspicious and more politicized than those in neighboring Chiduku. They were not talkative and met our overtures with stony silence. If they saw us first, they sprinted off into the bush to hide. One second, they may have been talking to their neighbor; the next second, there was a flash of color as they bolted for the trees. No shouts or threats stopped them, not even a warning shot. I had not encountered civilians deliberately running from us, and had assumed that Mr Bob Killer choked them by the throat. A villager trailed my patrol – hanging back, shielded by the rain – before disappearing into the waterlogged bush. Later, we sighted him again – skulking 200 meters away before merging into the scrub.

While we trudged through the constant rain, a November Troop Land Rover and Hyena were swept off a concrete bridge into the flooded Mare River. The vehicles halted at the foot of the low-slung concrete bridge, where muddied water foamed – obliterating the structure. One man volunteered to walk on the bridge to gauge the depth of the swirling water. The boiling water surged up to his knee, so after he paddled a quarter of the way across, the driver honked and waved him back. Assuming the bridge was level, the driver punted that the knee-deep water swirled evenly right across. The Land Rover idled forward and, at the half-way point, abruptly plunged headlong into the torrent, followed by the Hyena. Later, once the floodwater subsided, investigators found the river had completely swept away the middle portion of the bridge – leaving a huge, gaping hole. Fortunately, everyone was rescued. Two constables, who couldn't swim, were plucked hanging from tree branches over the raging waters. Equipment and rifles stowed in both vehicles were lost. The vehicles were banged around and waterlogged. Afterwards, Gray faced a ton of paperwork – diligently explaining vehicle damage and equipment loss.

At this stage of the war, section leaders wrote about equipment lost as part of a contact report penned after every brush with the enemy. All details – such as the location, time, date, weather, a hand-drawn map of the contact scene and a list of equipment expended or lost – accompanied a brief explanation of what happened, what should have happened and the result. The report should have been a useful tool if someone actually took the time to read it – evaluating tactics that worked against those that didn't and then updating the troops – but this didn't happen and the formality of writing them, as the war intensified, soon petered out. The only portion that bounced back to the troop was the equipment lost. The radio aerial lost, for example, had 'please explain' penned by the Q staff and sent back. In a very short time, I found that a detailed bullshit reply, that emphasized we searched high and low for the lost aerial, sufficed. Later, I discovered a shortcut: just swipe one from the army.

After returning to base, sodden and cheerless, the section commanders and I pooled information over a hot cuppa. The data collected joined rumor to gossip to fairy tales. The terrorists were here, there and in the treetops. The words were intangible – whispered gossip neither factual, nor complete fiction. I sifted through the distilled notes and matched up the most promising area – a zone worth combing. This was the first tour where I set the agenda. As usual, the local gossip was tardy, but it was better than the offerings from formal agencies. After a day in camp – drying out kit and munching on hot, solid food – all four sections plunged back into the solid CT rumor mill. They were definitely out there – protected by the villagers' fear of reprisals.

After two weeks in the bush chasing shadows, my section sat in the cool shade on a wooded spur, eating lunch, east of the Mtukwa Range – overlooking old maize fields and enjoying the short spell of hot weather. Moyo sighted six CTs and a number of civilians walking rapidly towards our clandestine position.

"Boss, *gandangas*, down there," said the unflappable Moyo – slipping another handful of *sadza* into his mouth.

"Yeah, sure," I answered sarcastically, as I eyed the puffy white clouds floating overhead.

"He's right," hissed Sergeant Chewa, his face ashen.

I rolled over onto my stomach, parted the stiff grass and peered below. A fighting unit and hangers-on walked on a worn dirt path that cut between the flat maize fields, straight towards the hill we occupied. The path then circumnavigated the bottom of the hill. Rapidly assessing my options, I concluded they would stick to the track, so a quick, close-range ambush would put lead into their pants.

"Leave the gear here," I whispered to the wide-eyed constables, "an' pull right back. We'll nick down the slope and hit 'em up at the bottom."

Chewa raised his eyebrows.

"That means your *sadza*, Sarge."

Leaving our canvas rucksacks and part-eaten lunch, we silently scuttled backwards on our bellies along the grassy ridge, out of sight, and then scooted down the side of the hill to rustle up an instant attack. Only lightly timbered, with some granite boulders, the slope wasn't an obstacle. The men dodged, skipped and hugged the available cover and arrived at the base without being detected. Stopping within meters of the dirt track, the constables eagerly spread out among the granite rock and long, dry grass to set up a hasty ambush, and waited in anxious and nervous anticipation.

My eyes focused on the point where the lead person should magically appear. With my stomach bound in a tight knot, thoughts bounced around my head – each considering our concealment, our cover from return fire, our arcs of fire, the precise point to spring the ambush and whether our position was solid. A quick survey of each individual position confirmed they weren't great, but the best available. A surprise barrage of rifle fire outweighed the lack of great firing positions. My eyes flicked back to the foot track. They should be here, I gauged, stroking the trigger guard in anticipation. No one appeared.

Meanwhile, the CTs – unbeknown and opposite to my predictions – walked off the main track and climbed directly through the long grass and up onto the hill. They clambered straight through the timber and reached the top, exactly where we had been eating lunch minutes before. If I had elected to stay, they'd presented ideal targets, but such are the fortunes of war. Now, the positions were reversed. While they were standing on top of the hill, we sat agitated below and waited and waited.

Finally, after what seemed hours and no sighting, I decided to clamber back up the hill to reoccupy our initial position and find them once more. I whispered the changed circumstances to the men and we scampered back up the hill, running and stumbling, but before we reached the top, a constable called out: "There they are!"

We froze on the timbered slope and pivoted to the left to see the whole CT group and their hangers-on running across an old maize field, at right angles, 150 meters away. Caught short, we simply swiveled and immediately opened fire – unleashing a blistering torrent of bullets, half aimed and half pointed. The target group scattered and sprinted hard towards heavy timber on the far side. The storm of bullets increased their speed, and they ducked and weaved – galloping towards a small, low-slung, thickly timbered hill. I aimed at one individual on the left flank and concentrated on him – sending single shots off. Bullets punched grainy dust clouds around him without any discernible effect, apart from spurring him along. Gaining on the woods, the terrorist began to break running speed records. From the corner of my eye, I noted the MAG red tracer flying too low and knew the gunner had not compensated for the height above the maize field. Fuck that!

"Give me that!" I shouted at Tutani.

I snatched the hot MAG off the astonished gunner, rapidly scrutinized the scene below and set the metal bipod on a suitable rock. I picked out the slowest runner (the bastard I had tried to shoot), yanked the trigger back, adjusted the aim – using the red tracer as pointers – and peppered him as he dashed for the thick bush cover. The fine dust from bullet strikes obliterated him. Confident of a hit, I switched targets to one runner within meters of the granite and timber cover, and again splattered bullets all around him. Alone, he ran inside the beaten zone. The MAG veraciously sucked in the bullets and showered out expended brass cases. The brilliant-red tracer bullets blitzed into and around him – the fine dust curtain obscuring his body – but he still managed to scramble into the green jumble at the base of the small hill. I fired a 10-round burst into the lush screen behind him; then stopped and studied the maize field. I'm amazed at the hundreds of bullets in the air, but most having nil impact. Any more? The field looked empty. They'd gone – dashing straight into the flourishing green bush, out of sight.

"Where are they?" I asked more to myself than anyone else.

"They're all gone into the bush. Jeez, they could run," marveled Moyo – grinning from ear to ear.

"Fire a mag into where they disappeared," I called, and burnt up 40 rounds through the MAG – the tracer scorching into the green canopy. Heat steamed off the hot barrel. "Reload!"

I swapped the MAG for my rifle and didn't muck around. The general metallic clatter of metal on metal ended. The section once again scurried off the hill – skipping and dodging the boulders – and lined up on the deserted track at the base. It was a beautiful African day, with a light breeze and a muggy temperature hanging over the landscape. An eerie silence draped over the dead maize stalks – the dregs of last year's harvest. There was not a visible sign that a short, violent clash had just taken place. The only evidence was the acid aroma of burnt cordite and fried rifle oil, which increased the heart rate. Combat cocaine! A quick glance each side confirmed the men had strung out into an extended line.

I weighed up my options on the scramble downhill: we could swing left or right and flank the hill that sucked in the terrorist gang – seeking to jimmy them out – or we could proceed straight up the guts to close the gap quicker. I stepped forward … up the guts it was.

"Let's go. Spread out. Shoot to kill."

Spread 10 paces apart across the untidy field – conscious of spacing between men – we deliberately paced forward through the knee-high, broken maize stalks and clinging blackjack. The tension tripled, as the sweep, immediately after the firefight, can be the most dangerous time. Wounded and trapped terrorists – sincerely believing that their time was up – maneuvered quietly to take someone with them. The stomach cringed on this journey. A shot boomed.

"One dead here," Mandaza called calmly.

The constable delivered a *coup de grâce* to the first terrorist hit by the MAG. Once again, we couldn't afford to walk past – presenting him with our unguarded backs. They're not dead unless their brains are splattered on the ground. An AKM assault rifle was recovered.

Abruptly, immediately in front, a figure bounded up from among the dry brown stalks and began to sprint off. The men saw a flash of movement and a blur of blue, and opened fire. Before the flurry covered five meters, several bullets smashed into the body, which crashed head first into the dry stalks. Swiftly moving in, we discovered the target: a village woman, in her thirties, wearing a blue and green dress. I knelt down for five seconds beside her and a very quick examination confirmed death. There was no pulse on the carotid artery. Unfortunately, tragically, she had a baby wrapped on her back with a towel, in the traditional manner, and the baby died also. Tsumba paused and knelt down to see if he might help – fossicking in his medical pack. Chewa, ashen, squatted down also.

"Don't stop!" I urged, as I leapt to my feet, "we need everyone in the line."

We were still in an open field – facing the hostile jungle.

In this war, combat was so close that men actually saw bullets strike the clothing, the human body crumple and fall, and the sparkle fade in the retina. You had to be quick, or very dead. Everyone in the contact scene was considered an enemy and, when movement was spotted close up, there was no time to discern whether it was armed or not. Your own life floated on the split-second response – particularly in a sweep line after a short, sharp battle. Armchair critics dispute this because they do so from the comfort of their leather lounge chairs.

Guerrilla warfare always produced civilian casualties. CT formations included civilians as guides, recruits, general hangers-on, *mujibas*, girlfriends, pack mules and so on. At close quarters, when the shit hit the fan, there was no time to differentiate. To survive and win without incurring unnecessary casualties, we knocked out all comers – and anyone running with the CTs was tainted with the same brush. They knew the inherent risk. Armed or unarmed, grouped together, they endangered their own lives.

The line of police walked beyond the dead woman – scouring the shriveled maize field ahead and moving into the looming hill. The line surged out of the open field – seeking cover. We paused at the base of a colossal granite boulder and caught our breath. My body was at a heightened alertness and charged with tingling adrenalin pulsating through the rushing blood. The hill was about three meters high, with low-slung granite boulders interlocking with mature trees that had grown wherever they had achieved a toehold. I stared back across the brown, broken maize field from whence we had come; then around the edge of the boulder, into the green shield, and swallowed … here we go. Licking my dry lips, I waved the men forward – stepping away from the granite shield – and we ducked into the gray shadows, where the terrorists sought sanctuary. The men treaded warily – their eyes wide and searching cautiously – combing the undergrowth: bit by tiny bit, rock by shadowy rock, tree by shady tree. It was a slow, methodical and high-tension search.

Terrorist cadres were taught to expect no mercy (we took few prisoners), but even if they successfully evaded detection, the wounded had no immediate access to trained medical help, so unless the local African farmers found them, death was agonizing, slow and lingering. If they were lucky to be found alive by the local people, and given even rudimentary medical help, they were still a long way from surviving. Sometimes, the seriously wounded were shot dead by their own comrades. Others were taken to a secure place, like the Catholic Mission or a hidden cave or, if they had a military rank, were manhandled all the way back to Mozambique. For a wounded terrorist combatant, the future was bleak. This part of the sweep got the arsehole tweaking. Boom! Boom! Boom! Boom!

"What the fuck's going on?" I roared, when four bullets zapped across the tense sweep line and smacked hard into the dirt five paces to my front.

Dry soil flung into the air. This was definitely 'friendly fire' – the FN's cannon roar. Friendly or not, I would be just as dead. I crouched, with my rifle tucked hard into the shoulder. The shooting ceased.

"What's goin' on in there?" I called into the green canopy.

"One dead here," Mandaza called – clarifying the situation.

The dead man had hidden in a large, dark crevice that split a mammoth granite boulder and had finished his camouflage by snapping off a fresh tree branch and hunkering down. He probably lost his nerve as the combing troops trod close. After the action, Mandaza said a wounded CT, without a smidgen of warning, had cast aside his green shield, popped up into view and, with an AK-47 in one hand and a Chinese stick grenade in the other, attempted a die-hard last stand. Luckily, Mandaza noted the hazy movement first and fired off shots from less than three meters. The terrorist was killed instantly, shot in the head. He didn't have time to toss the grenade. The Chinese stick grenade dangled alone by the thin string over the rock, with the metal ring still attached to his little finger.

"Jesus, Moyo, your pack's lying there," observed Tsumba dryly.

"Bullshit," snorted Moyo, as he swung around.

Sure enough, at the base of the hill, lay a police-issued rucksack. I scrambled free of the rock and tree jumble, as Moyo bent to pick up the pack. I scratched my head and wondered, for a few seconds, how it landed here. Only then did I twig that the CTs had climbed the hill we had first occupied. They must have walked into our abandoned rucksacks and helped themselves. No wonder they didn't reappear on the track. Afterwards, we counted four rucksacks missing, including mine.

I stared at the abandoned backpack and mulled over the events. What were the chances of the enemy walking off the track at that time and climbing that particular hill? I wouldn't have bet my car on it. I believed they climbed the hill to carry out a visual reconnaissance of the land. I wondered what they thought when they stumbled into the rucksacks abandoned up there – and the half-eaten lunch!

The survivors from our contact had fled east, smack into Garry's section, who was poised three kilometers away and, in the fleeting firefight, had dropped two rucksacks (one was mine, with the starlight scope inside). Surviving that brief encounter, the terrorists sprinted onwards and, 30 minutes later, slammed into Van's section. After a short firefight, blood smear confirmed at least one CT wounded. (The remaining backpack was recovered in Mutasa South TTL nine months later.) Sergeant Nguruve's section had been operating further south and had not seen its share of the action.

While secondary clashes with Garry occurred, before Van's surprise action, I radioed base to recover the deceased CT and the woman and baby. This was a real road haulage job. The main road from the base camp traveled north – the full length of Wedza – before looping west and tracking south to our location. It was the only road in and out – a dangerously predictable route. I didn't like the road option, but air support was not available. Tambe dispatched a two-vehicle convoy. The convoy couldn't avoid 'Ambush Alley' – the notorious winding section of main road that was a torturous stretch, which forced vehicles to slow right down and change into a low gear in order to negotiate the sharp corners dug into the steep banks. The winding road was textbook ambush country, with a record of successful attacks from thick bush hillsides. The twisting section offered the CTs a free kick every time we motored through.

As the convoy slowly whined around the sharp bends, a dozen ZANLA (concealed above the road) ambushed the two vehicles – scoring hits on the Bedford's cab and wounding Constable Ndhlovu, the driver. Without armor, the bullets sliced through the sides like puncturing cardboard. A bullet broke his leg and Ndhlovu couldn't work the foot pedals, and so missed the next corner. The truck, consequently, careered off the narrow road and slued onto the embankment. A November Troop constable riding escort on the back was shot in the hand. Only the terrorists' poor shooting skills avoided more casualties. The six escort constables on the back instantly debussed and raggedly engaged the CT.

Inside the stationary cab, the wounded Ndhlovu remained calmly seated and radioed for assistance via the base camp. Fireforce was summoned, and he sat inside the cab, alone. The passenger seat always remained empty because it was not armored. If you hit a landmine on the front left wheel, any passenger would be literally lacerated – and fatally. Unable to extract himself from the driver's seat, Ndhlovu remained seated – enduring rising pain – and fixed behind the steering wheel, with bullets zapping past. Fortunately, the RLI Fireforce had been airborne when they received the radio call, so they diverted and arrived within 10 minutes – their helicopters kissing the earth, while the CTs were busy extracting. The RLI troops bowled over a couple of CTs within minutes of stepping onto the ground; then two or three stubborn terrorists dug themselves in and began a serious fight. They pinned down the Stop Group – seriously wounding one RLI trooper before melting into the heavy timber. Three CTs were killed.

Ndhlovu was evacuated out by a helicopter with the other casualties, and November Troop sections were sent in to clean up the ambush zone. Gray drove the Land Rover with another driver to extract the truck and continued the journey to join up with my section. They uplifted the dead from the contact scene, deposited them in the Land Rover's tray and departed. I radioed my callsigns and dispatched Garry and Van's section to sweep the countryside east of 'Ambush Alley' to trigger any slow CTs, but they found nothing.

Three days later, after a half-day rest, Special Branch announced they'd be down to our base to brief an urgent action. They arrived the next morning, driving a Land Rover, and accompanied by a hairy PATU section seated in a Rhino. The two SB men parked in front of the house and stepped onto the muddy ground. With hair over the ears, civilian shirts, short shorts and long white socks, they looked like country gentlemen out on a stroll. The detectives greeted the white police they knew – especially Gray – and stood chatting and sipping tea. When the tea finished, the briefing began. The senior detective strolled into the operations room and, with India section commanders standing inside, began his brief.

"The ZANLA unit is 15 men, armed with AKs, an RPD, RPK and one 60mm mortar," stated the Special Branch officer – brimming with confidence. "They will be entering the Dendenyore business center in the next five days."

His white pointer tapped the wall map. The business center sat in the flat country north of Mount St Mary's.

He continued: "That's almost a certainty. They are conducting a recruiting sweep through north Wedza, and will be fed by the general store's owner. I expect that they will enter at night and depart before daylight. These guys are so confident that they'll probably use the main road to walk in on."

In the bag! Or was it?

I planned to infiltrate the troop – walking all the way; I briefed the section leaders – carefully plotting a route on the map. The long, weary, night walking cross-country was split over two nights. Garry and Van weren't enthusiastic – giving the 'what the fuck!' expression during the briefing. Walk all that way? They sat restless and uneasy. Van suggested we truck in to the half-way mark; I brushed that aside. The 'Ambush Alley' attack reinforced the need to minimize vehicle movement. I also wanted to ensure that the troop movement remained undetected. Van moaned under his breath. He didn't complain out loud, because I'd be walking every step with them; they couldn't skive or evade the night march. They then disappeared to brief their men. The stoic constables shrugged and got on with the job.

We walked throughout the night – trudging cross-country and using landmarks to gauge our progress. Early morning, we hid in solid bush – observing life's pattern the next day and then completing the final 10 kilometers the following evening. Split into three sections, with each tasked with ambushing one of the three approach routes, we separated and found individual section hides for the day. Surveying the target zone, I was shocked that the area was so open, just wide, flat, cultivated fields and stunted grassland. That night, we slinked into a pre-observed ambush position and waited. A long, dark, tedious stretch of time crept by before we carefully packed up before dawn, vanished into the wooded hills to the south and waited up all day. That night, we occupied a different ambush position.

Nothing moved at all over the five nights. Apart from the odd yapping dog or the rustling breeze, the eerie night silence reinforced the lack of movement. Five days were wasted. The most frustrating part was trying to figure out why the operation failed. Was it our fault, or poor intelligence? We never knew.

These episodes were written off as a 'lemon' – and there were orchards of lemon trees. When the open terrain forced us to move out to avoid the encroaching daylight and inevitable detection, the action was fraught with difficulty. Our boot prints found anywhere coming in or departing was a dead giveaway, or marks in the wet grass in our ambush position, or an item of gear left behind, or actually being seen in the first visages of daylight, or an alien noise detected by a light sleeper, and so on could spell the end. Coupled with our concealment in the local hills during the day, away from the road, that could be compromised by an eagle-eyed villager. All this aside, perhaps the information was simply wrong. Maybe the terrorist movement date occurred before we had arrived or after we had departed. The ambush area could be wrong, or the terrorists had changed their own schedule, or the informant was just stringing the Special Branch along. Any one of a dozen things blew the ambush. Whatever the cause, it was labeled a 'lemon'.

Meanwhile, Sergeant Nguruve's men concentrated on *kraals* around Mount St Mary's Mission. Nguruve discovered that by wearing a camouflage jacket inside out (to expose the light tan inner lining) and slinging his rifle over the shoulder like an AK, in the murky dusk light, to untrained eyes, he resembled a CT. He never, ever stated he was a CT; he simply acted the part and the responders assumed he was a 'brother'. The balance of his section remained close by, but out of sight. He owned the stage. He talked the talk of a liberator – his smooth words winning over the confidence of the villagers. They chatted unabashed about the 'brothers' and their comings and goings. The Mission certainly had become a honey pot for them.

At dusk one evening, at the Mission, the African nuns spotted Nguruve's section strolling on the outskirts and mistook them once again for terrorists. They almost flew across the open ground to greet the liberators. Laughing and skipping and chortling, one of them seized Nguruve's hand to lead them into the Mission safe haven. A younger nun, momentarily caught up in the ecstatic welcome, suddenly recognized their error.

"'Ma-Sojer'?" she cried, in shock.

"No," replied Nguruve politely, "'Ma-Police'!"

One nun pissed herself in fright. Urine ran freely down her legs. They stood frozen in horror – the electric realization knocking out their welcome. Fuckin' police. That put a cold shudder up their skirts.

"Get out of here," hissed the sergeant – uncertain how to deal with these untouchables.

They didn't need to be told twice.

Later, when a landmine explosion wrecked a vehicle within a kilometer of the Mission's gates – and consequently, a Support Unit constable was burnt by battery acid – the Irish priest refused point-blank to render assistance, even though they had a small hospital with medically trained staff. Just like Avila, they existed on a sanctuary island for terrorists and were, politically, untouchable. A cocoon separated them from the consequences of their actions.

After a particularly ugly firefight, Sergeant Chewa displayed a serious character flaw: back in Salisbury, he portrayed the model African NCO – sharply dressed, uniform lightly starched and pressed, black leather sparkling and his head shaved to the dome. He instilled the pride of a parade ground and inspection king – good enough to bring a flush of satisfaction on a regimental sergeant major's rosy cheeks. On long endurance runs, he'd exhort the tired constables to a higher performance – falling out and setting a cracking pace from the front. A saluting 'Yes Sir, No Sir' drill baron and PT king, I had been impressed, but unexpectedly, at the end of a drawn-out firefight, Chewa pronounced blindness. He showed all the symptoms and, horrified by the affliction, he called out loudly in distress. I left Moyo to console him, while we got on with the business. He may well have been blind from a psychological perspective, brought on by the shock of close-quarter combat. He waited out the sweep seated on a rock – panic arising from the misfortune. Blindness had to be the ultimate curse when surrounded by armed enemies. After the clash, Moyo led him back to the pick-up vehicles – guiding his footsteps like a shepherd. Once Chewa arrived safely back in base camp, within 24 hours, a miracle: the 'blindness' lifted and he saw once again. Once his sight had been inexplicably restored, he stayed behind to contend with the camp administration.

The flaw struck again: months later, Chewa suddenly announced he had fallen 'deaf' immediately after being ambushed, and he blinked and looked around, confused. Now a liability, as we attempted to extract ourselves, he couldn't 'hear' shouted orders – his face gray, astonished and bewildered. We bypassed him to suppress the enemy action. Chewa waited stunned and perplexed until the shooting ceased. After not 'hearing' orders, I shunted him back to camp. I felt sorry for him because he couldn't master fear. The constables sniggered and undermined his authority behind his back. I strongly suggested to Support Unit HQ that Chewa be transferred to the Training Wing, where he would be a useful asset as an instructor, foot drill and PT, but they refused. When I wrote his annual appraisal report, I stated clearly that in base camp, he presented himself as an excellent model NCO, but in the bush, he turned timid. I used mild words to muster some support for his transfer. The report was duly returned, with a note attached instructing me to amend it, because my opinion wildly fluctuated from his other appraisals over the past 12 years – but during the other years, he had conducted tame border patrols or guarded detention facilities for political detainees, and so had not experienced cruel warfare first hand. My argument fell on deaf ears. Told that my appraisal could seriously impact a fruitful career, I amended it. I wasn't a career policeman, so why rock the boat?

Chewa's stint in camp allowed me to send Sergeant Tambe into the scrub on the final week, as in my opinion, two NCOs in camp was one too many. Tambe was unimpressed. He had feathered his own nest and was probably wheeling and dealing in an underhanded way. The only hardship was skimming through 'Batman' comics on the late-night radio shift. In camp, he was warm and dry, with hot meals on tap – oblivious to the lashing rain. When I gave him the news, he looked shocked and then angrily stomped off to collect his gear – grizzling to anyone who listened. Grumbling and hissing, as Tambe departed on foot in the drizzling rain, he shot Chewa the look of death.

The rain continued. Garry's section walked unexpectedly into a number of CTs resting on the outskirts of a *kraal*. The constables opened fire. The CTs panicked, dropped two AK-47 rifles and fled. A tenacious follow-up by the tracker discovered a CT base. As the section entered, the CTs – sitting unseen, on the fringe – fired a ragged volley before vanishing for good. In the base, one wounded woman (shot in the arm) sat waiting patiently. Six CT nylon sports bags, two cases of Castle beer, a rusting bicycle and a Singer sewing machine stood abandoned. If one joined the SF for looting, the pickings were slim.

From our perspective, the wet weather bogged down the war. Besides the trial of living in the waterlogged bush – with sodden equipment, rotting clothing, moist bedding, mold attacking leather and rust settling on metal – the rains invigorated plant growth, greened up the treetops and provided more shelter from prying eyes. The tree canopy trapped the view of the enemy – particularly from the air – and the kill rates dropped sharply. Dry, sparse timbered hills transformed into emerald-green carpets. The hardy grass grew tall and the green maize crop stood shoulder-high – affording easy escape or hiding places. What is God's bounty to the commercial farmer was not so to the combatant. Worst of all, for a Security Force highly dependent on tracking, rain washed away footwear imprints so vital to closing with them. ZANLA carried out sabotage and attacks with almost impunity.

We happily departed a thoroughly unseasonal wet Wedza and drove back to the capital to utterly dry out. Van completed his police contract in Support Unit and departed the force.

We spent every penny we earned and pissed it up against the wall. You couldn't take it with you! To foreigners, white society was hard to breach because it was small, tight and everyone knew each other from nappies up. If I couldn't talk about turbulent times on the cricket field at Churchill, or who fucked whose sister on the graduation ball steps, or which aunt had dropped her houseboy with a roundhouse punch, or which boy was suspected of having sex with Africans, then I was on the outer. They were a cheerful, friendly, boozy bunch, but a closed society. It was like settling in a small rural town. Everyone was friendly and neighborly, but you were not one of them. To be called 'local', a relative must be buried in the town graveyard.

On R&R, Tutani stole a police Land Rover, got drunk and pranged it. No one was hurt, but the vehicle copped some damage. He was under arrest and sitting in jail when I finished R&R. I convinced the boss to release him for the bush trip and to leave the punishment to me. When we were at the base, after each time he came in from patrol, he would run around the camp with a full pack of rocks and the MAG until he collapsed. I'm sure, in hindsight, he would have rather endured the boss' punishment, but mine did not incur a loss of pay.

To hedge against continuous shortages, I purchased a second metal trunk and hoarded WP rifle grenades (liberated from the army), a captured 60mm mortar tube and Soviet HE bombs, 7.62mm NATO tracer bullets, a spare A73 radio and anything else I scavenged from the army or the enemy. We once turned up for deployment to find the Support Unit armory bare of tracer bullets. The tight police budget allowed the MAG three 50-round linked belts and three 20-round magazines for each FN. As this wasn't enough to feel comfortable, individuals took up theft as a secondary career. Woe betide any army unit that didn't have a ball and chain on the warfare necessities. We stole more belts for the MAG and more magazines for the FN rifles. They vanished in a flash, in a war trunk, so that the troop was never lean on the vital tools. The trunk was stowed in the Fife Ave room cupboard.

Wedza, May 1977

We returned to Wedza, but this time as a solo troop. I split the troop so that the trucks with the bulk of the men steered straight into Wedza, while the two Hyenas drove on to Rusape, where I reported to the JOC. After receiving an update from Special Branch, which included a comment that an army company was also based in Wedza, I sought permission from JOC to relocate the base camp. The police didn't have a problem and the army wasn't interested, but opposition arose from Internal Affairs, who wanted someone to babysit their real estate. They insisted on an SF presence in the camp, but I was adamant. Tactically, the camp was too far south and constantly threatened from the scenic hill. The JOC relented. Internal Affairs huffed and puffed, and then presented the facilities to GC.

After sorting out the camp issues, I departed Rusape – driving a Hyena on the main highway to the Wedza turnoff. On route, the Hyena burst a rear tire, the light trailer fishtailed and, with a high center of gravity, I lost control. The armored personnel carrier sharply dipped, screwed suddenly to the right and instantly flipped, all in split-seconds. The Hyena ended on its side after a complete roll. Everyone wearing seatbelts were fine, but Constable Christopher Chikwavira, for reasons unknown, had not secured his seatbelt and, as a consequence, was tossed out through the canvas roof and onto the tarmac road. The rolling armored personnel carrier crushed his head.

I vividly recall Sergeant Chewa attempting desperate mouth-to-mouth on the man with a shattered skull, whose skull bones appeared to float inside his skin. The Rusape police attended the fatality, began an official traffic accident investigation and later stated no blame or charges would be laid.

The troop was naturally shocked with Chikwavira's untimely death. Sergeant Tambe eyed me furiously, as if I deliberately set out to kill the young constable. Totally unapproachable, he shunned any discussion. I was not sure if he was close to Chikwavira, but he acted like a next of kin. To relieve the growing tension, I dispatched Tambe and two constables to Salisbury to represent the troop at the funeral.

After the worst possible beginning, I threw the troop into dismantling the base at the Intaf camp. Police GC moved in. GC were police seconded to the war effort – using their training to gather intelligence on the ground. They were courageous and hard-working – driving their Land Rovers about the tribal areas and seeking information at great personal risk. Some GC operatives grew slightly eccentric living on the edge. Both SB and GC combed tribal areas in small numbers at considerable peril.

We transported the recovered equipment to a fenced site with two small buildings located midway up Wedza, in the Chisasike Dam area, which was sandwiched between the main road and the Ruzawi River. Sited on flat, open grasslands, the camp was less exposed to a direct ZANLA attack. The terrorists risked real casualties attempting an assault. The two sheds were converted to radio and operations rooms. The men spent a sweaty week digging trenches, building bunkers from sawn logs, siting four-man tents and ablutions, as well as local patrolling. At dusk, many of the locals ignored the dusk to dawn curfew, so a couple of MAG bursts over suspect *kraals* reminded them of the consequences.

While India Troop was the only Support Unit troop in Wedza, a Territorial Army company based itself in Mount St Mary's Mission to prevent its informal use by ZANLA. They pitched their tents right in the Mission grounds and operated out. Just this one action neutralized the ZANLA use of the facilities. The Territorial Army, the Rhodesia Regiment was made up of eight battalions of white citizen-soldiers who had completed 18 months' National Service and were now subject to an annual call-up that had become increasingly onerous. They gladly undertook their compulsory service in the beginning of the conflict, but sadly, as the war ground on for years without an end in sight, the call-up played havoc with their careers and trades and marriages, so increasingly, families emigrated to avoid the impost. Men went on holidays overseas to spot opportunities, returned and began to cautiously untangle their social ties, but not announcing their intention, which was to finally depart without a ripple.

This company operated the northern swath of Wedza – leaving the bulk of the middle and south to India. While the army company's presence clearly inhibited the CTs' movement, there grew emerging discomfort among the officers that their men had been unable to kill even one CT. Right or wrong, success was measured in the body count. Frustrated, the company commander tentatively raised the subject of integration – in a nutshell, mixing the Africans in my unit with their white soldiers. He discussed his plans with army officers at Rusape JOC, but he didn't bother to do so in consultation with Support Unit. The major cited the effectiveness of what he termed the 'white killing machine', coupled to people who understood the nuances of the local population.

The JOC floated the proposition; I flatly rejected the suggestion. Support Unit never won in these hybrid formations, as the constables were either treated as mates, or as servants. Either way, the troop was later left to pick up the disciple problems that evolved – and these took at least two more bush tours to iron out. Also, the white police section commanders were irrelevant in this model and were left in base, reading novels. I was happy to conduct joint operations, where our people scouted for the enemy and called in the army boys on a sighting, or we could adopt an OP posture, where the African eyes sized up the activity and radioed the army unit to engage the enemy. That was not acceptable to the major, so stalemate. JOC began to insist. Badger (Jim Collins) stepped in to squash the idea once and for all.

Kiaran Allen, Paddy Allen's younger brother, joined India Troop as a temporary fill-in section commander. We first met on the same Support Unit training course. Dark haired and of average size, Kiaran was quieter than the extrovert Paddy, but he endured his 15 minutes of fame when ambushed by a crocodile while rubber rafting in the Nyawidzi River. He fought it off with the famous 'thumb in the eye trick' and added another 'tall story, but true' to the BSAP legends.

Kiaran spoke Shona fluently, which surprised the constables. He garnered this language proficiency as a boy, playing with African boys in remote areas, and spoke with all the slang and colorful language, which made the constables laugh. His Shona was so good he corrected the constables' grammar. Knowledge of the native language enabled him to conduct one-on-one interrogations with locals without the frustration of an African interpreter.

Few Rhodesian-born whites spoke Shona or Ndelebele. This was partly due to an education system that ignored the native language in favor of the British syllabus – offering Latin, German and French – and partly because many urban whites existed in a bubble. They lived, worked and played insulated from the African world. Most whites communicated with Africans in English or Chilapalapa – a bastard pigeon tongue borne in the South African mines. Chilapalapa allowed instructions to be imparted to black workers, but was unwieldy as a conversation tool. Used extensively in white-operated–black-worker commercial establishments, most rural Africans did not understand this language.

My expertise in foreign tongues stretched to first year French at high school, which I failed. An elderly farm cook painstakingly taught extremely basic Shona, but I was unable to pick up the words when spoken in full flight. I translated words that were spoken slowly and, if I concentrated, I interpreted the gist of a conversation. Some people have the gift for foreign languages, but I don't, so like most white police, I relied on translation by African constables; however, this was not always satisfactory.

For instance, the questioning of a villager proceeded like:

"Ask him if *macandangas* visited his *kraal*?"

The bored constable repeated the question in Shona.

The tribesman answered quickly, in a long, rambling explanation over two or three minutes – gesturing with his face and pointing with his hands; then he'd stop.

"What did he say?" I'd ask.

"He said no."

Two minutes' talk to say no? To employ the constable to translate, literally, word for word was a task in itself, and sometimes I wondered how much subtle intelligence was missed when constables dismissed large blocks of the answer as 'irrelevant'.

While the base-building activities were under way, my section departed for a three-day recce to judge the lie of the land. I liked to see first hand what was what. During my absence, an African male covertly approached the main entrance to our base; then made himself visible – his hands in the air. Described as a lean and hungry six-foot-tall man – stripped of any fat on his toughened body – he was dressed like a ZANLA in a blue denim jacket and jeans, with blue and white plastic beads strung around his neck. His hair was in plaited strands and he was shod in Superpro runners. The man stood outside the camp and called out. With his arms held high, he was clearly unarmed. His appearance dumbfounded the constable on guard duty, who immediately challenged the trespasser. The stranger stated he needed to speak to Special Branch. The guard called the white section leader (I'm not sure who) and they both approached the man warily. He handed over a piece of paper with a telephone number and name, and asked them to call. The constables escorted him into the camp, briskly searched his clothing for hidden weapons, offered him a camp chair and then gave him a hot cup of tea and a can of sour bully

India Troop lads at Wedza TTL, 1977. (Kiaran Allen)

beef. He ate hungrily, but said nothing. Within 30 minutes, a helicopter flew in to pick him up. He jumped aboard and the aircraft flew off. The rumor suggested was that the visitor was a Special Branch agent who had slipped into Mozambique to train as a CT and had then operated the Wedza area as a ZANLA security officer. If that was true, that's one gutsy man.

I returned and inspected the base construction progress. We didn't aim for comfort. Base meant a stopover; a sleep and mail spot; a place to return to – stinking and knackered; a cot to crash in for a restless sleep. Extreme comfort lay inside a cold bottle of Coke. We didn't allow alcohol in an operational base. Once back, the full glory of our pungent odor whiffed through the tents, which was caught by men who had showered first and then returned washed and refreshed. The late bathers usually were sucking on a letter from home – the highlight and a morale booster. Letters were savored, treasured and sniffed before opening – the delicate pages extracted and read over and over again. Some readers retreated to a quiet spot to absorb the written word. Men carried the letter inside plastic wrapping so they could reread in a quiet moment: read, interpret, dissect and enjoy.

My own personal policy precluded mail. Girlfriends were not informed of my forwarding address, as I figured that if they were still happy to date when

I re-emerged, then great; if not, party! Once on R&R, I told a girlfriend that India Troop had suddenly been called out for an unexpected deployment – a 'national emergency' (the word had spread about an animal party on a Saturday night and I didn't want her company). I turned up, ready to rave, and ran straight into her – Busted! – but I had no desire to be bound up in a close relationship. I had witnessed antics in the married quarters in an army post, when husbands had been posted overseas. There was a general joke at mail call: the spreader of good words began with: "Nothing here for you, O'Brien!"

The camp entertainment was minimal: thumbed novels for those who wanted to read, rereading letters from home, a sharp game of volleyball, a potluck stew slopped up, lounging in directors' chairs to catch a tan, the Currie Cup commentary on a transistor radio, winding each other up and playing practical jokes to break the boredom. There were no other distractions. This is an age long before DVDs and Xboxes and computers, with their dating sites and email! We stayed bored only long enough to clean our kit and prepare for the next sortie.

Sergeant Tambe returned to our base from Salisbury, sullen and moody. Chikwavira's death doomed our shaky relationship. Where I was impatient to dive out into the bush to score points, he just wanted the quiet life, where he dabbled in things that interested him. While he was polite and civil, he couldn't remove the sneer that emerged when I talked to him. I needed to wangle a way to move him out.

In base for a break, a surprise visit was sprung on us. Assistant Commissioner Jim Collins – accompanied by the Minister of Law and Order, Mr Hillary Squires – drove into our base camp. They breezed through 'Ambush Alley' using minimum escorts and without raising a sweat. I set up morning tea in our operations shed and gave the Minister a comprehensive briefing on Wedza. Using an up-to-date map board, the appraisal kept revisiting a long series of *kraals*, where the population openly and defiantly supported the resident ZANLA detachment.

"What do you plan to do about it?" Squires asked, as he delicately sipped his tea.

"There's nothing we can do," I replied. "We reported it, so it was a matter for JOC."

"And what's your solution?" He asked – raising his eyebrows.

"Simple: round 'em up and lock 'em up for the duration. Burn down the villages afterwards," I replied forcefully.

He smiled. He said he would look into it. Needless to say, we heard nothing more.

More visitors dropped by – and we were becoming a Wedza roadside café! Zulu Charlie Troop had deployed to regions south of Wedza. Their troop commander, the pirate Ron Hein – accompanied by Phil Smith, who was now a Zulu Charlie operator – sailed into our base camp on their way through. Over a hot coffee, Ron voiced his disgust that a hot party in Salisbury brewed and that his overtures to the CO for time off had been curtly refused. He laughed at our ribald ribbing and suggested a nice, simple flesh wound could park him back in the party zone. Of course, we shared the joke – loudly suggesting which body part the bullet should end up. Ron was miffed because he loved a good party. A few days later, I received a radio call from Sunray Mantle Zulu Charlie.

"Mantle India One, Sunray Zulu Charlie."

His familiar voice garbled very faint through the earpiece.

"India One, go ahead," I chirped, "you're strength two, over."

"Sunray Zulu Charlie, roger that," stated the barely audible voice, "we've been ambushed an' I've been shot in the leg, over."

"India One, yeah sure," I replied sarcastically – knowing that Ron wanted to hit the party scene in Salisbury. "If you think I'm driving down there to pick you up, you can piss off, over."

"Hey, O'Brien, this is no bullshit," replied the muffled voice, "I need a casevac right now, over."

"Go fuck yourself, Ron," I laughed into the handset, "fucking walk back, over."

His reply was not decipherable – the voice very, very weak.

"India One, it's Zulu Charlie Three," Smith's voice was loud and clear. "Ron's not bullshitting mate, he's been hit badly in the leg an' I need a casevac urgent. I can't get through to relay, so please relay for me. Our locstat … "

A bullet had hit Ron in the top of the thigh – a dangerously serious, heavy bleeding wound. It was a ticket home, but I don't think he upstaged the party.

Once we established base camp, I began to send patrols further west. The region west of 'Ambush Alley' interested me, so I sent two patrols out there, but before I decided exactly where my section would scour, a red-hot Special Branch report swore that the CTs would cross the Morris Bridge that spanned the Ruzawi River on the border with Chiduku. The intelligence had to be actioned immediately. Armed with this gem, we planned an ambush of the concrete slab bridge. I drew the three Claymore mines issued for the troop.

Each night, we carefully sited three Claymore anti-personnel mines. The Claymore mines were slightly curved slabs – dark-green plastic, with two adjustable legs at each end to stand and aim the beast. A USA copy was emblazoned with the words 'Front to the Enemy', so dumb shits didn't point the business end at themselves. Seven-hundred steel balls were moulded into plastic explosive and, if fired, blasted anyone standing in a 60° arc for 50 meters out, at two meters in height.

Once the Claymores were set, the men laid down at a safe distance, with the MAG machine gun focused on the bridge approach. With Claymores zeroed on the end of the bridge and a MAG focused down the middle, there'd be devastating consequences to any foot traffic, but the weather broke once again: the rain started. From the slow patter of heavy drops, the rain steadily gained momentum until it pelted so hard that the individual drops actually hurt as they whacked the unprotected skin. At its worst, the solid rain cascaded almost horizontal – bouncing off the hard clay ground and completely soaking everyone. Even a rubberized groundsheet wrapped tightly around the cold body failed to ward off the assault. No one slept. Rainwater ran down our exposed faces and the fine spray snorted into our chilled nostrils. Everything soaked up its capacity for water: webbing harness, woollen blankets and canvas backpacks – the material swelling and distorting. To add to the misery, the runoff bubbled over the sodden clay road and, next thing, we lay belly down in a small, swift running stream. Chilled from the teeming rain and soaked underneath from rising waters, I gritted my teeth. After all, the intelligence was hot off the press. Once daylight glimmered, we retreated into the sopping bush country, changed into spare dry clothes and shivered under huge granite boulders that blocked the rainfall. St Anne's Mission lay tantalizingly close for warm shelter, but we sucked in the weather and stayed bush. Each evening, we changed back into our wet uniforms – gnashing our teeth against the shock of chilled cloth scraping warm flesh – and re-set the ambush. I debated whether to up stakes and leave, or wait out the weather conditions and stay. The lure of a perfectly executed ambush enticed me to stay put. After four deplorable, cold and wet nights, the JOC – from the warmth of the Rusape bar – called it a day and we happily chucked it in. If the terrorists had any brains at all, they'd have been inside a dry *kraal* and tucked up in a comfortable bed with a warm woman – and they probably were.

The millstone of infantry work has to be the night sentry. I imagine former infantrymen worldwide shuddering at the memory of guard stints. To be awake and alert, in staggered shifts throughout the night, is an absolute necessity for survival and counter-attack. Two hours on – every night, night after long night, week after drawn-out week – guard duty robbed the body of useful sleep and frayed the nerves. On the odd occasion, a lazy sentry shortened his own spell of duty by winding the watch hands forward, but this also robbed others of sleep and sowed the grains of bad temper. On operations, I always did my equal share of sentry duty, but if I was really whacked and wanted more than my ration of sleep, I found an African graveyard, which was normally indicated by white rocks surrounding an anthill. After casually dropping my rucksack, I announced that we were sleeping there that night. There would be protests, of course, but I wouldn't hear any of it. I slept like a baby, while the men sat up, wide-eyed, waiting for the spirits to appear.

In another hoax, I presumed to hear a hyena coughing. The constables looked at me skeptically – knowing that hyenas were extremely rare in the TTL – but back in their folks' era, intoxicated men who attempted to walk home at night were in danger from prowling hyena. A number, over the years, had their whole face bitten off when the animal sniffed the alcohol fumes. There was also a lot of mysticism and magic tied into the hyena, so once again, they'd be more alert than I.

Sometimes, sitting on static guard, I dwelt on my men. What did they think about the conflict? Openly, the constables displayed neutral feelings. I never heard one mouth off his feelings one way or the other. They appeared apolitical on the surface. I never engaged them on the merits, so I just assumed we were all on the same team. Most were here because service represented paid employment, or their fathers were in the police, or they had an axe to grind, or some other reason (too numerous to isolate), but one would be naïve to think some did not lean towards Mugabe's crowd. Now asleep around me, they could easily dispatch me while on sentry, when I slept – rise up and kill the white man. I heard that three Support Unit constables absconded into Mozambique to join the enemy. One was subsequently killed in Chiweshe by the RLI. Pinned down, he called out to the army chaps that he was police – a red rag to some RLI blokes! Whatever the reason for being involved, one thing was clear: without them, the SF could not possibly contain the enemy and win. They were the heart and soul – the unglamorous footslogger. Their loyalty was to Support Unit first and the BSA Police second. Like the Foreign Legion, the unit watched over their welfare and they gave solid service in return.

This tour had numerous false starts – chasing shadows. Apart from long-range shooting, we did not come to grips with the enemy. Kiaran experienced a couple of sharp contacts and Garry had one. There was no evidence of ZANLA casualties. We had quizzed scores of surly people in dozens of villages without a crumb of anything interesting. Sergeant Nguruve continued his night theater. Bluffing and acting like a CT in *kraals*, he scored reams of information about the elusive enemy. Locals opened their hearts and were eager to talk to this unknown 'CT', but he was unable to pin down information that could be acted upon.

In the final week, in the early morning, the section accidentally blundered upon a ZANLA base. The tracker found *spoor* and we were off. The fresh tracks crossed the Ruzawi River into Chiduku. We followed. After losing the *spoor* late in the afternoon, near Denga School, we laid up in a small *gomo* and studied a lone *kraal* squatting on the edge of flat timbered land. At least three cooking fires burnt, and the young women clustered together to work on their beauty points – laughing and giggling, as if pop stars had arrived. Two girls were clearly seen clucking and plaiting another girl's hair. Scanning with binoculars, I spotted a mangy dog tethered to a tree on the main foot track into the village: the early warning system. The constables were absolutely convinced the CTs were ensconced around that village. They hadn't been sighted, but the vital signs were crystal clear.

Mentally, I reviewed four options:

1) Do nothing – not an option I wanted.

2) Wait till early morning – using the night as a shield to encircle them – but we had few men and only one radio to cover a large block of terrain. We hadn't pinpointed a base, so stumbling around in the dark to find one was fraught with hazards.

3) Wait until early morning and attempt to find them. This ran a risk of the terrorists moving on in the night, and we would be forced to start tracking all over again, with a high chance of losing their *spoor* due to rain or ground conditions.

4) We attack directly into the *kraal* and take what comes.

I opted for the fourth option.

"We're going in after dark," I briefed the section, quietly. "We'll move in an extended line into the trees over there," pointing to a clump on the village border – away from the mongrel tied on the dirt track – "an' we'll ease in an' drop down in a firing line. Tutani, bring the gun in next to me. Sarge, you hold the left flank. Once we're down, don't fire unless I do."

Creeping in after dark – avoiding the dirt path where the dog reigned supreme – we closed right in on the unsuspecting *kraal*. Gently crawling along the forest floor – through the crackling, dry leaf carpet for the last 20 meters – the men stopped in the dry grass verge on the edge of the *kraal*. We waited, coiled like springs, to see if signs of compromise arose. Had we been seen or heard? I held my breath. The dark activity swirled unaffected. Things appeared normal. I was always surprised at the high level of noise that could be generated on a night move, undetected. Fortunately, no alien sound like the clanging of metal rang out. Sounds were more the twigs cracking, the swish of clothing against branches and the creak of canvas straps. Still, some of the noise could be muffled better. We lay within spitting distance of one of the open fires and listened and watched the long shadows move.

"They're *macandangas*," Tutani whispered in my ear, as he silently strung out the 100-round MAG belt. I was sure he was right, but black shapes were hard to define with the shifting gray and black shadows, the wispy smoke, the flickering orange flames and anonymous shuffling movement. Unfortunately, the starlight scope had been lent to another section, so I relied on Eyeball Mark One, but the eyes could not distinguish who's who in the zoo.

I settled down ... the plastic FN rifle butt was locked into my shoulder and the black foresight blade covered the hip region of a dark shadow. I gauged that they were terrorists from their general posture, but I couldn't see a weapon to absolutely confirm it. That single, nagging doubt prevented the forefinger from the final squeeze. Around the second dying fire – five paces further back – huddled a darker group. They formed a black blob, from which bits broke off, wandered away and then drifted back and merged together again, like a huge amoeba. A solid mass split off from time to time, as an individual broke away and faded out. I interpreted the comings and goings as restlessness.

"They're *macandangas*," hissed the gunner again – the MAG butt locked solidly into the shoulder.

When I still did nothing, he added viciously: "They're going to get away."

I fired, and the rifle roared. As my FN bucked and reloaded, the section fired. Giant red tracer balls jetted through the black night – the brilliant-red phosphorous glowed like fiery comets. The roar of the MAG and FN combination consumed everything. The air vibrated. The powdered dust blasted into the still air, and the gloomy shadows sunk – sucked into the dancing dirt. We kept up the rain of bullets for a long 60 seconds.

The challenge with a firefight inside a *kraal* was to minimize civilian casualties. The CTs, being animal-wary, instantly hit the dirt. They rolled over to study the lines of red tracer bullets and crawled out at right angles from the red lines to escape. The civilians, on the other hand, frightened and disorientated, ran upright like headless chickens.

"Stop!" I roared.

One or two single shots rang out.

We waited – scrutinizing the hazy darkness – the fires masked by floating dust. The silence sounded noisy. My ears protested the muzzle blasts. Apprehension grew. No shots were returned. Were the shadows terrorists? Had I just shot up a civilian gathering? Will we find dead civilians who had been minding their own business? The seeds of doubt began to gnaw; however, my gut instinct said we were right. If there were only farmers, a short, sharp fusillade of bullets should keep the overall casualties down; however, if they were entertaining terrorists, there was scant pity.

Ordinarily, at the end of a night contact, I'd stay put, or pull back in case of mortar fire, and wait; then move through the contact area in the washed-out, early-morning light. That night, because of the uncertainty, I decided to press forward into the *kraal*.

"Reload!" I called, and metal scraping rang in the night. "Let's go!" I shouted, and rose to my feet.

After the initial hesitation – likened to 'what the fuck does he think he's doing' – the constables scrambled to their feet and stepped forward. Till now, there had been no return fire and I feared the worst.

"That means you, Sarge!" I hissed at Chewa, who was hesitant about joining us.

We stepped out of the black shadow and into the gray open. Floating dust particles blurred the scene ahead. A short burst from an AK rifle – fired from beyond the perimeter of the *kraal* – unwound the concern about CTs. I breathed easier. The men were right once again. We stepped past a dark body huddled close to the flaring fire, but we didn't stop to search or attempt to establish who it was. It was a shadowy lump. The aim was to clear the village and get out. Past the firelight, I slowed down to survey the seven buildings in the compound. Each house stood silent, with no lights visible. Mandaza seized a young woman who had attempted to duck into an open doorway. She struggled and swore. He tightened his grip on her arm.

"I'll clear the huts!" he called.

Chipangora joined the two and knocked on each closed door: two or three sharp raps. The rest watched the looming dark bush surrounding the *kraal*. Twisting the woman's wrist, Mandaza insisted the wildcat call after each sharp knock – demanding that the residents come out. Once they emerged, the capture was instructed to enter the hut and declare it empty. She vanished into each doorway. When she came out, she spat that the house was empty; the men tossed in a fragmentation grenade. The shocked residents were escorted to the baked ground in the center of the village and were left seated in a huddle. We cleared house by house until we hit the *kraal* perimeter; then marched to the nearest forested cover outside the village.

The next morning, on the cusp of dawn, we walked straight up the dirt path to the smouldering village. For good measure, Moyo shot dead the scrawny guard dog, which was still tied to the tree. A halo of wispy gray smoke hung low over the *kraal* in the cool dew-filled air. One house had been completely gutted. The exploding grenade torched the tinder-dry thatched roof, which erupted into a fireball, burnt fiercely and caved inward. I walked over to the blackened, decapitated hut, while the rest of the section surveyed the quiet village. I ducked down to peer inside the open door. The blackened burnt straw thatch and charred roof poles jumbled across the burnt personal effects. A blackened iron-framed bed stood above the rubble.

An abrupt movement caught the corner of the eye: against a sooty wall, a black chicken stood on a blackened human shoulder – happily pecking at a charred human head. I was spellbound. Was the Christmas chicken getting its revenge? Role reversal?

"Hey, Sarge!" I called to my blind NCO, who now had custody of the wildcat, "I thought that bitch cleared the hut?"

Something went off the rails here.

"She did," whined the sergeant, as he dragged her to view the chicken and human affair.

She jabbered something in a frightened, but indignant tone.

"What did she say?" I asked.

"She says that there was no one there last night," Chewa stated, in an offended tone.

"So what's that?" I asked, pointing at the blackened head, as the frightened hen made its escape – scooting straight out the doorway.

The body was so badly burnt that I couldn't tell if it was male or female. The girl emphatically denied there was anyone in the hut. I walked off before

Chewa translated her gibberish.

The villagers were still seated on the ground, just where we had left them. They experienced a sleepless, cold night under blankets – pondering their options. They hadn't ventured into the darkness, and there were too many armed men in the vicinity. When asked, the village spokesman emphatically denied the burnt body was one of them. I never found out the identity of our cooked friend.

One male was slain. The body lay stiffly across the cooling embers in the open fireplace. His right trouser leg was badly scorched and his right hand was in the dust. I judged he was in his early twenties. Tiny dirt particles were embedded in his skin from the face striking the earth. A bullet tore his jaw off the rigid face; surprise still registered in the dead features. A Korean-made AK-47 lay in the dust four meters away. I didn't know if the dead man was a terrorist, as he didn't wear the usual canvas webbing or Eastern Bloc equipment. He was a question mark.

Blood was splattered across the baked, hard village courtyard, with big blobs and smear marks heading to the outskirts. The tracker took note and followed. I was not impressed with the result. The shooting was too high. The red tracer shot steadily airborne and gained too much height by half-way through the village. I estimated that after 20 meters, the bullets were over two meters high and climbing – resulting in one possible dead out of a possibility of how many? Regrettably, two villagers were also killed in the flurry of bullets. A young boy, about 10 years old, was killed. Unbeknown, he had been deployed as a sentry on the village perimeter, right in front of our rifle muzzles. He must have shat himself when we crept in – sitting frozen in terror and then shot dead in the first volley. He lay on his back, spread-eagled, with a bullet hole smack in the chest. Tsumba gently cradled the boy – grief creasing his face. An adult male crawled off into the scrub and died from blood loss from a leg wound.

Once the bodies were evacuated, along with the angry girl and one villager we found skulking on the rim of the village, we once again started out on the *spoor*. Moyo strode alongside the shoe prints. Next to the path, blood splatter lashed the dirt like a modernist artist. Small pools of dark blood had been splashed at intervals – accompanied by mists of blood spray. Lopping along, the further we traveled, the less blood spray we found. After two Ks, Moyo knelt down to examine the ground: the blood spray had stopped. Lots of blood did not automatically translate into a bad wound. The extremities, like the hand or foot, can bleed profusely without being fatal. After five Ks, the CTs conducted a tactical bombshell and we hooked onto one individual, but his tracks faded to nothing.

Mantle Base decided to intervene with a helpful suggestion: "They just can't vanish, you know. Search the hills thoroughly."

"Thank you for the tip," I smarted.

The hills were a mixture of house-sized boulders interspersed in thick timber, which stretched for kilometers. With seven men, I'll winkle them out in no time.

Cash rewards were offered by the Rhodesian Government to pinpoint CTs or to locate weapons of war. Notices, similar to Wild West wanted posters, were disseminated and stuck around the TTLs. Fashioned along the successful reward system used by the British in Malaya in the 1950s, the cash rewards were infinitely lower. The offer was cash up to $US5,000 for a CT leader (compared to $US400,000 in Malaya), $US1,000 for a CT and $US500 for a weapon.

A tribesman stumbled on an AK-47 and webbing (which contained magazines) stashed in the bush and walked to the Wedza police station to hand them over. Thank you, they should have said, and handed over the cash reward, but the police – after checking the rifle's serial number – stated that it belonged to the Selous Scouts, who had discarded it during a botched job, so there'd be no money. The man was, naturally, aggrieved. The AK was the terrorists' weapon of choice, he complained. In the end, they fobbed him off with a second-hand bicycle. Five-hundred dollars was hardly worth sticking your neck in a noose, but a used bicycle? I wondered if someone else pocketed the reward money. Finally, India was relieved and was off!

On departure from Wedza, Special Branch asked me to stop at the police station. Over a cup of tea, a serious SB detective had a casual word in my ear: they'd heard through their grapevine that someone had impersonated a CT in Wedza and had told me to STOP – in big letters! I nodded gravely, but added nothing. They explained, like talking to a dimwit, that such antics played right into their province and that I was undermining all their good work. I'd hear that statement again and again. I nodded, agreed to avoid that tactic, finished my tea and departed for the City of Continuous Piss-Ups. Meanwhile, the troop motored to Salisbury for R&R. Garry finished his stint and departed the unit.

In August 1977, shortly after India departed Wedza, a Selous Scout OP inside Wedza spotted 20 CTs moving into the base of the hill the Scouts occupied. They summoned Fireforce, who zeroed on and promptly dropped the RLI straight in. A fierce firefight erupted. To contain the ZANLA group, K-Car – the command helicopter – asked Support Unit sections operating kilometers away to reinforce the RLI. They sat down on the edge of open ground, suitable for a landing zone, and began the wait – their hearts pumping in anticipation. Phil Smith's section was the closest. Picked up by two helicopters, they were deposited right into the gunfire.

An RLI corporal was shot and missing, so the Hawker Hunter jets called on wouldn't bomb the area until the corporal was located. Witnesses stated later that Phil distinguished himself – sprinting across open ground with bullets punching all around him (just like the movies), and attempted to pull a wounded RLI corporal out of the shit (later found dead) while shooting a couple of CTs at point-blank. We joked later about his Hollywood act and called it 'Phil's Run'. Later, the rumor spread that the Fireforce commander recommended a bravery award to be pinned on Phil's chest; however, the police offered a different mindset: Phil, an excellent and courageous bush soldier, flagrantly mocked discipline in town. At the recent Salisbury Agricultural Show, a superintendent spotted Phil walking with his back to the officer. The superintendent proudly mentioned to a VIP that there walked a fine example of one of his men, but when Phil turned his head, the officer's jaw dropped in shock and horror. Phil had applied full-face makeup – red lipstick, long eyelashes and eyeshadow – on a wager to walk the entire show without getting into a fight, but not to the best tradition of the BSAP! Later, the unit's 2IC – Chief Superintendent Pugh, who was a gentleman and a good guy – awkwardly asked Phil if he needed counseling for his 'unusual tendencies'.

The outcome of the Scouts/RLI battle resulted in all 20 CTs engaged killed for the loss of one RLI soldier.

I stalked into the Prospectors' Bar in the Monomatapa Hotel with my wallet full and burning to spend. The launching pad to a week of hard drinking, the Prospectors' Bar became the haunt of foreign soldiers to drink and bullshit. This day, standing and sipping a beer in a group of six RLI soldiers, I recognized a face: it was Chris Rogers – an ex-NZ Army soldier who had served in the exact same units as I. We were both surprised. We laughed, chatted and drank. An extremely fit soldier, he was currently serving in Support Commando, RLI. Chris soldiered for three years in Rhodesia – eventually buggering his back through parachute mishaps. Wounded in 1979, Corporal Rogers was awarded the Military Forces Commendation for action in a close-quarter contact. A quiet, thoughtful man, he was the last person I thought would be out this way. We met thereafter every few months when our R&R coincided.

8

Beitbridge: July 1977

I staggered drunk into the Fife Avenue cubicle at four in the morning, slept heavily for an hour and then woke up in a fright – wondering where the Land Rover had ended up. I scooted outside to find it unblemished and parked perfectly. Relieved, I stood under an ice-cold shower for 30 minutes before loading my metal trunk and driving to the depot. I vaguely remembered the last party – an all-day and all-night drinking session – but I don't remember driving home. The deployment preparation was another blur. Thank Christ Kiaran and the NCOs knew how to pack. The team manhandled the base tents, freezer, cook top, gas bottles, folding tables, camp chairs, desert lilies (portable urinals shaped like a funnel and rammed into the loose soil), toilet bases, shower tanks and nozzles, and the rest of the paraphernalia required to set up a 35-man base in the scrub, while I sat bamboozled in the shade.

Two new section leaders arrived: Wayne, a regular cop from Dog Section, was posted to India after unit training. A senior patrol officer, with several years of service, he found life difficult adjusting to a commander who had completed much less service. A tough and stroppy individual, who moved in the inner circle of long-serving, low-ranking police, he guessed he wouldn't fit in and immediately agitated for a transfer to a troop led by an ex-Dogs inspector. We'd barely deployed from Salisbury before he made his first overture. Graeme, the second arrival, had a freckled and youthful face. This fair haired, beardless lad – straight from high school – had elected to serve his two years' National Service in the police. By the time he reported to India Troop, he'd spent three months in Morris Depot and another two months in Tomlinson Depot. A quiet, unassuming teenager with university aspirations, it didn't take long to drag him out of his shell. In this first bush trip, Graeme was shuffled between sections to acclimatize him to the reality.

The convoy rolled out of Salisbury on time – driving the main highway south to Beitbridge. I drove the lead vehicle and dozed twice, only to be sharply awakened each time the Land Rover drifted into the loose gravel on the roadside shoulder. The crunch of gravel on tires set off the alarm. Without doubt, I was still pissed – an accident praying to happen! Throughout the long drive, sick as a dog, I quietly prayed to God that if I got through the day, I'd never drink again. Famous last words!

The convoy stopped at Fort Victoria to eat and stretch and use the toilet facilities before heading south to the border. After hours of driving, the hangover slowly dissipated, like a sluggishly dispersing swamp mist. By mid-afternoon, we drove into Beitbridge – a tiny border town 585 kilometers from Salisbury. The sleepy, dusty settlement sat on the Limpopo River (the border with South Africa) and offered petrol stations, cafés and the Peters and Beitbridge Hotels for transit people. The town seemed lightly coated in a fine brown dust that suggested drought in the surrounding countryside. The convoy parked on the roadside, while I sought out the police station. The men scattered to spend some money.

Feeling marginally better, I sauntered inside the brick establishment to run the gauntlet of shrugs and pointing when I asked to see the man in charge. Finding my way into a small office, a police inspector and a Special Branch operator presented me a thumbnail sketch of the bandit activity, which as usual, was closer to tourist information than hardcore intelligence. Two CT characters named Soweto and Jesus were loose in the area. Jesus! Preaching door to door? The inspector suspected my hangover (the eyes give the booze away) and fobbed me off quickly. He pointed to a crossed pick on the map.

"Your base," he announced briskly and walked out.

I screwed my eyes to see.

The crossed pick represented an ore mining operation in the Diti TTL: the Pande Mine. I noted the map location, picked up sheets of 1:50,000 maps and a shackle code, rustled up the men and the convoy rolled out of town.

The convoy drove through the arid Diti TTL to the isolated mining outpost. The Pande Mine stood only a few kilometers from the South African border. As we turned into the access road, the town outline crumbled. It was built on a flat-top promontory – overlooked by scrubby hills and a large white slagheap. The convoy stopped and Kiaran and I inspected the outpost. The empty houses were severely vandalized. Entire windows and doors – including frames – were missing. Large holes were kicked into the sheeted walls and the ceiling was riddled with craters. Inside, the porcelain basins and toilets were deliberately smashed, and shards of sharp white porcelain were scattered over the dusty concrete slab floor. The houses were reduced to wooden studs on concrete slabs, with a denuded roof.

With the basic shelter infrastructure in place, there was no need to waste time erecting tents. Each section took on a part-house, swept out the loose rubble and erected the portable toilet and shower facilities. The least damaged house served as the HQ. One room was used for the communications center and another to stow spare stores. Trenches from a previous army squatter were upgraded. Everyone worked to improve their home away from home.

The derelict township had been attacked twice over the previous months. The CTs had fired a 75mm recoilless rifle from the flat slagheap directly across the dusty road. Standing on the slag pile, our camp looked easy pickings. I saw every one of our houses and every movement in the camp. The troop didn't have enough men to provide a permanent standing patrol on the mining rubble. To do so ruled out one section for permanent 24-hour guard duty. With another section resting in base, half the troop would be diverted just to protect itself. A company-sized unit might consider the position, but for a platoon-sized force, it was untenable. I bet the CTs penciled in their next attack date. We needed to move out, so I immediately lobbied hard, but this simple request got bogged down in the Upper Command. The protracted and considerable verbal jousting between the JOC at Chiredzi, Police Beitbridge, Support Unit HQ and India Troop began. Whilst talk began in earnest, operations started.

Large swathes of Diti were hot, dry savannah – flat as a desktop and covered in four-foot-tall spiny scrub. The Nulli Range ran roughly north-west to south-east, like a protruding backbone, and hovered – shimmering blue in the background. There are no *kopjes* to climb and silently observe the comings and goings of the tribe's people, so the practiced art of OPs – perfected in the eastern province – was useless here. The impression painted a scrubby desert with few local people. Even ploughed fields were few and far between.

When a troop deployed from Salisbury, they towed a water bowser filled with town water, which was used as the basic source, but in the field, we resorted to natural running water. In the eastern regions, streams and rivers flowed freely; pebble and rock-based bottoms had clear water flowing over the top. The residents were clean and scrupulous about water use, and washed and bathed in the same place, not polluting. We drew water direct from the rivers without using any purification tablets and I don't recall any problems.

In Diti, the streambeds were dry. Even the mighty Limpopo River on the South African border had been reduced to a series of stagnant pools. With no running water, or a history of reliable rainfall, the government drilled boreholes. Each borehole was numbered and section leaders diligently plotted them on a map. The surveyor-general produced good maps, but useful information was out of date, so I requested the sections log each bore number and anything physically on the ground, but not featured on the maps. We gradually updated the operations map. When talking to the locals, they stated that so-and-so walked to borehole 32 – information which was of little value unless we knew exactly which borehole was number 32.

We soon discovered that boreholes were awkward to approach unseen. Located in the center of a cleared area 10 meters in diameter, with a number of paths leading in, like spokes on a bicycle wheel, not a single blade of grass survived; the dirt was trodden down by cattle. Even the scrappy scrub that grew on the circumference was completely devoid of grass or ground cover underneath – foraged to the roots by goats. Anyone operating the hand pump was a sitting target. The locals constantly walked the pathways into and out of the boreholes – particularly the women fetching and carrying water – so siting an ambush undetected under the border scrub was not an option. Anyone who chose to bend down saw straight through the ragged vegetation, but the fighting centered on these boreholes.

Three sections dropped into an area south of the Nulli Range, where clusters of CT-related incidents had occurred. Within hours on the first deployment, Kiaran's section engaged in two fierce contacts within the tight scrub. Graeme walked in the section, so it was an early baptism of fire. On each occasion, the section patrolled a foot track and bumped into a CT unit walking the same path, but towards them; both sides blasted a mad minute of automatic fire and rifle grenades before the CTs burst off the track and fled through the dense brush. The split-second sighting heralded a few minutes of intense, heart-pounding stuff for everyone.

We held meetings in the *kraals* to talk with the Venda people. The majority of the Venda tribe lived in South Africa, south of the Limpopo River, with smatterings to the north, inside Rhodesia. They were, effectively, cousins cut off by the colonial border. They looked poorer than their eastern Shona cousins – dusty and dressed in disintegrating clothes. They sat edgy, like delicate gazelles watching the circling lion. A close-knit community, they stubbornly supported the 'see nothing, hear nothing' line. Even Sergeant Nguruve's night act was canceled. The villagers were extremely wary of strangers – especially those trying to pass themselves off as 'brothers'. The real 'brothers' had integrated tightly into the community and each individual CT was personally known to the villagers. When Nguruve wandered by at dusk, they simply gawked in disbelief and mumbled amongst themselves. They weren't buying. His act

Kiaran Allen and a troop sergeant at Diti TTL, 1977. (Kiaran Allen)

lacked credibility, but still, he was an inventive leader looking for an edge. His section concentrated on wooing the children to see what they could harvest. Children were free thinkers, not bound in a world of political straitjackets. The section chatted and handed out food bits, but did not ask about CTs, just about strangers. They innocently steered him onto the trail, but we were not in Diti long enough for him to sink his teeth into the puzzle.

Two weeks later, my section night ambushed the main Lutombe store axis road. The road stretched east from the Beitbridge Highway, past Nulli for kilometers and into the Sengwe TTL. After a fruitless night, in the weak dawn light, the men packed up the ambush position. Tutani, standing and stretching, noticed a car headed our way. From where he stood, the car was Matchbox toy-sized and pumping up dust clouds. Usually, road traffic didn't begin until well after the sun bobbed over the horizon, after the night curfew hours. I was curious.

"Moyo," I instructed the sentry, "go out there an' stop the bastard. Give it the quick once over."

I expected a routine check – scrutinize the driver's license and an eyeball search of the vehicle.

Moyo groaned that 'why me?' groan, stepped away from his backpack and waited in the shadows on the roadside till the car drove closer; then casually stepped onto the white dirt and flapped his arms to stop the vehicle. I clipped my webbing belt on as I kept half an eye on the vehicle. Tutani watched the sentry amble half-heartedly onto the road, while he strapped his bedroll to the bottom of the pack.

Moyo's wave triggered a series of jolting reactions: the white Datsun braked fiercely; the wheels locked and the pick-up skidded along the loose stone surface – fishtailing slightly and grounding to a jarring halt. The female driver flung open the door and, in one fluid movement, leapt clear from the cab, scampered across the road and burst into the dense bush on our side of the road. Her whirlwind action concluded in a few breakneck seconds.

"Hey!" shouted Moyo, with his rifle swung into the shoulder, but she had vanished.

A thick cloud of white dust kicked up by the Datsun overtook the stationary vehicle and hung in the cool air like a pall. The male passenger slowly opened his door and eased out. He leisurely unfolded and stood upright. By now, all seven police stood tingling, alert, with weapons ready. Although the driver's reaction was unexpected, uncertainty hovered about who they were. The driver could easily be a startled civilian running from someone they thought was a terrorist. African constables had been mistaken before – particularly in the half-light – but then again, people don't like government SF personnel either.

We were still unsure of the passenger's status as he stood a meter away from the open door – obscured from his chest down by the Datsun's white cab and blurred by the descending dust cloud, so we paused; then, unpredictably, and with breath-taking speed, he stepped away from the passenger door (still facing us), whipped an AK up and fired from the hip. The weapon had been hidden by the brown suede jacket flap and obscured by the floating white dust. Once he fired, the spell was broken, but his sudden, startling 10-round burst put us off balance for a couple of seconds and he slipped straight into the thick roadside thicket. One second he stood there; the next, swallowed by the roadside bush.

"FIRE!" I bellowed.

The rifles boomed.

Without warning, two terrorists, who were lying flat and unseen on the back tray of the vehicle, launched themselves off over the tailgate – hitting the road with bullets pinging through the metal tray – and fled at the high port. The section put a weight of rifle and machine gun fire into the thick tight scrub where they had vanished, but apart from a brief spurt of RPD fire, they had disappeared.

The action was over in less than 20 seconds. No one was hurt. I felt mesmerized, like I was passively watching a film, with the action slowly unfolding before my eyes. My lack of assertive action when I first sighted the vehicle flowed right through our mild response and we ended up empty-handed. I simply didn't expect to find terrorists coolly driving a car in the tribal lands. As the spellbound feeling broke away, I became angry at my sluggish reaction. I should have fired earlier, when the passenger shuffled away from the door. Isn't hindsight a wonderful thing?

After the small arms bombardment, the men rushed in on the parked Datsun whilst still guarded against a counter-attack. Surrounding the static vehicle, we began a rapid search. Bundles of propaganda leaflets, bigger bundles of *Zimbabwe News* magazines, a ZANU propaganda magazine – a Mozambique Department of Information professional publication, with lots of black-and-white photographs – were stacked in the Datsun tray, along with three backpacks and three sealed metal cases of 7.62mm Intermediate ammunition. A loose AK magazine and a Chinese stick grenade were lumped together on the vinyl bench seat in the cab.

"Shit, we captured our own troop car," Sergeant Chewa announced happily. "Let's drive off in it."

"No, you don't,' I warned – still hyped up and ready for action. "What about landmines?"

"Mines won't be a worry," replied Chewa, pleased with his logic. "If there were any in the road, *they* wouldn't be driving."

"Can we drive it?" asked Tsumba, licking his lips.

"Go on," I said, as the promise of a counter-attack faded.

He leapt into the open driver's door – beating two others. The ignition keys dangled in view: clutch in, gearstick to neutral, start the engine – nothing happened. They tried and tried, but the engine failed to respond.

"You killed it, Tutani," they accused the squat gunner, laughing.

The bonnet bore bullet holes, so something vital was smashed. I called Police Beitbridge for a tow.

While we waited for the tow truck, the men scoured the tight scrub for signs of the escapees. The interconnected branches had effectively shielded the runners. Fleeing at high speed, their shoe prints were hidden under the scrub branches. The trackers found nothing, so they returned back to the roadside.

Before the tow truck with police escort arrived, the constables lobbied hard to keep the vehicle as a war trophy – an India Troop piss-up vehicle. After all, they had captured it, which was a good point, but Special Branch insisted on its confiscation – for evidence, of course! Later, it transpired that the Datsun was registered to a Beitbridge African businessman and his wayward wife was the driver. The constables sulked when the grapevine confirmed that SB used the Datsun in town as their private car.

Shortly afterwards, the poor tactical location of our base camp at Pande came to a head and Police Beitbridge reluctantly agreed to India Troop moving, but only after a shit fight. We located an old Intaf camp sitting close on the main Beitbridge-Fort Victoria Road. The new camp was much better placed to be serviced and to deploy into the TTL. As we had not erected a tent camp, the evacuation process was quick and uncomplicated. A rumor circulated that a couple of senior people retained a financial stake in the abandoned mining camp and wanted their money protected, literally. They arranged for GC to sit on their investment after India pulled out.

The troop motored to the new base and sized up the job. Utilizing an empty building as headquarters, we marked out the tent sites. To effectively defend the base, more physical labor was required. I decided not to stop operations, but rather appoint Sergeant Tambe to run the base camp with a list of jobs to be completed – using a spare section and bludgers. I had lost faith in his trustworthiness in the scrub long ago. His constables openly boasted about the lack of work ethic to other constables. I didn't bother with an investigation, as his time had run out. Besides, in camp, with a job list, his work progress was measurable and I diligently checked on the improvement, which led to further erosion of our poor relationship.

In the midst of completing the camp puzzle, Police Beitbridge radioed for help: a GC Land Rover had detonated a landmine on the main Diti Road – the same road we'd unsuccessfully ambushed. My section hurriedly drove out to assist. Some kilometers down the road, we spotted the matte-green police Land Rover, which was parked on the roadside and partly obscured by curious onlookers. The mine blasted the front left wheel to smithereens – mashing the engine compartment in the process. Their Police Reserve escort vehicle was parked on the roadside and the Reservists milled about like inquisitive civilians gawking at a road accident. On our arrival, the men debussed and Moyo and Mandaza sniffed about the shattered vehicle – searching for the escape route the perpetrators employed after planting the mine. Tsumba checked the two stunned police agents who rode the landmine. Both were shocked, but unharmed.

While we scouted around the wreck for a foot trail, two army trucks thundered past – heading east to Sengwe TTL. The six guys seated on the back tray saw our predicament, laughed and joked, and jeered. One stood up and gave us the fingers, with a huge smile. They disappeared in a cloud of white dust. We gave them the two-fingered salute and then settled down to find *spoor*. In less than a couple of minutes, a loud blast boomed and reverberated, and I flinched. The men automatically stopped and stared down the long, straight road.

"Here we go," I called to Tutani, Tsumba and Moyo, and waved them into the Hyena parked on the road, "Sarge, you take Mandaza and follow the *spoor*. I bet I know where it goes."

I signaled for the driver of the second Hyena to trail the trackers.

Before Chewa protested, I accelerated east and found the stricken truck two kilometers further up the road. It sat askew on the dirt. A mine had detonated under a rear wheel – shredding it. Although the tire was filled with water to dampen a blast, and the steel tray was lined with sandbags, the ferocious explosion flipped the six soldiers off the slat seat – causing serious injuries after landing on the hard turf. Two wore broken bones; now, it's not so funny. I parked and Tsumba leapt out, with his medical pack flapping in his hand. The lead army truck reversed up to the lame one and a sergeant called in a helicopter casevac on his radio. Before long, Chewa and his team rounded the bend – following the *spoor* from the police scene.

"Keep going," I said to Chewa, as he glanced at me.

Mandaza led the way.

With the casevac on the way, we deserted the soldiers and laboriously followed the teasing *spoor* – trailed by our two vehicles – and discovered the third landmine in the dusty road about two kilometers further east. The terrorists were busy boys: three landmines on the same stretch of road. The terrorists had planted the third one on the opposite side of the road for the returning traffic. I radioed India Base for the army's Engineers to come out and lift the bloody thing. Half an hour later, I was informed that the Engineers weren't available and that I had to deal with it. Now, a course in mine disarmament would have been handy. Mandaza meticulously scrutinized the road top for signs of other mines. He nodded to confirm he saw nothing suspicious. I cautiously edged closer to the mismatched soil, knelt down and warily scraped around the outline with my fingers. My eyes examined the gritty road surface just beyond the disturbed area and looked for anti-personnel mines – those small, shitty explosive charges designed to be detonated by foot pressure. There was nothing obvious. Making sure the constables scattered into shelter, I drew in a deep breath and attacked the job.

Using a dessert spoon, I scooped away the loose earth surrounding the mine and uncovered the beast. This one was a Yugoslav TMA landmine, which was made of solid explosive and encased in a thin, green plastic membrane, with three black plastic detonator pins screwed in the top; this was designed to deceive mine detectors. My fingers delicately stroked the cool casing and found a canvas strap embedded in the body – unearthing it. Moyo then handed over a nylon cord, which I tied to the strap. I knew scant about anti-handling devices, and so took extra care. Moyo attached the other end to the Hyena tow bar. I retreated from the mine, climbed into the Hyena and, once everyone was well away, drove gently forward and slowly towed the explosive device to the surface. The circular device slid onto the road surface and I braked. Clambering out of the Hyena, I returned to sit down on the road and delicately unscrewed the three black detonator caps.

While I detested playing the game 'dismantle the mine', I was happy that one ingredient of the modern guerrilla warfare cake was applied only in very small numbers (i.e. anti-personnel mines and the booby traps). I personally never ran into AP mines. From reports, they were present, but not in the huge numbers found in other civil war conflicts. The isolated cases were printed out on the daily sitrep, but not in the numbers that created unreasonable fear. AP mines caused enormous trepidation wherever they were used – and countries like Angola and Mozambique were littered with them.

Afterwards, I brewed tea and chatted with the constables about life and its vagaries. I eyeballed a very old – and soiled – *Playboy* magazine, which was treasured because it was illegal to sell in Rhodesia. The only magazines available were the limp-wristed *Scope* or *Illustrated Life Rhodesia* – both so bland that you couldn't raise a hard-on. Scanning one of the semi-nude white beauties (in the days before *Playboy* got into full-on nudity), I noted a curious glance from the tracker.

"Like that, do you Mandaza?" I asked – turning the page to give him a full-on view of it.

The others laughed.

"No," he said academically, as he dug his spoon into the hot *sadza*, "too skinny. They need to be nice and plump, so you can get years and years of work out of them. She wouldn't last two weeks."

The men burst into a chorus of laughter and general agreement. Everyone had different tastes.

Kiaran brought back tales from patrol of wild game so, to supplement rations, we lobbied Internal Affairs for permission to hunt. The District Commissioner granted consent to shoot for the pot. This was the first operational area where wild game roamed. Kiaran led the expedition and bagged two smaller bucks. Versed in the art of *biltong* manufacture, Kiaran cut one beast into meat strips and processed them. *Biltong* ('jerky' in the USA) was lightweight protein and easy to carry. The second beast was handed to the constables to cook as they wished. This was a welcome change from the corned beef or Spam, or we would jet into town for a chilled beer and a tender steak at the Peters Hotel whenever the chance arose.

Other wildlife stalked Diti. I once walked over a small, wooded ridge and almost stepped upon a giant python sunning itself in the wood debris. It was the first and last one I ever saw. There were a number of snake species: tales of the deadly black mamba entwined in trees, which heralded the possibility of being bitten in the face, were retold in the pub, but I never saw any. Puff adders were the visible snake and they were dangerous because, unlike most snakes that feel vibrations of walking feet coming, they slithered away, the puff adder tended to stay put. This snake did not seek attention, but the danger came when the walker failed to see the snake and stepped on it.

A couple of days after the army landmine, we received another radio call for help: an Internal Affairs convoy had drove smack into a CT ambush. We scrambled onto two vehicles and drove up the road to the ambush scene. Everyone was keyed up for immediate action, and our weapons were cocked and ready. From the back of the Bedford, Moyo sighted movement in the scrub.

"Fuck!" he cried in wonder, "look at him run!"

An African district assistant sprinted through the tight scrub parallel to the main road. He was visible from the waist up. Hatless and with no rifle, he ran hard – focused only on getting the hell out of there. His fawn shirt, stripped of buttons, flapped about like loose washing. Focused totally on his flight, he didn't hear the truck. Mandaza banged on the truck cab roof and the driver braked and stopped – the air brakes hissing and dust overtaking the motionless vehicle.

"Come 'ere!" called Chewa.

The shout broke the runner's spell, and he slowed to a jog and turned – pausing to catch his breath – and then headed to the idling truck. Eager hands helped him on board. He scrambled over the side and launched himself onto the hessian sandbags. The first thing I noticed was his bare feet. Where were his boots?

"You're runnin' away?" I asked the flustered man.

He gasped – his chest heaving, his fawn shirt open and his bare feet on bare legs sticking out from the rumpled fawn shorts, completely disheveled. I wondered where his socks were.

"No, boss," he mouthed – catching his breath – "I fired all my bullets, and then I run for help."

Yeah, sure.

"Bullshit," I snapped.

"There was hundreds of 'em," he pleaded – trying to compose himself – "they fired and fired an' I run out of bullets."

"Where's your rifle?"

Dead silence.

The man slunk down on the sandbagged tray like a deflated doll and fiddled with a piece of torn hessian sacking. His fighting spirit had obviously fled.

Five kilometers on, a dark-green Internal Affairs Bedford truck sat square in the middle of the dirt road, with the driver's door hanging open like a broken bird's wing. Confused district assistants shuffled about – pale in shock and disbelief. An overweight, aging African NCO – cuddling a vintage Sten gun – herded his men together using liberal tongue lashings and the odd smack around the ear.

"Any casualties?" I called out to him.

"No, boss," he replied casually, "but I've lost three men somewhere."

"One's up 'ere, Sarge," I replied sarcastically, "running 10,000 meters for the country."

"Get here, you bastard!" growled the sweating, porky sergeant.

The runner trembled as he stood up, paused and then jumped down onto the road before timidly standing to one side. The sweat-stained sergeant growled in his direction and then promptly ignored him. The man eased away – trying not to be seen. The CTs had scared the living daylights out of him, but the NCO's wrath may have been worse.

The India section dismounted and surveyed the ambush site. The CTs had fired from behind good-sized rocks and were hidden by scrubby camouflage.

At least 12 CTs had shot at the two trucks point-blank and had missed everyone. A 3.5-inch British shoulder-launched rocket had completely missed the second truck and had blasted into the ground – digging a small smear on the opposite side of the road. A second blue-green rocket lay abandoned in the ambush position and looked deadly silhouetted in the dried leaf. Squatting down, I wondered how they had missed. They could have thrown rocks at the passing trucks and had more success. ZANLA believed if they applied a solid weight of fire – a sheet of bullets pointed roughly at the target – someone, somewhere, would be hit and their job was done. Sometimes they did and sometimes they didn't. Very few had capable individual shooting skills, which was fortunate for government forces. On the other hand, Internal Affairs personnel presented mobile pop-up targets for ZANLA. A non-lethal force of civil servants bumbling along the road presented ideal targets to practice their shooting skills. Recruited for monitoring and advising the general African population on civil matters, African district assistants experienced sketchy military training. Sporting World War II vintage Lee Enfield .303 bolt-action rifles, they were no match for the sophisticated modern weaponry employed by the ambushers. The Internal Affairs casualties throughout the war were severe.

I presented the lost British anti-tank rocket to Special Branch in their Beitbridge office. As I laid it on the desk, they almost trampled me fleeing the office.

"You fuckin' idiot!" they called in alarm, "don't bring live ordnance in here!"

The rocket still had the safety cap on and was harmless, but still, it brightened their morning!

Days later, the entire troop deployed early one morning, along with sticks of RLI, on an unusual operation in the Mtetengwe TTL, which was west of the Beitbridge Highway. Selous Scouts had been active in Mtetengwe for some weeks and had requested troops to provide a cordon. India Troop strung four sections along the main dirt road, which cut a straight swath through the tight scrub in order to form block groups. The RLI set up another series of blocks further along the same road. The block groups covered kilometers. Once we sat in place, Special Branch and Selous Scouts chauffeured a number of Land Rovers straight through the scrawny scrub in an extended line, like Scottish beaters trying to scare pheasants towards the shooting party. Here, *we* represented the shooting party. Three helicopters circled lazily overhead, like vultures looking for stray runners. All day, we squatted in the searing oven heat – sheltered by sparse and spotty shade, and growing steadily weary and thirsty.

The author at Diti TTL, 1977; the Nulli Hills are in the background.
Note the starlight scope hanging off the neck. (Kiaran Allen)

Nothing happened. No one got up and fled. At dusk, we picked ourselves up and trudged home – another big fat 'lemon'.

After that, I revved up operations in Diti. With the absence of high ground to spy on the main routes or villages, the troop was left with ambushing and patrolling options. There were a number of short and sharp confrontations – resulting in nothing, or only one CT being killed. My section walked into an ambush at Nulli School and survived without casualties by only the slimmest of margins. Their RPD machine gun pinned us down, whilst they escaped unscathed.

One evening, my section strolled into a borehole area and straight into four CTs. The enemy saw the scout a split-second early. Moyo copped a quick glance as the terrorists bolted into the wiry scrub. Both sides dived into immediate action and exchanged an intense wall of rifle fire. The sharp crackle of AK fire made us wince. We blindly concentrated our rifle fire at waist height and into the dense scrub. Twigs were snapped off and branches chopped down by the hail of bullets. The CTs broke off the engagement and melted away – leaving us to intimately search the matted scrub and quickly finding signs that at least one CT was wounded. Fresh blood was splattered on the ground and smeared on the green leaves. We camped overnight.

The next morning, we pushed through tiresome, waist-high, spindly scrub. It was like walking kilometers against the tide in a waist-deep sea. While we stuck to the wiry scrub, the ZANLA gang walked on a foot track, so they were not difficult to pursue. After 12 kilometers, the tracker spotted the top of conical roofs jutting above the scrub. Moyo vigilantly approached the village – alert, and with sweaty fingers on the trigger. I decided, before we entered the complex, to undertake a clearance sortie outside the *kraal* first. As the men carefully circled the huts in the ragged bush, Tutani suddenly spotted one CT seated upright in the scrub. The enemy noticed our MAG gunner at the same time, and attempted to dive from view. The MAG roared. Tutani fired first and killed the CT outright. An RPD machine gun and an AK-47 were recovered, and the enemy fled.

The captured AK was filthy dirty, but once cocked, still fired. As a rule of thumb, most terrorist weapons were in shit condition. Brand-spanking new AKs had not been cleaned since they had come out of the packing grease. Some recovered weapons had working parts jammed solid simply through the lack of nominal cleaning. Even the Kalashnikov needs a tiny bit of love. The AK had certainly lived up to its reputation as the 'weapon made by experts for peasants'. In one common practice, the barrel was plugged with a cigarette butt to prevent dirt entering. The butt sat snugly inside, stayed in there forever and was blown out with the first bullet.

Once again, we locked onto another single CT. The quarry tried anti-tracking from time to time, and even walking backwards – a trick that a novice tracker can easily detect. (The walker's heels would sink further into the dust when they walked backwards, and also flicked the sand forwards.) After hours of relentless trailing, Moyo finally sighted and shot dead the lone terrorist. Kiaran's section also reported contacts; killing off the terrorists one at a time!

Between patrols (at least twice), Kiaran, Wayne and I drove over the border into South Africa in the police Land Rover to shop in Messina, which was a town 16 kilometers south. The South African Immigration and Customs just nodded their heads and gave a half-smirk as we motored through. They didn't bother with passports or paperwork. They acted like a big brother letting the small brother out to play. Johnnie Walker Red whisky, Gillette razor blades and other small personal goodies not available in Rhodesia were snapped up. The Gillette blades were purchased for personal use, as the Rhodesia-made

Lion razor blade plucked the facial hair out one at a time. We always timed our return for six in the evening, which was when the Rhodesia border wearily closed and the Customs people were tired and in a hurry to shut up shop. They knew what we were doing, but closed their eyes. It was small-time and, as long as we didn't tear the arse out of the undocumented border crossings – carting back goods for consumption and resale – who cared?

JOC's daily calls for assistance blunted offensive patrolling, with sections scrambled to investigate a CT ambush of the main Rutenga railway line, as well as other scattered incidents, which faded into nothing. We responded more and more to incidents, rather than taking the offensive. A local terrorist identity, Jesus, had met his end at a borehole in Diti TTL when he mortared a PATU stick. The policemen sprinted in quicker than he had slipped away and shot him dead. It was hardly a biblical end.

Wayne complained about this and that, and made contact with his troop commander of choice. His service allowed him to use the 'Old Boys' Network' to further his aims. I didn't care much, as his abrasive attitude rubbed up against mine. I knew we circled each other warily and he would never settle in. When he announced that his next deployment would be in another troop, I didn't stand in his way. The relief troop drove in and, after the handover, we scrambled back to Salisbury.

Once a deployment finished, troops became anxious about maximizing their leave. From the operational base, a lady at Rhobank was rewarded with a big bunch of flowers to ensure that cash payments were ready to go. The departure was radioed to Support Unit HQ and the troop motored home. Broken-down vehicles were left abandoned at the roadside, with a sharp call into CMED to tell them where to find them. Vehicles that stopped due to mechanical problems irritated me so much that I could have easily set fire to the bastard things. The RL Bedford trucks, in particular, were beyond their 'use by' date. Old and worn out, the mechanics did a sterling job to keep them running, but they were now beyond mechanical patchwork. They broke down with regular monotony.

The only legitimate stop on the long road back was at the Women's Voluntary Service canteen, where homemade cakes, sandwiches and cups of hot tea were a welcome respite. These amazing ladies worked long hours to produce goodies and hot tea in canteens parked around the country to serve troops on the move.

Once back in Tomlinson Depot, all hands were on deck to hand back clean vehicles, to clean and stow weapons and ammunition in the armory, and to complete any outstanding paperwork. If the boys worked hard and the base warriors cooperated, we were in the pub by Wednesday afternoon.

The 'Travel and Subsistence' claim at PGHQ always provided a hurdle. On one trip, I reported to PGHQ to pick up the check, only to be told by a junior, well-clipped section officer to come back the next day, as the people with authority to sign were playing golf. I stormed back to Tomlinson Depot, herded all the constables on a Bedford truck and drove them to PGHQ. I told the section officer to personally tell 30 angry Africans why they're not getting paid. He found the signatures in 10 minutes.

Starting R&R, I was shocked to learn that Detective Patrol Officer Francois Erasmus had been killed in a vehicle ambush up Inyanga way. I had met him two months prior, when he first arrived in the country. We enjoyed several beer sessions at the Monomatapa Hotel during his shortened police training. An ex-Hong Kong police inspector, he entertained the rigors of a shortened basic training once again. It was a shame that a quiet, unassuming, well-mannered young man was killed on his first deployment for Special Branch in a forgotten corner of a shithole TTL.

By the time we formed up for the five-day retraining after R&R, the troop lost a number of key people: Kiaran had departed to take his experience to another troop (Support Unit was expanding and urgently needed experienced leaders in new troops); Wayne swapped to another troop; Tutani was promoted to Lance Sergeant and Nguruve was to become a full Sergeant – and both were posted out to other troops; among the constables, a smattering of sickness, some transfers and discharges, and some extended leave meant that numbers were depleted, so the India numbers were reinforced with new African blood from the last recruit training.

This batch handled themselves well. They were cocksure, good shots and better trained. One of the new fellows came with an interesting story: in a party of ZANLA recruits heading for Mozambique, they tripped an SF ambush and he survived, captured. His brother – a police sergeant – found out, seized hold of him and gave him a brutal hiding; then forced him to sign up for Support Unit. He became one of our stars.

On the down side, among the reinforcements, an ex-RAR soldier turned constable joined India. I never trusted the man. Most constables oozed an easy-going appeal (there was never too much standing to attention or that kind of bullshit), but this guy always marched in a regimental fashion, even when alone, and if he addressed one of the white guys, he slammed to attention and rigidly reported whatever he had to say. Now, if you like that sort of shit, fine, but I didn't encourage it. The other constables thought he was a laugh. To cut a long story short, he was the only person in operations I suspected of raping a local – twice. I nearly caught him the second time, on the next bush trip. He was in the sergeants' section, and when I linked up with them, we carried out joint operations through villages. While a sergeant and I were engrossed in interrogation of the villagers, I suspected that the constable had lured a teenage girl and raped her in the outlying bushes. As we abruptly pulled the pin to leave ahead of schedule, a flurry of activity pinpointed his position and the young girl jetted off into the scrub. I asked him to explain, but he emphatically denied it – standing rigidly to attention, of course. The grapevine, naturally, came closer to the truth. I got rid of him at the end of the trip.

India had lost all the white section leaders except for Graeme, so a new batch arrived. The first was Mick Busby, an ex-policeman from London, who I had met before the posting. Mick had fierce eyes, a skid-ramp nose (flattened once by a swinging pool cue), a wicked smile and a short haircut on top – allowing the sides to grow long. Mick became the troop raconteur, with the gift of being able to hold an audience enwrapped with his storytelling and jokes. Plenty of the tales related to his experience in the Met, and his ability to maintain a level of cheerful humor kept the morale high in difficult times.

The second was Ray Hughes, who swapped with Wayne. Ray and I had endured the same Support Unit Training Troop. He was a supremely fit and assertive policeman, with a great sense of humor. The smallest in physical height, but with a proportioned body, he had fair hair and a bright, intelligent face. A native Rhodesian – keen to mix it with the terrorists – he displayed a sense of urgency to win. Ray was second to none in a contact: gutsy and aggressive. Immediately after the six-week tour, he'd dress in his 'drinking suit' (brown cap, brown overalls and sandals made from car tires), spend a couple of days partying with the lads and would then go quietly home to Umtali, where he lived with his *fiancée*, who was also in the police.

9
Chibi Twice: September 1977

The troop motored to Fort Victoria – the oldest white settlement, with a population of 18,000. The town grew in the early 1900s as a mining and cattle ranching center, but as Bulawayo expanded in the west, Fort Victoria stagnated. In town, we parked on the roadside on Allen Wilson Street, opposite the Chevron Hotel, and the men stretched and relieved themselves. In bunches, the crew scoured the town for last-minute purchases, while I journeyed to JOC to be briefed. Fort Victoria JOC was the command center for south-east operations, under the code 'Repulse'.

JOC allotted the India Troop Chibi TTL. Walking through the sprawling buildings, I tracked down the intelligence officer. The briefing was typically lightweight, not worth stopping to hear. It also included *chimurenga* names (war names) – personalities such as 'Monomatapa', 'Fast Mover', 'Dr Mao', 'Zebra' and 'Hungry Gun' – followed by the usual scattergun of incidents, but there was nothing useful.

Chibi TTL lay 30 kilometers south of Fort Victoria and brushed the Beitbridge Highway right down to Ngundu Halt – a tiny commercial hub and bus stop at the junction of the Triangle Road. The land swept west from the Beitbridge Road to the Fort Victoria-Shabani Highway. The countryside was semi-arid mopani, which was not much good for commercial cropping and prone to drought. Chibi was bordered by other TTLs and touched on extensive cattle ranching near the Shabani Highway.

The convoy chewed up the dirt road, which led from the highway to the Chibi village. The countryside either side of the road grew scrappy, with dust-coated bush that sighed poverty. Finally, we steered into the police camp, where we parked ourselves just inside the entrance, away from the station buildings. The substantial police grounds, spread over at least an acre, squatted at the base of a picturesque granite *kopje* that was protected from the world by an eight-foot security fence. The station buildings included the actual police station, cell block, single police messes, married personnel houses and spare buildings. The police complex was part of a tiny Chibi community made up of a cluster of government workers – mainly Internal Affairs.

I introduced myself to the inspector in charge of the police station and we agreed the troop would set up just inside the security fence. The men dropped straight into the routine. Sergeant Tambe, now an accomplished base warrior, strutted about – cursing and shouting at the work crew. The heavy canvas tents were erected and pegged down, slit trenches were dug, desert lilies were put out and cold-water showers and portable toilets (with their hessian walls) were put in place. Tambe swaggered back and forth – the camp slowly clipping together under his shifty eyes. The main tent served both as a kitchen (with a gas deep freeze, a gas four-burner camp stove and a folding metal table), as well as an operations room, with radio communication and map board.

The section leaders were beginning to get to know each other. Mick mercilessly teased Graeme for his short-back-and-sides haircut – pronouncing 'Ray-mond' with a French accent, 'from the left bank of the Seine'. As much as possible, I kept Graeme out of the firing line and used him for OP work and radio relay. Graeme wanted to study to be a chemical engineer, which sounded better than a footslogger. To be killed in this shitty little war would be a waste of talent.

Living in tents, showering in cold water and shitting over a long drop on the fringe of civilized creature comforts brought squabbles with the 'Brown Boots', who were not happy with the loose arrangement. The guys liberally helped themselves to the single men's mess for decent hot showers and to listen to the record player, which understandably, led to petty complaints. The occupants, naturally, became irritable, with the men's growing habit of calling their home 'Home'.

Two days later, the member in charge (MIC) laid down the law. He sent down a runner to request my presence. I wandered up to the station and into his office. The first thing I saw was the MIC's wife standing behind his chair, glaring at me. Why was she there? Had I stood on her toes? I'd hardly stepped into the doorway before he commenced to dress me down; no greetings, no formalities.

"Your men are to stay away from the station buildings," the inspector ordered, as he leaned back in his chair, "particularly the messes. That's the single men's home, not a facility where you can come and go as you please."

"Not even for showers?"

"They have no cause to be there. You have your own facilities."

Of course, like cold-water showers.

He didn't want Support Unit personnel at liberty in his sphere, so we were restricted to our lines. Although rankled by the formal style of the message, it was a fair decision in order to avoid accusations of theft and misuse, but the tone underscored the 'them and us' attitude in the police. I didn't understand then, but I quickly became aware that the wife was the power behind the throne in his camp, and whatever she wished became law. To resolve the niggling problems, I made sure that we stayed away from the police facilities and they stayed away from us. Tambe was instructed to keep tight reins on the constables. Still, the men sneaked in the odd hot shower and the niggling complaints were ignored.

On the second day, I sought out the Special Branch representative and was shocked to meet a young National Serviceman. Special Branch employed hardcore CID personnel – professionals with years' experience – but with intelligence assets stretched thin, Chibi wasn't a gold-plated posting for the old hands. Clearly, Rob worked the best he could with what he had, but with little practical police experience, he battled to produce anything worthwhile. He conscientiously typed reports and logs to his masters in Fort Victoria, but produced no information that could be acted upon. Deathly afraid of venturing out beyond the wire, he relied totally on snippets that walked in through the gate, or via the District Commissioner's office. We were stumped.

In his cramped office, he walked me through the history and expanded on nationalist supporters and known subverted areas. Again, the briefing was full of stuffing, but of little value. I studied his wall map and traced the logged incidents. The usual incidents were marked in colored pins that were dotted here and there. The history log spelled out the incidents. In terms of casualties, no CTs had been killed here. They must be on the ascension.

The Chibi area totaled around 250 square kilometers – far too much terrain for one 30-man troop. There was also lively activity around Berejena Mission, south of our base, but I couldn't be in all places at once. The Mission conjured up thoughts of Wedza and Inyanga North, which were places to avoid. I decided to operate north and west of Chibi village and concentrate sections around Takavarashe – a township at the base of large granite hills – and St Joseph School, which was to the north in the flat, agricultural land. The incident map was dotted with the history of CT sightings and contacts in those areas.

Once again, armed with zero intelligence, three recce patrols left base to get the feel of the tribal lands. It was step one in drawing a picture of the nationalist grip on the population and to pinpoint geographical areas most likely to produce quick results. Early success kept our people motivated. After four days, all patrols returned and reported the population was totally subverted and completely obstructive. Whole *kraal* lines evacuated in front of a patrol and disappeared into the ragged bush. It was the worst subversion I had witnessed to date.

My patrol shot and killed a youth running away. He was one of at least three killed in the tour. Once the youths sighted us, they fled at top speed. Despite shouting out: "Halt!" and firing a warning shot, they didn't slow. The second shot killed them. They knew the game: if they'd stopped, they'd be alive. We were not hampered by a political set of rules on when lethal force could be used. If they ran, refused to halt when warned, and then ignored the warning shot, they were CTs and shot.

The CTs had successfully entwined in the social fabric. We heard that the elders worked with spirit mediums to bridge the gap between the young ZANLA fighters, who originated outside the area, and the locals to provide a format where tribal customs and law flourished. The CTs had usurped the District Commissioner's role. The war had stunted the District Commissioner and his courts. The District Commissioner had not personally ventured out of the Chibi village for months. When I broached Internal Affairs with information that suggested ZANLA had taken over their legal role, I was treated with contempt. The Intaf men adopted a defensive posture. What would I know? We combined OPs with open patrols to flush out targets.

Firstly, just to get an idea of the CTs' movements, the daily questioning in the *kraals* began. We sat for hours – looking into defiant, stoic or ambivalent brown eyes – listening to the adamant and sharp (or whispered and fearful) rebuff of our questions. Denial piled upon denial: no, they hadn't seen the *macandangas*; no, they had never heard of them; no, they had not fed them. They remained stubborn and emphatic. It was a grindingly slow, painstaking and time-absorbing process. Talk, question, yell, threaten, talk, appease and the next one please – at a rate of three to four *kraals* a day – was an exhausting process. All the section leaders reported a stubborn, anti-government population.

On patrol after a quick break, my section scoured the northern region. We planted ourselves on a small hill and surveyed the countryside. Hours later, the constables spotted something.

"Shit, there are three o' them," Mandaza muttered from the low rock overseeing St Joseph School.

"Where?"

"On the soccer pitch."

I saw them. They stood in denuded country 400 meters from our position. I snatched the Zeiss binoculars from the backpack and magnified the stoic faces and military equipment. There was no mistake. They were stood dressed in green and denim, with one wearing a black waist-length coat; two had AKM assault rifles clearly strapped to their backs on a canvas sling; one was holding an RPK machine gun. Two other males, dressed in light blue cotton shirts and brown cotton trousers, stood casually chatting to them in the goal zone on the open soccer pitch.

"Fuckin' bullseye!" I smiled.

With the fine-focus knob, I noted none of the three terrorists carried bags or packs, so they were based somewhere nearby. A radio call for Fireforce to India Base was relayed through to JOC Fort Victoria. The five men calmly chatted – waving their arms to reinforce points. They laughed. The call soon came back: Fireforce was not available.

"Shit," I spat – checking my watch.

To order a section from Chibi would take too long. By the time they had slipped into their equipment, mounted the trucks, drove and then humped cross-country, two hours would easily have slipped by. The two other sections operated the other side of Takavarashe. I briefly entertained the notion of shooting from our position; then instantly ruled it out. I was not a Paddy Allen when it came to long-range shooting.

"Here we go," I stated, as I tucked the binoculars away, "follow me."

Scooting down the small, rocky outcrop – bounding from boulder to boulder like baboons – we assembled at the base and then sprinted through the acacia trees and on to the border of the barren land adjacent to the soccer field. The CTs and their companions had gone.

"Shit!"

The CTs' tracks – strong imprints at first – simply vanished on granite slabs.

"Shit!"

Where from here? I scanned the scattered school buildings.

"We'll go back an' search those places."

We walked directly to the school; the grounds were clearly empty, not a soul in sight. The school consisted of two long classroom blocks – simple and stark in the brown countryside. Beyond the buildings, a hundred meters away, a cluster of small houses were visible. Leaving Chewa, Mandaza, Banda and Chipangora to search the school buildings, Moyo, Tsumba, Mandoza and

I strode over to the houses. The men began a house-to-house, building-to-building search. They were simple brick and iron sheeting roof cottages. The distinct scent of Africa tickled the nostrils – the aroma of dust, wood and campfire. Finally, after knocking on three doors without a response, the fourth door opened and a man answered. I stepped back. As he stepped into the light, I recognized him. He was the same man I spotted chatting with the CTs.

I greeted him and asked: "You're a teacher?"

"Yes," he stated – folding his arms.

"Then I'll make this simple," I replied. "Were you standing on the football ground an hour ago?"

"No," he responded flatly – his eyes widening.

"With the 'Brothers'?"

"Of course not."

"An hour ago?"

"I've been inside all day," he stated confidently.

"Can someone vouch for that?"

He hesitated; his angular face twitched.

"Chris ... Hey Chris!" he called.

Anger swelled deep in my gut – the lying fuckin' bastard!

Another male emerged from the darkness behind him.

"Chris, tell these people I was here today."

"He was here ... inside."

Fury shot through my blood like hot pokers.

The second man was definitely the other man on the field – still dressed in the same light blue cotton shirt and brown cotton trousers. He hadn't even changed.

"You weren't out on the football field an hour ago?"

"No, I've been marking school papers inside," his voice warbled in fright.

"You fuckin' liars! I saw you and you standing out there – cuddling up to those three ZANLA bitches!"

Rage spurted forth like hot vomit and tweaked the muscles. I could seriously hurt these bastards! Fuckin' defending the indefensible! Cunts!

Both men tightened up – fright and despair colored their faces.

"I fuckin' saw you two with these fuckin' eyes!" I spat – pointing my finger at my eyes.

"It wasn't us," murmured one – looking nervous at the ground.

"Moyo," I snarled, "bail 'em up an' I'll get Acorn on the blower. We should

A burnt-out store; Chibi TTL, 1977.

shoot you lying bastards!"

After a year in the bush, I found it difficult to remain calm and objective in the face of continual rejection of the facts. After scores and scores of days over months filled with our questions and their passionate denials, their two-faced words grated inside me. The rebuffs particularly riled if the party questioned absolutely and emphatically denied something I just witnessed, but they knew that if they stubbornly held onto that line of bullshit, they might get a punch at worst. Sometimes, I obliged and other times, I did not (it was dependent on my mood and the circumstances), but the retribution meted out by ZANLA – if they cooperated – made any beating pale in comparison.

I switched tactics to mount a series of OPs overlooking prime suspect regions. At dawn one morning, still bathed in the clearing dawn light, my section – together with young Graeme – lay an OP on a heavily wooded ridge overlooking the area east of Takavarashe. Entrenched on the second day, there was an expectation of at least another day on the rugged hillside. The sun had not peeped over the horizon.

'*Macandangas!*' hissed Moyo – observing the valley below. "At least 40," he added nonchalantly.

"What?" I choked – freezing automatically – my plastic water bottle suspended half-way out of the canvas carrier.

The OP had not been set up based on intelligence, just a gut feeling. Most OPs accomplish nothing. Maybe a spotter sees CTs once in 10 different OPs or, more likely, whatever they see allows us to interpret the signs of the terrorists' presence. These were long odds, if it meant remaining hidden – sweaty and grubby, bored, tormented by insects and weather, and always low on water.

"Where?"

"Walking across the mealie field … down there," he nodded – his head indicating the flat plains that funneled into the scenic defile – "towards our *kraal*. See 'em?"

You bet! Two Y formations, each of 20 terrorists, traversed the open fields. One Y was leading, with the other stomping directly behind. Awash in the first rays of the new day, they walked arrogantly in plain view – silhouetted perfectly against the dead maize stalks. There was no mistake: the rigid formation, the striding pace, the natty clothes all screamed *macandanga*! My adrenalin leapt up two notches. My stomach knotted. The cheeky fuckin' bastards! I snatched the plastic handset from the A73 pack radio and squeezed the transmit bar.

"Mantle India Base, this is Mantle India One," I croaked into the mouthpiece – still mesmerized by the tactical formation gliding through the broken maize.

"Mantle India One, this is Base, read you fives, good mornin', go ahead, over," boomed the cheerful voice.

"Mantle India Base, roger. I have four zero Charlie Tangoes visual. I say again, four zero, over."

"This is India Base, copied, over," the voice tone sobered instantly.

"Roger. My locstat is unchanged from last night. They're below my loc, 400 meters to the north-east, moving west," I said into the mouthpiece, as my whole mindset focused on the prey below. "I request Foxtrot Foxtrot for this one, over."

India Base read out the exact grid location.

Although I committed the locstat to memory, I still squinted at the scrawled handwriting squeezed into the white margin on the map, where I had penciled my present location on the first night.

"That's affirmative, over."

"This is India Base; can you confirm weapons visual, over?"

"India One, course I can," I snapped and immediately regretted it. I knew that weapons would be the first question the sad tacticians at the JOC asked, so I added light-heartedly: "Do you want the serial numbers, over?"

"Negative," laughed the operator, "I'll be straight back to you, over."

"Roger out," I smiled.

The comment about weapons irritated me. Why radio if I wasn't so certain? I lowered the handset and switched my attention to the field. They had walked three quarters of the way across the stubble-filled field. I raised and focused the Zeiss binoculars. The enemy figures jumped sharply into view, as they traipsed directly towards our *kraal*: denim jeans, different colored shirts, travel bags slung over the back and assorted headgear. Armed with a combination of light automatic weapons and at least three RPG rocket launchers, they strode comfortably and cockily.

The binoculars swung across to the village: an older man stood on the fringe – his arms outstretched in welcome. The girls hustled – giggling and skipping – anticipating the arrival of rock stars. Kids flocked to the village perimeter. Older women scattered into the brush to gather dry wood for fires, while others scurried off to bordering villages to round up mealie-meal to accommodate the 'Brothers'' hunger. The bed and breakfast hostel was open for business … let the games begin.

JOC vacillated for over an hour: "Yes, Fireforce is ready … no, there's been another sighting … yes, but are you sure they have weapons? Hold on, no, there's other activity, so wait … "

Meanwhile, the elder guided the Y formations into the thick scrub – 20 meters from his *kraal* – and shook each man's hand as they filed past. The formation broke up and the terrorists followed each other into the trees – merging with the thick vegetation. Fortunately, their exact position remained visible, with the odd one or two emerging from the scrubby green belt to talk to the local people. I diligently wrote the village map coordinates on the white margin – ready to read out to the Fireforce commander. I then carefully studied the topography for suitable cut-off routes.

The OP hill formed the east arm of a wide re-entrant into very craggy hill country. The village sat opposite on the west side – jammed up against trees and solid granite. The land south consisted of a jumble of rough granite hills, which were amply covered in wild woods – presenting generous escape routes. To the north, wide fields, flat *veldt* and arable country spread out for kilometers – dotted with chess-like *kopjes*. Even an unskilled tactician could judge that parachute troops in the northern, flat, ploughed country would provide an immediate cut-off to ZANLA survivors racing north. The deforested, flat, sandy soil was ideal for parachute landings. Once in place, they'd completely block off the mouth to the re-entrant and seal it shut. Helicopters could then drop Stop Groups into the twisted rock valleys to the south in order to shut off straightforward escape routes.

The scenario below was a perfect killing ground. The village was hemmed in by solid granite hills on three sides – east, west and south – with the northern end a chokepoint if troops sealed off the re-entrant. It was like a natural inland harbor. Trapped inside this arena, the CTs should be lambs to the slaughter – an easy elimination of 40 enemies.

We laid back and studied the unfolding events. Two CTs emerged from the shadows and entered the village to confer with the villagers. The logistics and supply machine cranked up: women on the move – their colored cotton frocks spotted in the scrub – were carrying aluminum buckets on their heads and fetching water from a nearby stream; others carted in bundles of tied dry firewood – balanced on their heads – back to the *kraal*. Village men entered the tree line, where the enemy squatted. Whilst the activity had kicked up a notch, it did not appear frantic. I wondered whether they were staying for the day. Meanwhile, the silent A73 radio earpiece hovered close to my ear … come on, you bastards, I willed the JOC – do something.

Another hour crept past. Two outdoor cooking fires were lit and the cooking brigade set up kitchen. The fires burnt fiercely, with little smoke. I scrutinized the village activity: a crew manhandled two large black pots, many surplus folk had disappeared and the two CTs who had ventured in the village were no longer visible. If we had just turned up now and observed the village, questions would be asked about the amount of cooking. The radio suddenly squawked.

"India One, Base."

"Go ahead, over."

"This is India Base. Foxtrot Foxtrot is airborne. Change to channel five, good luck, over."

"India One, roger, out."

We waited and watched. The activity below remained unhurried – oblivious to the preparations from our end. Two active cooking fires supported black iron pots astride, and a steady stream of women, men and kids visited the square of bush that hid the enemy. They acted like long-lost family had arrived.

Ten minutes on, the K-Car commander's mottled voice suddenly burst on air.

"Mantle India One, K-Car, over."

"K-Car, Mantle India One, read you fives, over."

"Roger that," his tone was brisk and clipped. "Confirm your present locstat."

He read the six-figure reference.

"India One, affirmative."

"K-Car, copied. Confirm the gooks are at … "

I quickly rechecked the map margin for the tenth time and confirmed the locstat.

"K-Car, what's happening now, over?"

"This is India One, the Charlie Tangoes are stationary in scrub at the head of the entrant. The locals are preparing a meal in the *kraal* on the west side. You'll see the smoke, so they'd be settled in, over."

"What sort of numbers, over?"

"India One, we counted four zero, over."

"Copied that," his voice pruned off the words. "What's the terrain like there, over?"

"India One, to the south, it's extremely rugged *kopjes*, no good for parachutes," I confirmed, as my eyes reassessed the terrain, "but to the north, it's fairly open, flat country – a mixture of maize fields, paddocks and light scrub – much better for a para drop. You'd cut off escape routes to the south with chopper Stop Groups, an' seal 'em in the northern re-entrant with the paras, over."

"K-Car, I'll determine the tactics," snapped the aloof voice.

"Shit," I thought, as I pictured an arrogant puss in charge.

"India One, K-Car," the voice continued, "I'm two minutes out, an' will be flyin' in from the south. Let me know as soon as you hear us, over."

"Copied," I replied into the handset and then turned to the constables: "Listen out for choppers … they're on their way in."

"I can hear 'em," stated Moyo within 20 seconds.

I relayed the message to the K-Car commander, who grunted a reply.

The four Alouette helicopters flew gracefully up from the south – low and nicely tucked behind the mass of granite hills – with the jet turbine noise suppressed by the layers of gray rock. They neatly rounded the rugged hills, where the rocky slopes met the timbered riverbed, and soared over Takavarashe to appear magically over their target before the CTs knew they were there – perfect, or it should have been; then it all went to shit …

The first helicopter soared low and right into the re-entrant – close enough for India to clearly see the two soldiers sitting in the open doorway. They looked tense, with their eyes fixed on the ground below, gripping their rifles. The Alouette banked slightly – heading directly towards the village and losing altitude rapidly. Everyone engaged in cooking scattered and fled.

"Why are they doin' that?" I asked no one, "can't they see the smoke?"

Chewa shot me a worried glance, but thankful we sat out of range for this fight. To my horror, the aircraft flared as it approached the ground, and the wheels kissed the grainy dirt 20 meters from the cooking fires, right in front of the ZANLA hiding place. Jesus! A storm of automatic fire shattered the air, with green and orange tracer rocketing from the tree line. The sharp rattle of machine gun fire rebounded off the hills – magnifying to a solid thunder.

In the split-second between the tire rubber hitting the dirt and the barrage of bullets, a lone RLI soldier jumped from the doorway – marginally ahead of the other three soldiers. As the man soared into space, the helicopter pilot noted the wall of green and orange tracer zapping around him, and didn't wait for an invitation; he took instant evasion action. The Alouette powered back into space to dodge the bullets and got the hell out of there, but the pilot unknowingly abandoned one guy. Left in front of the enemy's hornet's nest, the soldier fought a one-man war – shooting his way out – and, I believe, was decorated for this action.

A second Alouette swooped down to deposit troops behind the village, and again flew into a storm of RPG and small arms fire from a small group that had split from the main body. Suddenly, the sky and the bush sparkled and crackled with gunfire. An RPG rocket zoomed past the helicopter, but just missed and jetted off into the clear blue sky to self-detonate. A brown puff in the sky looked like flak. I watched in despair. Bullets ripped and whizzed in the sky – chasing the Alouette. Why are they determined to land on top of the enemy? Where's the southern block group? Within seconds of a heavy barrage, the helicopter pilot took instant action, banked sharply and zoomed out of the danger zone – chased by green tracer dots.

The third helicopter dropped a group of four soldiers east of the re-entrant. Why are they there, below our hill? What does that achieve? So far, in the opening minute, Fireforce had not blocked any escape routes plotted south of the village. One four-man stick waited on in the old maize field at the base of our OP, just opposite the village – the only boots on the ground. The other two sticks were still airborne, with one soldier lost – a terrific start!

An overworked DC-3 Dakota droned overhead and dropped parachutists.

"Ah ... shit," I swore, as we watched the parachutists launch from the open aircraft door – their parachutes bellowing open and plunging through the sky, and straight towards the granite rock outcrops to the south and east of the village (not into the soft fields, as advised). I couldn't believe it. After tumbling out of the aircraft door, the parachutists had only about 15-20 seconds in the air before they landed heavily amongst the granite. Their green silk canopies disappeared into the tree cover. They looked like they were sucked into the tree vortex.

Time ticked on. Suddenly, the parachute stick leaders shouted on the radio about leg and back injuries among their men. Their talk burst on the radio net – back and forth to K-Car. The K-Car commander – impatient and concerned – snapped at the circling helicopters to extract the casualties. The two laden helicopters swooped down, landed in the maize field and ditched their men to make room for casualties. No one had been positioned to cut off the CTs; the helicopter sticks were simply dumped to empty the helicopters. Once the injured men were aboard the waiting helicopters, they were shuttled to Fort Victoria. Their evacuation became the priority, so within 10 minutes, one RLI soldier was missing and at least six soldiers were injured – unable to continue. Two helicopters were out, as they raced back to Fort Victoria – carrying injured parachutists. The force on the ground was now substantially whittled down. The parachutists and chopper sticks were jumbled together and paralyzed. The stick leaders were uncertain what the priorities were. The southern escape routes were not sealed off. The northern escape possibilities remained completely open. All the infantry waited – clumped untidily in the south and east of the target *kraal* – and time ticked on.

Slowly, disorder on the ground began to untangle as K-Car resumed the battle. The commander issued brisk orders. Small firefights suddenly erupted, but the enemy broke into small packets and sneaked out without being pinned down. The contacts ebbed and flowed, but from where I sat, there seemed to be a lack of cohesion. There were a number of scattered firefights, but no shouts of triumph. The vast majority of gunfights occurred under the green leaf canopy, so we were unable to see anything other than the stray, colored phosphorus tracer zipping through the treetops. We could hear the cacophony of weapons firing aggressively and one-sided radio calls from the K-Car. It was rather like trying to watch a game of rugby from outside the ground, through the tiny cracks in the fence. We heard the throaty roar of the crowd and the shrill cry of the whistle, but saw little of the action.

The K-Car commander was scathing: 'India One, stay awake up there!' he warned. That was his total motivational contribution – as if I'd go to sleep!

He must have skipped breakfast, and now he was a grumpy sod. He certainly didn't get a tight grip on the situation: radio transmissions bounced between the Stop Groups and the commander, but still there were no confirmed kills. Fortunately, the wayward soldier had been recovered. Helicopters returned from Fort Victoria and dived down to uplift troops and juggle their locations to get a bite on the enemy. The CTs retreated back into the main re-entrant and began to fade away, one at a time, into the mishmash of rock and bush. Understrength and poorly positioned block groups failed to plug the major escape holes from the initial trap.

A Lynx joined in – flying high overhead. A solitary airplane circled far above us – a black dot in the blue sky – out of bullet range. The pilot advised K-Car he could get a Canberra bomber to stir things up. A bomber was primed – sitting on the runway. The K-Car commander readily agreed. He eagerly grasped the lifebelt and ordered his Stop Groups to disengage, pull back one click and wait. (Walking back a thousand meters was the minimum safety margin for a bombing run.) Obviously, this maneuver gobbled up more precious time.

I listened to the progress on the radio and thought: "Why?"

He still had time to maneuver Stop Groups and shuffle them into a position; compress the Stop Groups over a tighter area to trap slower-moving CTs. With a little foresight and a touch of bravado, they might snare at least a dozen and just concentrate on eliminating them.

More time ticked on. India sat on the grandstand hillside for 40 minutes and watched the broken terrain in silence. Agitated by what I concluded was a wasted opportunity, there was nothing I could do but watch. Nothing moved down there; all firing had ceased. The smoke still emitted from the cooking fires. The helicopters flew off, one at a time, to the Chibi village to refuel. The occasional broadcast from Stop Groups garbled over the radio waves. The only consistent sound was the steady drone of the lonely Cessna flying high overhead. Using binoculars, I closely studied the battlefield; every African eyeball strained as well. Apart from a leaf rattling in the hot breeze, even a gnat was invisible. The cornered enemy were either long gone, or had decided to camouflage up and sit it out.

Time ticked on. The Lynx pilot burst on the airwaves and talked to the Canberra pilot – asking about the ordnance on board, the approach run, the estimated time of arrival and all the technical stuff. The K-Car commander interrupted and suggested some fancy approach to the target, to which the Canberra pilot snorted: "I'm a fuckin' bomber, not a fighter."

While we intently studied the quiet re-entrant, unexpectedly, there was an almighty WHOOOSH! The dark shadow of the Canberra shot close over our position and dropped hundreds of Alpha bombs up the re-entrant. We didn't even hear its approach, just WHOOOSH; then bombs away! The round Alpha bombs, much like a large lawn bowling ball, were dumped from the open bomb bay as the bomber climbed and showered them over the re-entrant – a carpet bombing exercise a hundred meters wide and a thousand meters long. The bombs were designed to bounce when they struck the ground – arming and exploding about six feet off the ground, which was super-deadly to exposed bodies.

The twin jet engines roared distinctly as the Canberra accelerated and climbed to fly over the hill country, followed by the sounds of bombs exploding below. Unsure of their capability, we all ducked behind a granite wall and waited till it was over. We were well out of range, but hell, why tempt fate? The explosions ended, and their roar echoed off the hills. The jet engines dimmed in the clear blue sky; then the quiet soaked up the residue noise.

The show was finally over: the block groups sat a kilometer away; the CTs still in the re-entrant hung their blue denim jackets in the trees to attract the helicopter gunners, while they slunk away. There were plenty of bullet holes in the denim, but the wearers got clean away. Suddenly, Mandaza saw six terrorists attempting to maneuver their way out.

"K-Car, India One," I radioed, as I scanned the enemy flitting from rock to rock.

"India One, K-Car, get off the net!" snapped the K-car commander viciously.

"K-Car, we have six 'floppies' visual under a rock outcrop," I called into the handset – ignoring his response.

"India One, K-Car, get off the fucking radio net now," growled the army commander, as he switched to one of his callsigns.

I watched helplessly as the six ducked from rock to rock, and then finally disappeared from sight. I had talked to some snotty commanders in my time, but this one was the worst. I put the low rate of kills directly in his lap. If he had followed my directions, the result would have been much, much better.

Four CTs were confirmed killed and six weapons were recovered – a very poor payoff, considering the large target, the corral re-entrant they were trapped in and the resources applied. The RLI rapidly wound up and pulled out – leaving us with the quiet battlefield. My lasting impression was the large number of unexploded Alpha bombs that lay in the bent grass.

Some days later – still patrolling the OP area – a short, sharp contact crackled as we engaged the unseen enemy; we had uncovered a CT resting area. A woman in her twenties was flushed out – slightly wounded (a bullet had creased her arm). Forcing her to sit, we vigilantly skirted through the undercover. My gut rolled into a tight ball once more. Tsumba glimpsed blue cloth, aimed and then, inexplicably, paused. He eyeballed a CT – hiding in the scrub. He nearly stood on him, the man lay so still. Fortunately for Tsumba, he wasn't a 'fight to the bitter end' type. Wounded with a gut shot, he still had his webbing harness strapped on, with AK magazines and two stick grenades, but had lost his rifle. Dressed in three sets of clothing – the standard escape and evasion plan, where the top set is discarded to confuse a spotter – he also sported *chimurenga* colors: a dual-colored cloth, worn inside the three shirts, to identify the detachment. Tsumba squatted down and examined the wound. The bullet had passed through the midriff and had punched a tangerine-sized hole out his back.

"You should have shot him," I snapped at the medic – angry like a parent who has watched their child suddenly wander onto a busy highway. I was angry, but relieved.

"This is old … maybe from that OP contact," Tsumba commented, as he opened his medical pack – ignoring my rebuke.

"Is he fucked?" I asked.

Without replying, Tsumba scrupulously applied two field dressings. He worked without talking, while the section secured the area. He set up a saline drip, while Chewa and Chipangora constructed a makeshift stretcher. Once Tsumba was satisfied with his handiwork, the men gently slid the capture onto the makeshift rig. Although in acute pain, the terrorist didn't moan. Walking the woman out, Mandaza and Banda manhandled the wounded CT on the stretcher as gently as possible to an open field.

In his early twenties, and with good English, the wounded man and I chatted as we waited for a helicopter to uplift him. The conversation was light-hearted; I'd leave the serious shit to Special Branch.

"Is there any room for whites in your new Zimbabwe?" I asked out of curiosity.

"Sure," he smiled smugly, "we'd need you all to stay to hoe the mealie fields."

I laughed.

I wonder if I'd have the guts to say something like that if I was wounded-captured. Excruciating pain prevented him from getting too chatty, so we made him comfortable till a casevac arrived. The helicopter whisked him away, but unfortunately for SB, he died on the way.

Some days later, my section reverted to the St Joseph School area – patrolling along the boundary with the cattle ranches.

"Hisssss!" Mandaza sounded through his teeth – his arm up, signaling STOP.

We froze.

A movement in the dry riverbed caught our eye. Five young women walked and skipped across the coarse sand – laughing and chatting excitedly, like they were on the way to a local dance – and then they scrambled up the small, sandy embankment opposite and melted into the ranching country. In less than a half a minute, the green and brown mottled scrub swallowed them. They were so engrossed in their light chatter, they didn't see us. Instinct tingled like light electricity; I sensed something was on. I nodded to Mandaza to follow. Crossing the sandy river base in the women's footprints, the section vigilantly climbed the small embankment on the other side.

Standing on the opposite bank, we were greeted by wiry trees and long grass. A rusted wire cattle fence ran at right angles from the riverbank and a dirt track snaked next to the boundary wire – disguised by knee-high brown grass. There was no sign of the women. Mandaza bent over and studied the baked, hard footpath. Walking behind him on the concrete-like surface, I judged finding *spoor* to be near impossible. Mandaza shuffled a few meters – his eyes fixed on the track surface. I covered him by watching over the fence into the trees on the right.

Abruptly, an old man blundered straight into the tracker. He burst out of the tall grass – almost tangling with a startled Mandaza. When he banged into us, the old man suffered an instant attack of nerves and a sudden voltage of muscular spasms, as well as managing a fidgety, flickering smile. If the situation were not so dangerous, I would have laughed out loud. Mandaza shoved him to one side. The man stumbled, with fear stamped in his wrinkled face. The men smelled the enemy … very close. Blood pumped through my ears and my stomach curled up. The elder fled across the sandy riverbed.

The men guardedly crept along the rusted fence line – all senses finely attuned. Without having to be told, everyone knew a clash lay tantalizingly close. Safety catches clicked onto fire. All sets of eyes scoured the dry grass and thorn scrub country. The tall grass angled down to ankle height further away from the fence line. Up ahead, I saw nothing but dry and jaded grass country.

A movement caught my eye … it was a smudge at first; then – striding out of the tarnished bush – two armed terrorists walked idly, parallel to us, as if on a city stroll. Both were dressed in light blue jeans and a greenish shirt – one with a blue baseball cap and the other donning a black beret. Mandaza signaled 'enemy' with the classical thumbs down, like the Roman Emperor giving the death sign to the vanquished. They hadn't seen us, because they were too busy chatting. The sighting was surreal, like partaking in a movie. The enemy fighters traipsed across the brittle grass – one with a cigarette dangling from his lips. I cautiously swung the section in an extended line – pivoting 45°. The maneuver was risky, but brought all weapons to bear. We waited for a few seconds … I nodded and we followed the two CTs discreetly – maintaining a suitable distance.

They linked up with eight others standing together in the speckled shade. The eight stood in a semi-circle – most with their backs to us – engrossed in conversation. The danger radiated from the three standing at the fringe being alert enough to see us slinking in through the light timber and stark scrub, with nowhere to hide. They stood visible from the knees up and, no doubt, so were we. I tensed up – anxiously searching for a sentry standing alone. I minutely surveyed the timber for a man hidden in the shade who might shout a warning.

I thought: "How long should I leave to luck?"

My heart pounded heavily and sweat beaded across my brow. My mouth dehydrated. I thought it was better now than later, so I nodded to Ray and then paused momentarily – targeting one CT. His blue denim jacket filled the whole aperture sight and I squeezed the trigger. The FN roared and the empty shell ejected. The man dropped – poleaxed. Ray fired – pleased to use the red spot optical sight he'd purchased.

"Got 'im in the guts!" he cried.

The rifle fire exploded and the bullets tore into the group. The MAG entered the fray with tidy bursts. A bullet shower smacked into trees, dirt and flesh. Powdery dust burst from bullet strikes and tainted the air. Tracer lit up and sizzled bright red; the thunderous boom of firearms echoed; a burnt cordite and rifle oil aroma filled the nostrils; hot brass zinged through space; the adrenalin gushed to the head. The enemy fell – blurred – a mess of color. They slumped to the ground like wooden puppets that'd had their strings suddenly slashed. It was all over in a minute. Three had attempted to run, but had sprinted straight into a barrage of bullets.

Our extended line walked straight in and Ray sighted a movement: a seriously injured terrorist raised his head above the folded grass and mouthed some words.

"Fuck you," Ray spat – a split-second before he fired again, and the bullet hit the wounded terrorist in the head. The force of the bullet slammed the head backwards – blasting out the back of the skull. Brains and muck and red slop flew out at high speed. We stomped past to claim the bloody ground and then formed a defensive half-circle – waiting for a possible counter-attack (perhaps other terrorist formations that might be lurking close by). My heart pounded with excitement and anticipation – the adrenalin surging through the blood. The counter-attack never arose. Five CTs lay dead or mortally wounded, and seven weapons were scattered in the ankle-long grass.

Once settled into a defensive half-circle, I radioed base with the news. Squatting with the handset to my ear, one new constable broke position and wandered over.

"Can I have a look at these bastards?" he asked mutely, as he knelt.

"Yeah," I replied – waving him off to concentrate on the radio call, but then eying him with mild curiosity. He paced up to each deceased, knelt down next to the inert head, rapped their exposed forehead with a closed fist, like knocking on a door, and mumbled: "One dead, two dead" and so on. I found out later that Constable Mandoza, who had completed a degree in Agriculture at Chibero College and had managed a white-owned farm, had lost his entire family to a killing frenzy up in the north-east. After attending the funeral, he immediately enlisted in Support Unit for the sole purpose of exacting revenge. That day, he confirmed to himself that his revenge was now beginning.

Ray and Mandaza conducted a quick follow-up on blood *spoor*, which led them back to the dry riverbed. The duo crossed over and lost blood signs not far from the opposite bank. The footprints were conspicuously stamped in the gritty sand on the riverbed, but not on the opposite bank, where the soil was baked hard. The ground on the TTL beyond was open and flat. They surveyed the terrain, but could not see a person trying to make headway under an injury, nor any blood splatter. I told Ray not to press on too far, as we lacked a second radio. (Six weeks later, SB uncovered another body buried in the riverbed.)

I was ecstatic. Generally, we killed in ones or twos. Once the shit hit the fan, terrorists took to their shoes and quickly raced out of the danger zone. On our own, we had neither the numbers, nor the communication equipment, to ever effectively cut off escape routes and inflict high rates of casualties – and rarely did they go toe to toe with us. Their job was to get out alive, and some were very good.

Later, Special Branch reported that the dead terrorists were part of a 50-strong unit drawn from both the Chibi and Belingwe TTLs, who had attacked railway sidings near Shabani two nights prior to their death. They were on their way back when we sighted the vital signs and got stuck in.

At the scene, I pocketed a Tokarev pistol. Pistols were in demand on the lucrative black market in Salisbury. A Tokarev 7.62mm semi-automatic pistol fetched $400; cash on delivery, no questions asked. The cash supplemented the drinking money. Any salvaged 60mm mortar tubes were traded. Communist M60 HE and HEAT rifle grenades – a steel green body, with white plastic fins – fitted our rifles perfectly, and so were stowed, as well as 60mm mortar bombs and spare AK ammunition. All other weaponry was handed over to SB.

After a successful contact, the constables looted anything worth taking. They favored foreign-made transistor radios – brands like Sony or Phillips – carried by CTs across the border and stowed in a cloth carry bag. Due to UN sanctions, they were not sold in Salisbury shops, and so were valuable. Cash, Japanese watches, cosmetic jewelry, good spare clothing, travel packs – anything but weaponry. Naïvely, I once handed everything over to Special Branch under the guise of 'intelligence gathering'. Told that intelligence people formed a clearer picture if they possessed every little thing recovered after a contact, it didn't take long before I discovered the property in the hands of 'Jam Stealers'. Once at Rusape, I saw an army store man wearing a Seiko watch we had recovered in Chiduku. Thereafter, the men took first pick of the prizes.

The constables plundered the spare clothing like bargain seekers. Most CTs carried good spare clothing inside a sports kit bag, so shirts, jeans, underwear and jackets of all sizes were tried on, removed and sized up again; however, by now, the removal of spare clothing ceased, by proclamation. The Special Branch's 'Dirty Tricks' Department began to lace the seams in underwear and denim jackets with a poison named parathion, which entered the body through the hair follicles and caused massive internal haemorrhaging and breathing arrest. The spiked clothing was seeded among CT contacts, so any clothing recovered thereafter was burnt – and without telling the constables why (all based upon the 'need to know' premise). They looked upon us as being spiteful pricks for denying them the good-quality clothing.

Canned food fell into the same category. SB had poisoned selected brands of tinned Spam and European canned fish – and, through their slick contacts, the cans fell into the hands of the terrorists. Occasionally, we recovered canned goods and fed it to the dogs – those scrawny canines that lived in the TTLs. They were bag-of-bones mongrels covered by bloated ticks – not a pretty sight. Either the canned stuff was the best feed they'd ever had, or it'd kill them.

Many CT dead carried school exercise books as diaries. Inside, literate CTs painstakingly entered their operational details. We read the paragraphs with a smile. The dates and times and places were accurate, but the contact details were outrageously exaggerated. In one contact, they claimed to have shot down the entire air force! The books also logged a weapons list (with serial numbers), comments on the peasantry, a few names of helpful tribal contacts and justice meted out amongst the CT ranks. The documents were prized by Special Branch and readily handed over.

The base radio announced terrible news: Paddy Allen – my good friend from Delta, who had subsequently taken command of the troop – had died as a result of a vehicle accident. He had rolled a Land Rover when returning to Salisbury and then died days later in hospital. In shock, I motored back to Salisbury for the funeral. I had met his family once, when I was invited to a picnic in Salisbury, and felt for their loss. The police chapel was packed. Family members said their bit in the chapel, and someone spoke the eulogy. I listened to the words feeling detached and separated – the words spoke of a man I did not know. For a second, I thought I was at the wrong funeral; then I realized that I had only met the one dimension: I only knew Paddy the party man, the bushman and the larrikin.

Afterwards, we hit the bars and got seriously pissed. That night, unfortunately, his brother Kiaran was injured in a motor vehicle accident. Gray Barker – driving a Land Rover, with Phil Smith and Kiaran as passengers – miscalculated a corner and collided with a tree on the way back from the party. The three were injured and then ferried to hospital. That news placed enormous stress on his good folks, but fortunately, Kiaran made a full recovery.

I wondered about the pledge Paddy and I had forged: the first to die would reach out and contact the other. I half-expected to see something, as Paddy's reckless determination enabled him to trespass across the abyss between the living and the dead, but there was no signal; no final hurrah. His death confirmed for me that there was no life thereafter. Death was death. Final.

Meanwhile, operations continued. Mick's section entered a *kraal* at night.

The Paddy Allen memorial; Warren Hills, Salisbury.

A woman sorting kindling outside the kitchen hut saw the dark outline of African constables and assumed they were 'Brothers'. She talked to the section sergeant and told him they must flee this place because the 'Ma-Sojers' here were hard men and would surely catch and kill them. The section slipped out of the *kraal* to ensure the lady did not discover her error. Maybe easing into *kraals* after dark more often may result in show and tell? Where's Sergeant Nguruve when you need him?

A call from JOC dispatched the whole troop to patrol the Tokwe River in south-east Chibi, near the Nyoni Hills. It was the first time we had bothered with the southern area of this sprawling TTL. Special Branch stated it was crawling with terrorists. We walked and watched that river valley and ambushed at night. It was a prick of a place, with daunting, towering granite rocks to clamber over. The SB assessment was probably right, but we couldn't find them. The only action was a long-distance running contact that petered out to nothing. The intelligence was too general to be acted upon; we should have stayed in the north. The troop handed over to the incoming troop and fled back to Salisbury.

Sergeant Tambe had found a cushy number back in Salisbury that suited his cynical view. (I had assisted, with a little push.) He had landed among other senior African police that ran gambling schools in the barracks, as both the bank and the lender of last resort, who used stand-over tactics to bully the young, naïve constables. Their income included loan sharking, theft of government petrol, theft of petrol ration coupons, spotter's fees for married accommodation and so on, so it was right up his alley!

Phil Smith was up to old tricks! Once again, he volunteered to extend his bush tour. He switched to the troop that relieved his troop, before rejoining his troop once they redeployed. In theory, this meant he spent 15 weeks on operations before coming back to Salisbury on R&R. It was to make more money, he said. The Support Unit HQ wasn't excited about men staying on operations for extended periods; however, they grudgingly agreed, as experienced manpower was at a premium. Once he changed troops, Phil organized parties in Salisbury, hijacked the troop's Land Rover on some operational pretext, and zapped back on the odd weekend to blast off with booze and women. He finally overstepped the mark when an officer sighted him among a rowdy crowd at a rugby match in Salisbury, when technically he should have been footslogging it north of Bindura. Extended tours of duty were terminated forthwith.

During the hectic R&R, at a low-key dinner function, I met Christine through a mutual friend. English-born, she once had a career in the British Consulate Service before she and her folks emigrated. Her posting to the USSR made for interesting discussions over dinner. A warm-hearted woman with a challenging brain, she was too good for a self-absorbed drunk. Christine and I stayed a few days at the Montclair Casino Hotel, outside of Juliasdale. It was a beautiful hotel set on 200 acres, with luxury facilities including a casino. I felt insecure, as the facility was extra-close to the Makoni hunting grounds. Having spent months scouring the countryside for ZANLA, it was surreal to be wining and dining at a classy hotel within ZANLA's reach, unarmed.

After R&R, the troop reported back to Tomlinson Depot to spend a week retraining. The first day heralded vigorous PT to flush out the week's boozing, followed by small sessions of foot drill and kit inspection under the scrutiny of Sergeant Chewa. From there, troops were scheduled to attend four days out at the battle camp in Concession – practicing minor tactics and honing in the shooting skills.

I avoided Concession. My relationship with Paddy Baldwin had soured, so I saw the boss – Assistant Commissioner Collins – and asked permission to train my own men. He gave the OK and I steered clear of the formal training regime. Thereafter, I would withdraw communist weapons from the main police armory in Morris Depot, equip and dress a section out as terrorists, and have the other sections practice and re-practice the contact drills – using these 'terrorists' on the outskirts of the battle camp. The men reckoned seeing this group dressed and armed like the enemy got the adrenalin pumping. We received a frivolous complaint about the terrorist exercises from a Concession farmer, so I sent my 'gooks' to visit him when he was working alone in his tractor sheds. His life unraveled before his eyes – and there were no more complaints after that heart-starter.

Chibi TTL, November 1977

In November, India returned. In my mind, the first deployment was a success because we had shaken up the resident detachment and inflicted casualties, but I was stunned by the reception at Fort Victoria JOC.

After the standard briefing at JOC, a message arrived from Special Branch asking me to attend an urgent meeting. I strolled among the semi-permanent demountable buildings to their office, knocked on the open door and stepped inside. An African servant wandered in straight behind me – carting a tray – and began clearing away the three empty teacups sitting on the wooden desk. I moved aside – giving him room. In clear view, on the varnished desktop, lay a manila file on a proposed operation against the terrorist camps. Curious, I flicked open the cover and skimmed the first page on the situation. Impulsively, the anti-establishment streak urged that I snatch the file to demonstrate the pathetic security. I was sorely tempted. Fortunately, sanity prevailed, as I had trod in enough shit without making another enemy. Besides, the tea boy had probably read the dossier and had taken notes.

I was astounded by the lazy trust many white people put into their black servants – particularly when bound up in a war of ideology. Farmers like the boss in Centenary religiously padlocked his security fence every night, but slipped the cook an entry key to enable him to unlock the gates from the outside to make the first pot of tea at 4:00 a.m. There seemed little point to meticulously lock themselves inside the fence if a person on the outside pocketed a key. A number of white farmers were murdered after a 'trusted' employee palmed the key onto the CTs. The neighbors' voices stung in surprise and shock that a loyal employee had willingly handed over the key to the murderers after 20 years of service.

Inside Security Force bases, African servants enjoyed an amazing degree of unfettered access to offices and operation rooms – cleaning and serving unchecked among secret maps and documents. The busy batman washed their soldier's clothes and cleaned boots, while sniffing out gems. A coy African barman – hand washing and stacking glasses – would be carefully listening to the tactical conversation among half-pissed officers over their cold beer. These people would have been wonderful sources of information. India Troop was also guilty of this relaxed security – employing a batman from Salisbury to accompany each tour. ZANLA didn't need any 'Mr Big' traitors in the Security Force HQ.

The senior detective burst into the prefab office and the African ducked out, unseen. He glowered as he strode across the floor and stabbed a finger on the wall map, without introducing himself; then he angrily launched into a stormy lecture. He loudly claimed India were hooligans in Chibi – 'undoing' the good work. By whom? What was he on about? The furious verbal assault shook me. Special Branch had given up absolutely nothing. If they were working away in there, I never saw an inkling of their work.

"Shooting civilians, beating *povo*, reports of theatrical stuff and other indiscretions," his tirade continued – his voice raised in a genuine, five-star dressing down.

I had expected muted congratulations on our success in Chibi, but instead had been greeted by a red-faced, angry man. When I objected to his invective, he snapped back.

"There are civilized standards in war, O'Brien," he growled irritably, "and I expect you to abide by them."

What was he talking about? He harangued me as if we were in the business of wholesale butchery – lining up slabs of people and executing them. Apart from two or three young men fleeing, who were shot in the heat of the moment, our brutality was a few thick ears and a boot up the arse. Some people receive worse in custody in a police station for a petty crime. I thought we were remarkably restrained. Special Branch could hardly be so righteous with their clandestine poisoning and dirty tricks campaign.

Offended, I counter-attacked on my hobby horse: "If we disappeared and just hid in the bush and did nothing, you'd be happy because there'd be no complaints," I rattled off.

It boiled down to the fact that impotent units didn't attract the attention of the JOC committee. They simply became a non-entity and the commander was not rebuked for a lack of success, but if a unit approach was aggressive – and a few toes were squashed in the process – that 'terribly British' attitude would then spew out from some senior officers; that bullshit code of 'fair play' – attributed to the British by its former colony. The joke was that the British proved ruthless in Northern Ireland when it came to suppressing dissent.

"That's not what I'm saying," he grunted. "You can be aggressive without being bastards."

"Using whose intelligence?" I asked in a smart-arse fashion.

He just glared at me – hostility lit up his eyes – but he didn't retaliate.

"You're not goin' back in there. That's final!" He snapped and rudely brushed past me, and stomped out of the room. "Wait here!" he barked, as he disappeared down the path.

I stood alone in his office – well, thank you very much. Fuck, do you think I care? Chibi, Chiduku, Wedza, whatever … they're all the same. Banned from Chibi, I'd be chucked into some other shithole. What difference did it make to me? None. This dressing down had the bitching District Commissioner's fingerprints over it.

On our last tour, the District Commissioner attempted to maneuver the troop into situations that suited him. He wanted more guard duties – particularly of his own convoys in Chibi – but that was not our role and I resisted his meddling. Also, no doubt, complaints would have filtered back from the tribe's people. They were not happy with our assertive actions, just as we weren't overjoyed with their open support for ZANLA. The legitimate complaints were mixed with hearsay and propaganda pushed forward by ZANLA to undermine our role. There was always an element of lies and twisted facts shaped by the CTs and fed back through the population to the government authorities. Unfortunately, the DC never confronted me directly about any concerns laid at his feet – thus we caused ripples in his kingdom, and the DC sniped back.

We could have also inadvertently trodden all over a Special Branch project or threatened a Special Branch informer. There were no limitations placed on our plate, so how would we know? We were not guided by orders to stay clear of an area or persons. If we tripped some secret operation – to advance the campaign from our perspective – we wouldn't know. It was the blind leading the blind.

Unfortunately, propaganda shot out by the government-enforced silence. Everywhere, colorful posters challenged people to remain silent. One pictured showed a soldier, dead in a pool of blood, with the caption: 'Who talked?' The repression of loose talk was understandable, but some commanders used that cloak to avoid criticism. The imposed silence isolated halfwits in charge from direct questions and robust debate. The senior men were imbued with all the talent – and questioning the commanders' performance was almost unpatriotic.

I believed that certain senior commanders saw the writing on the wall and decided the war was not winnable. After all, they coveted the bigger picture and had a grander view of the overall security situation. As a result, they silently modified their own behavior and expectations to salvage their pension entitlements and, for the more ambitious, sought ways to ingratiate themselves with the new regime should the unthinkable happen. As they had all their assets tied up in the country, it would be natural not to jeopardize them. In the end, self-interest surpasses other considerations. I believed that then, and still believe it.

I ambled outside and sat in the sun – and I couldn't believe the dressing down. The troop toiled vigorously. We were hard-nosed about results, and used every tool at our fingertips to complete the mission, but we weren't thugs. My biggest mistake was thinking it mattered what I thought. I'm just a gnat on an elephant's bum – and a bloody foreigner to boot. I tossed around whether to pull the plug and leave, to fly off to Europe. I stewed over the sharp, verbal dressing down. After 30 minutes, he stormed back to the office and angrily told me to piss off. He had been overruled; Badger had ironed matters out. The angry man didn't even bother to clarify his concerns so that we could avoid treading on his campaigns in Chibi. I walked out – shaking my head.

India Troop drove out to Chibi. As I drove out of Fort Victoria, I seethed with the ticking off and the lackluster intelligence briefing. What should I tell my section commanders? The last trip into Chibi offered no intelligence whatsoever, or any strategy from JOC Fort Victoria. The briefings were sparse again – devoid of any useful titbit … absolutely zip. I told Ray about SB's outburst and he sat back and laughed loudly.

"That's it," I bitched, "a swift kick up the arse for the good work and no intelligence in exchange."

"A good swap," he smiled.

Once again, the overall strategic plan that required certain action from each individual Security Force unit had not been forthcoming. A tactical jigsaw that required the troop to sweep, search, block or OP in conjunction with other Allied forces, as part of a masterplan to outmaneuver the enemy, was absent. The JOC was too reactive. Special Branch may have succeeded in Chibi in some subtle, underhanded way – and being a mere troop commander certainly didn't entitle me to know what they were trying to achieve – but there were scant instructions that proposed that we conduct our operations in a certain fashion because other forces were working to undermine the enemy. Each unit worked in isolation. I knew we had to go back to the drawing board.

The troop slipped back into Chibi and quickly got down to business. The MIC wandered down to our base and reminded me that all the old rules applied: no unauthorized visits to the single men's quarters. Welcome back.

Billy Pring joined the troop – bringing his extensive PATU experience. A stocky, fit, moustached policeman, Billy was a touch vain. His two concerns were going bald and getting fat.

For a joke, Busby might say something like: "You're putting on a bit of weight there, Billy."

Naturally, Billy vehemently denied it, but the next minute, he'd be spotted jogging around the camp or grinding out sit-ups. When the story did the circuit that wearing a hat increased the chances of baldness, Billy refused to wear one – even in the most searing heat.

Billy quickly learnt about humping unnecessary loads in the bush. Anyone new to the troop was seconded with my section for one or two four-day tramps, so I could impart practical knowledge. Generally, if I am not on a specific assignment, we would cover 20 kilometers and more a day. On the first day on a grinding walk, under the boiling sun, Billy's overloaded rucksack weighed down on the shoulders, but he humped that pack without complaint. After stopping in cooler shade for a break, Billy finally stripped the weight from his rucksack and out came a number of cans of fruit. He distributed them to the happy constables. Observing the number of cans handed out, he was a tough cookie humping that lot.

One night, while I was on patrol, the Chibi police camp came under attack from the beautiful *kopjes* to their rear. The CTs sat on the heights and served up a barrage of small arms fire and lopped in 60mm mortar bombs. Green and orange tracer bullets jetted across the darkened police property. Rob, the SB officer, leaned out of his bedroom window to return fire with a captured RPD. He poked the communist machine gun out the side window and let rip. A troop MAG gunner heard the RPD's distinctive chatter and thought the police mess had been overrun, so he blasted the building with the MAG. The SB operative ditched the RPD out the window, dived under the bed and stayed there. The attack was accompanied to the rock music of Queen's *A Night at the Opera* booming from the record player inside the mess – a surprise attack to music! No one in the camp was hurt, but one CT was mortally wounded and the body was recovered the next day, five kilometers away.

Rob – shaken by the camp attack – grew timid and withdrew, so he dabbled in one or two projects from the comfort of the office. The two or three times Ray tried to coax him into accompanying the troop into the field, he avoided the impost. Once, Mick was involved in a shoot-up with a terrorist section in a dry riverbed and radioed for reinforcements. As fortune happens, Ray drove his section Hyena to another incident, accompanied by Rob. When he heard Mick's radio call, he diverted off the main road and drove madly cross-country in an attempt to cut the runners off. Laughing and chuckling at the wild ride – and passionately attempting to head off the enemy – Ray tested the Hyena. The vehicle bucked and rocked violently – cutting through scrub and old maize fields. The SB agent sat inside the armored car mortified – pleading with Ray to leave him with the vehicle guard, and not with the cut-off group. He was left behind thereafter.

To assist the lone SB intelligence gatherer, JOC posted a Territorial Army RIC sergeant to Chibi. He wandered down to our camp and introduced himself. From Salisbury on call-up – keen to roam outside the wire to sniff out information – he joined Mick's section in the field. To Mick's surprise, the man spoke only schoolboy Shona, so required translation services. There was that language barrier again. I expected an intelligence expert to speak the local language; it's like sending a British agent into Germany who couldn't speak German. The section doggedly talked with locals in the west border region, while he tried to paint a clearer intelligence picture.

One night, the section ambushed a path that connected two villages, where they had spent the day eliciting intelligence fragments. Later, it was alleged the RIC sergeant had dozed on sentry and that CTs simply wandered through the killing ground. The section woke in the morning to find the fresh *spoor* imprinted on the dirt track, right in front of their noses. How the CTs' presence didn't alert someone I'd never know. After a little confusion, India Three chased after them and a contact ensued around a cluster of small hills. No casualties were reported on either side and India avoided inviting outside help thereafter.

While I rested in the base, Rob the operator received a garbled report of a murder at a business center. The operative asked India to investigate. Rob declined to attend; too much paper war. I rode out with my section to the deserted center, where we found the two general stores and a flourmill firmly locked up. The place was completely deserted … warning sign number one! The men bailed off the truck and wandered up to the closed stores.

"Where are they?" asked Moyo, as he searched the store frontage.

"Round the back," Mandoza called, as he juggled the MAG, "you can smell them" – and sniffed the air.

Sure enough, four bodies were sprawled in the dust at the rear of the general store. They were young people: three males and one female – and all less than 25 years old. Dirt and grit was embedded into their skin like a fawn mask, and their simple clothing was clustered high. At first glance, they appeared to have been machine gunned and bayoneted to death. Empty brass, green and chocolate-brown cartridge cases littered the dirt. The female looked to have had her genitals mutilated. Next to her, a young man lay spread-eagled, with his right leg severed below the knee and a blood-caked *badza* tossed alongside. A congealed blood pool harbored hordes of flies. Five meters away lay two other crumpled males – their clothing screwed up and both shot to death. The swarm of flies lifted off the deceased like hundreds of tiny helicopters – angrily buzzing in the warm air because their feast had been interrupted. Another ZANLA massacre, as timeless as murder, with all the essential components: the ripening stench, droning flies and untidy corpses.

"Sarge, take Moyo and find the *spoor*," I uttered, as the putrid smell of early decay wafted under my nose.

The bodies had cooked in the hot sun for at least one day. The black skin tightened as the body gas expanded.

Tsumba stood silently with his medical pack drooping from his hands.

"Nothin' I can do here," he murmured.

"I guess not," I added.

Chewa and Moyo wandered away into to a fallow ground.

I radioed base to ask the Chibi police to take over the murder scene. They could transport the bodies, while we looked for the perpetrators.

"Come here, boss," Sergeant Chewa called out in a hoarse whisper.

"What is it?" I snapped back impatiently.

"Have a look at this," he insisted.

"Better be good," I answered, as I walked over.

Impatiently, I stalked up to 'Mr Courageous' – my 'blind' and 'deaf' NCO.

"Over there," he said – pointing into the broken maize field.

Staring down his outstretched arm, I saw something move … I squinted at the small rustling. Something dark shuffled – camouflaged by the brown maize stalks. On closer scrutiny, a brown and black blob formed – a dog … a mangy, brown village dog. I concentrated, and then straightened … the dog chewed on what appeared to be a black log. Focusing harder, I realized the log was a severed lower leg. The dog slobbered over the exposed red muscle like it was a big supermarket bone. The critter barely took any notice of us. Disgusted, I aimed and shot the mongrel – smack in the chest. The dog yelped in pain and bit savagely at the entry wound, and I shot the beast again, but this time in the head. The bullet impact flipped the dog onto its back. I stomped over to the quivering mongrel and recognized the human leg as the joint severed off the young man.

"Get the leg over to the body," I said to Moyo, who ogled me. "I'll get on the blower to find out where the 'Brown Boots' are."

While we were busy, Internal Affairs sent out tax collecting teams to scour the villages south of Chibi. The residents were informed in advance, so clearly the CTs knew. A tax collector's Land Rover had detonated a landmine. Once again, a low speed and seatbelts had assisted, but they endured bruised backs – another four-wheel-drive vehicle shattered. A few kilometers away, another Intaf team lazed under the cool tree shade at the cattle dip – eating pre-packed lunch – when they were rudely attacked by RPG-2 rockets and small arms. Fortunately for them, the rocket man missed by miles, but who likes tax collectors anyway? Once the CTs had established the geographical route of the tax collection, their own tax team jumped ahead of the government workers and collected the money themselves. Once the government boys arrived, the village coffers were bare – and Internal Affairs was red-faced. Consequently, the national tax base collected in tribal areas steadily declined. Billy's section attended, but the chase fizzled out.

Days later, India One sat in the cool shade whilst preparing a midday meal, right next to an arterial road. I decided to make use of the time by stopping and searching any traffic. Moyo – lounging on the roadside and chewing on *biltong* – stepped out and stopped a rural bus plying its trade (just a random search when the war tempo dropped off). The bus lines were the only dependable transport from the cities to the remote rural areas. All sorts of wonderful things could be found aboard – a treasure trove of oddities. A bus could be the preferred means of transport for couriers, *mujibas* and, if we were really lucky, a CT incognito.

"*Chitupa!*" snapped Moyo, as he boarded the front steps. The passengers fidgeted as they searched for their identification documents. The driver, in his grubby white shirt, reached inside his pants pocket. I wandered along the outside – aware of hostile eyes following my movement. The fatigued bus displayed the usual lack of roadworthiness, with paint peeling and small bits about to fall off. If we played 'Policeman', an infringement notice book would be overwork; this was a real traffic ticket bonanza: bald tires, shock absorbers stuffed, headlights broken, a generally dubious mechanical condition, a window wiper missing, whole windowpanes absent, rubbish strewn everywhere inside, luggage blocking the aisle, and so on. As usual, the suspension was broken on one side and the bus appeared like it was traveling with its rear end sagging, slightly side on.

I boarded behind Moyo to survey the passengers' faces.

"Your bus is in shitty condition," I snapped at the pudgy African driver, as I gazed at the dirt and grime inside.

"It's not mine, boss. What can I do?"

"Tell your boss that if I see it in this condition again, I'll 'ave it impounded."

"OK boss," he said, as driblets of sweat ran down his face and onto his soiled white shirt. Why would he give a shit? He tucked his *chitupa* into a plastic holder.

The vibrating heat inside had a life of its own. Mixed with sour, unwashed body odor, stale smoke and hemmed-in goats, the tart aroma fiercely struck the nostrils. I winced to steady myself. Twenty-two people sat mortified – waiting for Moyo to study their papers. Battered suitcases, crumbling cardboard boxes and packed plastic bags were jammed in the aisle and provided an obstacle course. I noticed five young males seated on the bench seat at the rear of the bus; they sat like village delinquents. One chuckled as he exchanged his blue ID document with a mate. My eye caught a blur of movement. Did he do that for a joke?

"Get those five bastards off the bus," I ordered Moyo, "with their luggage."

They paled collectively, while the other passengers stiffened in anticipation. Their tired eyes roamed the seat in front – anywhere but at the police. Icy stillness settled. Moyo hissed the order in Shona and the men rose, uncertain, from the worn seat – shuffling and tugging their shirts.

Normally, as a matter of routine, after checking everyone's *chitupa*, the passengers would be escorted off the bus one seat at a time, quickly pat-searched and then seated outside on the dirt in exactly the same order as they were seated on the bus. By seating them outside in the same seating plan, they could not deny ownership of parcels and luggage in and around their seat. When they were all out, the personal effects inside would be searched. Once the internal search was completed, a constable would climb up the rear ladder onto the roof. Slowly, he would establish ownership of each piece of luggage strapped to the roof rack before opening, so a thorough search occupied a number of arduous hours.

I decided to skip that process today; I had a hunch about these five. They dragged their feet awkwardly down the cluttered aisle – pulling down their shirts in agitation.

"Got your luggage?" reminded Moyo.

They nodded blankly.

"Sarge!" I called out the door, "there's five comin' off."

They stiffly clambered over the aisle jumble, walked past the statue passengers and the rigid driver, and scrambled down the dirty steps in anticipation of a heavy whack around the ears. I assisted each one off the bus with a token push. They landed on their feet on the dirt road and huddled together.

"Come 'ere," called Chewa, who swiftly rounded them up like a fussy mother and escorted them into the roadside scrub.

I stepped out of the vehicle – all passenger eyes staring straight ahead. See no evil, hear no evil and smell no evil.

"Go," Moyo told the driver, as he alighted.

The sweating man didn't need to be told twice. A plume of dirty diesel smoke billowed from the exhaust as the driver accelerated away. All passenger faces were frozen – staring straight ahead. No one dared look out at the fate of the prisoners.

The five were marched to our resting place, separated and sat down. They stared at the ground in silence. The constables slowly finished off their meal and methodically packed away the utensils.

"Bring the first lucky bastard in," I called to Moyo.

The constable cut one out of the herd and marched him up for a talk.

The first man forward appeared calmer than when fingered inside the bus – and a defiant spark had settled in his brown eyes. He looked about 20 years old and was dressed in a threadbare cotton shirt, with tan trousers and bare feet. After a brisk interrogation (the usual questions of where, when, how and why of terrorist activity bounced off him) and a few slaps around the ear to emphasize the pertinent points, the first man refused point-blank to acknowledge that ZANLA had ran riot in Chibi – giving the usual bullshit 'see nothing, hear nothing' answers. He was marched off, with a bleeding nose, to sit near Mandoza.

The second one witnessed the physical activity and, after being escorted to where I stood – and being a little more sensitive – pissed his trousers and admitted that they were going to a *kraal* in an adjoining TTL to be inducted and spirited to Mozambique for training. Unfortunately, the precise area he nominated was outside my reach. Once he confessed, he became a regular chatterbox. Moyo had to slow him down to translate, while I jotted down notes.

The third youth – being escorted for questioning – paled. He shook and quivered. As soon as Moyo brought him forward, he quickly blurted the second man's story – fiddling with his cotton shirt. He shivered as he answered the questions – his wide eyes looking about for an escape.

The two remaining lads, with nowhere to turn, agreed that they were recruits journeying to the start point. I called Special Branch Chibi and organized the prisoners to be uplifted to the station, so that Fort Victoria Special Branch could spirit away the five youths for processing.

Afterwards, JOC Shabani directed two India sections to spend a number of days escorting the Psyops boys into Rundu TTL, which was north of the Shabani-Fort Victoria Road; Mick and Billy landed the job. Psyops was a new concept in the army – a psychological approach to the war. It was a vehicle to push the government line to the skeptical population. They carried out impromptu meetings to explain the benefits of assisting the government by reporting the CTs' presence. I thought this concept was a hard sell. Why ever would the Africans do that? Helping us encouraged a hideous death. Where was the benefit? What was in it for them? What were the long-term gains? We couldn't promise freedom from CTs, as there weren't nearly enough boots on the ground. We weren't promising political or economic change. It was like shoulder pushing a laden truck uphill; it could lose control any moment.

On the other side of the same coin, ZANLA spent considerable energies politicizing the population. They invoked the traditional spirits (the fact that the country belonged to their ancestors) and the 'lost lands', in that it was their historical right to the land, which had been expropriated by white settlers. They kept the narrative simple: chase away the white settlers and their productive farms, their new cars and their large houses – even the white towns – are yours for the taking; just kill the whites and all that belongs to them becomes yours.

To a peasant farmer, it was an extremely lucrative proposition.

The gap between the stories was enormous. On one side, the government said that if the villagers took the risks and supported the government, everything would remain the same, but the CTs' story was that if they got on board with the Revolution, they secured rights to all the white man's treasure. It wasn't hard to figure out who presented the best sell patter.

Moyo told me one interesting sideline that highlighted the gap: the white people from Psyops did not speak Shona. They were Territorial soldiers from a Salisbury city advertising agency, which had been commissioned to advise ways to conduct a government media campaign – leaving their African companions to do the talking. Apparently, according to Moyo, the Africans stood up and undermined the white administration!

I never quite got with the Psyops program, and I couldn't understand what the government had to sell. In Malaya or Kenya, the British colonial rulers agreed to hand over the government to the people and completely withdraw, which was a major incentive to get with the program, but this government was not contemplating that. They talked about 'responsible majority rule', but eliminated any militant nationalist group. 'Majority rule' was code for a moderate African politician who could be manipulated to never match the demands of the militants.

One major hurdle in any psychological operation was, plainly, that military men understood military action and therefore had developed little interest in political or social enterprise. Men who had taken up the sword had hardly earned a social welfare mindset; they judged their own performance on the destruction of ZANLA units. Pacification programs required the leadership of professional non-military thinkers – with some even implanted in military units – but closely supported by military, which linked into the aims of the program. Along with the common purpose, a colossal bucket load of cash was required to lift the peasant farmer from subsistence living to a modest life expectation. The minds and hearts of the thousands of people are, purportedly, the prize. I suspected there was no money in the kitty to make Psyops work.

One Psyops program – touted as the 'Harmony campaign' – had been under way. The television campaign centered around a white kid and a black kid walking hand in hand with each other up a grassy knoll, while accompanied by a 'Harmony' melody.

The army sang the theme tune (albeit slightly altered): 'Harmony, harmony, har-many gooks have you killed today?'

The RLI chatted about loading their rifles with 'harmony pills'; far too little, far too late.

One tiny bit of 'hearts and minds' we reserved was for the babies with serious eye infections. Many infants' eyelids were gummed together by yellow pus. The mucus wept from the eyes and attracted squadrons of flies. The sight of a babe in arms with weeping, pus-filled eyes crawling with flies was heart-rending. During the hours of painstaking interrogations, Tsumba kept busy washing the gummy eyes clean and applying a strip of tetracycline paste into the watery pupils. Generally, the antibiotic cleaned up the infection within hours.

The medic also applied basic medicine wherever he could. Medical supplies were inadequate, with training only going so far as advanced first aid, so his expertise and medicines were limited; however, where able, he'd bandage sores and apply healing antibiotic pastes. Many tribespeople's minor ailments were sorted within his supply restrictions.

The foot patrol operations were concentrated along a riverbed to keep the pressure up on roaming bands. Walking the dusty embankment, I sighted a lone CT sprint from a *kraal* located right on riverbank. It was a snap glimpse and then he was gone. The village was located at the junction of two dry riverbeds and the CT had slipped into the dry tributary to escape. I fired off six shots, but I was far too late. We swooped hungrily on the seven-hut complex – dodging amongst the light timber and heading right into the village center. An AKM rifle was found lying in the dust next to a full set of canvas chest webbing – including four full AK magazines and two Chinese grenades; then, to our surprise and amusement, Moyo pointed to a set of clothing (brown shirt, denim jacket, dirty underpants, blue jeans, Superpro shoes and scrunched socks) all jammed up against an iron bathtub full of hot, soapy, warm water. I deduced from that scene that one CT was now on the loose – completely naked.

The quick and violent confrontations kept occurring; Ray's section was engaged in a firefight near Takavarashe. The CTs escaped and one African male was wounded – a CT bullet striking him in the left extremity of his forehead, which then followed the skull around before zapping out behind the ear. The pink and white brain protruded, and he sat quietly as Ray sought to prevent the rest of his brain from creeping out further. Ray and his medic cut the saline bag and roughly taped the plastic drip to the villager's head. Their goal was to keep the brain sterile and moist. He'd lost enough brain matter to cover half the palm of a hand, so Ray thought he was a dead man walking – but no! The next visit, about two weeks later, we ran into him, in town, with a dirty bandage wrapped around the skull – his eyes bright with the light of the resurrection.

We kept finding the enemy, but not eliminating them. Billy's section had 20 CTs visual and so called for Fireforce. After an hour of radio talk back and forth, Fireforce established it would not be coming; once again, it was not available. Billy watched, frustrated, as 20 CTs walked off. With no time to insert troops by truck, the JOC opted for an air strike. Within a half-hour, two Hawker Hunters screeched in and rocketed, bombed and strafed the barely visible CTs. When they flew off into the wild blue yonder, the OP section left the hill and investigated. Not one body or piece of equipment was found; it was a complete washout.

Meanwhile, on another OP (under young Graeme's eyes), 20 CTs emerged near Takavarashe. He calmly requested Fireforce through JOC Shabani, but the strike force was not available. My section – including Ray – patrolled north near Jenya School, which was 15 hard kilometers away in the flat, agricultural country. Listening to the negative answer to Graeme's request, we unfolded and scanned the map, pinpointed the enemy location and elected to move up. The flat terrain sloped gently uphill from our location south, to the Takavarashe Hills. This was a real long shot in the vibrating heat.

"We'll jog south, heading for Takavarashe," I announced to the constables, "to intercept these gooks."

Six 'what the fuck' looks creased their faces; I ignored their astonishment.

We checked each other's kit to ensure all straps were set tight, settled the backpacks on our shoulders and distributed the belts of machine gun ammunition, and then we broke stride and began the long haul. The heat shimmered and pulsated, and the target hill country floated on a blue, shimmering line. Once we began to jog, sweat burst from every pore. I gritted my teeth and trotted silently. The men sucked it up and jogged along the baked turf. The only sound was the rattle of machine gun belts, the creaking of canvas straps and the hoarse breathing in the midday sun.

After a sweltering five kilometers – running past a deserted village – I spotted a donkey hitched to a cart and standing in the shade. It wasn't a difficult decision to hijack the donkey and rudimentary cart, so we surrounded the stationary beast and tossed our packs into the empty scotch cart. The harnessed donkey looked at us with rising panic.

"She's yours!" I shouted at Banda.

The young constable snapped off a green branch.

Mandaza clamped the bit in the mad animal's mouth and we broke back into a run. Banda lopped alongside the gray beast – whipping its butt with the branch: the poor man's logistical support! We ran hard up a beaten track – aiming for the distant hills. After only a few kilometers, the exhausted donkey suddenly collapsed. We snatched our rucksacks and hightailed – abandoning the stricken animal and leaving it to stagger upright, as it gasped for hot breath.

Unfortunately, the CTs got bored waiting to be killed, and so split into small parties and ambled off. Everyone's frustration was running as hard as possible in the oven-baked heat (our equipment bouncing, as well as sweat pouring from every conceivable pore, our inner thighs suffering friction burns and the canvas webbing belt rubbing our skin off the hips), only to hear a running commentary over the radio that the quarry had nonchalantly walked away. By the time we finally puffed into the OP's view, Graeme was only able to talk us into a five-man group – the only portion of the original 20 visible.

Steered by Graeme's radio voice, we jogged closer and, on his say-so, changed down to a cautious walk. Ahead, a section of thick scrub shielded the hill base. The voice in the radio handset, stuck in my ear, told me ZANLA had vanished. Shit! We spread out and walked towards the last sighting. My heart pumped renewed energy into my tired body. With the enemy a fly's whisker away, the weight of equipment vanished, the tiredness evaporated and all eyes were riveted on the shady bush. The patchy scrub filtered into a number of large, dry gullies, which had been caused by massive soil erosion. Rain and wind scoured yellowish soil into long, narrow ravines with crumbling sides and bases, and we stumbled into one.

Suddenly, the ZANLA boys broke cover like startled gazelles – galloping at full throttle – as we fast ran out of puff. The men quickly opened fire and ZANLA retaliated in a short, vicious firefight. Blood splatter found later indicated someone had been shot, but no enemy bodies were left behind. Exhausted, the men flopped down for a rewarding cuppa and rest. Recovering on a granite rock at the end of the short, sharp contact, Ray – a superbly fit man, who had ran up Christmas Pass (outside Umtali) on his R&R – decided that there must be an easier way to fight the war, and resolved there and then to apply for pilot training in the air force. On R&R, he applied.

Back at Chibi camp, the District Commissioner still complained. In his jaded eyes, India had been naughty boys again. He never directly confronted me with his objections, but rather filtered them through the Chibi police or Special Branch in Fort Victoria. I decided to do something: after the naked CT fusillade, we recovered three backpacks in the dry riverbed. I instructed Sergeant Chewa to draw a rough map plan of the District Commissioner's camp – penciling in CT attack groups and a recoilless rifle, aimed at his house, and dated it a week hence. The next night, in the Chibi bar, I slipped the penned map to a district officer who worked closely with the DC and said we had recovered it from a rucksack found after the fleeting contact.

"I'll need your troop to provide protection," he stated, as he paled – slowly grasping the possibilities drawn before him.

"Sorry," I replied, with relish, "we're fully committed. You've got plenty of your own men. Besides, it could come to nothing. You know what Charlie Tango is like – a tendency to exaggerate."

He said nothing, folded the paper and walked out of the bar in a huff, and I heard no more complaints.

One night, while patrolling, my section heard someone approach an isolated track. The shadow flitted on a dirt track and the scout fired; then there was a sharp squeal and a moan. We closed down on it fast … a dark shadow was found seated on the track.

"You've shot me in the leggy only!" he called out in shock and surprise.

"Who are you?" snapped Moyo – fidgeting with his rifle.

"Simon. I'm a student from the city."

A student? Out here? At night? Long after curfew? On a barely used trail, far from the villages? The bullet had punctured his left thigh – high in the muscle. Chewa shone a small torch on the wound, which was now spurting like a small hose. Tsumba knelt down and concentrated on stemming the flow, but he couldn't grip the artery. It was like trying to block a broken water pipe without turning off the source. The spewing blood made the leg slippery to handle; a tourniquet didn't work. Field dressings which were rammed into the wound only marginally slowed the flow. Within minutes, they were soaked and useless. He tried tweezers, without success. Red blood pumped on, and the man slumped. He was going to bleed to death. Tsumba attempted every trick to shut off the blood flow, but each came to nothing; Tsumba had exhausted his knowledge. Unfortunately, we didn't carry fine steel pinchers to shut off the artery, and a helicopter rescue was not possible on a pitch-dark night, plus we were too isolated to manhandle him back to a main road. Simon didn't survive. What was a university student doing wandering alone, in the wilderness, in the dark? I still wonder to this day.

As our last act, Ray's section escorted a forensic scientist from Salisbury and a policeman from Chibi to unearth three Africans who had been (allegedly) shot by white farmers. The allegation stated that the Africans were caught red-handed rustling cattle and that the frustrated farmers had taken matters into their own hands. Cattle rustling was an enormous growth business. Cattle stolen from white-owned ranches were hidden in makeshift pens in the tribal regions and then slaughtered to feed the expanding terrorist numbers. Rustling increased by a hundred percent within a year.

The constables uncovered three shallow graves. The pathologist loved his work and played with the stinking bodies like a kid in a sandpit. He called Ray over to the grave site and explained the bruising found on the skulls was consistent with a *coup de grâce*. The Chibi police opened a murder docket and we never heard whether the matter ever went to court. We trucked out of Chibi and, no doubt, the DC and the MIC celebrated. Sergeant Chewa tacked three weeks' leave to his R&R and did not return to India when his leave finished, as he was posted to another troop.

"Combined Operations Headquarters regrets to announce the death in action of … " The soothing RBC Radio voice once again informed the melancholy nation of its war losses. "Security Forces Headquarters announce the death in action of three members … blah blah blah … Security Forces killed 15 terrorists … "

The fatalities were broadcasted like motoring deaths, but divided into two teams. It was like motor vehicle fatalities; the score was noted, but it was not intimidating.

Mick and I flew to London and stayed with his folks. We literally handed in our rifles at the depot, rushed out to Salisbury airport, boarded an SAA flight and arrived in London. Walking off the plane – dressed only in a T-shirt and jeans – we stepped straight into chilly, wintry British conditions. Looking at the people there, they were all whiter than white. Once settled, we soon opened the door to the first of many pubs. The beautiful ladies Mick knew thought I was either insane or a criminal by the wildness in my eyes. Tipped straight from the no holds barred Bush War to the sophisticated city, I felt no different, but after four weeks, the same people said the 'look' had disappeared. I had a great, drunkard time through the packed clubs and laid-back pubs of Mick's hometown.

Mick's little tiff occurred flying back: a big Dane – a business-class passenger – leaned against the wall that divided business from the cattle class and annoyed the economy passengers. Clearly pissed, he heckled and insulted total strangers. I ignored him as part of the background noise. Comfortably watching the in-flight film, I noted this big Dane suddenly tossing a screwed-up paper ball at a woman sitting not far from us. Within seconds, Mick leapt over my seat, took a couple of strides and punched the Dane out – a knockdown at 30,000 feet! The crew escorted the woozy Dane back to his business-class chair and injected him with a knock-out syringe. We were treated like royalty on the way back – plied with free beer and snacks. The Dane was taken from the aircraft by the South African Police in Johannesburg and put on the first one home.

Overseas travel costs could be offset by returning with Levi jeans, Wilkinson razor blades, digital watches and calculators, which were all unavailable in Rhodesia, and so carried a great sales mark-up.

10

Chiduku Yet Again: January 1978

After returning from London, the whirlwind holiday still sparkled. While I absolutely enjoyed the big city atmosphere, I felt like an outsider looking in. There was still little appeal in staying and dropping back into the civilian world – a world of time clocks, rent payments, tedious work schedules, public transport and a weekly pay check that barely stretched the seven days. I wanted the adrenalin buzz and, at this point, that was in Africa.

After a brief stop in Salisbury to collect the war kit, Mick and I scrambled straight to Rusape, where India Troop was stationed at Mantle Base 151A. When we arrived, the troop was patrolling Chiduku and I elected to join them. Mick was more circumspect and remained in base with the Reservists. At a snap briefing, Fred Mason pointed to the India callsigns pinned on the operations map. I squinted at the chart: this time, India worked the northern end of Chiduku – away from our playground around the Dorowa Road. The India pins were stabbed into the Devedzo Hills, which was a massive escarpment that dominated north Chiduku. The map showed how high the landscape was by the tight contour lines, but I learnt soon enough how steep it was.

A Mantle convoy dropped me off that night and I was met by Ray Hughes and his section at the roadside. The escarpment loomed like an enormous black cliff.

"Yes," Ray grinned, as I thought about the climb.

We quietly hiked cross-country – across flat stubble and open grassland – to the foot of a steep escarpment. At the base, Moyo found a goat's track and the men commenced to climb. The summer rains had churned the wet track slimy and we had fun maintaining a sound footing in the treacherous conditions. The muck track wound up the line of least resistance – a zigzag up the sheer slope on the escarpment face and I immediately discovered how unfit I had become after a month drinking beer in London. Fatigue slammed the quadriceps and my knees threatened to buckle. Using regular stops on the way up the slope to ease the legs and regain my breath, I soon regretted my keenness to get out in the field. I was relieved when the section finally stumbled onto the flat top.

Dawn revealed a flat plateau surrounded by mild, hilly country. The population remained hidden. Only dark trees, green maize fields and the peaks of thatched huts were visible. Ray led the troop into a reconnaissance of the plateau – familiarizing himself with the topography and probing for terrorist gangs. Once again, each section was assigned a prescribed area. We zigzagged through the villages to speak to residents. Now, if they spotted us first, they simply stopped whatever they were doing and fled; if they were walking along a path and saw us, they abruptly sprinted into the scrub; if they were working, they abandoned their tools in the field and vanished.

The war entered its third year in this area and the population had developed expertise in avoiding the Security Forces. If they couldn't escape, they'd shut their mouths. Every reply was monosyllabic. Their eyes were hostile, but fearful. The elders allowed the questions to blow over their heads; they hardly spoke and just shook their heads. The men acted dumb and refused to admit the CTs lived in Chiduku. The women scrambled their kids to hide in and around the *kraal*; then they faced us with flat expressions – tempered with 'don't know' answers. In the 18 months since my first venture in Chiduku, the population swung from friendly and inquisitive to stonewalling any effort to engage them. There was not an offer of anything.

Billy's section was shot at entering a prominent business center, but no one was hit; however, the local terrorists knew we were there.

"The boss up here is some gook called Bata Hana," said Ray, "as slippery as an eel."

A new senior sergeant had replaced the wily Tambe. Senior Sergeant Kembo trudged in the bush with Ray's section to get a feel for the men and the troop's élan. Solidly built, with no neck and a craggy face that burst into laughter at the least provocation, he had accumulated 14 years of service. I was impressed that he insisted on accompanying the troop in the field, as Tambe's attitude had made me a touch skeptical of long-serving NCOs. During this tour, I judged he had earned the wherewithal to run a troop himself. He knew how to play the games necessary to get things done, he displayed good man-management skills and he got the work done with little fuss. He knew who was who in the zoo, so no one pulled the wool over his eyes; I liked him immediately.

A second new face was Lance Sergeant Ncube, who replaced Chewa. Selected from a younger crop of men who had proved their mettle in the field, Ncube demonstrated exceptional common sense. A tall, charming man, with a charisma that constables valued, he was one of many constables with combat smarts that were prized and, consequently, was quickly promoted. He joined a new wave of younger NCOs who had replaced the old peacetime Support Unit hands – men who no longer had the ticker for counterinsurgency operations.

After the reconnaissance, the troop gathered on the roadside. A stream of RL Bedford trucks conveyed us back to Mantle Base. Sitting on the Bedford slat seats, with the sandbagged tray underfoot, I watched the countryside slide past – hating our vulnerability. The road wound around the base of hills, which was perfect for an ambush. While I was not keen on the Mantle Base atmosphere, I felt very strongly that trucking the troop from Rusape to the area of operations wasted time and placed the constables in constant danger of a vehicle ambush or detonating a landmine. Too many unnecessary casualties had been inflicted on other troops by landmines, so I thought hard about how to avoid the roads.

After hours of contemplation, I tossed my solution out to the section leaders: I was keen to try an experiment where the troop hulked in all supplies and cached them in the TTL. The plan envisaged humping six weeks of food and surplus ammunition to hide in a cave, or to be buried anonymously right in the tribal area; then we were to live like guerrillas and spend our entire time there – six weeks easing among the *povo*. We could move closer with the events and the population, and knock out driving back and forth; we would not have to protect a formal base, nor waste time and team effort chasing shadows, but to instead just concentrate solely on north Chiduku by living right amongst the population.

The section leaders were underwhelmed; they were not keen. They saw the sense in terminating the constant trucking in and out, but they liked a little bit of base life. The absolute minimum requirement was a safe, static position to eat and curl up asleep. To be constantly on the move without a base unsettled them. Even the aggressive Ray Hughes didn't like the plan, so I walked away to modify it.

Later, I proposed that we station on a farming property adjoining Chiduku and erect a small base from where we would walk back and forth – without using vehicles, in our time, at night – thus avoiding the local scrutiny. That proposition was more acceptable and I sold the idea to the Mantle Base commander before I drove out to visit the farmers.

I visited the Smart family – the owners of a Lesbury tobacco farm, which was flush with the border of Chiduku and separated only by the Macheke

River – and discussed the plan to base there for the duration of the operation. Two generations of the Smart family lived on the vast tobacco farm in separate homesteads. They were delighted with the proposition, as the close presence of the troop was good security.

The troop trucked out from Mantle Base with lightweight kit and a small camp was erected close to the tobacco barns. We had the minimal requirements – a cluster of tents accompanied by slit trenches. It was a simple affair – sheltered by the 30-foot brick barn walls and rows of cut logs – and without even Mantle Base's limited comforts. A patrol roster set out which section took a turn in the tent encampment to rest and sleep. Senior Sergeant Kembo stepped into the role of base camp commander with practiced ease. The camp was his baby and it ran like clockwork. He conducted a daily run for the men along the river, after which they dived in for their wash. Once, I accompanied a section on its run and, at the finish, they scrabbled down the riverbank to leap naked into the cool water. Noting some of the swinging dicks, I pleaded administration duties and jogged back to the tent town. The Smarts visited spasmodically – bringing gifts of food.

Chiduku was squatted only kilometers away from our base. The Macheke River, adjacent to the farm, ran deep and swift – thwarting safe crossings. We either marched about three kilometers through the farm to find a shallow crossing point, or we walked down on the main dirt road and over the low bridge – at the junction of Chiduku-Dowa APA-Willows – to land a foot in Chiduku, but we now enjoyed flexibility and unannounced entrance and exit.

On 25 January – patrolling jointly with Mick's section, early in the morning on the Devedzo escarpment, just south of Twatswa School – Moyo sighted four women a hundred meters away walking through medium-dense bush and balancing aluminum buckets on their heads. The ladies hurried along a finger of light timber that shielded them – and although swallowed by moist bush, glimpses of the aluminum bucket caught the diluted sunlight. Cautiously, the section skirted the waist-high green maize – staying well inside the scattered scrub – and headed directly to where the finger joined the main undergrowth clump.

At the finger intersection, we bumped into a *kraal* – a small four-house configuration. At first glance, the *kraal* looked deserted; then the scout sighted a girl (about 10 years old) standing alone outside a doorway. She appeared more perplexed than anxious when we emerged. Sergeant Ncube knelt down in front of her – his eyes level with hers – and softly questioned the shy girl, and she volunteered that her mother had gone to feed the 'Brothers' … as simple as that! We thanked her and eased away from the village – steering through the vegetation and towards the point where the women were last sighted.

All eyes anxiously scanned the shadowy trees as we delicately moved along a wooded spur. The woods narrowed, and one section traveled in front of the other. Eight pairs of eyes in my section scoured the speckled bush. Ahead, a faint footpath ran down the spur. Shadows flitted through green leaf: darker shades, gray tree trunks and smooth granite boulders. The sunlight dappled the leaf into a mosaic of light and dark – and the noses did not detect foreign smells. Creeping on sensitively laid boot soles, the stomach contracted … my rifle butt was tucked in my shoulder, my heart thumped wildly and our eyes rapidly interpreted the ground ahead. We sought to find them first.

Alas, a hidden sentry fired – a high-pitched automatic burst. Bullets crackled sharply overhead, like a stock whip. They snapped the warming air and pinged off the tree trunks. I saw the women standing 15 paces away. The biting crackle jolted them and they weighed up the situation in a flash – dumping the food containers like poison and fleeing into the underbrush. They were visible for only a couple of seconds – a smudge of color, and they were gone. The CTs – hidden 20 meters further, inside the green screen – joined the sentry with an intense small arms barrage.

With the first fusillade, the men swung into supercharged action – fanning out into extended line and firing as they doubled forward.

"Follow me!" was the only call to action.

My section led, with Mick's further back.

The bullets harshly crackled, but the opponents remained hidden – unseen.

Rattle … cathunk!

The metallic sound of a mortar bomb minutely trembling on the journey down the mortar tube sounded alien; then cathunk! Cathunk!

"Jesus! Take cover!" I bellowed above the din of the rifle fire.

The forward rush crumpled as we all dived down onto the leaf-coated forest floor to avoid the hot shrapnel. I shut out thoughts of where the bombs might land; I couldn't control that. The wait for the detonation dragged on …

CRUMP! CRUMP! CRUMP! Three bombs exploded close by. The mortar tube must have been near vertical to hit us. There was a theory doing the rounds that one could suddenly roll on their back and look straight up into the sky to catch a glimpse of the mortar bomb at its peak trajectory; then your eyes could follow the bomb path down to gauge its impact point. It was nice in the desert, but not so practical in the trees. The only trick was not to be standing when the bomb exploded. Unfortunately, the men did not hit the deck quickly enough. Mick Busby's section – bringing up the rear – didn't hear the mortar fire, or my shout. A 60mm mortar HE bomb exploded in a gray cloud right next to Constable Chipangora – a supercharged sliver of hot metal slicing into his chest, which punctured his heart and killed him outright. He collapsed without a peep. Shrapnel from the same blast slashed Constable Banda in the left-arm bicep, but he said nothing until the action was over. Mick, who scrambled in line with them, was lucky not to receive a scratch.

"Let's go!" I yelled, when the last bomb of the trio detonated.

In the front section, unaware of Chipangora's death, we launched to our feet and surged forward once again. Stampeding through the timber and undergrowth, we broke out among large boulders into a natural, granite-rock fortress. The gray stone flashed by as I stormed inside – furiously scanning for the enemy. A minute passed before I realized that the rifle fire had ceased. The policemen scuttled through the enemy base – poised to fight at close range – but our opponents were gone. The mortar bomb explosion had signaled the CTs to pull out and, on the last explosion, they fled out the back and straight down the steep escarpment.

After the rush, I paused before mounting a detailed clearing; the priority was to secure the enemy base. Quickly, a wounded youth was uncovered hiding. The young man lay in the lush undergrowth – saying nothing and afraid to move – hoping we'd soon go away. Discovered by the vigilant team, he was roughly hauled from his hiding place. His squeals revealed a bullet wound in the rump and he was laid to one side (sitting was a problem for him) until we had time to rattle him with questions. Tsumba, in the search team, peeled off and knelt down next to the youth to stem the bleeding, and quietly chatted to the teenager to calm him down as he tightened a bandage.

"Chipangora is down!" called Moyo, as we secured the base.

"Where?" I asked.

"Back there," he signaled, with his hand, "a mortar, I think."

"Anyone with him?"

"Banda."

I looked around: the enemy base camp sat on a small knoll at the end of the spur – protected by giant, house-sized granite boulders and good-sized quality trees. If they made an aggressive stand, there'd have been serious trouble, but I believe that with African troops, there is only one tactic: SAS

(Speed, Aggression, Simplicity). If the leader pondered or attempted some fancy flanking movement, the lack of inertia can paralyze the advance and, once the troops go to ground, a crowbar is needed to lever them up.

Reloading the FN with a fully charged magazine, I quietly searched for any hidden enemy. An abandoned SKS rifle lay on top of one gray granite boulder. Moyo and Tsumba bolted back to find Chipangora; Banda knelt beside the flattened constable – his eyes wide in shock; Mick knelt on the other side and shook his head. A quick examination confirmed Chipangora's death. Tsumba could do nothing for him, so he turned to Banda and applied a field dressing to the bleeding bicep.

Chipangora was dead! The ramification slowly sunk in. Dead? What do you mean, dead? Had I not just chewed him out this very morning for slack carriage of his rifle? Jesus, dead! The notion of death didn't engage. Chipangora – a baby-faced youth; the butt of jokes, who bumbled through on patrols and steered clear of trouble in base; the boy who hovered on the edge of activities; the lad who needed a poke to motivate him – had suddenly died. The young constable lay huddled in the leaf carpet – a single, fatal wound to the chest … dead in a rat-arse, anonymous Chiduku forest.

As I studied the map and prepared to radio a contact report, Mandaza – standing on the perimeter and covering Mick and Banda – absentmindedly kicked the dead leaf blanket in nervous agitation. His boot tripped on a metal object … he looked down and, scraping the leaf aside with his boot toe, saw the rim of a metal case. His boot had uncovered a sealed green metal container.

"Have a look here," he called to Sergeant Ncube.

"What?"

"I've found something."

Ncube slipped across to Mandaza. He sidled up to the constable and peered through the timber. He saw Mick in the woods to their front.

"Not there, here," hissed the constable.

Ncube looked down. He saw the metal container and dropped to his haunches. His hand felt around.

"There's more here."

Astonished, he raked his hand around and uncovered a small ammunition cache: ten sealed cases of 7.62mm x 39mm ball rounds. He extended his search – scraping the leaf aside – while Mandaza watched and Tsumba and Mick carried Chipangora. They uncovered landmines, rifle grenades and TNT and mortar bombs.

"Boss, look at this," Sergeant Ncube called – fiddling with a TMH landmine and dusting down the flat body. He held it up so I could see.

"Shit!" I exclaimed.

I walked over to the pair.

"How'd you find this?" I asked Mandaza.

"That was easy," said Mandaza offhandedly, "they could have found ours just as easy if we lived in this area."

I stared at him, but said nothing – a sarcastic shot at my guerrilla proposal! A point taken.

In quiet sorrow, we collected Chipangora, gently wrapped his body in a groundsheet and one section tenderly carried him out to a road. The second section manhandled the ammunition dump and our wounded prisoner to the road to await Mantle Base vehicles. Ncube amused himself by talking to the boy with the sore backside. He shyly divulged that he was supposed to remain behind to guard the ammunition by keeping it under surveillance. Sergeant Kembo headed India's funeral arrangements.

The same evening, a landmine blast claimed the lives of an African businessman and his wife when their Peugeot 403 ran over the device, which was dug into the road at the entrance to the Chiduku TTL (the same one we walked in on). The French-made vehicle was demolished, and neither stood a chance. The CTs had laid the mine – waiting for our reinforcements to be trucked in – but the victims drove in the wrong place at the wrong time.

Also that evening, three young *mujibas* walked casually into Billy's night position – calling out cheerfully as they walked, as they believed the section to be CTs. One was shot dead by the alert sentry and the other two hid in the scrub till dawn – too frightened to run. One explained (when captured the next morning) that they had seen the dark figures walk in at last light and had assumed the fuzzy outlines to be their mates – a fatal mistake.

A few days later – patrolling the flat country below the escarpment – we brushed the perimeter of St Terese's Mission. The white building cluster, which was distorted by the heated air, looked like it sat in a lake. Whilst we had not been warned to avoid the Mission, I elected to stay away unless in pursuit; they were legal tripwires. Within minutes, we noticed a person strolling in our direction. As he wandered closer, his shape was better defined. It was a European … it was the Irish priest. I watched him from the bush line – a bearded, stocky man in his early fifties, who was dressed in a white short-sleeved shirt, fawn shorts and leather sandals. Relaxed, he strolled alone on a dirt path that circumnavigated the Mission grounds. When he drew close, we stepped out of the bush shadow. At first, he blinked with surprise, and then his face changed to open contempt when our eyes met. I greeted him cordially and he reluctantly stopped three meters away. He didn't return the pleasantries. I tossed a couple of general questions about the area around the Mission, but he answered cautiously and in monosyllables. His sparkling blue eyes said it all: he just wanted us to go away.

"What about a cuppa for the boys?" Ray asked the Irishman, who turned to face the speaker.

"I can't," stated the priest firmly in his Irish brogue, "I don't know who my friends or my enemies are."

"What?" Ray raised his eyebrows in astonishment. "You won't even boil the water for the tea?"

"No," stated the priest adamantly.

"Where's your Christianity?" smiled Ray sarcastically.

"You're hiding behind the bloody Christian cloak like some tribal mystic," I said to the casually dressed priest before he could answer. "You've already taken sides."

The priest glared at me with open disdain and then withdrew without another word. I riveted my eyes into his retreating back. They were but men. How could they take sides with terrorists without any comeback? I thought missionaries had much to answer for, as they laid the groundwork for the breakdown of African tribal traditions that eventually undermined the centuries-old authority of the chief. They scorned tribal religion, clan morals and belief systems to replace them with the white man's idols. I imagined him indulging in a cup of tea with the ZANLA commander – chatting about this and that – only hours after the commander had bloodied his hands murdering local people. I intensely disliked their holier than thou attitude.

"You should have kept a mine from the cache," said Ray wistfully, when the priest was out of earshot, "an' planted the bastard under his car wheel. That would've given them something to bitch about ... first-class pricks."

I watched as the priest vanished into the shimmering heatwave. It was a waste of time and energy confronting the religious order. Once he had disappeared, we tramped away towards the main dirt road. I decided to head to the main Chiduku thoroughfare. The temperature soared and the humidity sucked the energy reserves. The exercise rapidly soaked the clothes in sweat. Crossing a field on the hot slog, suddenly, Moyo froze.

"Look! *Gangandas!*" hissed Moyo, as he flashed the FN into his shoulder.

"Where?" I replied hastily.

The country was open, with old ploughed fields returned to long grass alongside blossoming six-foot maize and small tree clumps. A small village sat squarely on the side of the road, with the conical roofs barely visible through the outlying tree shield. I squinted along Moyo's rifle barrel; the other men were spread out – sharp, alert and pulses racing.

"Going through the *kraal*," Moyo added quietly.

I didn't doubt him, but I just wanted to see for myself.

In a flash of movement, an African in a faded yellow shirt and denim jeans – armed with an AKM – sauntered between two huts. A wall blocked my view. Shit! I signaled thumbs down. It was the enemy – without question! The team looked at me for instructions and I silently waved them forward. We carefully picked our foot movement as we edged closer – trying to identify the numbers. The terrorists were there, but how many?

A sudden blur and another scurried movement … I raised my rifle barrel. My eyeballs lined up the iron sights. The post foresight matched the rear aperture sight on the indistinct target, and the forefinger brushed the trigger. A white man filled the iron sight – wearing a Rhodesian camouflage jacket and light-blue shorts, long cream socks and brown leather shoes. Fuck! The rifle lowered marginally.

"Who the fuck are you?" I bellowed.

The man spun and faced us – blanched and fumbling for his AKM slung over the shoulder, as constables stepped into the open, with their rifles leveled.

"Acorn," he replied; a millisecond separated him from death.

"Jesus, we could've killed you, you stupid bastard!" I roared – fright generating into rage.

The African wearing the yellow shirt joined him.

A four-man Special Branch team had conducted a lightning raid into a specific *kraal* – targeting a known sympathizer – but they did not bother to inform JOC of their presence in our operational area. They assumed a 50-meter jaunt from the roadside, where they had parked their vehicles, was close enough to the main road. They were very, very lucky. That was the closest I came to killing or maiming one of our own.

I never encountered a death in a blue on blue contact in Support Unit. A blue on blue was where Allied forces mistook friends for the enemy, and this tragic mishap occurred in other troops in Support Unit from time to time. The two main causes of blue on blue came down to a mix-up in grid references, or nervous sentries firing on friendly forces. Sometimes, a ground unit can be attacked in error by aircraft. Once, my section came under machine gun fire from a circling helicopter, but we found large granite slabs to hide behind, as I hurled abuse at the air gunner. Some deaths related to an accidental firearm discharge. I never witnessed or had cause to reprimand African police for the unauthorized discharge of a firearm.

Another Support Unit troop OP – operating silently and further along the top of the same Chiduku escarpment – spotted 30 CTs. I listened to the excited radio conversation. Fireforce deployed from Grand Reef and was talked cleanly onto the target by the OP operator. Initially, the CTs' movement was not sighted from the air, so the K-Car commander roundly ticked off the OP for wasting his time. The K-Car commander was reluctant to drop off troops, but finally acquiesced; 2RAR troops landed. As time rolled out, the K-Car commander snarled about another fuckup – orbiting high above the steep country – and, just before he wound up the sweep, a Stop Group stumbled into 10 CTs attempting to snivel out and some vicious firefights erupted. Suddenly, CTs scurried everywhere. As the rotor noise whined along the steep slope, the CTs scattered and ducked down the escarpment. Six CTs scuttled down the wooded escarpment – desperately seeking shelter. They attempted to hide behind a prominent waterfall, but unfortunately for them, they were spotted just as they ducked behind the water spray. They huddled together in a shallow cave entrance and were shielded directly behind the water cascade – a perfect hiding place if they hadn't been seen nipping in there. A helicopter hovered opposite and pounded the waterfall with automatic fire. Their blood turned the water pool light red, rather like a horror movie. Fireforce killed 10 CTs and 12 people running with them – not bad for a scene that the K-Car commander threatened to throw away.

There was a growing tendency developing in Fireforce to abandon the hunt before it began. As the helicopters flew in, if the K-Car commander personally could not see credible evidence of terrorists, they were reticent about deploying any troops. Commanders sought to actually see the enemy running, or their aircraft suffer machine gun fire, as tangible evidence that the OP had done its job correctly. Too often, the CTs heard the airborne assault come in; then did a shuffle to the left or right, held their fire and the helicopters did nothing. The CTs learnt that by holding their fire, there was a chance to persuade the gunship to pull the plug. The Alouettes fired a few bursts of the .303 MG or a couple of rounds of 20mm cannon to see if they provoked a fight and, if nothing happened, the helicopters departed.

I understood that Fireforce commanders were reluctant to drop parachute troops into something that may not be genuine. The time wasted floundering about in an attempt to flush out something, as well as the retrieval of the parachute canopy after the jump and the logistics of packing up and leaving, compounded a headache; however, they could at least drop two helicopter-borne sections to test the OP sighting. Either Fireforce commanders were choosy, or there was enormous pressure for kills on every landing, or they had so much work on their plate that they only took the targets that were sitting ducks; however, on the other side of the coin, some Support Unit troops that operated from Mantle Base 151A Rusape initiated a number of successful Fireforce talk-ins. Darryl Brent's Lima Troop was particularly successful in OP work and, based on the Lima Troop OPs, RLI bowled over 30-odd around the Dorowa Road in a fortnight. His troop had built an outstanding record for OP and operational kills.

The monotonous humping carried on. Winding in and out of *kraals* and rough terrain, occasionally Mantle Base called and ordered a section to move several Ks. To Mantle Base, in the comfort of the office, the map suggested mildly hilly scrub; to the man on the ground – standing in dauntingly remote parcels of bush and staring at clusters of huge boulders interlocked with tight scrub – it was a different story. Because the piled boulders did not reach the minimum height required for a mapper to draw a contour line, the base assumed the ground was a walk in the park, whereas the man on the ground saw a backbreaking, ball-busting effort.

After receiving a transmitted order with the coded grid reference, I studied the contour lines on a map, which gives a sense of elevation and connects the points of the same altitude.

"Mantle Base, India One, go ahead, over," I replied.

"This is Mantle Base, I want you to move in there in two hours to begin a search north-west, copied, over."

"Mantle Base … India One … ah … I read you strength two, transmission breaking up, over."

"India One, Mantle Base, how do you read me now, over?"

The voice became anxious.

"Mantle Base, India One, you are breaking up, can't read, over."

"India One, Mantle Base, go to higher ground, over."

"Unknown station, this is India One, you are totally unreadable, out."

"India One! This is Mantle Base, over!"

My handset was clipped on the webbing harness and the caller ignored … fucked if I'm going to scramble through that country!

On the closing raining days – acting substantially on a tip, mixed with our experience and instinct – we trailed a CT group … reeling them in. Sometimes, sharp *spoor* mocked us; other times, the shoe prints were simply washed away. When *spoor* was obliterated, we leaned on the population for answers. Sometimes they told, but mostly they didn't. Finally, Moyo spotted a hazy human cluster on a rocky knoll – shoved next to an undistinguished *kraal*. Through the steady rain, he wasn't sure if they were the elusive enemy, but instinct shouted: "Yes!"

"It's them," stated Moyo, with certainty.

"Sure?" I asked, as I tried to distinguish outlines in the steady rain.

"Yeah, it's them," Moyo said firmly.

"Do you think we'll be able to outflank them?" I asked Sergeant Ncube – watching the murky figures.

He shook his head – a firm no.

"They're packin' up and goin'," replied Moyo.

"They're leavin'," added Mandaza.

I observed the fuzzy outlines merge and separate. Why would they stand around in the rain, when they could adjourn to a cozy house?

"Let's get closer," I said, and we sneaked up as close as we dared.

Using another granite lump as a shield, we strode to close the gap. The men ducked onto a small granite slab about 40 meters from the movement.

"Try from here," I hissed, as the men spread out.

Ray squatted down and set up the captured 60mm mortar tube. Using an old leather sandal as a base plate squarely on the wet rock, he guided the mortar tube base square in the center of the sandal. He positioned two Chinese mortar bombs on the wet rock, with a third one poised in his left hand over the mouth of the mortar tube. He glanced at me and I monitored the enemy. The CTs began to evacuate the knoll position – heading towards the village. I nodded. Like the CTs, Ray used the white vertical line painted on the mortar tube for direction and guessed the elevation. He dropped the first bomb into the tube mouth, while I simultaneously fired a communist M60 HEAT anti-tank rifle grenade from the FN muzzle, with the rifle butt firmly implanted against granite. The rifle grenade arced through the rain and exploded on solid granite rock with a loud BANG! Great for shrapnel spread! The mortar bomb exploded in a steel-gray cloud; then the MAG joined in, with bright-red tracer balls that blistered across the dead ground and smack into the granite hill – ricocheting off the rock in dangerous trajectories. Ray fired two more mortar bombs in quick succession, one after the other. All three landed smack on the target area in a red flash burst and gray cloud eruption – and, as if on cue, the rain geared up and belted down. The teeming rain wiped out the enemy outline. Thoroughly soaked, with the ground bathed in water, the men dodged and splashed around the undergrowth to clamber over the granite protrusion. The flat granite outcrop sat naked. We found no bodies, no bloodstains, no *spoor*, just pelting rain and a miserable village next door. I sat down in a cold puddle and sulked. Ten days later, Special Branch was led to the grave of a CT who had died of wounds in that attack.

We packed up the farm, said goodbye to the Smart family and India motored to Mantle Base before cruising back to Salisbury. In Salisbury, Phil Smith sought permission for an overseas holiday, which was summarily refused. He was really pissed off when he was told his troop would be deployed to Shabani to cover an emergency, so Phil, being Phil, drove straight to the airport and flew overseas anyway. He mailed the CO a postcard from the Greek Isles, that began: 'A funny thing happened on the way to Shabani … ' When he was ready to come back, he telephoned the CO from London and negotiated his punishment: three weeks in the police cells in Morris Depot, his head shaved and made to run around like a recruit.

On my return from R&R at Troutbeck Lodge, I met up with some Support Unit mates at the Fife Avenue police mess. The usual drinking marathon occurred there – coupled to a thunder flash tossed (a grenade assimilator used in military exercises, which explodes like a big firecracker) in jubilation in the downstairs bar, which blew out windowpanes, and I locked the barman in the backroom so we could help ourselves. I was banned forthwith from the Fife Avenue police bar, but there was always the Support Unit bar.

Constable Banda, with his arm wound bandaged, but mostly healed, rejoined the troop; Constable Dube – transferred from another troop – replaced Chipangora.

11

Mangwende: March 1978

India Troop motored out of Salisbury to a Mantle Base in Mrewa. The town was a sleepy agricultural hub, some 70 kilometers north-east of Salisbury, and astride the main highway to the Nyamapanda border. Once in town, the police directed the convoy to Mantle Base – a flat paddock populated by dreary gray tents. From the moment I arrived, I didn't like the 'Boy Scout' look of the base and decided to worm my way out. I was not happy as a pawn in a larger operation.

Superintendent Julian Twine, the base commander, had been newly posted to Support Unit for a second tour – the first tour prior to the 1973 insurgency operations. Awarded the Police Decoration for Gallantry in 1974 for his courageous actions when his police launch on the Zambezi River came under rifle fire from Zambia, he was still an unknown quantity to me.

Like the north Chiduku tour, I negotiated an independent operation to base the troop on a farm on the rim of Mangwende TTL. I once again discussed the proposal with the farmer and his wife, before unveiling the plan to Superintendent Twine. He agreed without an argument. Words of my unconventional behavior preceded me and Twine happily packed the troop off.

Mangwende TTL surrounded Mrewa and, in stark contrast to other tribal lands, lacked large wooded areas; instead, open, rolling, grassy hills dominated. The grass grew so short that it looked like someone had cut it with a lawnmower. Below the grassy hills, the lush, flat country grew eight-foot maize crops. Without substantial woods, the countryside was wide open, which therefore restricted unnoticed foot movement. If we sought to roam undetected, patrolling could only be undertaken at night.

During the daylight, the enemy was one step ahead; they fostered an excellent intelligence network. The African juveniles formed a protective shield around the CTs as an early warning of our approach. The village kids ranged out far and wide in search for the Security Forces, and their runners swiftly updated the CTs. With innocent-looking kids constantly roaming on the lookout, they formed a thin membrane that shielded the terrorists. Those junior scouts partially insulated ZANLA.

The Mangwende inhabitants were extremely politicized and totally supported ZANLA; they made no bones about it. They had wrapped their lives around the terrorists. The war had been spluttering in Rhodesia's north-east zone for six years, so the African civilian population was well versed in the art of survival. Here, they did not flatly deny they'd heard of the terrorists; when asked, they agreed they knew them, had seen them, had attended meetings with them, had actually fed and entertained them, but always two weeks ago. Every interaction was two weeks old – a smart change from the usual dogged denials. They did not cop a smack around the ear for defending the indefensible, as they agreed with what we said, no matter what we said, except that it happened two weeks ago. Again, we experienced little cooperation. To force a result, the troop switched to night patrols, where the *mujiba* eyes could not pry. They were in mortal danger if they walked after dusk, with the shoot to kill curfews, so we had a slight edge. I smiled how events had changed: once, to be effective, the terrorists slunk about in the dead of the night; now, it was us. We'd patrol 5-10 kilometers at night and pop up well away from where we were last sighted. We would then lie up on the clear, felled hills and carefully scrutinize the area in the emerging daylight. While the wooded areas were sparse, the maize crop was high and provided the enemy with excellent cover from view.

Regardless of the *mujiba* screen, daytime operations continued to wave the flag. If we all disappeared in the night, the CTs would have a propaganda coup – telling the locals we had been driven off. Two sections worked the night, with one during the daylight hours. One morning, Billy's section walked straight into gunfire. I sat back in a hiding place on the side of the hill and watched the green and red tracer bullet show. My section was too far away to offer direct help, so I just observed and talked to the section commander. The section was pinned to a contour ridge by an RPD machine gun for 10 minutes before the CTs broke off and escaped through the plump maize fields. Even from our height, we couldn't actually see the terrorists, who were hidden by the mature crop.

On a daytime patrol, my section walked into an abandoned *kraal* and, around the corner, found a natural holding pen jammed with stolen cattle. Two giant granite boulders formed a V-shaped wedge at the rear, with the front opening penned off with rough-sawn logs. The imprisoned cattle stood listless – standing in their own shit and busy flicking the maddening flies with their tails. There was no water or feed for them; the branded cattle had been stolen from the white farmers. Cattle rustling became a growth industry, despite a mandatory nine-year sentence for perpetrators, which had been forced onto the government by irate farmers. This case was handed over to the Mrewa police.

By now, people started to venture back to Mangwende from Salisbury for the Easter holidays. The main road supported more vehicle traffic, with old Zephyrs, Austins and Peugeots packed tight with happy people returning home to their families. For their sake, I hoped they knew more about the mining of roads than we did. I wondered if any would end up bayoneted and burnt to death, just to round off the Easter celebrations. Those on foot carried transistor radios and travel baggage. The men stopped one dapper African gentleman, who was walking cross-country and wearing a three-piece suit, a white shirt and a red tie, and carrying a black briefcase. Moyo was so intrigued that he asked him to open the leather briefcase. Embarrassed, the young man unclipped the lid and opened it up. Inside was a stale sandwich and some worn underpants; he was just out to impress an old flame back home.

We continued to openly patrol – talking to tight-lipped villagers. Frustration ripened with benign political outcomes, the lack of useful intelligence, the multiplying ZANLA numbers and the tribespeople's open support of the enemy. More particularly, the long, drawn-out war – with no discernible light at the end of the tunnel – contributed to the whittling down of patience and civility. Irregular warfare does not adhere to the certain rules and customs of conventional war. The nature of the conflict – the 'anything goes' mantra – brutalized those who remained fighting for years. We walked on the border of lawlessness in the pursuit of the enemy – and both sides displayed elements of bandit mentality.

By now, the African villagers' suspicious eyes and hardened facial expressions summed up the mood: we were not welcome. Once, in 1975/1976, I conducted rural police duties in the tribal areas outside Inyati – a small police station 69 kilometers out of Bulawayo. The area slept peacefully and I received a genuinely warm reception whenever I patrolled the villages. The people offered food and drink, and were happy to talk about their lives and local gossip; they exuded a natural culture of hospitality. In 1978, in the Mangwende *kraals*, hostility radiated from the population. It was here – squatting and talking to the guarded people – I recognized that the war was not winnable. Whatever was required to reach into the local population's hearts had slipped away irretrievably for the government. The government simply had too few men, very little money and little political appetite to seriously change attitudes. While we patiently sat and listened to denial pile onto denial, the roughhouse stuff still consisted of a couple of thick ears and a boot in the backside.

Occasionally, I resorted to theater to loosen lips – for instance, where a *kraal* head had openly and publicly thrown their lot in with ZANLA. Where they were contemptuous of our presence and had made it known to others, a piece of theater was used. In these cases, the villagers were rounded up and seated outside the *kraal*. Sergeant Chewa quietly congratulated the *kraal* head, shook his hand vigorously and explained to the silent masses that their gallant leader had showed courage and fortitude for telling the police about CT-related incidents – referring to specific, known activities. He added that the government had rewarded the *kraal* head with a Post Office savings account filled with cash, but we were authorized to hand over two dollars to assist him in the journey to a town to collect. I handed the crisp, red two-dollar note to Chewa, who grandly palmed it off on the grayish-looking *kraal* head. We invited the villagers to talk about the benefits of the reward system, and we left the CTs to read between the lines; however, if we were in hot pursuit of enemy fighters, we were particularly harsh. When the *spoor* had suddenly dried up and the populace left behind stood around agitated and anxious, but tight-lipped – and when it became obvious that the same villagers had assisted in wiping out the terrorists' *spoor* – we shocked out answers, but we didn't go further than a quick beating. Critics state that the use of force must be avoided, but when in pursuit of barbaric terrorists, whose escape equaled more grisly atrocities, the rules were severely bent. I make no apology for these actions; however, the torture of suspects for the sake of being suspects rarely worked. Men in physical pain, or in total fear, will blurt any story to release them from the agony; they'd implicate their grandmother if that stopped the torture. Police General Headquarters were worried about the trend towards mistreatment and sent out blistering memos to cease forthwith. They were frightened that heavy-handed tactics learnt in the Bush War would be liberally applied to ordinary suspects back on the police beats. No one at the coalface took much notice.

Sitting on an OP one warm morning – overlooking the flat green Mangwende expanse – Mandoza, the gunner, gave me some of his homespun philosophy.

"You white people are too soft," he stated quietly, as he oiled his beloved MAG for the tenth time.

"What do you mean?" I asked, as I gazed out at the light-blue African sky.

"We must kill everyone living here," he stated matter-of-factly.

"Oh, yeah?" I asked curiously, "and what would that achieve?"

"If we kill everyone down there," he continued thoughtfully, "then those who are left must be the *macandanga*."

"Oh," I stated – not surprised by his statement.

The only problem with his theory was that many tribal people had relatives not connected with nationalists, with some working for the government and even the Security Forces, as well as plenty who did not want to be involved.

"That was the way we used to fight," he said fiercely – closing the top cover.

"If I agreed to that Mandoza, CID would investigate; then the axe would fall."

"Then we kill all CID," he said unemotionally.

Knowing Mandoza, I was sure he would.

One night, sitting on a hillside, we sighted vehicle headlights bobbing up and down like a ship at sea. The bright lights wound along a dirt road running parallel with our hill. The engine growled as the vehicle labored in the wrong gear. I wondered who the vehicle belonged to – surely not a hapless, lost civilian? A dusk to dawn vehicle curfew had been fixed in place for years. I doubted they belonged to SF, because a lone vehicle ploughing through the TTL at night was unlikely. The engine noise sounded more like a four-cylinder car, not a truck's heavy rumble. I radioed Mantle Base, as they would know if troops were deploying. We patiently waited on the hillside and the lights toiled closer … Mantle Base returned the call to confirm Security Forces were not driving in our area; then we took off – running hard down the hill, in the inky dark, before veering across the open grass fields. We ran flat-out at an angle to cut off the car. This was one car that was not to elude us, after the experience of a carload of enemy in Beitbridge. The men ran hard through dead maize stalks and light scrub, which scraped and slapped exposed skin. The hollow sound of rubber soles thumping on the earth, and the creaking of webbing and rasping breathing surrounded us. Fortunately, no hidden holes or sharp dips tripped up the runners. The team just managed to cut the car off with a half-minute to spare.

Mandaza burst out of the scrub and jumped onto the center of the dirt road, within the frame of the car headlights, and signaled the car to stop – a hand up like a traffic cop, but the car did not stop; the engine roar did not diminish. In fact, the motor accelerated.

Before the dazzling headlights loomed too close, I yelled: "Mandaza, get outta there!"

Mandaza – momentarily hypnotized – frantically leapt back into the thorny scrub.

The car roared past without braking.

As the dark sedan dashed past, Mandoza stepped onto the road and opened fire – the MAG tucked into the shoulder. Bullets bit into the black outline and the car wobbled – veering to the left and crashing into the scrub that lined the roadside. The left wheel flattened the immature trees before the car shuddered to a halt; the engine was racing. Before the driver contemplated escape, Mandoza and I ran up to the rear bumper. Peering through the back passenger window, I saw nothing. We slithered along the length of the car and I snapped open the front door. A picture revealed two African males bathed in the yellow, flickering ceiling light. They were slumped over the blood-splattered vinyl bench seat, with a pool of shimmering black blood spreading on the blue vinyl console. They were both dead. Subsequent police investigations discovered that the driver was a district assistant who had deserted from Internal Affairs in Headlands, and who was believed to be running with and assisting the CTs; the other was unknown.

On 26 March, I set up a night ambush on ground as flat and open as a bowling green. Dividing the men between an old fallen tree trunk and a dark anthill, I lay in the middle. From snippets of intelligence, terrorists were moving in and about a specific *kraal* line. We traced the fragmented information to an actual *kraal* parked in the open, which was surrounded by flat grass eaten down to the roots. It sat rather like a small housing cluster in the middle of a huge, empty car park. The lack of hiding places made the village difficult to sneak up unseen, and closing in on the village ran a profound risk of the scrawny dogs barking, which would alert the owners.

I laid the ambush using the usual tools of a MAG and FN. From our position, we observed the darkened level ground that stretched into the fuzzy village. The houses were far enough away to merge into a low lump, but nothing could move in or out without being sighted. Satisfied we were undetected and that we had an easy observation of the village, I organized the sentry roster before I placed my head on the backpack pillow and dipped into a shallow sleep.

A hand roughly shook me awake, and I blinked rapidly. Looking across the plain, the dark shapes were unmistakable: at least 10 smudgy figures were hiking rapidly across the grassland, from the *kraal*, and directly towards us. I snuggled in close behind my FN. These were not civilians, I deduced. They strode purposefully – spread out in a tactical formation. The tension mounted … a faint moonlight caught them. The dark shapes were visible from their boot soles to their peaked hats. Do we fire now, or wait?

The forefinger curled on the trigger … the heart drummed – pumping deep inside the chest. A sneak-peak out of the corner of the eye confirmed the constables were poised ready. The constables said later that they'd heard the walkers mutter something about shooting one of the people with them – an execution party? Their shape became sharply defined as they advanced closer, with low banter drifting in the still night. I wanted them right on top of us before we opened fire.

Unfortunately, when they closed the gap, the RPD gunner saw something suspicious and called a warning: "'Ma-Sojers'!"

Mandoza opened fire the instant the CTs were called out – decking the gunner. The night blasted off in rifle and machine gun fire. Green and red tracer bullets intersected – shooting fiery orbs in the night. The wounded man rolled behind his RPD machine gun and let rip. In a wild exchange, I fired ball rounds smack into the man. I witnessed the shock of the bullet strike, but the bastard did not stop; he kept returning fire. The RPD's brilliant muzzle flash sparkled in the darkness. More red sparks leapt from the gas regulator – he wouldn't stop. I concentrated solely on him and aimed and fired more bullets into him. He jerked with each hit.

When I thought: "He's a goner," a short pause followed; then he fired back! An icy-cold edge ran inside me.

The other terrorists opened fire. Their AKs honed to automatic, the bullets zipped high and were ineffective. The darkness burst into an array of tiny red, orange, white and green meteors, as tracer bullets zapped everywhere – burning out in the distance like shooting stars. Both sides were stitching up the night in colored tracer and the air trembled in the crackle of gunfire. Sergeant Ncube, on the left flank, pinned down the AK boys as best he could, but the real danger lay in the RPD.

The CT gunner's next burst killed Constable Banda outright and a bullet punctured my chest. (Banda had been privately fatalistic about his chances of surviving this tour.) With the high-pitched excitement and awash in adrenalin, I felt the hit, but ignored it. There was no excruciating pain, just a hard punch in the chest; however, the coppery taste of blood rapidly filled my mouth and my breathing became labored, and warm blood pissed everywhere. The invisible energy source associated with being alive rapidly dissipated and began to fade – and only then did I become concerned that the wound was serious.

Another machine gun burst chewed up the old log. The men remained cool and continued to fire – finally neutralizing him with a sheer storm of bullets.

The firing stopped.

"Anyone hit?" I mumbled – barely conscious.

"Banda's dead," Moyo stated flatly.

"Dead?" I muttered, "how do you know?"

"His brains are on my shirt," Moyo replied unemotionally.

"Get Base," I croaked to Mandaza.

I shouldn't have bothered. Mandaza had the handpiece jammed to his ear – calling Mantle Base. He had summarized our situation and that Sunray definitely required an urgent casevac. He listened intently as I hovered, semiconscious.

"They're sending out trucks," he said cautiously.

"Fuckin' tell 'em to get an air casevac … I won't survive trucks."

Sergeant Ncube snatched the handpiece and stated the case bluntly. He listened hard, and shook his head.

"They're insisting on a road casevac," he finally said.

"Jesus, I'm fucked."

The base probably thought that Ncube was overstating the case, but the sergeant argued fiercely for an airlift. His voice sounded detached and remote, like he was inside a tunnel. I was fading and flopping in and out of consciousness. Tsumba slipped out of the ambush line and, after a quick examination of Banda, scurried to my side. Working frantically, he stemmed the chest bleeding and got a saline drip into the collapsing veins. I felt someone buzzing close, but the image was tarnished. I was sinking.

The skirmish was over, but Mandoza scoured the littered plains for signs of life.

"Get out there an' do a quick sweep," I slurred to Ncube – unaware he was talking on the radio.

He looked at me quizzically, as he jammed the handset to his ear.

"Make sure there's no one out there ready to put up another fight … Moyo, take Mandaza and Dube, an' clean up out there!" he then ordered, before he returned to his conversation.

Moyo, Mandaza and Dube (the new constable) withdrew on their bellies and sneaked out the long, roundabout route across the flank – tiptoeing behind the enemy group. They found the CT gunner still alive; his head was propped up in his hands. Unable to fire, he was hit more than a dozen times. He was a hard son of a bitch – a combat veteran and a detachment commander – sporting Bob Marley dreadlocks. They shot him dead. Three terrorists were killed that night.

Ncube's transmissions were interrupted by a new callsign, and the pinched-nose voice of an air force pilot broke in. Reality flickered on and off as I faded in and out of consciousness – losing awareness of events. A helicopter pilot, asked to fly to Mrewa to wait there for the road casevac, had heard the radio conversation and jumped on the air. Assured by Sergeant Ncube that the firing had ceased and the area was safe, the pilot changed course. Ignoring orders from Mantle Base, the pilot flew direct to the contact scene. Flying helicopters at night was hazardous without night-vision goggles – and without a horizon. Consequently, the pilot can become quickly disorientated, but fortunately, the night was very light, with a clear sky. The pilot's selfless act, without any doubt, saved my life.

One of the unwritten caveats to fighting was the understanding that the wounded get rushed to medical help as soon as humanly possible. The Rhodesian Air Force, even with the serious lack of funds and world-class flying machines, provided exceptional casualty evacuation throughout the country – unimpeded by a long chain of command. Stretching the bounds of the possible, they pulled out all the stops to rapidly transport the wounded out of very dangerous situations, and I am still humbled by their courage and tenacity.

The helicopter flew direct to the Andrew Fleming hospital in Salisbury. On that flight, I recall a strange sensation – one of hovering on the ceiling of the helicopter and looking down on the army medic working frantically over me … a hallucination? Morphine? I don't know, but the vision was real. (For a long time, I thought it was supernatural – the spirit leaving the body – but now I believe that a close-to-death experience was caused by portions of the brain temporarily shutting down, and that the chemical reactions the process released had put me in a dreamlike state.) On landing, the expert medical staff jumped into gear. Fortunately, Mr Standish-White – a top thoracic surgeon – was in the team, and I needed his skills. I remembered the doctors and ward persons wrenching the stretcher out of the helicopter, and then I blanked out again.

A single bullet had struck high on the right side of my chest, above the nipple. It had tunneled through the right lung, diaphragm and liver – minutely

The Wilson Banda memorial; Warren Hills, Salisbury.

nicking the vena cava – and puncturing this and that on the way. They cut the bullet out from the top of my right buttock.

In Mrewa, Support Unit withdrew India Troop from the farm. As soon as the troop departed, the farmhouse was burnt down by marauding CTs.

12

Recovery: April–July 1978

I lay in the Andrew Fleming hospital's intensive care unit for 10 days – and it was touch and go. The bottom third of my right lung had been removed, and my liver had been cut back and stitched; the liver is the only organ in the body that regenerates. I don't remember anything except a blur of a nurse rushing at me with a syringe. I was told later that the liver had caused considerable trouble and that the stitches kept bleeding. Ron Rink's sister, a theater nurse, told me later that I had a foul mouth when I was unconscious – good to know. For Ron's sister, at the time I'm hovering in intensive care, things got darker: she was notified that Ron was wounded and had been casevacked to another hospital.

Once shifted out of intensive care, a parade of mates marched through the hospital ward carrying bottles of Mazoe orange cordial stacked with vodka. The nurses thought I was a cordial freak, but soon discovered the potent drink. We became merrily inebriated and rowdy around the bedside – and I slowly recovered. The staff and the hospital provided exceptional care and expertise; the nurses maintained a sense of humor and a definite sense of duty. They put up with the jokes, teasing and unbecoming behavior, but were able to draw the line without rancour.

The worst part of recovery came with physiotherapy – particularly the painful, forced coughing to rattle up the blood and mucus that lingered in the damaged lung. To actually cough blasted the lungs worse than the bullet strike. If I heard young Jo coming, I waddled off to the toilet and waited behind closed doors until I thought she had gone, but she hovered nearby. As I sneaked out, she'd be waiting patiently.

While hospitalized, Support Unit comrades broke into my locked cubicle at the Fife Avenue mess to find personal stuff to bring to hospital. They just wanted to supply the necessities of life; however, they found a spare A73 radio and enemy munitions stowed in my locker. There was a 'please explain', with one superior rank keen to lay charges. The incident finally went away when I later explained to Collins I was just hedging against shortages, but one officer still pushed to have an official enquiry, which was thwarted.

Ron Rink sitting on a keep wall; Nyamapanda, 1976. (Ron Rink)

In June 1978, Ron Rink and I were dispatched to Durban for 10 days to recover at the Malibu Hotel – compliments of the Victims of Terrorism Relief Fund. Shrapnel had zapped Ron in the throat (he didn't duck when a grenade presented itself) – a fine 'singing voice' destroyed! Ron and I had met at the Morris Depot when he was enduring National Service, while I was a volunteer. He had returned to Rhodesia from overseas to serve and was older than most of his companions. After training, we met once again in the same Support Unit training squad and drank plenty of the good stuff, as well as whirling through many parties. Once again, I was at my animal best, with acts ranging from being drunk and disorderly to completely obnoxious.

As a civilian, Ron once worked in Durban, so he knew quite a few people. Being a keen surfer and a gregarious man, his nose was fine-tuned for parties. Ron loved a chilled beer, and we certainly drank merrily. He ducked out occasionally to surf, while I remained on the bar stool. I met a lovely nurse at one of his parties, who escorted me to her family estate, where we had a good time. Despite the parties, I managed to dip in the ocean to allow the sea salt to heal the wounds – and it did a damn good job.

After Durban, I ended up at Tsanga Lodge, which was a recuperation hostel run by Dick Paget and situated in the Inyanga Mountains. This was an excellent environment – among the scented pine trees and the cool, high, country air – where I began to slowly build up through controlled physical activity. Daily workouts in the lodge gym and graded runs on the dirt roads that wound around the pretty hill country slowly brought the battered body back into operational fitness. All the training was closely supervised by staff to ensure no further damage. One character, the 47-year-old Pop Gentry – a Brit serving in 1 Commando RLI, who had fought in the British Army, French Foreign Legion and Australian Army over 30 years – assisted the damaged men. He had injured his back in a parachute landing and remained to aid others with their recuperation. His 'if I can do it, you can' flavor worked, and he was a 'no bullshit' kind of guy, which leant itself well to broken bodies (and, in some cases, spirits). Unfortunately, I heard in the months ahead that he had to leave for the UK for medical treatment.

Once again, I ran into Jim Datsun of the army's Engineers at the lodge, who was totally immersed in physical training. I had known Jim for a couple of years of fierce drinking in the Copper Pot, along with his sidekick, 'Stingray'. An ex-British Army soldier, Jim had lost a leg below the knee on an anti-personnel landmine in our own minefield. The rain had shifted the mines in the loose sand and he stepped on one that shouldn't have been there – and his leg evaporated. Jim road-tested a new prosthetic leg and ran for kilometers along the empty roads. Once he was satisfied, he returned to work in the minefield again.

After the lodge, I hung about in Salisbury and was then readmitted back to the Andrew Fleming hospital for a second operation to remove an infection in my chest. After 10 days on the road to recovery, as Mr Standish-White did his morning rounds, I asked for permission to attend a rugby game at the Police Club and told the surgeon I'd be back at four. He agreed. I returned drunk and disorderly at four in the morning – and the matron was not amused. Fortunately, Mr Standish-White retained a sense of humor, as I slept through his morning rounds – and the liver passed a critical test!

I grew increasingly restless as my recovery finalized. With nothing much on the agenda, I spent days drinking and being a pest. The South African nurse that I enjoyed a brief fling with in Durban sent me a letter to say that she was coming to Rhodesia to visit. That spurred on the desire to drop out of sight, as I needed a relationship like a hole in the head. The time had come to vanish into the bush.

In June, Inspector Dawson was killed in a vehicle ambush; he was the second Echo Troop commander killed in action. Of the scores of rounds in the air, only one hit his Land Rover – and it struck him in the heart. A respected policeman, a Rhodesian representative rugby player and a swimming champion, who was married to the daughter of a serving policeman and who had a dynamic career ahead of him, his loss jolted Support Unit. A second blow came with the death of Johan Steyn – a quiet, serious young man, who had been tied to the same Support Unit training course as me. He was killed in a vehicle ambush in Nyajena TTL, just south of Fort Victoria.

I elected to divorce the Salisbury booze joints to conclude my recovery. The bush beckoned, but it was premature for me to return to India Troop. Whilst I recovered physically, I decided to dip my toe into combat when an opportunity presented itself, to 'test my bottle'. Reflecting on the Mangwende punch-up, I pondered on my reaction under fire … would I chicken out? Mentally, I didn't think so, but a germ buried deep in the subconscious might be triggered in a dangerous moment – causing muscles to go to jelly – and I didn't want the India Troop people to witness the event if it happened.

So why didn't I just get out? Wounded twice, with the second one close to fatal, I had earned a ticket to a quieter life. Why not apply for a desk jockey job? There were plenty of other opportunities in the police. Why not transfer to traditional policing in a city? Go back to a rural station? Or join the intelligence arm? It was difficult to logically answer that question: patriotism was not the driving force, or simply a duty to the men under my command, or to the Support Unit. Secretly, the driving force was a selfish love of combat and life with a complete lack of routine – none of the repetitiveness that dominated most mortals' lives … no nine-to-five job; no clock-in and clock-out; no ordinariness; no humdrum existence, like my father. I was hooked on the adrenalin rush – the intoxicating, natural chemical high; living right on the edge, which pumped adrenalin into every nook; the electricity spike of feeling utterly alive; the thrill of the unknown; the plucking of the arsehole; the perception of slow motion under enormous pressure; the frantic activity under accurate fire; the wind-sucking triumph in surviving … adventure for the sake of adventure. There was nothing in the world like it – and I was hooked.

In July 1978, to stop my antics in town, Support Unit HQ obliged and I was dispatched to Mantle Base Nyanyadzi – a tent city located behind the police station on the main Umtali-Fort Victoria Road. My orders were to offer hands-on experience and assist Superintendent Twine, the base commander. The appointment did not exactly excite me: Twine was in command of Mrewa Base when I was shot and, I thought – rightly or wrongly – that my casevac lacked urgency. He clearly wasn't pleased with the posting either, as he barely greeted me on arrival, as if I'd turned up with a contagious disease. My anti-establishment attitude ran counter to his police mindset, so we were complete opposites. He didn't want some upstart to fiddle in his kingdom, but he had no choice, as I had been thrust upon him. I felt like a delinquent who had been thrown into a monastery, so I decided to find combat, test myself and then go.

From my perspective, Julian Twine was an unusual individual. As skinny as an Ethiopian in a drought, he seemed to relish postings to remote and obscure police stations, like a lost soul. No doubt though, he was a model policeman – admitted to the holy of holies … a commissioned rank … the 'Machine' establishment had certainly lined him up in the career stakes. A bachelor and a fitness fanatic, he ran to the top of the big hill behind the Nyanyadzi police camp every afternoon. I slumped in a canvas director's chair in the camp and, with a cold beer in hand, watched him sweat. He returned sweaty and breathless and insisted I accompany him next time – no thanks.

Each morning, after a cup of hot instant coffee, I wandered to the operations tent, read the overnight logs and settled back in the director's chair while listening to the radio chatter reporting small incidents. There were at least 14 Support Unit sections spread through Mutambara TTL and the adjourning tribal lands. On my first two days, Quebec sections deployed north into Mutambara TTL and soon reported a contact, as well as recovering an SKS rifle. They consumed an extraordinary amount of ammunition, so I drove out a resupply. Another Quebec callsign sighted 15 CTs and fired at them, but with no result; a Foxtrot section was mortared at night. A startled voice called Base for comfort – alone in the dark, with bombs exploding – but what could we do? Romeo rounded up a number of *mujibas*. These youngsters cemented themselves as a local menace. Another Romeo section sighted a lone CT, who quickly evaded them. The Romeo Troop commander had set up his night position in the late afternoon and wondered out loud why his section had attracted a hail of small arms fire just before dark. The Quebec section sighted 12 CTs, but failed to engage them. There was plenty of 'contacts, no casualties either side' and no follow-up.

Over the days ahead, the number of small incidents and sightings escalated

– creating a continuous radio buzz describing CT-related activity, but producing no concrete results. The sections did not get a firm grip of the enemy, and the daily frustration of listening to a string of small incidents mounted. I wanted personally to reach out there and pummel the enemy. Sightings were fleeting, just seconds at long range, before the CTs engaged their running shoes. By the time someone spotted them – and the police brain had registered 'enemy' – the terrorists had already disappeared. A bullet fusillade blistered after them – slicing into the scrappy leafy shield as they ran. With one section alone, there was no simple means to tie the enemy down, or to block off all escape routes, so small, fleeting contacts became part of the weekly grind. The superintendents commanding the Mantle Base were guilty of reprimanding their men for too many contacts, no casualties either side. The caustic comments didn't help either, as they offered no solutions.

On some pretext, I drove to Umtali, where I met up with John – an ex-British Military policeman and ex-constable from an English county police force, who had enjoyed the same training course as I in Morris Depot, 1975. He was stationed at the Umtali police station and we met for a beer at a local hotel. John malingered his way through police training with exquisite skill, and he had no desire to be treated like a raw recruit for the third time. He had completed basic army and police training in the UK, and was underwhelmed when he found out that he had to endure basic training once again in Rhodesia, so he played on an old parachuting injury to avoid the hours of foot drill and PT. By producing a medical certificate, he avoided marching everywhere. The instructors were miffed, but indulged him. When the bush training phase arrived, the training staff delighted in informing him that if he could not complete the bush bash, he would be held over till the next training course. Suddenly, a miracle occurred: the back popped into first-class shape, but the moment the bush phase ended, he leapt off the back of the parked truck and immediately reported a twinge in his spine. His first posting landed him in the Marandellas police station, where one night, he terrorized another policeman in the single men's mess and chased him with a shotgun when the terrified man escaped out onto the lawns. Allegedly, a couple of rounds were fired off – and fortunately, John got away without being charged by the skin of his teeth.

Mantle Base reacted to convoy ambushes inside our operational area. The national highway from Umtali to Fort Victoria traveled through large slabs of untamed tribal country and received a share of attacks. As the Mozambique border ran less than 40 kilometers east, terrorist units tramped into Rhodesia and aided local detachments by nobbling the main road. At Hot Springs, the motel had been abandoned and, with the help of energetic vandals, began to crumble; a passing motorist stopped at the police station and reported seeing more vandals. A lone salesman, driving south, found himself in a hail of small arms fire and three rifle grenades sailing over his Peugeot 404 sedan. The shaken driver had escaped injury and then ducked into the Nyanyadzi police station to report the incident. Alpha Troop, who replaced Foxtrot, was ambushed on the main highway, with nine hits on an RL Bedford truck; one constable was slightly wounded. A civilian fatality occurred soon after I arrived: an RPG-7 anti-tank projectile blasted a sedan driven by a farmer's wife – killing her.

The Police Reserve organized a convoy system for the protection of motorists along major national highways that cut through wild terrorist country. Designated routes between Point A and Point B were advertised. At the start of the journey, travellers rendezvoused at signposted staging points at set times on the outskirts of town; then the convoy drove in a column from A to B – protected by an armed Police Reserve vehicle in the front, the rear and sometimes in the middle (depending on the length of the column). The Police Reserve used a civilian light truck pickup, with a belt-fed MG on a rig mounted on the tray, which could swivel through 360° and send out a devastating volume of fire. The police vehicle's passenger maintained radio communications with fixed stations along the route.

Although the Police Reserve provided protection, the convoy system was not compulsory; anyone could travel alone if they were so inclined. Some lone cars traveled at high speed and bristling with rifles from every window. The risk of ambush was not only blindingly obvious, but even a simple puncture left the driver stranded in unfriendly territory, on their own. Consequently, the convoy system promoted the 'herd instinct'.

A convoy was ambushed not far up the road from the base, as we heard the distinct crackle of gunfire. The radio called – urgently seeking help. Fortunately, there were no reported casualties. All Mantle callsigns were deployed and I told Twine I'd handle the response. I rushed from the radio room and grabbed two white section leaders, who were resting up in base. The two surprised men were the only spare people. One dashed off to grab the spare MAG, while I rounded up maps, codes and an A73 radio set. We boarded a vehicle driven by the station police and soon arrived at the convoy. The cars had driven through the shower of bullets, but were now parked on the roadside, with the Police Reserve assisting a shocked driver.

"Where's the ambush?" I asked the older Police Reservist, who chatted to the stricken driver.

"Two bends up. You'll see a small cutting on the left … " he arched his eyebrows, "are you it?"

"We're it," I replied, as the Hyena accelerated up the sealed road.

The police dropped the three on the roadside and swiftly U-turned and departed. We stood alone on the tarmac road and looked around for likely ambush points. A cutting in the road 30 meters away flagged itself as the probable spot. We tramped over and quickly found 20 firing positions. The grass lay flattened and warm expended 7.62mm Intermediate cases littered the ground. A lost Russian HD hand grenade sat in the grass – looking lonely. Behind the warm ambush site, a dirt track meandered parallel to the firing positions. Clear-cut *spoor* was stamped on the grainy surface, as plain as marks on wet concrete.

"OK boys, let's go."

We were off: three strangers – striding alongside the well-beaten dirt track. The shoe prints stayed on the track that cut straight into the Maranke TTL. This tribal landscape was a large, isolated slab of timbered country, which claimed to be the 'Wild West'. A semi-liberated tribal land, Maranke swarmed with CTs. I shrugged off the possibility of running smack into a large group who'd salivate at the prospect of three lightly armed white men walking straight into their ambush.

We chased the clear-cut *spoor* for 10 kilometers. The ZANLA ambush team made no attempt to cover their tracks and walked on worn dirt paths for the entire course of their escape. Their shoe prints glowed in the grainy dust – displaying confidence in their status. We alternatively jogged and walked the trail, and had no difficulty in latching onto the *spoor*. The tracking was so easy, even for non-trackers, that time was not wasted attempting to find them. My fitness proved good and I felt unaffected by the fast foot journey. The path scorched a line through flat grass country, which was broken by tidy bunches of bush and shadowed by lush timbered hills. Along the route, we sighted no one; the population had made itself scarce.

Eventually, the shoe prints walked off the main thoroughfare and up a minor pathway to a lonely *kraal*. An old man, dressed in a shoddy sports jacket and gray flannel trousers that were past their 'use by' date, was mucking about in a vegetable patch on the trackside. He looked up and called out a loud warning.

"Good afternoon, boss!" he called out loudly, in strained English.

A frightened quiver ran through his old body. Jackpot! I shoved him off the track and elbowed past, as we instinctively broke into a run. He wobbled and staggered off. We automatically spread out – jumping through the newly planted vegetable gardens – and ducked around the perimeter houses. As I encroached on the *kraal*, I slid up against a house and peered around the cracked pole-and-*dagga* wall. Out in front, a basketball court-sized hardened clay pan baked in the sun. Across the matte-brown flat clay, on the opposite perimeter, stood three relaxed CTs talking to four women and a male. The heart conducted a double flip! All three young men were engrossed in conversation with a middle-aged man seated on a hand-carved stool. Their AK rifles were casually slung over their blue denim shoulders, and the terrorists focused on the villager's words. They stood upright, side on to me – listening intently. Four youngish women stood behind the seated man – listening to the conversation in awe. The danger lay in the female audience, as one woman stood directly facing me.

My two companions had slipped around the other side of a second house – out of sight and out of whispering range. Should I wait for them? How long do I wait? Concerned that I'd been compromised, I lifted the FN rifle barrel, quickly aimed and fired one shot. The other Support Unit partners fired immediately without asking what was happening. The MAG thundered at close range. The sheltered village burst alive with machine gun fire, red tracer bullets, a dust veil from bullet strikes and loud shouting amongst ourselves. We dashed forward into the heat-warped dust cloud. A flash of color here and an ear-splitting MAG blast were the only foreign infringements.

I sprinted to occupy the CTs' position and, within a few strides, I crossed the clay pan. The handmade stool lay discarded on its side, but the speaker had vanished. A terrorist was sprawled in the gritty dust – clutching an AKM rifle. He was huddled down, with his clothes askew, and his skin was embedded with grains of sandy dirt. His face was a sandy mask, with blood pouring from his mouth. A 60mm mortar tube lay abandoned, about 10 meters away. Only one down? A few paces away, large puddles of warm blood had splashed across the baked earth, like someone had tossed out a bucketful. One or more badly wounded? I was constantly surprised how quick the ZANLA boys could vanish in a firefight. There was no sign of the girls, or the village speaker.

I paused, as the two section leaders snatched the AKM rifle and the mortar tube. There was fresh blood, splattered in pools, surrounding a perimeter hut, but then it appeared to separate. More than one badly wounded? Pools of blood were splashed heavily towards the outskirts, with another along the back of the huts. Follow which lot? Choosing the most liberal blood *spoor*, we dashed along to where the red stains led to the edge of the *kraal*.

"We go after 'im?" asked the MAG gunner.

"What do you think?"

"Let's do it."

The balance of the CT unit – resting unseen in the shade of thick scrub, behind the dry thorn fence at the back of the *kraal* – sprinted when the gunfire blasted. We didn't know they were there, but within a minute, we heard mortar bombs fired.

"Shit! Mortars! Down!"

There was a longish pause; then three HE bombs exploded so far away that we didn't see the detonations. Once the echoes died, we stood up, brushed ourselves off and laughed at each other – the dusty apparitions. The blood still pumped and the adrenalin tingled, and we were keen to get on with business. We chased the copious blood splatter along a main path and down a slope that led into the forest. The path carved through virgin forest – following a dry riverbed. The treetops shut out the sun – settling in the gloom. As the shade enveloped us, we slowed our pace to a cautious walk.

In the gloom, with the adrenalin still swishing, I began to feel a touch uneasy. The forest was comprised of towering trees and a lower foliage canopy, plus a dry riverbed littered with fallen logs and large boulders. We had trespassed into ideal ambush country, so how far should we push our luck? Staring across to the opposite bank, I suddenly spotted a flat green color and sidestepped for a better view. The green cloth – splurged with dark bloodstains – was tangled in dry wood. Shit! I ducked. Using rapid hand signals, the MAG deployed to where the gunner could clearly see the opposite bank, with his mate squatted next to him. I waited until both were in position; then, covered by the MAG, I scrambled alone across the sandy riverbed. Was it a wounded CT? I ducked and dived through old tree trunks and large boulders, and surfaced on the bank close to the object. Hugging the bank, I debated whether to toss a grenade over onto the lip. I peered back at the gunner, and he made no indications of any immediate threat, so instead, I eased myself up to a crouch; then I raised my eyes above the embankment and drew level with a face … a pair of brown eyes looked back. My heart flipped and, before fright set in, I recognized the woman who had been talking to the enemy. She had collapsed into a loose heap among the wood debris. Her eyes were wide open in shock – the dullness setting in and her mouth dribbling dark-red blood. Her dress was drenched in arterial blood; the early flies had honed in. I reached out and touched her. She was dead.

I signaled the gun team to join me in the streambed.

"Shall we push it further?" asked the gunner, as he surveyed the deceased.

"No. We're too few an' that's thick shit in there," I replied, as I surveyed the tall timber, but I was secretly pleased. I still received the positive adrenalin boost and enjoyed the hunt.

I elected to return to India Troop.

A few days later – seated in the canvas chair in the operations tent – the radio squawked into action.

"Mantle Base, this is Mantle Papa Two, over."

"Mantle Base, go ahead," I responded to the early-morning call – yawning and stretching.

"Roger, I have eight, I say again eight Charlie Tangos visual, over."

"Roger that," I stated – sitting up smartly in the canvas chair, "confirm your locstat, over."

The voice read out a shackle code, my sidekick deciphered it and then plotted the spot on the operational map. The callsign squatted in their night position.

"This is Papa Two, request Foxtrot Foxtrot, over."

"Roger that, back to you later, out."

The operational wheels started to crank. I placed a call with JOC Umtali – stating the target and grid reference. They ascertained whether they had a strike force available. The decision now rested entirely in their lap, so it was time to just shut up and drink my coffee. After 30 minutes, they called to state that Fireforce was airborne and on the way.

"Mantle Papa Two, this is Mantle Base, Foxtrot Foxtrot is airborne, switch to channel one four, good luck, over."

"Papa Two, switching now, out."

I sat back and stared at the botchy canvas roof – imagining the OP focused on the target and the four inbound Alouette helicopters filled with grim-faced young soldiers, who would be keyed up for action, swooping in. The quarry was in the bag. I changed to channel one four and listened. The coy batman entered and brought in breakfast – a bacon and egg toasted sandwich, with a hot cup of coffee … the fruits of base camp! Within 10 minutes, the Papa callsign began the talk-in. His voice was a little flustered – the nerves crackling in his young tones. The helicopters soared on his grid reference and all eyes from the aircraft scanned the treetops for signs of eight terrorists.

"Mantle Papa Two, K-Car, we're over target, can't see anything. Where are you, over?"

The callsign repeated his coordinates and the K-Car commander snapped back.

"Mantle Papa Two, then we must be flying on top of you, over."

The OP spotted the helicopters flying kilometers away. Suddenly, it dawned on the section leader that the grid reference he had transmitted was wrong – kilometers wrong. The Papa team was not where he thought. Disorientated on the night walk, he sat now at least five kilometers out. The helicopter assault force had soared over the empty bush. The eight CTs – startled by the sound of the distant rotor blades – took the hint and ran. By the time the OP sorted out his true location, the quarry had escaped. A muttering Fireforce commander departed.

The Papa callsign was embarrassed into silence, but to their credit, remained static on the same OP – confident they had not been blown. Two days later, the same excited voice bounced on the radio waves and announced they had sighted 35 CTS. The exhilaration in his voice was palpable, but everyone in the Mantle Base radio shack held their breath.

"Roger, they're walking in single file, heading west. All in a matte-green uniform, all weapons visual, over."

We knew this time that the grid reference was solid; this time, the talk onto target was sweet. The RLI Fireforce landed right amongst the unsuspecting CTs – a perfect aerial ambush. The roar of gunfire began immediately and the sporadic, vicious fighting raged all afternoon, as the army Stop Groups engaged small bunches of terrorists right into the descending dusk. Elated with the success thus far, the RLI elected stay put on the ground overnight. The helicopters withdrew, and Papa OP switched to sentry and semi-sleep mode.

Before dawn the next morning, the fighting erupted once again. Up before a sparrow's fart, the bright-red tracer bullets sliced through the drab scrub. The enemy had been freshly trained and armed, and was on their way back into the country for the first time. They were so scared in the initial vicious battle that instead of using the cover of the long night to slink off and evade the attacking soldiers, they had simply stayed in the scrappy scrub in exactly the same place where they'd hidden when darkness fell – absolutely frozen in terror; the instinct overrode reason. Man has three survival instincts: fight, flight or freeze – and they elected freeze. It was a fatal decision: 33 CTs were killed, with 34 weapons recovered.

Later, a newly captured man (not from the Papa contact) was hustled into Mantle Base. Aged in his late thirties (possibly early forties), he wore dark-blue overalls, with the words 'Dairy Board' embroidered in red cotton over the chest pocket. Older than the standard terrorist model, he looked out of place, like a middle-aged man at a teenager's party. His lined face and mature countenance unsettled me. Was he with ZANLA, or was he a hanger-on? Maybe a senior leader? Or a nobody? The army insisted he possessed an AK and chest webbing when he surrendered, and SB asked me to accompany the captured man on air recce to see if he recognized any bases used by local detachments.

"What were you doing in ZANLA?" I asked to him, to get a better handle on his experience.

"I crossed over to Mozambique in 1975," he stated, in good English, "an' spent three years driving a truck. I used to drive for the logging company in the hills here before I joined the 'Brothers', so I was one of the few qualified drivers. I drove the boys and supplies to camps near the border."

"So, how come you ended up here?" I asked, with interest.

"One day, I was told to take up arms and cross back into Zimbabwe," he shrugged nonchalantly. "This is the second time."

His stiff demeanor and offhanded attitude did not sit easy. He played a bumbling oaf – the ignorant worker. While innocence was stamped on his lined face, his constant fidgeting and reddened, flickering eyes said something else. He didn't look commonplace to me … there was an underlying self-confidence that didn't sit right. He might be a senior commander, who was trying to disguise his status, but I wasn't sure. SB confidently assured me he was nobody.

We flew in a Police Reserve Cessna over the eastern border TTLs – seated together behind the farmer pilot. This was his first ever flight. I examined the map and pointed out relevant features on the brown and green terrain below – features he should have known if he operated in the area. He shrugged and stated he didn't recognize anything; he acted disorientated and unsure. We flew for almost 30 minutes, in which time he stated plainly he didn't see anything he could name. With no worthwhile intelligence gleaned from this escapade, we landed and handed him back to SB. I suspected he was a ZANLA commander trying to emulate an ignorant soldier.

By now, I had grown tired of the radio and quasi-administration work, and informed Superintendent Twine I would return to Salisbury to join India Troop. He had no hesitation in releasing me, so when the next available transport headed to the capital, I hopped aboard. In the meantime, substantial changes occurred at Support Unit Headquarters: new barracks had been under construction for months at Chikurubi – custom-built and almost ready to be occupied. The Support Unit structure was in the throes of being transformed into bigger, company-sized formations and new commanders were being drafted in from other branches of the police. The reformation made sense: scales of economy enjoyed by bigger formations rendered independent, troop-sized units impractical from many aspects – including command and control. Company-sized units were the natural progression from Mantle Base organizations.

Once I arrived back at HQ, I snooped about – eliciting more details. I found the transformation certainly had slipped enemies in positions that would have a definite negative impact. Men of senior rank who had their noses put out of joint in their dealings with me now had recourse. The Support Unit CO Assistant Commissioner Collins, who had shielded my antics from some of the keener disciplinarians, accepted retirement – his replacement yet to arrive.

The Command reluctantly offered a 2IC of a company where the commander, an inexperienced inspector, had been conscripted from the Traffic Branch. They suggested I would be valuable as an advisor. After the independence experienced thus far, I didn't want to play second fiddle – pushing administration and paperwork; in fact, I hated the paper war, nor was I interested in coaching someone with little practical combat experience. The new commander was likely to be a career man, with the 'Rulebook' firmly tucked under his arm – and therefore irritated by a non-conformist.

The Support Unit, once the police dumping ground for the unruly and those with discipline problems, began to exude a different aroma. As the unit's war success lifted its profile, police who avoided the posting were now knocking on the door. I knew these career inspectors and more senior ranks would be appalled by my cavalier behaviour; the boisterous, anti-social antics were detrimental to the BSAP myth. With these gentlemen logging into senior positions, with one eye on the career ladder, I definitely felt the icy winds of change. Whilst I loved the India Troop boys, I didn't need that bullshit. I decided to resign and promptly did so.

The news came through in August that Bill McClelland, who joined the

BSAP from the Royal Ulster Constabulary, was killed in a freak contact. At the time, he thought seriously of pulling the pin and returning to Northern Ireland. He was on operations in Rundu TTL with another section, and together they spotted CTs. In the ensuing battle, the CTs fired a series of mortar bombs at one section, with one bomb overshooting and landing right next to the Irishman – killing him outright.

13

Western Border: August–September 1978

In late August, Mick Busby and I drove 500 kilometers on the black asphalt highway – south-west from Salisbury and through the sleepy towns in the Midlands – to the city of Bulawayo. There we teamed up with an escort vehicle, and then headed south to Plumtree – a railroad town on the Botswana border. Busby had just returned from his holidays to rejoin the troop. India deployed somewhere out of Plumtree and we had orders to report to the police station for detailed instructions as to the troop's actual location. Although I enjoyed a short stint in Bulawayo and Inyati in the uniform police, this was the first time India had ventured into Matabeleland.

Matabeleland, the western province, was the home to the Matabele people – a warrior race descended directly from the regiments of Shaka Zulu. In the 19th century, the regiment rebelled against Shaka (so the story goes) and headed north from Natal – crossing the Limpopo River. They settled around Bulawayo, with their *impi* raiding the Shona tribes to the east for women and cattle. In 1978, ZIPRA CTs lurked here, with sole allegiance to Joshua Nkomo and the ZAPU party, which was based in Zambia. ZIPRA was the alternative nationalist guerrilla army, in a war where the African nationalists were split cleanly by tribal allegiances. Where ZANLA and ZIPRA operations overlapped, they did not hesitate to attack each other – and there was no love lost between the Shona and Matabele, with the ZIPRA combatants rumored to be better trained and tougher campaigners than their ZANLA counterparts. Other Support Unit troops reported contacts where the attacking ZIPRA unit pinned down a lone section with heavy small arms fire, before attempting a flanking move. The ZIPRA leader blew a postman's whistle to signal his flanking intent, and they'd have a serious crack at overrunning the section. At least one Support Unit section was mauled when they sought water – ambushed, encircled and hammered.

The escort vehicle from Bulawayo – a worn-out Hyena – finally broke down on the Plumtree Road and, impatient as ever with the delay, I elected to go on without them. We carried a cash payroll, which was stowed in a trunk in the back of the Land Rover. At the Plumtree police station, a bored section officer pointed out India's position in a border TTL, which was marked on his operational map by a white pin. The pin represented a Mantle Base that incorporated at least two other Support Unit troops. After a stop-off at the hotel for refreshments, we decided on the 'fuck it, let's go' strategy and drove straight through Plumtree and into the flat, scrubby countryside alone.

On the dusty road in the Mpimbila TTL, Mick and I saw a green blur sprint across the red road (about 30 meters ahead of the lone Land Rover) and vanish into the light scrub. The smudged apparition galloped three or four paces and evaporated.

"A fuckin' gook!" blurted Mick, as he snapped open his seatbelt harness.

As the metallic click announced the clip disengagement, Mick lunged from the cab. I braked hard and stirred up a choking, red dust cloud; then I skidded and stopped. I debussed rapidly and, using the stationary vehicle as a shield, scanned the gray scrub shimmering in the humming heat. The withered scrub stared back vacant; nothing was out there. Mick licked his dry lips as he attempted to spot the danger … nothing happened. I cautiously sneaked forward for a closer look, with Mick covering from the front fender. Clear military boot imprints were emblazoned in the reddish grit, but we weren't about to follow.

"We should shoot up the Land Rover," I laughed, when it was obvious that we were alone.

"An' nick the payroll."

It wouldn't be hard: using a folding-butt AKM in my metal trunk, I would fire a 30-round magazine through the windscreen, show our boot prints vanishing into the surrounding country; then follow it all up with a formal report that explained the missing cash; but I didn't follow up the statement, as one of my failings surfaced: I'm too honest. We boarded and drove on to Mantle Base. Interestingly, when I reported the incident, no one believed me.

We pulled up at the troop lines at Mantle Base, with lines of drab tents in a drabber countryside, and then alighted from the vehicle to stretch and observe (the long drive had numbed the backside). An HDF was under preparation – using Support Unit troops and a company of 2RAR. India Troop gathered together, kitted up, while other troops also milled about. The men greeted me with broad grins and we commenced backslapping. Senior Sergeant Kembo welcomed me back with an expansive smile and a firm handshake.

"You're fine now?" he asked.

"Good as new!" I replied.

Sergeant Ncube also shook my hand and looked at me in wonder.

"You are lucky!" he beamed – showing his neat row of teeth.

Mandaza ran his eyes over me from head to toe, as if measuring me for a coffin, smiled knowingly and wandered off.

Mandoza cleaned the linked ammunition with a piece of rifle cloth and chuckled.

Moyo stared quizzically … he was trying to spot the bullet holes.

"Don't worry Moyo, I'm invincible," I stated, as he laughed loudly. "The Very Reverend O'Brien can't be killed."

Ray and Billy came over to shake hands and slap backs, and Jim introduced himself. Jim was the new patrol officer who had replaced young Graeme. Tall, wiry and blond, with a sharp keenness to get the job done, he had settled into India whilst I was hospitalized. He hovered on the outskirts of the veterans to gauge where he fitted in. The troop morale was high, so I didn't tell them I had put in my notice to end my police service. That could wait till the end.

I'd hardly had time to unpack when the call came for a briefing. The section leaders and I reported to the main marquee, which was an operations center. A chief inspector I hadn't met, who didn't bother to introduce himself, didn't waste time on his plan; he launched straight into his tactical briefing. He split India Troop into individual sections to report directly to him. I thought that, clearly, he was another micro-manager. In one sentence, he had cut the troop leader out of the equation and I was just another section leader in his eyes. He took it upon himself to personally assign each section's area of responsibility, so how was it that the chief inspector, who had served in Support Unit for only two minutes, was already the expert? The knowledge must have come ready-packaged with the rank. He had not asked for comments, and he didn't even want suggestions.

"So, this is the new Support Unit regime," I thought, as I wandered off to prepare.

Thank God I was out.

Men with years of experience running a police station – handling crime and administration matters – were shipped to Support Unit. At the unit, they received six weeks' recruit training so that they joined their Mantle Base with the tactical training equivalent of a lance corporal. Unlike army officers, who trained at squad, platoon and then company strength, commissioned police entered with experience in PATU (four-man sticks, again corporal level), a short unit course and then undertook responsibility for company-sized organizations. I didn't stay long enough to see the transition, but wondered what they offered in tactical innovation.

My section patrolled the Tegwani riverbank for seven days 'to close off escape routes', the chief inspector had stated. Escape routes? I questioned the logic of one seven-man patrol versus dozens of kilometers of river frontage? His brief advocated that Support Unit sections operating further inland would stir up the resident terrorist group and force them to hightail to the river; then west into Botswana. India One had to block. One section, with dozens of kilometers, didn't sound practical, even in theory.

On the riverbank, an abundance of fresh elephant *spoor* and big piles of elephant shit signaled wildlife, but elephants were not sighted – only the overworked dung beetles. We patrolled extra-cautiously, not willing to bump into 'Big Game'. I had no reaction drill planned should we come face to face with a beast, apart from backing off at a hundred miles an hour. At night, we urinated on the game trails to scare off wandering animals and, to complete our protection, we dabbed a touch of rifle oil on low branches, as I didn't fancy an elephant blundering through in the night and stepping on people. I don't know if urinating or the rifle oil worked, but we didn't see game.

Away from the river line, the flat terrain made us reliant on pacing. Without a magnetic compass – and the absence of high country to fix a bead onto – pace counting became a clumsy, but rough estimate of our position. Once I established our location, we'd count the paces to the next bound. Every second step counted as one meter, because the sand and obstacles reduced the length of each stride. Once we counted the number of paces, all eyes were engaged in looking for confirmation that we stood at the end of the bound. We didn't get lost, which is saying something.

There were few villages, and the ones we spotted looked poorer than the villages on the eastern border. They were smaller, with ragged thatches and crumbling *daggas* – distinctly shabby and huddled in harsh, parched countryside, where the spindly scrub looked so dry it would disintegrate to the touch. The crops had yet to be planted, but plenty of mangy goats fed in this quasi-desert. The people appeared dusty and animal-wary, and talking to them produced shifty eyes and monosyllabic answers.

The HDF fizzled to nothing, and the patrolling inland sections did not force ZIPRA to dash to the river. If they were operating inland, a step to the left or right would have avoided our small numbers. We sweated and walked and cursed, and found nothing.

On a day that was back to shit, shower and shave, and resupply, the crisply-dressed chief inspector marched over and shoved us straight back in the *bundu*; we didn't even have a night in a camp bed. We continued the footslog operation south of Madyambudzi, which was across flat, gritty dust bowls that were punctuated with spiky acacia. Sweating freely under the white sun – criss-crossing the thirsty land and stopping locals to question them, with half an eye always out for water – water supplies were always low. Forced to enter the police station zone twice to replenish water (and to cadge fresh supplies), the police gave us the cold shoulder and a hard time about little things. They were definitely prickly. Assorted army and police units ambled in and out – disturbing their quiet rural outpost. It was shades of the Chibi police attitude, so I decided to shake them up.

Late one black night, India One silently approached the police station boundary wire from the scrub, and I decided to see how good these cowboys were inside their cage.

"Give 'em a rev?" asked Ray, with a cheeky twinkle in his eye.

"For sure," I grinned, and I set up the 60mm mortar tube.

I aimed the tube to drop bombs outside the perimeter, parallel to the police station building, but far enough away to avoid shrapnel damage. Three Soviet-made bombs were fired in rapid succession; then we stepped back and merged into the shadows – well out of harm's way. I heard later the brief rev caused anxiety and minor panic.

After the HDF operation, Support Unit dismantled Mantle Base to set up elsewhere, but to my delight, India Troop received orders to remain. The troop motored back to Plumtree to relieve 2RAR. Plumtree was a small rural town of 2,000 (621 whites: 1969 census) in population, with the railway and road junction from Bulawayo passing through into Botswana. Renowned for its high-performing boarding school, Plumtree also serviced the cattle ranching and mining. We found 2RAR based in an empty building that had been set up on the edge of town (possibly the veterinary department depot). This was luxury – an urban-based environment. Ray Hughes carried out the changeover administration with the army and, subsequently, was invited to dine in that evening. After a cold shower, he shaved and got dressed into a clean green T-shirt, with matching rugby shorts (all neatly pressed), as well as a pair of rubber thong sandals, and strolled over to the RAR officers' mess tent. Closer

Mick Busby, Billy Pring and the author at Plumtree, 1978. (Ray Hughes)

to the mess tent, Ray spotted the long table inside, which was laid with fine white cloth and adorned with the regimental silver. To his amusement, the RAR officers were smartly attired in their dress uniform (collars and bow ties), with miniature medals. Stopped at the entrance to the mess tent by a young lieutenant, the immaculately dressed officer stiffly told Ray that his dress code was totally unsuitable. Ray shrugged and ambled back to our informal base, as he couldn't fix his clothes. The police did not deploy to bush operations toting a dress uniform.

Stranded in Plumtree, with absolutely no intelligence, no briefing and no idea of enemy forces, numbers and even incidents, we had stepped right into a vacuum. The 2RAR company had packed up everything – including the operational maps and incident reports. Nothing was left behind of any value; we were just allotted an operational area – the small tribal areas south and west of Plumtree – and see you later! Special Branch didn't bother with us; we were just small fry.

Left to our own devices, the troop conducted a series of OPs for a week on the Botswana border. Three sections spread for 20 kilometers along the dry Ramakgoebana riverbank to observe locals casually walking back and forth across the border. I thoroughly studied each person who traversed the dry riverbed through our Zeiss binoculars – passing the glasses to the constables to confirm my findings. They corroborated my assessment: none of the pedestrians looked remotely like terrorists. They were just ordinary folk walking across the crumbly sand in the drudgery of the hot day – probably visiting relatives in Botswana, who had been separated by a national border arbitrarily drawn in by a British colonial government. We spied a Botswana military Land Rover cruising slowly along the riverbank, on their side, and we wondered what they were doing. Whatever it was, they were entitled to do it, but we didn't see any CTs.

When the OP time expired, I ordered pick-up of the troop. On the way to pick up our sections, a convoy led by a Kudu (a landmine and small arms-protected vehicle, which was built on a Land Rover chassis) drove into the jaws of an ambush. Crossing a dry streambed, the hidden enemy fired a solid volley from the opposite bank and struck the vehicle cold, but Jim buried his accelerator pedal and drove the Kudu hard through the ambush, with bullets pinging off the armor plate. After the event, an examination found that the bullet strikes on the metal plate were at such an angle that if the vehicle had have been a soft-skin Land Rover, the driver would have been killed – a sobering thought.

On 3 September, the horrifying news broke that an Air Rhodesia civilian Viscount – carrying 52 passengers and four crew – was shot down by an SAM-7 missile as it took off from the Kariba airport. The pilot managed to control the airliner sufficiently to crash-land the stricken airplane into a cotton field. His skill enabled 18 passengers to survive, but ZIPRA terrorists intruded onto the crash site and cold-bloodedly murdered 10 of the shocked survivors. It was really, really tragic. Imagine surviving an airplane crash, only to be then lined up and machine gunned. The nation was utterly appalled. The world remained silent – and still does today. The foreign governments all looked the other way and no one outside Rhodesia condemned the murder. To win, we needed to take the gloves off.

With no intelligence to operate upon, we began at zero, so I decided to switch to spying on villages from small, scattered, rocky outcrops. Whilst the landscape was boringly flat, occasionally the odd clump of huge granite rock lay in strategic locations. The rock clumps looked as if God had deposited one rock on top of another in some obscure game he had played. We observed one village, with the day creeping on, and the activities slowed to nothing. Hardly anyone moved, so it was like watching still life – the reverberating heat forcing animals and people into the cooler shade. Goats fossicked in the grass stubble – looking for a meal. After staking out a village for three hot and thirsty days – and observing nothing out of the ordinary – I tossed in covert spying and moved around.

The patrol moved among the scattered *kraals* – questioning and watching. The terrain was washboard-flat. India One walked unhurriedly towards a primary school with a disheveled youth, who had been found skulking in the bush, spying on us. With nothing specific in mind, the men noticed a group of village women striding ahead on the road, on the way to draw water, but looking back and displaying increasing signs of nervousness. Their flitting eyes became a dead giveaway; their drawn, anxious faces became wooden. They shot glances back at us, and increased their walking pace. Bingo: the symptoms are there. We picked up our walking speed and scrutinized the light woods – methodically searching the thin stands of trees. Our sudden presence created a frightened aura among the women that placed the terrorists very close.

Mandaza sighted four CTs walking hastily through the light timber, parallel to the road, some 30 meters off, but starting to angle away. They had sensed something was wrong, which was reflected in their urgent walking pace, but they had not begun to run. I wasn't sure if we had been seen, but imagined we had only seconds to react. I paused, shouldered the FN, aimed at a fuzzy figure lopping through the spindly trees, squeezed the trigger and fired – dropping him instantly. A brief, vicious exchange of small arms fire erupted, with both sides on the move. The terrain did not offer shelter from bullets. Fawn dust burst upwards – marking the indiscriminate bullet strikes and temporarily providing a smeared screen for the enemy to escape behind. Two fired on the run, with bullets cracking close by. We stopped, aimed and poured fire into the arcs to our front – the 7.62mm NATO bullets probing for exposed flesh. Red tracer spurted across the dust bowl.

"Stop!" I yelled, as the rifle fire spluttered. "Reload!"

Changing FN magazines – and certain that the enemy was too busy running to seriously oppose us – we shook out in a rough, extended line. A quick glimpse up the road confirmed the women had disappeared. My eyes flicked to the front and, satisfied we were ready, we stepped off to engage in an immediate sweep. We flitted through the light timber – alert for wounded stay-behinds – and carefully scrutinized the sun-fried terrain for the three survivors.

"There's one!" hissed Mandoza.

He pointed in the direction of a small *kopje*, and I peered along his outstretched arm. I saw nothing initially, and then sighted one African hopping desperately.

"Get 'im!" I growled, and we gave chase.

The hobbled man had a good lead – gathered up in a desperate survival attempt. If he'd continued with this momentum, he'd hop to the rock-and-scrub fort before we had caught up, so I stopped, stood beside a robust tree, rested the rifle barrel in the solid branch fork and aimed with infinite care. As the hopper rose up from the brown reedy grass and into the aperture sight, I squeezed the trigger. The rifle roared, recoiled and spat out the expended brass cartridge. The hopper collapsed and vanished into the dry gray scrub. We rushed in to finish the job.

"Look out, grenade!" a constable bellowed anxiously and, without question, I kissed the ground – belly down on the brittle soil. I imagined the armed grenade lying right next to my exposed face – separated only by a clump of sickly grass. The facial skin throbbed in anticipation. Time ticked by extremely slowly … I had only heard the shouted warning, and had not actually seen the grenade. Seconds stretched out, time drew on and, when nothing happened, I poised to jump to my feet and roundly abuse the man who shouted the warning, when the muffled explosion echoed. The wounded CT did not throw the grenade, but rather used the bomb to finish himself off. He hugged the steel head right in against his chest, over the heart. A huge crater blasted out the ribcage. By the time we sprinted forward, he lay askew – the chest cavity smoked with residue explosive. The blast cauterized the gaping wound, and the ribs were charred and reddish-black. A wisp of steam rose from the chest crater. These boys don't like capture. We recovered two AKM assault rifles and a full medic pack, plus some Botswana currency.

The patrols kept on. The continuous search and follow-up pressure mounted and, one morning, we heard automatic fire three kilometers off. The sound definitely emanated from Soviet Bloc small arms. Taking a general bearing on the gunfire, the men hoofed out through the impoverished landscape towards the source and, on the way, cut across the CTs' boot prints in the soft sand. Mandaza bored down on the shoe prints … the CTs smelt pursuit and had ran directly west, to the border.

"How far ahead are they?" I asked the tracker.

"Not too far, one hour," replied Mandaza, with a shrug of the shoulders.

The shoe prints were fresh in the loose sand – so fresh that the grains still slid inwards on the shoe impression, so we picked up the pace. We jogged to catch up. It was a hot and sticky exercise, with sweat pouring off our bodies and soaking our cotton clothing. The running pace drained our energy reserves as we strode, heavily laden, through the loose sand. The backpacks might have been filled with cement. The CTs had tossed aside any pretence of anti-tracking and fled. We threw caution to the wind and chased, but they beat us in the race. They crossed the border into Botswana about 15 minutes ahead of us. We stopped at the dry river border, squatted in the shade to rest and recuperate, and radioed in for permission to follow. Much vacillating took place before permission was finally refused. India Troop returned to Salisbury – a long and weary journey.

My application for discharge from the police – submitted at the beginning of this bush trip – had been rubber stamped; it was official. I was happy to depart, as the formalized Support Unit had become more structured, so therefore was less tolerant of the 'fly-by-the-seat-of-the-pants' leaders. It was finally time to say farewell to the men. At first, they thought I was joking, but when I wished Ncube and the crew good hunting, they realized I was serious. The constables were shocked; then amused.

"Where would you get another job like this?" they asked – and I wasn't sure.

These African warriors – the backbone of Support Unit – were the people I'd miss.

After the goodbyes and handshakes, I began the tedious discharge process: handing back my kit to stores and obtaining the required signatures. There was no debrief, and definitely no trumpets ringing out. I trudged from the warehouse to offices to strip myself of the last vestiges of the BSA Police. There were no handshakes, just sign here and go.

Whilst I considered myself among the better anti-terrorist exponents in Support Unit, no one encouraged me to stay. My in-town rowdy behavior did little to inspire senior people, and their career prospects could be blunted if they championed my cause. I brought the abrupt departure upon myself by not networking with men who held the strings of power. There is a price to be paid – assuming a moderate amount of talent was all one needs to get by.

Interestingly, throughout my posting in Support Unit, I do not recall ever

Ray Hughes receiving his wings, 1980. (Dave and Eileen Hughes)

being debriefed by anyone about the tactics and successes we enjoyed, as no one with any clout was vaguely interested. Only the previous head of depot training, Inspector Power – a veteran of the British and Australian Army, who had departed in mid-1977 for a commission in the South African Army – showed any curiosity. The middle and senior police ranks must have had all the answers, even though they offered little practical advice to the man at the coalface.

As I departed, I knew that India Troop and Support Unit would go on as if I had never been there. Someone said that the hole you left was comparable to the hole left behind after extracting a hand from a bucket of water. The Support Unit continued to contribute to the war effort in its understated way – and punching above its weight. Its continuous shortage of equipment was more than made up for by the fighting élan of its African warriors. I was proud to have fought alongside them. Hitching a ride, I took my final journey out of Tomlinson Depot and headed down to the pub.

Ray Hughes passed his aptitude exams, departed the police and joined the Rhodesian Air Force. He joined Training Squad PTC33, where he began the gruelling training schedule, before being packed off to pilot training in South Africa.

14

Interlude: October 1978

Unemployed and drinking aimlessly in the Salisbury hotels, I wasn't sure what was next. I'd departed the police on a whim, with no thought to what was next. I made no plans other than to party. One rowdy drinking session followed another at the usual haunts. One afternoon, Phil Smith surfaced in a bar – recruiting for farm security work. Phil completed his police contract in August and elected for discharge. Along with André Stapa, another ex-Support Unit policeman, Phil knitted together a private security format. He asked if I was interested.

"It's a 'bludge'," he smiled, at his only selling point. Light on cash, I agreed and together we drove east – 80 kilometers out of Salisbury to Marandellas – and then headed south. Our car glided through the low, rolling farming countryside before entering the Soswe TTL. A cattle grid across the road denoted the border. Soswe was a tiny TTL surrounded by commercial farms, like a tiny blot on the map, and the car drove through it in a few minutes. From the Soswe exit, the road led to the Mere Estate – a large tobacco and maize commercial property nestled into the northern border of the Dowa African Purchase Area. Dowa bordered my old hunting grounds in the Chiduku TTL.

The three-man security team bunked down in a small cottage, which was known light-heartedly as the 'maisonette' – a short walk down the road from the rambling Mere homestead. Christopher – a tall, gangly, logical Rhodesian – owned the Mere Estate and lived with wife Janice, his children Colin and Jennifer, and his mother. Chris had grown up on the farm, but had lived most of his adult life in Canada – pursuing his flying passion. There he met and married Janice. His father died and Chris and the family left a stable, provincial life in New Brunswick for the shaky uncertainty of Rhodesia to take over the family farm. Chris was his own man and did things his own way.

Janice, in her wildest dreams, never thought she'd be living in a Wild West show. An unflappable, bubbly and gregarious woman, Janice made everyone warmly welcome in her home. She exuded a quality of hospitality I had never experienced, but if a guest got on the wrong side, she was not shy to put her opinion bluntly and sharply.

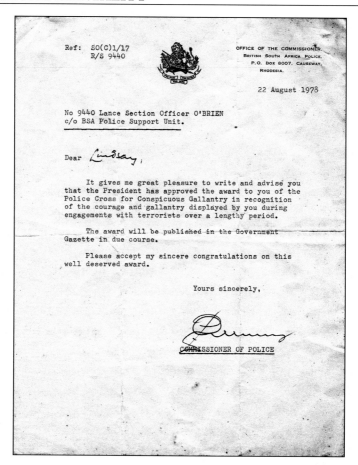

Ref: SO(C)1/17
R/S 9440

OFFICE OF THE COMMISSIONER,
BRITISH SOUTH AFRICA POLICE,
P.O. BOX 8007, CAUSEWAY,
RHODESIA.

22 August 1978

No 9440 Lance Section Officer O'BRIEN
c/o BSA Police Support Unit.

Dear *Lindsay*,

It gives me great pleasure to write and advise you
that the President has approved the award to you of the
Police Cross for Conspicuous Gallantry in recognition
of the courage and gallantry displayed by you during
engagements with terrorists over a lengthy period.

The award will be published in the Government
Gazette in due course.

Please accept my sincere congratulations on this
well deserved award.

Yours sincerely,

COMMISSIONER OF POLICE

The Police Commissioner's letter.

Like all farmers, they carried on life as normally as possible – taking common-sense precautions. The family house was one of very few without a security fence. Chris constructed a second brick wall, parallel to the main house, for the length of the house and strung chicken wire netting from the top into the steel guttering to prevent grenades from being tossed in the windows. A brick wall enclosed the courtyard at the rear, with a solid steel door to the outside. Inside the courtyard, a small sandbag bunker was constructed for the children. An antique two-inch mortar sat set up; I don't know where he had swiped that.

The farm security was organized and funded by a group of farmers who wanted a semblance of control over 'friendly forces'. Police Reserve topped up their money and issued FN rifles and ammunition. With the Security Forces stretched to breaking point, there was no guarantee of help if terrorists attacked a farm. Groups of farmers in vulnerable locations accepted that fact of life and elected to have ownership of the response.

Farm security equaled boredom – helping where possible and driving the quiet farm roads at night in an armored Land Rover. Randomly checking about 10 farming properties, we presented a floating target. To minimize the risk, we alternated the route and the timing – finding all sorts of interesting tracks to follow. Because some farmers resented paying for security, they'd phone in the morning to whine they had not heard the Land Rover; then Phil slipped on his diplomatic gloves and drove to the disgruntled farmer to prove that the Land Rover conducted the agreed checks. On Saturday night, before patrol time, we'd party away – sometimes at the main house. Phil – a flamboyant disco dancer – cranked up the music and took to the floor with such a flourish that John Travolta might blush. Also (as mentioned earlier), he perfectly mimicked David Bowie – much to Chris' astonishment. On Sunday afternoons, we'd all go onto the clay tennis court with tennis rackets – displaying a varying degree of skill – with the security team drinking from a flagon of rough Portuguese red.

One day, I drove into Salisbury for a break and the medal parade back at Tomlinson Depot, and stayed at André's father's house – a senior man in Customs – and, lo and behold, that night the main homestead came under fire. The terrorists humped an 82mm heavy mortar tube and set it up on the flat granite monolith behind our cottage. Without the benefit of a bipod or mortar base plate, they struggled to hold the tube as they fired. Nine mortar bombs were fired, but luckily there were no hits on the house. The children headed to the courtyard bunker as trained, and the bombard ended quickly. No one was injured, nor any property damaged.

The CTs ambushed the Land Rover one night – once again when I was partying in Salisbury. A long-range 'snotty' was fired across a ploughed field, which was aimed generally at the moving vehicle. The night burst alive with green tracer balls that hit nothing. A startled André accelerated and neither side suffered casualties.

During his time on the farm, André decided to attempt the SAS selection course and began earnestly training for the gruelling trial. During the day, in the intense October heat, he pounded the dirt roads, with large rocks jammed into his small backpack: off around the extensive maize fields; up and down the huge, gray granite *kopje* to the immediate rear of our encampment; then a solid workout with makeshift weights. He appeared motivated to pass, but I

Medal parade, 1978; the author receives the PCG wearing a hat
lent to Joan Stapa by the Honourable P.K. van der Byl.

wondered if that was just because he didn't know what to do next.

"Why don't you give it a go?" he asked me after one sweaty session.

"Too much like hard work," I answered offhandedly.

I was not sure whether he wanted a running partner to push him along in his training phase, or someone to egg on during the selection course. I helped with the former, but he could forget the latter. At heart, I was a lazy bastard.

In early November, the word drifted out that the army had created a new unit and required volunteers. Sniffing the air, a vague job description became visible – something to do with playing a liaison role in a political army. They required experienced applicants, and they trumpeted the pay as twice the police wage, with a month-to-month contract (the two most appealing job facets). Farm security had no future, and neither of us was prepared to sign contracts for regular service. We both required cash to zip overseas so, on a punt, Phil and I decided to join.

The political tempo in the country had altered substantially, as PM Ian Smith reluctantly acknowledged that black majority rule was reality. The USA had finally wrestled South Africa onto the floor by turning the economic screws hard – and South Africa, in turn, muscled Smith into a tight corner. Elections for majority rule were proposed for April 1979, with a number of moderate African political parties competing. As the two terrorist entities led by Robert Mugabe and Josiah Nkomo were excluded, the odds were stacked in the favor of the unlikely Bishop Muzorewa of the UANC and the newly moderate Reverend Sithole of ZANU. Both parties required a military wing to assist them to disseminate their political programs into the war-torn TTL. Without armed support, neither party stood a chance with electoral campaigning in the rural zones, when the TTL swam in banned ZANU-PF terrorists.

The rise of political armies burst into the public domain when the *Sunday Mail*, on 13 August 1978, ran the headline: 'Muzorewa Meets Guerrillas in Historic Ceasefire Zone'. The article splashed photographs of Bishop Muzorewa clutching an AK rifle and introducing 'Comrade Max', who loudly declared himself the commander of the Msana TTL. Max brashly claimed that he ran Msana, and all his men claimed to be former ZANLA fighters who had swung their allegiance behind Muzorewa. Peace has finally come to Msana, he cried. In reality, Max was a Special Branch creation, but the article infuriated the 'fight to the last bullet' white citizen.

By late 1978, the Security Forces were stretched tight. That meant large swaths of tribal land – thousands of kilometers of remote country – existed without an SF presence. The SF had not been defeated; they had simply run out of people. To fill the increasing void, the government drummed up a new 'guerrilla' force to provide a permanent presence in these areas, so that a newly elected black government could seize and hold gains. The recruiting also tapped into African human resources that were unavailable to the Regular forces due to education or political alignment. By shifting some of the unemployed youth into the government's pocket, this kept them out of ZANLA's reach. At least this strategy made sense, and so began a massive recruitment of loyal followers. The core guerrilla army – initially recruited and raised by Special Branch – utilized the expertise of selected SAS and Selous Scout soldiers. They set up ultra-secret training facilities on abandoned commercial farms – properties situated well away from prying eyes. The SAS and Selous Scout trainers largely withdrew from the training program as the shroud of secrecy lifted and the army presence became public. This gig was probably not sexy enough for the elite troops. From then on, the Special Forces HQ was handed the dubious task of running the new program.

Special Forces HQ originally formed as an umbrella organization to command the SAS, Selous Scouts and Grey Scouts, but the concept never got off the ground, and so, lost for something useful to do, took over the administration, training and logistics of the political armies. Based in a four-bedroom house on the edge of the old married quarters at King George Barracks in Salisbury, under the command of Colonel McVey, operations were split evenly into the two distinct African political camps: the ZANU-affiliated army – touted as more volatile than the UANC – required greater skill in diplomacy and political nous. They came under the wing of an SAS Major Harvey, an aloof officer, and his super-secret liaison officers. He ran his operation from a pre-fabricated building erected in the front yard of the main house – closeted away from the UANC mob. He always appeared to be stressed out – ricocheting from one crisis to another. The UANC responsibility fell directly into the lap of Major Tom Douglas, Rhodesian Light Infantry, who also appeared permanently harassed (that mental condition formed part of the job description). Phil and I were attached to the UANC element. The Special Forces had been raised from scratch at very short notice, so no doubt thousands of niggling supply, logistic and administration problems rebounded around the building. I'm sure the bevy of Regular Army officers and NCOs didn't know whether they were coming or going.

Phil and I, in simple terms, were hired as liaison officers in the UANC's fighting organization to provide tactical advice, organize the logistics and supply, and provide the vital communications to allow the African commander to get on with his work. We were the men at the sharp end of the business – out in the tribal areas, living rough, and working and assisting the detachment commander. To get on board (and to comply with bureaucratic military administration), we were drawn into the unit strength and army payroll as sergeants, with a Territorial Army number. Although officially on the army payroll, it was only an administration tie-in. No uniforms were issued, and there were no officers to salute (because we wore civilian clothes); there were no bullshit parades, no pedantic barrack inspections and no sleepless guard duties, but one thing SF did have in common with all military units was the 'hurry up and wait' syndrome.

Once on board, we reported to HQ for work at eight each morning – slightly worse for wear after a night's partying. Major Douglas flicked us off by asking us to wait on the rock – a granite outcrop in the front garden of the SFHQ – and, at about ten o'clock, someone wandered out and stated there was nothing on that day, so off we toddled to the pub. We didn't care; after all, they were paying. Fortunately, as liaison officers, we weren't immersed in the army bureaucracy – thrashing about trying to secure basic items from a government strapped for cash.

An Australian, Skip Dolega, faced the same flexibility on that rock. He arrived in Rhodesia on spec, and being a rugged Australian individualist who had served in the Australian Infantry, he refused to sign a contract to join the Rhodesian Regular Army. Other foreign soldiers – comfortable with the three-year contract – explained to him that if he didn't like the army, he should simply board an aircraft home and that would be that: the famous 'Out Clause'. Skip, not convinced, operated in the field for a few months with a Territorial battalion before volunteering for this lark. We nicknamed Special Forces 'Monty Python', which seemed apt, due to the comical disorganization.

Finally, Phil and I were assigned to a Muzorewa mob training on Retreat farm, which was north of Bindura. After a sketchy briefing, Special Forces issued a bright-orange Land Rover, AK rifles and ammunition, a briefcase of cash and a destination. Special Forces tried to disassociate themselves from formal army colors by painting their vehicles any color other than brown or green. They painted them bright orange, deep blue or plain white – hardly fantastic for bush concealment. Skip was assigned to a group operating in Rushinga and departed Salisbury on his own.

With our personal kit on board, we departed headquarters and Phil drove out towards the King George Barracks gate. Suddenly, an irate officer stomped straight onto the road and waved stop! Phil braked and eased to a halt, with the Land Rover almost touching the man. The officer stepped stiffly next to the driver's door and demanded to know what we were doing inside an army barracks dressed in civilian clothes, armed by the enemy and riding in a luminous-orange Land Rover.

"Get fucked," Phil replied, when he noted the beret badge – a major in the Education Corps … a commissioned schoolteacher! Always the fucking 'Jam Stealers'.

"What did you say?" the immaculately-attired major roared – so angry that his neck glowed brilliant-red. "What unit are you from?"

"Monty Python's Flying Circus," Phil smiled, and we drove off and cheekily waved – leaving him yelling at the retreating vehicle.

I wondered why some officers were like that – the 'kiss my arse' species. In my world, they'd have to serve two years as a private soldier in the muck; then – and only if they have the wherewithal – would they be offered an opportunity to apply for a commission and attend the college.

We drove north-east out of Salisbury and off to war armed with AKs and a briefcase crammed full of ten-dollar notes. Our instructions included the grid reference for an anonymous turnoff north of Bindura, so we finally guessed the offshoot and drove slowly down an unsigned dirt farm road. The overgrown road finally led into a secluded valley, and we noted a building in the distance. As we drew closer, scrub shielding a plain-brick farmhouse opened up and we saw three vehicles parked in front. I felt a touch uncomfortable when we finally drove up to the isolated house, as a score of Africans – wearing blue denim and carrying AK-47 rifles – were aimlessly milling around outside.

The scores of Africans involved in training had been sold to the public as returned terrorists who had seen the light, and who had swung their full support behind the good bishop, but as Phil and I soon discovered, those billed as terrorists deserting the Patriotic Front ranks (a name now used by the real terrorist forces, so as not to be confused with Sithole's ZANU) were nothing but a shower of dodgers dragged out of the teeming shanty townships surrounding Salisbury. Only one solitary man of the 150 flunkies had ever been a guerrilla fighter. After being shipped wholesale onto the farm, the mob received rudimentary military training, which was conducted with questionable discipline. Dressed in cheap denims, they struck arrogant poses with their AK-47s – hiding behind shades and cigarettes dangling from the corners of their lips: the black James Deans; the Security Force Auxiliaries; the SFA.

The vast majority did not have two cents in their pocket when they were swept up in the bulk recruiting drive and trucked like cattle into the wilderness; then clothed, fed and armed – compliments of the taxpayer. Every little whim had been catered for, from Madison cigarettes to plastic toothbrushes. Someone made a small fortune wholesaling cheap clothing – manufacturing canvas ammunition bandoleers – and also providing the basics needs, such as wool blankets and spare clothing, right down to the soap and green towels.

The commander was the only ex-terrorist. In his forties, he was an African gentleman named Albert, who had been captured soon after entering Rhodesia in the mid-1960s without completing his mission; then he was promptly jailed for life in Khami prison. After 10 years' incarceration, Albert delicately slid his allegiance behind the bishop, which was rewarded with an immediate release, on the condition he accept the dubious command of 150 questionable warriors. He was the 'token' ex-guerrilla: quietly spoken and an amateur philosopher, he sounded like a tired schoolteacher rather than a hardened terrorist. He grasped at the evolving concepts caused by the whirlwind political changes, but was clearly treading in water out of his depth. When I met him, his handshake equaled a wet fish and he avoided my eyes.

Phil and I spent days observing the motley detachment jump through its paces – the whole gambit: silent patrolling, fractured shooting and fumbling weapons handling. Scrutinizing the shooting, I winced. Shuffled into ranks of 20, each rank fired off a 30-round magazine into the open *veldt*, just blasting the shit out of the scrub. Bullets zapped into the wilderness; no targets to check. What did that achieve? An SAS instructor demonstrated the RPG-2 rocket launcher, as well as the 60mm mortar. A rocket and a bomb flew into the open paddocks and detonated with a sharp bang. For some unfathomable reason, the SFA members were not permitted to fire them, even though those weapons were part of the arsenal.

The detachment – about a traditional army company size – had completed five weeks' basic training before we had arrived, with a week more to finish. From a professional Security Forces viewpoint, six weeks would barely scratch the surface. Even the most optimistic trainer could not produce a reliable soldier from a raw African recruit in that timeframe. To produce a basic soldier, a minimum of six months' solid training was required, but this venture pressganged unemployed illiterates straight into service. Their primitive military skills were not the only challenge: large chunks of them were urban dwellers, with little concept of the primeval world they were about to be dropped into. They held distorted illusions of life ahead.

Phil and I mixed and chatted, and listened and observed. They were a diverse bunch – lumped together from different tribes with competing motives. Most said they were poor street kids – unemployed riffraff and unlikely to ever find jobs. Some saw the opportunity for self-enrichment, whereas a few exuded an animal political savvy – peering at us suspiciously, like we were the enemy. A small number looked in poor health, not having been properly medically screened. Nearly all were illiterate, and couldn't read or write any language, and many only spoke a meager amount of English words. Most couldn't even tell the time from a wristwatch.

Before deployment, Phil and I drove to the Zambezi Valley to check out the facilities set aside for the detachment. On the way through Centenary, I stopped in to see Doug. I worked a season for Doug in 1973/1974, where I learnt the fundamentals of tobacco farming. Doug was a community leader, a rural councillor in Umvukwes and active in the Police Reserve. A few days prior, Special Branch officers met farmers at the Centenary Country Club and explained our purpose in the neighborhood. Their words were not well received. The attending farmers voiced their opposition in straight talking – taking the news as heresy. Like many farmers, Doug chose not to attend the formal meeting. Busy fixing a Massey Ferguson tractor when we pulled up, Doug shunned talk about the changing events. The conversation was low-key and disjointed; we represented the future he didn't want to see.

15

Gutsa: November 1978

We drove on and down the steep road to Mzarabani, on the Zambezi Valley floor, and introduced ourselves to the police MIC and the DO at the Internal Affairs office. We also shook hands with a supervisor for Tilcor – a government agricultural arm charged with establishing commercial ventures in the TTLs. Tilcor planted vast irrigation fields that contrasted sharply with the dead matte-brown of the Valley floor, with the lush-green cotton crop looking misplaced in the harsh matte-brown wilderness.

The guerrilla war had incubated in the Zambezi Valley in the 1960s. Gangs roamed freely – trying to put down a conventional base – but were soon detected and killed, or driven out. The war had spluttered across the roasting plains for more than 12 years, and the sparse tribespeople were extremely wary. A generation of people grew into teenagers on a war footing, so this was a tough nut for the UANC to crack.

We drove out of Mzarabani – west, on the main gravel road. On the left side of the road, neat green cotton fields stretched out in regimented rows, with the dark Zambezi escarpment rising straight out of the plains – hovering in the background. The harsh, speckled African bush filled the land on the right. In this neck of the woods, the people were uprooted from their traditional lives in *kraals* and lumped together into a single, large town known as a 'Collective Village', which was shunted right next to the Mzarabani Road. A simplistic Collective Village differed from a Protected Village because it was not enclosed in a barbed wire fence, nor did it house armed guards and all the goodies that went with it. A CV dragged all the isolated villagers and simply dumped them together in a large town. The concept was much cheaper to erect and run, and had limited tactical advantages by forcing the terrorists to a central point for food supply, but with no fence or guards, the security was riddled with gaping holes. We drove straight past the village – seeing nobody.

Once we arrived at the Gutsa turnoff, we had a choice of two dirt roads: one risked ambush and the other landmines. They came together at a Y junction that led to the base camp. In the weeks ahead, we'd pause to toss a coin: heads, ambush; tails, landmine. For some reason, the enemy never laid mines on the ambush road, nor ambushed the mined road.

After driving kilometers along a bush dirt road, we arrived at the proposed SFA base – a crumbling Internal Affairs camp. The buildings, which were shaded under umbrella trees, looked flimsy. Fortunately, the main house – constructed of stout brick and plaster walls, with a fibro roof – although abandoned for years, was still in good condition. A line of brooms would sort out the dirt levels. As fortification, a waist-high wall of logs had been rammed vertically into the ground, which surrounded the house; a double-row palisade, with compacted rock-hard clay, was sandwiched between them. Millions of termites had attacked the logs and some simply disintegrated to the touch – hardly a stout defense against small arms and rocket-propelled grenades, but it was better than some camps we'd served in. We wandered the whole perimeter and discussed the future camp layout.

Satisfied with the base camp, we departed with pages of written notes. On the main Mzarabani Road – crawling at less than 40 kilometers an hour – Phil noted scrape marks that didn't match the road surface. We parked opposite and, gingerly using our fingers and a pocket knife, unearthed a TM46 landmine – not a good omen. Phil contacted the police station and we waited on the roadside until they arrived. After handing over the ownership of the explosive device to the police – still buried, but the top exposed – we drove off.

We returned to the Bindura training farm and organized the SFA deployment. Apart from calculating the logistics, we sifted out the command element. The day before departure, section and platoon leaders were distilled from the mob, along with headquarters staff. The HQ nominees needed one qualification: a minimum of primary school literacy. They needed to demonstrate an ability to read and write simple English, and to calculate basic arithmetic; a simple test sorted out likely candidates. I remember men seated in the dust – staring at a pencil and unable to comprehend how to use it.

We loaded sacks of mealie-meal, bags of red kidney beans, bags of cellophane packs of dried *kapenta* fish, and bulk packages of tea, sugar and salt. The HQ flunkies ticked off the dry food stores, and one of them was elected to calculate the rations per day, per man; we'd have to check the math. The detachment finally trucked out at night through Bindura and a darkened Centenary, to shield the black rogues from offended white eyes. The men were in good spirits and in light humor, like Boy Scouts on their first bush outing. None had any inkling of the hardships ahead, and they didn't know the wheres, the whys and for how long.

Phil Smith: the epitome of the warrior. (Fiona Smith)

The convoy spent part of the night camped above the escarpment and proceeded down the next morning – having hardly slept a wink. The trucks finally braked in a dust cloud outside their new home. The men slowly disembarked and some looked shocked, dazed and disorientated as they stretched their sore limbs. Staring at the landscape, the dusty, prickly bush shimmered in the oppressive heat and offered little comfort. We barked and pointed and harassed the men into unloading the stores and tents – dumping it off the trucks.

Once the kit was unloaded, the main body of the convoy departed. They left behind a blue Rhino, a brown Bedford and the orange Land Rover. Phil and I were the only licensed drivers, so there were three vehicles and two drivers. None of the 150 SFAs had any driving experience whatsoever. We couldn't find one unlicensed person to drive strictly on the Valley floor, not even a juvenile delinquent who had spun a wheel around a paddock!

"If there's time," I thought, "maybe I can teach someone how to drive, or maybe not."

I shrugged and just got on with it.

The detachment slowly settled into their new home. Phil and I patiently demonstrated differing skills to the platoon commanders so that they, in turn, taught their subordinates – the basics of setting up outdoor showers and long-drop toilets, and erecting tents and demonstrating how individuals can make life as comfortable as possible with the limited amount of supplies. I worked with Doc, the medic/storeman, to calculate food supplies and daily ration portions. Doc stood at an average height in his leather boots and was slightly overweight – an outward sign of an easy life. A serious man lurked behind his thick-lensed reading glasses – and that impression was reinforced by hardly ever smiling. A very sketchy knowledge of First Aid had landed him the medic's job. An opportunist, he saw the UANC as a path to easy money; as Albert's right-hand man, he slowly acquired the art of logistics management.

Phil plucked a couple of likely lads who spoke passable English and taught them the finer points of radio procedure. He imparted enough skill for them to sit on radio watch day and night, which released us for flexible duties. Satisfied the camp had been shook down to something organized, Phil and I drove back to Centenary with a shopping list. At the town general store, sacks of mealie-meal, bags of dried fish, red kidney beans, tinned corned beef, cartons of cigarettes, crates of Coke, crates of fresh vegetables, tubes of toothpaste and soap cakes were purchased. The Centenary storeowner smiled broadly every time we turned up with a briefcase of cash to empty his shelves and fill his cash register. On the return, I purchased a live steer from a farmer I knew and the men comically drove the beast onto the back of the truck, before wrestling it to the floor – fresh meat on the hoof.

For company, we brought a black Labrador dog, and we fed it meat and beer. Early in the morning, the dog could be found hard against a wall, with its front paws over its nose, like a man with a severe hangover. One evening, while testing out the old World War II Russian DP machine gun we had snitched for camp defense, the sudden firing fury frightened the dog shitless and he sprinted into the gathering dusk. We saw a black smudge vanish down the road at full speed, never to be seen again.

During this flurry of activity, our esteemed leader Albert stood aside, aloof. He didn't dirty his hands in the camp set-up; in fact, he hardly left his room. He saw himself as a political field commander – divorced from ordinary routines. Whilst thoughtful and quietly spoken, he was unable to generate any enthusiasm. He always vacillated – refusing to make decisions. Discussions always ended up going around the subject without ever tackling it. He especially shied away from talk of operations – continually lecturing us on how things would change. He was so certain, when the local terrorists recognized his terrorist pedigree, that they'd soon agree to constructive peace talks. It never occurred to him that the CTs would use their best endeavors to wipe out his command. I don't know who had tutored him in the realities of the political situation, but he slowly became disillusioned.

Finally, after a week of settling in, I convinced Albert to send out a routine patrol (based on the premise to build a political base), as they needed to circulate amongst the wary population and sound out the tribesmen's opinions, as well as to mingle amongst the locals and broadcast the qualities and benefits of a new country under the leadership of Bishop Muzorewa. They were new on the block and needed to build credibility. Albert (who stayed behind) briefed the excited men, before they exited the camp and wandered off in a ragged formation, like footy fans leaving a game, believing the myth that they were the saviors of the people. The unemployed bums from the African satellite townships knew as much about the African bush as an East End London trader. They were, unashamedly, here for the job and the prestige of wearing sunglasses and toting an AK-47; they believed their own publicity of being ex-terrorists out on a mission to bring peace to the land, which was sprinkled with the occasional armed robbery.

When the patrol ambled back, the platoon leaders insisted the people cried out for food, so they chorused to Albert an overwhelming cry for food. Albert approached me and we sat at the kitchen table. He stated firmly that to put runs on the board, the quickest way is via the peasant's stomach. He argued his case strongly – stating that his men needed grassroots support; food enabled them to step onto the bottom rung of the ladder. Sacks of mealie-meal, used as a token of goodwill, would build their credentials. I had the strings to the cash that supplied all the food, but he wanted to loosen the strings. He stared at the table top – his eyes round and pleading. Very skeptically, I caved in – partly to get them back out of the base camp and on patrol. Our commander reveled in the feelgood duties and saw food as the perfect tool to the hearts of the war-weary locals, but shortly after the handout began, our own intelligence gleaned that the maize flour had been swiftly handballed to the ZANLA boys, and I had quite a job trying rein in the commander's enthusiasm.

"You know the mealie-meal is going straight to the enemy," I argued every other day, "so why do you persist with this handout?"

"You'll never understand," countered Albert, in one of his more philosophical moods, before adding: "Maybe today they hand over, but tomorrow they will understand that only I have their welfare at heart. They will switch allegiances, you'll see."

"Until ZANLA murders a dozen," I reminded him, "then they'll be straight back in their pocket – if, indeed, they ever leave."

"You just don't understand."

I didn't. I kept tight screws on the excess maize flour.

Another big patrol was organized and a hundred men sauntered out of the front gates into the wild, speckled scrub. Laughing and jostling each other, with cigarettes dangling from their mouths and rifles handled slovenly, they wandered off in a party mood, as if they were on their way to a circus. It was real amateur hour. Phil and I watched in amazement until the last straggler disappeared from view, and then we entered the base, where Albert remained with Doc and 30-odd guards. Leading from the front was certainly not one of his strengths.

Three hours later, a vicious exchange of automatic fire sparked and echoed in the distance. Heavy and prolonged, we ran out to the perimeter to gauge the extent of the firefight. I could not tell who was attacking and who was copping the fire. Automatic fire ruled; no explosions were heard. The intensive exchange roared and rebounded, with the final crescendo, after five minutes, spluttering for a minute; then silence. The radio operator frantically tried to call the unit, but gained only mush static.

Now we waited – and waited. The surrounding bush wilted in the scathing sun. Within 40 minutes, the first breathless men sprinted into the camp gates, followed by the remainder. It was like watching the end of a marathon road race. The frightened leaders were in first – sprinting like possessed madmen – and were followed by the main pack, who were jostling shoulder to shoulder; then, finally, dribbles of the slower or older. It took about two hours for the last stragglers to stagger in.

"What happened?" I asked the exhausted participants, but the shock was beyond their life's experience.

"Hundreds o' them," volunteered one, as he sat on the hard ground – his eyes popping. "They asked us over to them, and when we come, they fired to us."

Albert wandered among his demoralized men – muttering to himself. Later, I deduced that they had not suffered any casualties, not even a slight wound, but they had lost five weapons. Trying to get to the bottom of the debacle was arduous, as no one admitted losing the plot. The only rational explanation forthcoming stated that a ZANLA group had spotted the company-sized force; had then called out to them to cross the open ground to talk peace; and had then opened fire once the SFA complied. Fortunately, ZANLA's shooting was as shit as the Muzorewa boys'.

I decided, after that example, that more training was paramount. There was an urgent need to sharpen the collective vigilance and tactical movement, so the next morning, we began. I immediately ran into the first hurdle: most of the men did not understand English, and my Shona was poor and rusty, so I roped in Doc to translate. He was not keen, but slowly grew into the task, although I sensed that he added his own flourish to my instructions. The men were not eager participants, and I quickly realized that I couldn't push them hard like the Support Unit constables. Too much goading had built up resentment, both with the leaders and the cadres. They didn't volunteer for hard work; they came here to bring peace! I made adjustments to my 'in your face' directness and toned down my instructions in order to make progress. We worked the basics over and over, but the work was painstakingly slow.

Within days, a platoon walked into an ambush a mere kilometer outside our camp. Phil and I sat at the kitchen table, eating our breakfast, when the roar of gunfire reverberated off the walls. Initially, I thought the gunfire had been directed at the camp, but discounted that when a guard pointed excitedly down the dirt road. We armed up, ignored Albert standing in his room, who was wringing his hands, and ran down the dirt road to bolster the men. Some were already running back home – their faces pasty in shock, with their eyes round and bugged out – breaking running records. When they saw us coming, they hesitated and then turned around.

"What's goin' on?" shouted Phil, as we ran on the side of the road – the crackle of gunfire thick in our ears.

"They're everywhere!" screeched a panicky voice from within the dark scrub, "we must flee this place!"

"Like fuck!" I bellowed – knowing that finding the enemy was the hardest part of killing them.

Now we knew where they were, I was determined to hook right into them.

I stumbled into a half-dozen frightened SFAs who, I found out later, had fled on the first volley; had then hared up the dirt road; and then, suddenly, had stopped and squatted in the shady scrub – safely out of immediate danger. From there, they fired blindly – trapping the main body of their own men in a crossfire. I had to lever them out of their comfort zone and haul them back to assist the floundering main group. We quickly joined the spluttering contact.

The wild firefight emanated just a few meters off the main road, in a thin stand of tall trees. From there, the fighting fanned out to a ploughed field, which had old and broken maize stubble. Thirty CTs had initiated the contact. I sighted 10 CTs jogging slowly on the far side of an open field – heading for a lonely copse of trees. I stopped, locked the barrel of the AK into a V-fork in a solid tree, quickly aimed and opened fire, and dropped one. With an FN, I felt I could have done better, as the AK feels and fires tinny compared to the trusted FN. Phil, meanwhile, harangued men to their feet and led them in a flanking chase. The CTs fled.

I grabbed six men and swept forward across the open ground. A dead CT – a youngster; a teenager; a mirror of the SFA boys – was stretched out sprawled in the tall grass and clutching an old PPSH sub-machine gun. The man wore Security Force camouflage trousers, Bata *veldskoens* and a dirty-gray shirt, with a cloth pouch slung around his neck, which held spare drum magazines. Gunfire still crackled fiercely through the trees. I hesitated, in a quandary, whether to press on, as the blood was fired up by the scent of battle, but I decided, very reluctantly, to withdraw – noting the undisciplined use of firearms and fearing that we could be easily shot by one of our own.

"Phil!" I called out, "better pull back before you wear one in the arse!"

"Yeah," he laughed, "don't know who's shootin' at who!"

We rounded up and ushered the sullen people back to base. Once back at the base, a role call discovered that one of the auxiliaries had been shot in the leg; the bullet had punched a neat hole through the muscle, without breaking any bones. Doc fussed – patching the wound. Two were missing; we called their names again, but no reply.

"Better go back an' find 'em," stated Phil, as he checked the RPD he borrowed. "Who's coming with?"

"I'm in," I smiled.

Three auxiliaries put their hands up without hesitation, while the rest silently looked away, hangdog. Phil shrugged; we didn't need the others. They were a millstone around the neck. I noted that Albert had shrunk from the restless gathering and had slyly entered the building. We ventured out again and jogged back down the empty road. The volunteers had their confidence boosted and were happy to follow.

"What happened to the missing men?" I asked one of the auxiliaries.

"When the enemy fired at us," he stated bluntly, "they surrendered."

"What, they put their hands in the air?" I asked incredulously – knowing surrender was never an option.

"Yes, they handed them their guns, an' went off with 'em."

The other two nodded glumly, as they had also witnessed them toss down their firearms and walk with their hands up to the enemy.

Jesus, did they have lots to learn.

After scouring the open agricultural countryside, we finally found one young man two kilometers from where the group of 10 CTs was last sighted. Huddled in a dip in the baked ground, steam lifted off the crumpled body. Once up close, we saw he had been gruesomely bayoneted and burnt to death. His blistered face laid side on and a charred right arm pointed upwards. His new AK rifle and webbing, with full magazines, had been stripped. I wasn't sure what accelerant had been used to ignite a fire, but he had endured a grizzly, agonizing death. The sight of their superficially charred dead friend finally rammed home to the urban cowboys that this was serious business – and secondly, it eroded the prevailing myth that the CTs would be happy to do business with these interlopers. The other man was never found.

Less than a few days later, a lazy dawn clearing patrol walked the same circular route at the same time, despite our lessons constantly reinforcing the dangers of routine. My protestations had made no difference; what more could an enemy want? The CTs had arranged a little welcome package: they had tied Chinese stick grenades to the exposed, hardened roots of some trees that grew along the banks of a dry stream – exactly where the dawn patrol walked each morning. When the switched-off patrol wandered sleepily amongst the static grenades, the enemy pulled hard on long strings that were attached to the 'O' ring to detonate them. The half-dozen grenades exploded together – showering the stunned slackers with hot, steel shrapnel and rock-hard dirt; then the ambushers ripped them with automatic fire. One frightened auxiliary immediately surrendered and was promptly shot dead; then he was stripped of his AK-47.

Once again, Phil and I dashed off to render assistance, while Albert pondered the theoretical world – and once again, bleeding, bamboozled men fled back to camp. We managed to recover two SKS carbines they had left behind. After organizing two men to carry one seriously wounded man back to camp, I rounded up three less traumatized men to close the ground with the elusive enemy. Phil and one SFA man began to track, with three of us behind in support. The follow-up was shitty: a scared auxiliary fired off a round from his AK, while stumbling through the tinder-dry undergrowth, and shot another SFA man in the upper back. I dove in to stem the gushing bleeding in a desperate attempt to prevent the man suddenly succumbing to shock, but apart from field dressings, there were no other medical supplies. The section commander and radio operator had fled the scene at the initial grenade ambush, so the communications were gone. The man bled heavily and, despite desperate attempts to stem the flow, he died within 10 minutes. I stood back, unmoved. With arms and hands soaked in warm blood, death didn't tug any strings. I prepared the body for carriage; then the four of us lugged the body back to a morose camp.

After this skirmish, a cloud of depression descended on the camp. Casualties were evacuated to Bindura from the Mzarabani airstrip, so I decided that it would be a good idea to vanish and organize the next resupply – leaving the detachment alone to chew on its self-pity. Leaving one truck at Mzarabani with a small crew, we took off in the Land Rover – carting an RPG-7 launcher and three rockets in case the ride up the escarpment turned hairy. We found that the sealed road made a difference in the road speed. Once at Centenary, we loaded up (with the storeowner once again grinning from ear to ear); then Phil and I sank a few chilled Lions in the Centenary Country Club before commencing the journey back.

Driving down the 700-meter Zambezi escarpment – winding around the gorges – Phil saw a herd of a dozen elephants lumbering gracefully along a single path. Phil, the wannabe 'Big Game' hunter, was keen to have a shot, so he braked and parked.

"Jesus, I'm havin' a crack at this," he smiled wickedly – grabbing his AK – and he bounded from the cab.

I watched him jog out across the low thickets, towards a winding path, and I sighed.

Thinking the AKM rifle was too light to take on an elephant, I grabbed the RPG-7 rocket launcher off the back and ran after him. An anti-tank rocket should pull the biggest bastard up! I hurried after him to a copse of trees above the dirt track. When we got in real close (I could tell, because my arsehole was tingling), we waited … and waited … They had not detected us; they ambled past – perfect targets – but we did nothing. They were so majestic that we just sat and marveled. That was the beginning – and the end – of our 'Big Game' hunting career.

At Christmas 1978, Phil and I partied back in Salisbury, and I had spent a fair amount of spare time at the Prentice home. Morris and Madeline lived in a gracious house with two of their three daughters, Lorraine and Jacky;

they were feisty and fun. Their son, Billy, served in Support Unit. Downstairs accommodated great bar facilities, which were utilized to the fullest. We partied hard and fired Para flares into the dark sky at midnight – much to the displeasure of the authorities. They saw them – and heard about them through dozens of panicked phone calls – but never found the source. I, once again, found myself banned from the bar for damaging the bar top with a corkscrew while making a drunken point.

On the dying days of 1978, we headed north out of Salisbury to Bindura (worse for wear) to pick up a terrorist who had been nominated 2IC of the Valley Detachment. His name was Lazarus and he was waiting with an SB sergeant near the police station. Lazarus was in his thirties and stood like a quiet, polite mouse. He spoke educated English and I assumed that under the quiet exterior, there lived a UANC political animal.

The three of us traveled back through Centenary – down the winding road to the Valley floor. The young, idealistic Lazarus had been tasked to observe and report on the progress of their boys. He sat sandwiched between us, quiet and demure, like a servant instead of our future promise. Driving unescorted on the Alpha track and down the escarpment to Mzarabani – through a steep, winding section, just minding our own business – someone fired shots at the Land Rover. The gunshots originated from the heavily wooded slopes of the steep banks rising above the tarmac road – and the rifle fire was neither heavy, nor accurate.

"Fuck, let's get 'em!" hissed Phil – dead keen to shoot them up.

He steered the Land Rover over to the gravel shoulder, stopped and clicked on the handbrake. We checked our AKs.

"The RPG-7 in the back could be useful," I thought – assessing the terrain.

"You let rip up into the trees," Phil stated briefly about tactics, "an' I'll climb up through that shit over there an' flank 'em."

I nodded.

"What about me?" Lazarus pleaded.

"Just wait 'ere," said Phil – standing on the road and figuring out his outflanking move.

"You can't leave me here," Lazarus begged – tears forming in the corner of his eyes – "we must just drive on to the base. It is urgent!"

I looked at the man: his face had collapsed; his eyes were wide with fear and apprehension.

"Please!" he begged again.

Two more rifle shots cracked above our heads.

I observed the woodland: thick trees and gray rocks immersed in shadow, on a steep slope. I doubted whether we could catch anyone hidden in there. The job was to convey Lazarus to our camp in one piece, not to chase down amateur ambushers.

"Fuck, Phil, let's go."

"What?"

"Leave 'em, an' let's fuck off to Gutsa."

"Fuck 'im. Let's do this!"

"Pleeaassee!!!"

Phil stared at the shaken Lazarus – the UANC official misbehaving like a child. He sighed and shrugged his shoulders, and then reluctantly stepped back and silently slid behind the steering wheel.

In the first days of January 1979, a bolder clearing patrol feeling their way five kilometers out from the Gutsa base walked into an 82mm mortar bombardment. Once again, the men had used the predictable and lazy route. ZANLA had targeted the zone and they waited patiently; the range had been paced out. Two men were killed outright and nine went missing, along with their weapons, never to be found again. They may have opted to join ZANLA, or had been clandestinely murdered and their bodies buried, or had hightailed it back to the capital city; I'd voted for the third option. The fun of being a fighter had significantly ebbed.

January brought Elias – an RAR sergeant seconded to us to assist in retraining. A short, squat man with 15 years of service, he brought a swag bag of training skills in the finer points of combat arts. His natural Shona, coupled with superb infantry experience, pushed the training forward. He mixed better with the men and trust began to build. Whenever possible, I joined the training to keep abreast of developments.

One afternoon, whilst squatting in scrub bordering the road, I saw a vehicle – a black dot trailed by a plume of white dust.

"Ah, Tilcor," I thought, and wandered onto the road to wave it down, to see what I could cadge.

As our base was more spartan than Support Unit's, I wondered if the Tilcor boys had anything to soothe a sweet tooth. The shimmering dot soon became clearer as it ventured closer, and it wasn't a Land Rover, but a blue Citroen sedan … now I was curious. The vehicle slowed down when the driver saw a large white man astride the road, and drew up alongside me. The dust cloud overtook the car, with powder coating everything. I peered into the open driver's window and noted a forty-something white man and his delicate lady seated beside him, and then I was completely surprised to see two children (aged around three and five) seated in the back.

"Can I ask what you're doin' 'ere?" I politely asked the driver.

The man wrinkled his nose; I was a stinking unshaven bushman – toting an AK rifle.

I leaned near his face.

"We've come down to see the elephants," the driver replied indignantly.

"Mate, this is the ambush and landmine capital of the world," I said – restraining myself.

What a selfish bastard! Fancy driving his family down the Zambezi Valley – one of the most seriously dangerous patches in Rhodesia! With a definite Rhodesian accent, the man couldn't be ignorant of the high risk.

"Go back now," I hissed between my teeth.

"But we've come all this way to see elephants," pleaded the woman – raising her sunglasses – "you see, we're emigrating next week and this is the last chance."

"Go to a bloody zoo," I snapped impatiently. "Get outta 'ere, or I'll set those bastards onto you," I warned – pointing to the 40 scruffy, dirty and armed Africans crouching menacingly in the shadows.

"We all voted on this," the driver insisted, before swallowing his words when he noticed the ugly crew for the first time: his eyes bugged out, his jaw dropped and the discussion was over.

Abruptly accelerating and circling tightly – tires churning up more dust – he sprinted back towards Mzarabani. Perhaps he was going to report a foreign white man running with terrorists! His brash statement that the kids had voted pissed me off. What would they understand? Luckily for him, the auxiliaries were not the real thing.

January blew in rumors that the SFA were up to freelance banditry – namely the robbery of bus passengers. The word hinted that enterprising SFAs had erected toll stations and extorted fees on the main road. There was no hard evidence yet, just murmurs. The SFA were yet to be paid cash, so they used their rifles to solicit money. That raised eyebrows.

The base continued to be plagued by radio transmission problems and Phil and I were forced on the dangerous run into Mzarabani police station to contact HQ. The precarious, time-wasting drive through cowboy country – waiting to be ambushed, or detonating a landmine – hardly caused a ripple in the capital.

Salisbury ummed and aahed and, after a week without direct communications, they sent a Signals Corps captain to Mzarabani by light plane. We met him at the airstrip, and just as his feet touched the ground, I indicated the orange Land Rover to whisk him off to our camp.

"No way," he stated firmly, as he glanced at vehicles parked with five motley AK-toting African pirates swatting away the flies, "we can run through the problems here."

"Sir," I said calmly, "we don't know much about the science of radio aerials. We'd like you to come to the base to be absolutely sure that we have comms."

"The plane is departing in 15 minutes," he stated crisply – dressed in the light-tan office uniform – "an' I'll be on it, so you either learn right now, or stiff shit."

I shrugged. What could I do? A base camp officer who showed real leadership.

These pansies saw the writing on the wall and were determined to stay safe. He supplied a spare radio and explained, on the safety of the airfield, the various radio aerials and how to set them up. After we fielded a number of dumb questions, the captain signed over the equipment and nimbly boarded the light aircraft – pausing momentarily to shudder at the sight of the unfriendly scrub that shimmered in the roasting sun. He was just ecstatic to fuck off out of no man's land.

The radio's first transmission ordered me to Salisbury HQ for a compulsory briefing. From around the country, liaison officers drove to the headquarters and milled about – unsure of the point of the exercise. At headquarters, a captain promptly told me that each LO was to present a verbal report of our progress; we were given no notice for preparation. One by one, in a small theater, the LOs delivered their summary to Colonel John McVey and his staff officers. To my utter astonishment, other LOs reported commendable conduct by their men. They stated emphatically that their men were getting on with the job – quoting specific incidents to back up their claims. In contrast, my briefing and that from Skip out of Rushinga reported the shortcomings experienced in our respective areas – the complete antithesis of the first speakers. Judging from our fellow LOs' impressive briefings, we either scored detachments scraped from the very bottom of the barrel, or our advice and counseling was marginal, but I was confident that our advice and coaching was as good as the best.

Afterwards, Skip and I circulated to chat to other LOs about their success. Obviously, I had much to learn. Later that night – lubricated with liters of beer

Skip in Rushinga with a UANC detachment, 1979. (Skip Dolega)

and spirits – the truth dropped out: their detachments fared no better than the Gutsa mob. In the midst of multiple glasses of beer and brandy, the penny finally dropped … many LOs had buried their greedy snouts in the gravy trough. They were on a good thing: well paid as contract soldiers, and handling easily tapped cash that flowed through our fingers. This was one gravy train they didn't want to derail. By colorfully painting success in their areas, they cemented their own jobs.

The gravy train was unlimited cash expenditure. Special Forces did not have the infrastructure to cope with an explosive growth, and the SFA size had ballooned from next to nothing to thousands of men in three months. They all had to be fed and clothed. We signed for cash at HQ, and spent the money on food and the other necessities of life for the hundred-plus men. Cash purchases ranged from fresh meat and fresh vegetables, through to cartons of Madison cigarettes and tubes of toothpaste. The SFA men were not paid, so the cash bought every little thing they required. As long as legitimate receipts for expenditure were surrendered (any receipt), the money was topped up. Bogus receipts became currency, so the first purchases included a receipt book. One LO went straight out and bought himself a luxury car and powerboat; others stayed at luxury hotels and had the time of their lives. Double invoicing became rife, so it's no wonder they didn't want the circus to end.

The cash grab didn't stop at LOs: the more astute administration staff also dipped their fingers in the pie – hedging against the possibility of a Mugabe victory. With large sums of money going out every day, it took little talent in the chaotic swirl of the infant unit to convert wads of notes to their own use. Officers flew to South Africa on purchasing binges and left large amounts of money in bank accounts in the Republic as future security. Inflated invoices on all sorts of military purchases became the norm: buy two-thousand denim jackets for $20,000, present an invoice back home for $25,000 and pocket the $5,000 difference. Middle-management hedged against a Mugabe victory, and I hadn't tapped the loose money because I was too stupidly honest.

I returned to Gutsa wiser and with another bucket of cash, while Phil left for the city to catch a breather and to sponge more supplies. On my arrival, rumors strengthened that a small team of SFAs had indeed robbed a bus … so we had entrepreneurs on board! I made a mental note to talk to Doc about the chitchat. He might be dour, but he knew who was who in the zoo. At the CV, Lazarus improved the political spin in the attempt to win over hardened hearts. Albert mixed freer with his men, but remained firmly glued in base. Sergeant Elias busily engaged himself in the mob's military skills, and I began to see a smidgen of improvement in their bearing and confidence. We got back to business.

16

Shot Again: January–June 1979

In mid-January, Sergeant Elias and I drove the main road to Mzarabani to link up with Lou, who was the Special Forces' mechanic. No one visited our isolated camp (we came to them), and Lou was running late, but we didn't launch off till early afternoon. Our vehicle fleet had developed mechanical hiccups: the blue Rhino had completely broken down and the brown Bedford was just being plain temperamental, while the orange Land Rover required an urgent service and oil change. Because Lou had arrived without an escort, I drove to Mzarabani so he could service the Land Rover; then we'd provide the escort to the base for his expert eye on the fleet.

Clearly, it was risky to drive solo: with it not being a routine run and in good daylight hours, there was an element of chance of getting away unnoticed. The journey on the rutted road to the main road was event-free, but driving along the main Mzarabani Road – thinking safety was closer at hand – a roar of gunfire ripped through the still air. An RPG rocket exploded on a tree and a hail of small arms splattered around the Land Rover. They shot tons of ammunition, but I ignored the cascade of bullets to focus only on driving. Changing down to third, I slammed the accelerator to the floor and increased the speed, but two bullets ploughed into my right leg and smashed the femur. I swore when I looked down at the damage … not again. The right leg was flopping and the muscle had been peeled back, which looked disgusting.

The bullet strike had also severed something vital in the engine, and the motor died. I desperately clawed at the ignition key, but the starter motor didn't fire. My good foot slammed down the clutch pedal, the left hand slotted the gears into neutral and I mentally urged the vehicle along. The firing ceased and the overlapping silence grew heavy. The Land Rover glided rapidly out of the ambush zone and then slowed down until it finally stopped; then Sergeant Elias leapt out from the passenger seat and sprinted down the road. Not being as nimble, with my right leg shattered, I swiveled gently in the seat before I jumped out on the left foot and hopped.

"Don't be a coward! Run for it!" Sergeant Elias yelled out at the top of his voice and, with that announcement, he grandly added: "I'm going for help!"

and instantly vanished into the dead ground.

Thank you for your continued support!

I broke a cardinal rule: travel required a minimum of two vehicles for mutual support. It was just common sense, but neither Elias, nor any of the SFA had any driving experience. The immediate priority was boots on the ground. The SFA's shortcoming (no trained drivers) would be fixed in the future, but this did not help the initial deployments. If either Phil or I was absent, the other did the unforgivable: drove without an escort. Once again, we used the tools on hand.

I frantically hopped along the gravel road to a large eucalyptus tree rooted on the roadside and flopped down behind the solid trunk. Sorting myself out in double-quick time, I assessed the position: I was up shit creek with an AK, five 30-round magazines and two Russian hand grenades. My leg below the knee lolled about without my help. Rolling delicately among the spiky grass and small pebbles, I saw the dreaded movement: about 15 CTs, in plain view, circled around on the edge of scrub country – slinking and weaving through the low trees (about 40 meters), and straight across a tilled field. They weren't looking my way and they carried their rifles low. To overrun my hiding spot, they were exposed traversing the crumpled, tilled soil before crossing the flat gravel road. Fortunately, the gum tree grew solo, with no bush cover, so they weren't able to creep right up without drawing attention. To sneak in close, they endangered themselves to lethal fire, so I relaxed a mite. I looked down at the injured leg: it laid snapped half-way between the knee and the ankle. The ankle lay at right angles to the leg – strangely, not the most comfortable position. The brilliant-white shafts of shattered bone contrasted against the red mashed meat. While the wound was disabling and looked messy, it didn't invoke panic. What would that achieve? Alone in the hot scrub, with gung-ho CTs milling about, the choices were stark: if they took me on, I'd use my AK rifle to fend them off and reserve a grenade for me. I had seen suicide acted out by wounded CTs and knew that the grenade did the job. Falling into the hands of the unpredictable ZANLA was not an option; I'd witnessed their bloody handiwork. Suicide, rather than capture, was a cold, calm, but rational decision. Later, in the comfort of a warm bar, the choice seemed extreme, but on reflection, I remained completely lucid while lying utterly alone without a radio transmitter – right in the heart of enemy country, with one leg shattered. Fortunately, they half-circled and disappeared into the bush.

After they slipped into the speckled foliage, my second worry popped up:

I conjured up images of an African civilian ambling up the road and casually spotting my predicament. If this occurred, the odds favored the excited person rushing off to bring ZANLA back to entertain them. I hoped circumstances minimized this occurrence, as the ambush was set up not far from the CV, and the civilians scattered and hid until dark in case the Security Forces decided to 'Skull Bash'.

I lay there for a half-hour or so. A third fear was losing consciousness, being woken by the sharp poke of a rifle barrel and then looking up at a circle of snarling terrorists. The thought of being tortured to death did not excite me. I imagined a local bitch hacking off my balls with a blunt, rusty blade – accompanied by the bloodthirsty cheers of an eager audience. ZANLA had accrued a grisly reputation for torture – and that shuddering thought spurred on the desire to stay awake.

Whilst baking in the humming afternoon sun – floating in semi-consciousness – the mind did not dwell on judgments about the past, nor any idle thoughts on regrets, or opportunities lost, love missed or making peace with God; none of these pillars of life filtered through. I still fervently believed in my 'invincibility', and that I would not die in this war. My mind remained fully occupied with staying awake and alert.

The leg still sat at a weird angle and, occasionally, I'd move the bottom half with the rifle barrel to ensure the acute pain kept me wide awake. The shock that automatically protected the body from the initial wave of sickening pain began to recede fast. Scores of tiny black ants covered the bloody parts – rushing everywhere, like kids in a candy shop. Meanwhile, in the Mzarabani police station, the unmistakable roar of small arms punctured their afternoon. Skip and Lou – expecting my arrival – guessed I was in trouble. Skip had departed the Rushinga bush scene in disgust a week before and now rode shotgun with Lou the mechanic. After rounding up a scratch police crew, Skip deployed on a truck with police and stood behind a MG laid over the cab roof. The Bedford and escort vehicle rumbled out of the police station and down the Mzarabani Road. Soon, they spotted Elias running along the road on his mission of mercy. The truck paused long enough for Elias to point roughly towards where I was last seen.

Recommencing the journey, Skip fired the mounted MG at likely ambush spots along the route. I heard the roar of the whining engine riding through the gears, which was overridden by the harsh stucco of machine gun fire as they ground closer. While the rescue mission was welcome, I grew more anxious of being shot than being found by terrorists, as he didn't know exactly where I was, and I had no communications. To save myself, I crawled out onto the roadside when the truck rose from the dead ground. The police scrambled from the truck and gently hoisted me onto the sandbagged steel tray, and the three-tonner returned to the Mzarabani airstrip. Now the pain really began: the men splinted the leg to support the break, but the tray bounced at every pothole – so much so, I had to scream out to the driver to slow down. I can remember every little pothole in the road, every little stone. The police had tossed a medical kit aboard, but no one knew where the morphine was hidden. Skip rummaged among the junk inside and found a morphine sack, but it required a tiny needle to pierce a hole, like opening a tube of glue. There was nothing that vaguely resembled a needle, and together we tried various ways to burst the seal, but to no avail, so I bit back the pain.

The truck drove straight onto the Mzarabani runway and parked next to a Police Reserve Air Wing light aircraft, which had been dispatched from Centenary. The agony intensified, with shooting and severe electrical pain stabs. I smoothly lowered myself down from the raised back of the truck, and hopped unsupported along the hot tarmac; then up to the aircraft. The wing was positioned below the fusillade, so I poised to climb on. A reinforced rubber-coated strut on the wing looked impossible as I struggled onto the low-slung wing, with Skip supporting the way.

"Watch the wing," warned the farmer-pilot, as Skip and I trod close to forbidden parts.

"Fuck the wing," I mumbled – pausing at the tiny cabin.

The door was open … the Perspex cabin and tiny door are not designed for big buggers. Peering inside, the passenger seat looked difficult to wriggle into for a fit man with two fine legs, so I wondered out loud how I was going to get in.

"The sun is just over the horizon," the pilot pointed out, "and when darkness sets in, and if I can't see a horizon, I can't take off."

I shot into the cabin – strapped leg and all – and wriggled down into the seat. I didn't need to be told twice: the pain had revved up to excruciating. Skip jumped down onto the tarmac, and the pilot nimbly hoisted himself onto the wing, eased through his door, settled down and fired up the engine. At dusk, the airplane smoothly taxied down the runway, accelerated sharply and lifted off over the matte-brown Zambezi Valley. I watched the clumps of gray bush shrink smaller and smaller as the plane rose above the escarpment; then we flew direct to New Sarum airport in Salisbury.

On the ground at New Sarum, I repeated the same scenario in reverse and finally hopped onto the tarmac; then into a waiting ambulance.

"Got any morphine?" I uttered to the medic.

The pain hummed and throbbed.

"Have you had any?"

"Nah."

A pause.

"Better not. We'll rush you straight into theater."

The driver took the morphine reference as an order to break all speed records. He shot out of the airport like a dragster, with lights flashing and the siren wailing – dodging through red traffic lights.

"Tell your fuckin' driver mate to slow down. Jesus, he'll kill me on the way."

The medic grinned and the driver kept the accelerator jammed to the floor.

The ambulance screeched into emergency at the Andrew Fleming hospital; Major Douglas and Phil were waiting. I asked them, while being wheeled in, to make sure the surgeons didn't cut the leg off. Scuttlebutt among the Security Forces stated that surgeons preferred to remove a leg rather than save it – and the cost of post-op treatment justified the rumor, so that was my only concern at that moment. In surgery, the doctors lined up the tibia and fibula bone splinters and bandaged and plastered the entire leg – pinning the ankle to a weighed pulley to keep the leg straight. They had not pinned or plated the bone itself, rather setting the pieces to heal without foreign bodies clipped on. Over time, the bone healed nicely.

I occupied the same ward as Jerry Lancaster – a GC policeman. He had been shot through the femur and the stricken leg was taut on pulleys and other serious weighted instruments to keep the bone together. It was a more serious wound than mine.

Finally discharged from hospital after four weeks, with the leg in plaster from the ankle to the top of the thigh – and wobbling on the new crutches – I roamed the town drinking at hotels and became just a general nuisance. The bullet exit hole refused to heal, and the wound remained open and weeping, so after close examination, the doctor decided on skin grafts. A South African military doctor at Andrew Fleming hospital carried out the skin graft, which went as follows: skin was stripped off the top off the thigh and laid over the hole. The graft still contained bits of meat hanging on, and soon withered and died, so he tried a second time, but with the same result (I think he was in

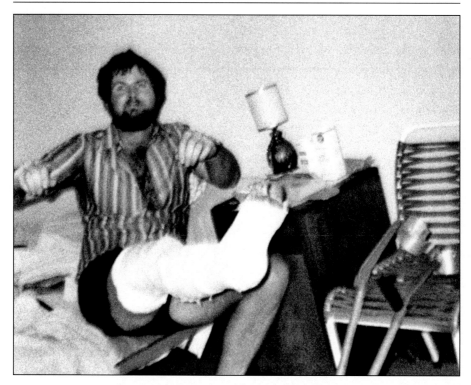

The author in plaster after the leg wound, 1979.

Rhodesia to get all the practice on live dummies). I refused to have a third one carried out and allowed the wound to heal itself slowly over time.

On 12 February, the second Viscount civil aircraft was shot down by a shoulder-launched SAM-7 missile while taking off from Kariba airport. All 59 passengers and crew were killed on impact. Once again, the world forums did not condemn the shooting down of a civilian aircraft; the United Nations sat silent.

I stayed with the Prentice family for a couple of weeks of my recovery, during which I attended the wedding of the eldest Prentice girl, who married an army major. The reception was held in a marquee erected on the front lawns of the beautiful Prentice home. Major General Sandy MacLean – the army commander, who was a guest – mingled in the crowd and circulated, drifting my way. The white ankle-to-thigh plaster cast became a conversation point, and he asked politely what had happened. I gave him a brief rundown on the incident, and then launched into a fiery tirade that senior officers were only concerned about their pension rights and that they didn't have the balls to win. I was clearly intoxicated and he was patient. He listened and, slightly embarrassed, replied he had a vested interest in the country and a building society mortgage as well. I didn't want to hear his soothing words – and fortunately, a colonel led him away before I made a complete fool of myself.

One Saturday morning, Skip phoned to say he was in prison for an act of hooliganism. Laughing all the way, I drove to Salisbury Central prison to visit. With the aid of an intrepid Bob the Para, they were inebriated and caused damage to a taxicab. They were detained by the police. I supplied him with lemons, suntan lotion, chili sauce and other jail necessities, and I also talked casually and informally to Special Branch contacts to see if anything could be done (nothing much, it seemed).

In March 1979, Phil Smith resigned from Special Forces and flew overseas, as we had originally planned. He flew home to England and, after a couple of postcards, the next thing he had landed in West Australia.

Over the coming weeks, two Australian acquaintances departed Rhodesia; they were formally shown the door. Michael was ordered out for allegedly biffing a priest whilst on operations, and Skip for being a hooligan. The authorities didn't need the negative publicity, so they found it easier to ship disorderly foreigners out of the country.

In April, I spent a couple of weeks off and on at the Mere Estate, as the country geared up for the first majority rule election. The election was comprised only of the African political parties who had complied with the aims of the Internal Settlement, which barred Robert Mugabe's lot. There was a subtle level of electioneering in the tribal lands, but the population there were firmly in ZANLA's grip. On the farm, all the workers wore UANC T-shirts; for Africans, the first-time vote was a novelty. The lines were long and the people were patient, and there was a solid vote for Bishop Muzorewa across the nation.

In June, Rhodesia evolved into Zimbabwe-Rhodesia – a country neither white, nor black. Whilst the UANC won the elections and formed government, in reality, the whites still firmly held onto all the levers of power. They still controlled the police, army, air force, civil service and the economy – and Ian Smith became Minister without Portfolio. Under Muzorewa's brief reign, the world did not change much for the whites: the war raged on, sanctions challenged businesses and families broke up under the pressure of continual army call-ups. Many whites sitting on the fence now firmly decided to pack a bag and emigrate, even though that option meant they were leaving behind most of their assets to begin a new life from scratch, but to continue fighting for something already lost to many didn't make sense. Within the white community, there were vocal voices to have the urban blacks eligible for military service – and for Africans living in the tribal lands, nothing changed at all.

During this time, the Special Forces' ZANU contingent destroyed one of its rebel detachments in Gokwe because both the SF hierarchy and the ZANU politicians had lost control of them; they had, simply, become bandits. Concerns also existed that they would defect to the enemy, so the LO met the rebels in their base and plainly stated they should wait until Sithole arrived to hear their grievances; then the LO left, ostensibly, to pick up Sithole from the airstrip. An OP placed to watch the camp radioed that the detachment was back on the move and that the LO had courageously returned to persuade them to remain in camp. They did so and Fireforce flew in and wiped them out: end and closed.

If the government had given birth to the SFA two years earlier, where the need to rush out underdone personnel would not have been imperative, the SFA may have influenced the political landscape a little; it may have.

17

Shangaan Army: July–December 1979

O nce the leg bone had healed and the plaster was removed, I circulated among the Salisbury bars. The leg, even after the bones had mended, still felt weak. After months encased in plaster, the muscle had wasted and the exit wound had dilated, but it still wept and required a clean bandage. Out of the blue, Detective Inspector John Davey made an offer: he asked if I would coordinate the Shangaan Army – and as I was under-employed, I was glad to. I remained on Special Forces' books while John wangled a transfer.

I moved down to Chiredzi – a sugar town population of 3,260 that was plonked in the south-east *lowveld* – dragging my black trunk. Chiredzi grew primarily from the irrigation schemes in the 1960s and, as a town, was unremarkable. As I motored through the countryside, I noted the monotonously flat geography, which had been gifted with rich, black soil. The region was intensively farmed sugar cane, with patches of cotton and winter wheat. Sugar cane flourished across thousands of acres – a vast sea of green streamers. The cane-crushing mills and the sugar infrastructure offered lots of employment.

I met John at the Chiredzi police station. John served the war years in Special Branch and, unlike some compatriots who had gradually turned feral, he dressed and conducted himself like a true professional – a real gentleman. An avid birdwatcher, John and I once drove to a large dam on one of the *lowveld* cattle ranches, which was away from the serious operational areas, and we spent the whole day bream and bass fishing. In the delicious silence, he pointed out – and named – every bird that popped its head up.

John laid out the Shangaan Army's *raison d'être*: the unit had grown from a Special Branch hybrid, which had been borne out of a niggling problem in that the flat south-east geography offered the CTs an unimpeded infiltration highway from the Mozambique border right through to Fort Victoria. The tennis court-flat terrain mitigated against Security Force Ops, so to stem the flow, PVs were established at Boli in the overgrazed Matibi Two TTL. The strategy of removing the entire population (the source of food) from the enemy was in full play, but cutting off the food supply in the Matibi tribal lands had left the African ranch employees, who were living on boundary, vulnerable to extortion and stand-over tactics. The terrorists found life less troubling to seize food from the unprotected farm workers than attempting to smuggle it out of the PVs, so to plug this glaring hole, Special Branch recruited and trained the Shangaan Army to provide armed protection for the African farm workers. By just loitering in the village, this dried up the easy access to food and supplies, as well as placing another thorn in the side of ZANLA on their push north-west. As a secondary role, they added a deterrent to cattle rustling, which was running at epidemic proportions.

The Shangaan Army recruited solely from the Shangaan tribe. This tribe lived in South-East Rhodesia and spilled across the border into Mozambique and South Africa. They represented a tiny one percent of the country's population. Historically, they are an amalgamation of various clans brought together when a small tribe fled Shaka Zulu and headed into the southern area of Mozambique in the 19th century.

Structured like the SFA, the Shangaan Army selected their commanders, who were chosen by education and common assent. The men dressed in light-green overalls and were armed with a full range of communist-manufactured weapons that had been captured from the enemy. As well as light arms, they owned RPG-7 rocket launchers and 60mm mortars. The Shangaans proved reasonably aggressive and better disciplined than the SFA political armies.

Once the briefing at the police station was completed, John dropped me off at the Shangaan Army's main base in the Hippo Valley – a former Internal Affairs establishment. The base stood on the lush banks of the Lundi River, sandwiched between the sluggish river and the sugar estate. The three whitewashed buildings contrasted sharply with the luxuriant greenery, but were comfortable and well-appointed compared to the Gutsa base. The complex overlooked a right-angled bend in the slow-moving river, where eight hippos wallowed. The hippos remained immersed in the muddy water at eye level – lazily watching the world go by.

I set myself up in the main building. My black trunk was stocked with extra food and basic kit, as well as a folding camp bed. The metal box had traveled with me for years – and everything I owned had a compartment inside. Before he departed, John presented me with a brand-spanking new RPK; even the woodwork shined – newly varnished. The Soviet-made light machine gun was, basically, a heavy-barrel AK with bipods. This model had a 75-round

The Shangaan Army lads lining up for the photo, 1979.

drum magazine and one spare, as well as 30-round magazines. Once John drove away, I arranged my kit in a small room and then roamed the camp. A dozen men lived here, whose roles included radio work and sentry duty – providing a semblance of security – plus there were two older (and larger) men for discipline. The elected commander stayed in a field base.

Once I had settled in, the Chiredzi police assigned Patrol Officer Trevor. A tall, wiry and dark-haired policeman, with a dry sense of humor, he was eager to try something new and enjoyed being away from mainstream police duty. He jumped straight into the duties, as we upgraded the camp amenities and observed the operational tempo. Unlike the SFA, here I wrote a list of food and requisites that John filled. Loose cash didn't float through this venture – and this assignment brought administration and paperwork. I smiled – thinking that I had left the police to dodge pen pushing; however, here there wasn't any pressure exerted by careerists: no 'norms', and certainly no code of behavior; I was left to carry out the duties.

We basically operated a trucking business that supported two satellite platoon-sized bases on the BJB Estate cattle ranches across the Lundi River. The truck dropped off food, radio batteries and ammunition supplies at the operational bases and plucked personnel to return to the home base for training, medical treatment and R&R. To travel to the bases, the two-vehicle convoy navigated a tight road network that zigzagged through the tall cane fields until it joined the main Chiredzi tarmac road. From the sealed road, we cut south-west onto the long Mtilikwe-Chingwizi dirt road before turning sharply east – following a sandy farm road. The vehicles traveled one road – going in one way or the other – in a circuit; there was no other alternative. As much as possible, the traveling times were juggled to break up routines – and as Trevor and I were the only drivers, we anticipated a vehicle ambush or landmine at some point, but it never occurred … I don't know why: a soft-skinned Land Rover and an armored Puma truck rumbling alone, through remote bush country, should have been a tempting target.

At the first ranch, I met Daniel, who was the commander. He was an ex-primary school teacher, who had become unemployed by school closures, and was happy to have paid work. He stood about 5'6" and had a skinny build, with an intelligent, smiling face – and he spoke flawless English. Over a mug of tea, we both reviewed their status and operational instructions. He explained that 30 or so Shangaans lived in each compound and roamed the area, and he laughed light-heartedly about ZANLA – saying that they tended to avoid the village. Before I arrived, the Shangaan Army had managed a few noticeable contacts with the CTs – recovering arms and ammunition – so now their presence simmered down the number of clashes.

Out of courtesy, we introduced ourselves to the ranchers. The homestead was built perched on top of the flat mesa, like a castle outcrop overshadowing the Shangaan base, with stunning views across kilometers of rangy treetops sweltering in the sun. The green-leaf canopy elicited a false notion that water was plentiful, as underneath the leaf treetops, the soil lay dry and arid. A young couple managed the ranch and, over a welcome cup of tea, they explained that they specialized in Cold Storage cattle. The cattle were trucked onto the ranch at a certain weight and, once fattened, were offered for sale, with the couple profiting from the increased weight price. We talked loosely about their farming routine, and they were firm that apart from repetitive driving, they acted as if there were no bands of terrorists loose in their backyard. They displayed the essence of courage I had lived among in Centenary. Their ranch covered many square kilometers and they were absolutely vulnerable on the lonely roads.

Departing the first base, the convoy ploughed a number of kilometers

Some captured weapons and ammunition by the Shangaans, 1979.

through sand drifts and knotty forests to the second base. In contrast to the first camp, the men here looked bored and slovenly. The camp had begun to look shoddy and unkempt, so it was time to start to stiffen up the training. The unit commander here was a big surly man, who was fond of his RPG-7 rocket launcher. His broken English and my even worse Shona were the tools used to patiently explain our mission, so I decided to begin with this team first.

At the ranch house lived a taciturn, rugged rancher, who lived alone in the house, which was fortified by a complex maze of sandbags – the 'Great Wall of Chiredzi'. In the event of an attack, he evacuated the house and scrambled via a sandbagged wall that led into a bunker positioned on the perimeter. It was one of the most protected fortresses I had yet seen, but scanning the options, I could see why: the house stood completely isolated on a sandy bush road in the middle of the wild *veld* – backing onto dense forest and huge granite boulders, which were many kilometers from a main road. If attacked, only the Shangaans could help; to stay took guts.

Both ranchers risked landmines and a-thousand-and-one places to ambush them while fixing fences, herding cattle, conducting dipping programs, repairing water pumps and driving the dusty farm roads. They didn't employ armed backup and worked without any hope of imminent rescue. They showed a steely determination to get on with life, despite the dangers.

After the first inspection, I decided that the main priority meant withdrawing a section from the Number 2 Base to retrain and then sending them on a well-earned R&R. Each journey, we picked up 10 men and conveyed them to the main base. Together, Trevor and I conducted training along the bank of the Lundi River – away from our eight hippos. The last thing I needed was an angry hippo taking offense to training in their territory. We started with the basics: weapons handling (load, unload, make safe etc.) and immediate action drills – all repeated over and over again using the AK, SKS and RPD. Once we were satisfied, we moved into basic contact drills.

The training injected confidence. Their section leaders began to enjoy the invigorating experience, and easily slipped into the role. The men were not expected to be assertive combat experts, just static guards who could be relied upon not to back off in a firefight – and they proved their courage doing just that. Once satisfied the men had brushed up on the rudiments of attack and survival, they were trucked to Chiredzi for a spot of R&R before being dropped back at their forward bases. They showed one vice allied with mine: a fondness for beer. Once their R&R had expired, they haphazardly wandered back to base, which made organized deployments a challenge. Senior Shangaans combed the beer halls and the brothels to round up the strays – and to bring a semblance of compliance, the odd man who wilfully disobeyed orders found himself tied to a post in the main camp and flogged across his exposed back with a thin supple cane, which was wielded by a huge older Shangaan.

By now, Phil Smith had arrived back in the country. He had returned to Zimbabwe-Rhodesia from overseas restless and unable to comprehend civilians and their lives, and so had joined the RLI. With a month-to-month contract and no basic training to slog through, he happily jumped into the job. Avoiding parachuting as much as possible by claiming he was a qualified tracker, Corporal Smith landed on both feet and was back in the thick of the fighting. He experienced one close call when a burning hut, used as an ammunition store, violently exploded near him. The RLI were up to their necks in daily and fierce action, as the number of terrorists multiplied inside the country. He tried to convince me to join the RLI for a final fling, but I saw little point; Zimbabwe-Rhodesia's time was running out fast.

Special Branch had heard whispers that the CTs had formed a temporary base upon a huge lone hill, Chiyumburra, which was surrounded by thousands of acres of nothing. They asked me to investigate, but rather than bumble out there on foot, I chose a short air reconnaissance. The Police Reserve provided the Cessna aircraft and pilot, and we soon took off from the Buffalo Range airstrip into a brilliant, African clear-blue sky. I surveyed the wild trees that rolled out below like a green chunky carpet. Chiyumburra easily stood out, as it was the only huge hill feature squatting in the steaming plains, and we flew directly to it. It didn't take long before the tiny Cessna hummed over the hill, with the massive blue feature slipped underneath and its dark shadows cast over the natural folds in the ground, but I saw nothing untoward.

"Fly lower and around it once," I asked the middle-aged farmer-pilot.

He nodded.

We flew around it once lower, but not low enough to draw in ground fire. Layered with scattered scrub, I studied the grassy ground floor and saw nothing of interest … no trampled grass, or new signs of occupation. Below, unfolding tree and grass country was lapped in bluish and speckled shadows, with no sign of humans.

"Around again?" asked the pilot, as we came close to completing the first circuit.

"No, let's go home," I said.

There were no visible foot trails, worn grass tracks, flattened camps or anything suspicious, so I was going to wait until intelligence precisely pinpointed the information.

The pilot completed the circuit and leveled out; then headed back to Buffalo Range, which was the Chiredzi civil airport and JOC base. I gazed absently at the ground passing underneath – thinking about nothing in particular. Thousands of acres of natural bush spread out to the horizon without a sign of human interference, not even a road. Captivated by the treetops flowing underneath – flying straight in the blue, cloudless sky – the engine suddenly spluttered and the single prop stopped and started; then stopped.

"What's goin' on?" I asked the pilot – uncertain if he had caused the engine failure.

The pilot said nothing – furiously pulling and poking at levers and buttons, while I stared straight ahead – mesmerized by the static propeller.

The plane glided, but lost height rapidly.

The pilot made noises like: "It's alright, it's just one of those things," as he conducted the checks to get the engine started.

"Can I do anything?" I asked – feeling helpless.

"No, no, I'll get it going," he muttered, while pushing and pulling on knobs.

The airport loomed in the distance, with toy-like buildings and a sealed runway, but at the rate of descent, even a non-pilot realized we weren't going to make it. Soon, the pilot acknowledged that the airport was out of the question. He dropped his attention from the mechanics and seized the flight column – anxiously scanning the ground for likely landing spots. The aircraft skimmed through the air – losing height in big chunks. As the treetops flipped dangerously close, he brought the plane around and pointed the nose at the main Chiredzi Highway; I got the message. Sitting back in the co-pilot seat, I found myself surprisingly calm. I mean, what can you do? Your fate lies entirely with the anxious pilot, as he attempted to land on the main road.

The Cessna coasted down right over the sealed road. Fortunately, at this precise moment, there was no traffic. The Cessna glided to touch down, with the front wheel lined up on the middle white stripe and the right wing's tip narrowly missing the power lines. I unconsciously held my breath as the power poles rushed by. The aircraft hit the road surface – a slight bounce and, just as I breathed a sigh, a rural bus crabbed around the corner 200 meters ahead and was driving towards us. I laughed out loud at the comedy of errors – a fucking head-on collision with a bloody bus! How would my death be explained in the situation reports? The African bus driver saw us, and the bus suddenly plunged off the road shoulder and furrowed into the long grass. He had probably shat himself. The passengers popped their heads out of the missing windows and gawked at the airplane rolling along the main road.

Once the plane parked, I alighted without comment – leaving the stunned pilot. I walked back up the main road and crossed to the JOC buildings at Buffalo Range and radioed my base; then I adjourned to the pub for a beer or three. I found out later that the airplane ran out of fuel, and I couldn't believe it. The pilot had not physically checked the fuel tanks before take-off – relying on a faulty gauge. If I had agreed to fly around the hill once more, we might have been in dire trouble – IF I had agreed.

A week later, Garry, an Australian – and one of the first foreigners to enlist in the RLI in 1973 – arrived in Grand Reef. He contacted me to assist in a clandestine job Special Forces HQ had assigned to him. I had met Garry socially sporadically over the past months – and the last time, we were drinking at the Terreskane Hotel in the company of a Brit ex-French Foreign Legionnaire. The Brit provoked a loud argument with a big Afrikaner standing at the end of the bar, and fists flew. The Brit, who wore the worst of a sudden fracas, decided to leave and, as he staggered by, Garry said we'd be with him in a couple of minutes. I sat there, slurping on my beer, and the next thing, an AK barrel was shoved between Garry and I, and the rifle opened fire. I was so pissed that I saw the white sparks leap from the muzzle flash in slow motion. Garry leapt off his bar stool and wrestled the Brit to the ground – disarming him. The man wore chest webbing, with two full magazines and two stick grenades … out looking for a private war! Fortunately, the bullets missed the intended target – a now speechless, blanched Afrikaner. Garry sat on top of the Brit until the police arrived, but to keep him calm, we accompanied him to the police station – sitting with him in the rear seat of the police car. While the ex-Legionnaire was clearly nuts, the young, green policeman had provoked him with smart comments, so when we arrived at Salisbury Central, the Brit was wound up to fight the world. A welcoming committee headed by Inspector Bothwell – once 'Mr Rhodesia' – waited at the station. The Brit went berserk and they had a hard time restraining him and getting him into the cells. Garry and I shrugged and left them. The long and the short of the incident was that the Brit jumped bail, popped up in Mozambique and began broadcasting on Radio Zimbabwe about war crimes he had alleged were committed by the RLI.

Garry had a secret job to do for Special Forces HQ, and so he recruited me in a short foray into Matibi Two to sort out some problem at Boli. He never divulged the mission, so I had little idea why we were driving into the TTL. When we arrived, there was nothing the matter anyway, so Garry returned to Salisbury.

While visiting a Shangaan base on a resupply, 10 CTs inadvertently walked into the position and the shit hit the fan: one second, I was talking to one of the Shangaan men; the next, bullets zapped everywhere. The sharp crackle of AKs and light machine guns split the air. For a moment, I wasn't sure who was who, as both sides used the same armaments, and men were dashing and hiding in the failing light; I easily could have shot one of our own people. A ragged and disorganized firefight exploded, where both sides poured bullets in the futile hope of hitting someone. The firefight soon withered to a vicious splutter and wound down to nothing. The CTs smartly withdrew.

I organized a quick sweep through the low scrub on the edge of the encampment to clear the zone just out from the village. While edging around the gloomy timber, I glimpsed a faint movement in the light scrub, almost at my feet: a flit and scurry, like a small animal. Instinct guided me … too close to swing the RPK into action, I thrust out my hand and snatched the PPSH sub-machine gun straight out of his hands, by the cold barrel (the weapon had not been fired). The terrorist – a mere teenager, about 14 and shit-scared, with his eyes bugged out – was crouched frozen in the spiky scrub and so close to me, he could have easily reached out and touched my leg; luck had shielded me. The others quickly scooped him up and marched him away.

The CTs that had swarmed into the south-east in the last half of 1979 carried older weapons. Instead of the modern AK range, more and more entered armed with the World War II Russian PPSH sub-machine gun and SKS semi-automatic rifles. The odd bolt-action rifle had crept in and a couple of FN rifles had been recovered, so were their stockpiles drying up? Was it a result of SAS cross-border raids and sabotage, or was it simply that there was so many ZANLA volunteers that they were dragging out the stuff from the bottom of the barrel? I wasn't privy to that information.

The war was racing to a climax. Security Forces delivered blistering attacks on ZANLA and ZIPRA base camps, railways, bridges and infrastructure throughout Zambia and Mozambique. In September, the news exploded through the radio that a helicopter had been shot down in operations over in Mozambique – killing 14 white Rhodesian soldiers and three crew, including Captain Charlie Small (the army's explosives expert). To the war-weary white population, it heralded another sour blow – particularly when they sensed that the war could not be won. John asked me what I thought … what could I say? I thought that the news would further undermine the morale of the whites in the cities – the most skittish portion of the population.

As the weeks crept on, JOC began to request that the Shangaan Army carry out other assignments. Blistering-hot intelligence sent 20 men scurrying into the Gona Re Zhou National Park, which was right on the south-east corner of the country, to spend a few days on reconnaissance. JOC stirred up the swift deployment to allay fears that a big mob of more than 200 ZANLAs had trampled through the park. I joined Daniel's group for the walk. The park was fortified by thick virgin scrub, steep sandstone cliffs, ancient baobab trees, tons of biting and annoying insects, and little water. Stories floated about the number of CTs who were said to have died of thirst trekking through, so we went prepared. There were also fables of a giant bull elephant with enormous tusks that were so big they ploughed a groove in the dirt if it lowered its head. The same story also claimed that the Games Department had attached a radio transmitter to a collar around its neck so it didn't fall victim to the war. We didn't see any game at all (and certainly not the elephant for which the park was famous), just thick, hardy scrub and rich green trees as far as the eye could see, as well as a million flying insects and some of the hardest country I had attempted to move through in Rhodesia. Needless to say, there were no recent signs of the CTs.

With the political uncertainty, South African troops – dressed in Rhodesian camouflage – slipped into Beitbridge and sealed the border with South Africa under an arrangement with the Zimbabwe-Rhodesia Government. Within a couple of weeks, they suffered unnecessary casualties in Sengwe TTL through a lack of tactical common sense. Asked by JOC to journey to Sengwe to demonstrate the necessary skills to avoid casualties, I agreed, but the mission never got off the ground. I held amicable discussions with two South African captains at Buffalo Range, but they blithely brushed off any assistance and stated firmly they would work it out themselves. They weren't having their little brother telling them what to do; they were here to save us!

After months of wrangling, the British Government – determined to solve the Rhodesia problem – summoned all parties to a peace conference in London. The Zimbabwe-Rhodesia Government, the ZANU-PF terrorists and the leaders of the African States bordering the country were brought together at Lancaster House to negotiate a way to a ceasefire and free elections. As the political squabbles in London intensified, men at Chiredzi JOC quietly found new jobs. Vital jobs sprang up like 'swimming pool attendant', 'corporal in charge of pinning colored pins for operational charts', 'private in charge of sorting out pins into different colors', 'sergeant in charge of reorganizing army stores' and so on. In this charged atmosphere, many rumors floated. One rumor circulated that certain units were offered a cash bonus for CT kills – and a general reluctance to go to the bush started to gently permeate the operational units. Superintendent Felix Cuttler, the Chiredzi JOC boss, strongly suggested I move my HQ base from the Lundi River and into the direct path of terrorist incursions. He named a point on the map just outside Matibi Two, which was closer to the two farm bases. His advice was tactically sound, and three months prior, I would have seriously considered the proposal, but now I decided not to put myself at risk and remained unmoved. Many rumors circulated – a swirl of fantasy and hope, but even a blind man saw where the wash-up would be, but many, many people were in denial.

Any downtime relaxation was spent in Triangle – a company town owned by Triangle Ltd., which grew in the 1920s around sugar production. For night entertainment, I drank myself stupid at the Triangle Country Club. Like all

Rhodesian drinking holes, a rifle rack stood by the entrance like an umbrella stand outside a wet UK pub. Guns were everywhere … GUNS. They were hanging off soldiers, policemen, farmers, council workers, salesmen, contractors, miners, maintenance people, visitors, retirees, bounty hunters and their wives and girlfriends, and even some kids. Looking at all the guns, I believed that the whites would love to sink back into a gunless life. I slipped into my usual drunkard, abusive self – calling a spade a fucking spade and breaking up some of the furniture – only to be thrown out and banned. It followed a long trail of banning orders. I had drastically slimmed down the number of drinking establishments that opened their doors.

In November, John announced that the Shangaan Army had been officially handed over to the Special Forces. It made sense, as Special Branch had too many things on their plate. In the past months, the Security Force Auxiliaries had undergone a number of evolutions and had begun to relieve Guard Force units on PV duties so that GF could be used as infantry. (Guard Force was raised from scratch in 1975 as the permanent guardians of Protected Villages.) The blue denim and AK fad was tossed out, along with the pretence that they were ex-terrorists, and now they wore a standard chocolate-brown uniform. The unit's new motto: '*Pfumo reVahnu*' ('the Spear of the People') – a spear on a cloth badge – was sewn to the arm sleeve. The Heckler & Koch G3 rifle replaced the AK range of weapons. The rabble started to shape up like a disciplined army, but fell short of being one; they still robbed and fought amongst themselves.

With the police withdrawal, Trevor was posted to a police station and so I was left alone with the Shangaans. Promoted to WO2, I was summoned by radio to Fort Victoria Special Forces HQ. I tried to cancel the meeting, as both vehicles sat broken-down in the mechanics' workshop.

The insistent officer at SFHQ snarled something like: "Catch the bloody convoy. This is an urgent meeting."

I cadged a lift to Chiredzi, where I hitched a ride on the Police Reserve vehicle, on the convoy that motored through to Ngundu Halt on the main Beitbridge-Fort Victoria Road. The farmer-Reservist driver said the convoy's final destination was Beitbridge, but that it would meet the northbound convoy at the Halt; however, when the convoy reached the intersection of the Beitbridge-Chiredzi Road, the northbound convoy had not arrived. The Police Reserve driver radioed the Fort Victoria-bound convoy and established that they were an hour behind schedule. As all the cars in this convoy were driving south to Beitbridge, they had no choice and dropped me off. I stood by the roadside – stranded at Ngundu Halt.

I turned to observe a collection of wretched rural stores facing the road – smack in the middle of Indian country. I was not impressed. Ngundu Halt was a pimple in the southern Chibi TTL, where India Troop had rustled up the people in 1977. I surveyed the faded storefronts: curious and hostile Africans squatted on the veranda and radiated the evil eye. Some milled about – chatting in low tones – but the Africans' roving eyes calculated my every movement. In my imagination, I saw a runner link up with the CTs and urged them to dash to Ngundu. He'd tell them of a perfect target: a white boy, standing alone – an absolute free kick! I eased myself next to a large eucalyptus tree and squatted down, with the RPK ready for action. Without communications, the hour dragged out extremely slowly. Waiting impatiently for the connecting convoy, the hands on my Seiko watch dragged round. I decided that enough was enough, and that the time was ripe to resign. This bullshit was the last straw.

I arrived at the Fort Victoria JOC fuming with pent-up anger. Left alone in the scrub, in hostile country, this meeting had better be extremely vital. I asked for directions to SFHQ and, after locating the temporary office building, I entered. Inside, a corporal ushered me through to a separate office, where a captain and lieutenant waited. The immaculately dressed, office-bound Captain Nobody took an immediate dislike to the non-regimental soldier: my canvas runners, denim jeans, green army shirt and FRELIMO cap didn't impress Mr Neatness. Not bothering with even an introduction or nominal greeting, he instantly noticed the RPK in my hands and stood up sharply from behind his desk and demanded the machine gun. I was ordered to hand it over. A rude, arrogant bastard, I told him to sod off. He rounded the desk and launched into a raging tirade, which was backed up by the snot-nosed lieutenant, who was fresh out of the School of Infantry.

"I command the Shangaan Army!" he raged, "an' there'll be no more independent operators! Starting today, there are immediate changes! The Shangaans' machine gun ratio is too high, so you'll withdraw eight of them for other units. I need the three RPGs. Blah, blah, blah. Got that, CSM?"

Got that? "Sure," I seethed to myself.

He could have radioed for the extra weapons. There was no need for the road journey and all that pissing about: cadging lifts, jumping convoys and squatting alone in Ngundu Halt, just to hear this nonsense. He might have even got off his lazy arse and personally motored to Chiredzi to introduce himself and assess the Shangaans. Once again, I was snookered by a know-all base camp warrior. Neither officer looked as if they had been within 10 kilometers of a firefight. I quietly told him to fuck off, and then stormed out – leaving him speechless; then I returned to Chiredzi, where I promptly quit. There were too many bullshit artists in charge.

More bad news started to filter in: I heard that David James had been killed in a vehicle ambush in Chibi on 29 August. Attached to Special Branch, he drove straight into an ambush while responding to a tip-off. I had met David in 1975 when I was stationed at Inyati, and he had served down the road at Fort Rixon – both tiny, rural Matabeleland police stations. We first met when both of us were shunted off to Gwanda on an assignment to assist in protection duties of the Prime Minister, Ian Smith, who was in town for a series of speaking engagements. A Special Branch unit provided the PM personal protection, and we had drawn the short straw, which was to guard the private house where Smith was lodging. In uniform, we were the police presence outside the brick dwelling. Posted together at the bottom of the driveway, we shivered through the cold night. I recall that Ian Smith arrived back with his genial host and, when he spotted David and I standing outside, invited us inside, handed us both a beer and then talked a little before tottering off to bed. In 1975, he looked tired and gaunt.

Afterwards, David and I met occasionally on weekends off to drink copious amounts of beer – and we both ended up competing for the same woman. Once, after compulsory PATU training in Bulawayo, we both drank to excess at a bar and I slipped away. Later, David staggered to the woman's house – knocking on the door and calling through the closed window – as she and I lay in her bed, laughing … another fine young man lost.

By December 1979, the Lancaster House negotiations ushered the war to a spluttering climax – the months of tedious talks in London finally screwing down to an agreement. Under the arrangement, the warring parties withdrew their armies into controlled zones prior to a democratic election in 1980. The Commonwealth Monitoring Group – a mix of UK and Commonwealth army units – flew into the country to oversee the disengagement. CT forces were assigned assembly areas in tribal lands that were calculated so they could walk directly to them. Small Commonwealth army units were tasked with monitoring the terrorist forces at each assembly area, and they welcomed the suspicious terrorist hordes, as well as keeping an eye on SF behavior. It was a tense period for the Security Forces, who wondered both individually and collectively what the outcome would bring.

18

The Final Months: January–May 1980

I spent New Year 1980 at the Victoria Falls Hotel playing ordinary tennis, drinking liters of cold beer and being a nuisance once again. I watched the fine spray mist rise from the famous Falls from the bar – not venturing out for a closer inspection. Steve – studying for a university degree in South Africa – was also there. While one-legged, he still played a mean game of tennis. I tried courting a glamorous woman staying in the Victoria Falls Hotel, but fell well short of the mark. Agitated and unsure of what was next, I drank beers with some Australian and NZ members of the Monitoring Force, who stopped to take in the sights and anyone else in a mood to party. It was time to consider future options: should I return to New Zealand? I was not convinced yet.

In January 1980, a woman named Debbie and I drove my VW down the main highway and past my old hunting grounds to South Africa for a holiday. I needed time out to think … where to next? We toured Natal, from the Zulu battlegrounds at Rorke's Drift and Isandlwana, to the beaches of Coffee Bay in Transkei. We enjoyed each other's company, but we also fought a lot. I mulled over the future: Zimbabwe looked rocky; a move to South Africa could entice the lure of combat, but I didn't want that; the Western World lacked the will to win. Also, I was not a supporter of the Afrikaners' philosophy and gauged that South Africa's government would topple in 10 years.

We returned to Zimbabwe-Rhodesia and I ventured back to farm security work at the Mere Estate, which lasted through to the national elections held in March. The security team had passed through a number of hands since my last venture. Months before, one bleak night, a farmer's son, who was home on a break from university and seeking to earn some coin, was accidentally shot and badly wounded whilst playing 'Security Guard'. Now, the mixed bunch included a red-haired ex-RLI dope fiend and two African ex-RAR soldiers, so I resumed the nightly farm patrols whilst pondering. South Africa still strongly beckoned like an alluring, but unreliable lover: the South African Consulate furiously recruited Rhodesian servicemen for their own war in South-West

Africa (Namibia) and Angola. Many contemporaries headed south to join the South African Army – including Phil Smith – split between 32 Battalion and 44 Parachute Brigade, but I wasn't too sure.

Friends in Salisbury tried to dissuade me from going back to New Zealand – pointing out that I would arrive only to find the very reason why I left, and it made sense, so studying possible opportunities caught most of the spare time. Was there any work in the new Zimbabwe? My toolbox of civilian urban skills lay empty – and besides, employers were jittery. The nation teetered on a razor's edge. Farming sprang to mind – capitalizing on the two years spent as a farm manager in Centenary during 1973-1975 – but working the land involved risk: land division must come into sharp focus for the next government and large chunks could be appropriated to meet the African aspirations.

As political events turned sharply against the white ruling elite, I watched fascinated as the white farmer changed allegiance like a chameleon. Men in the district who were sworn life-and-death Ian Smith supporters quietly hedged their bets with the local ZANU-PF Party. One no-nonsense Smith fanatic threw his name in the hat to be the Marandellas ZANU-PF agricultural advisor, and even the loudmouth farmer who publically espoused that Ian Smith was too soft altered his ideals in a big hurry – backpedalling at a hundred miles an hour. One grizzled farmer offhandedly told me that he'd happily hand me over to any ZANU-PF committee investigating the war; after all, I was an expendable foreigner. I was shocked watching a stampede of farmers – the backbone of Smith's government – elbowing each other to leverage support from a new terrorist government. Self-interest illuminated brightly, and their actions became the defining 'lightbulb moment'. The swing from one political extreme to the other within weeks warned me that it was time to go.

The *Herald* newspaper reported that the ZANLA and ZIPRA terrorist gangs had moved seamlessly into assembly areas pitched across the country, in accordance with the Lancaster House Agreement. The Commonwealth soldiers stationed at the assembly points greeted and guided them in, and the terrorists had to be housed, fed and entertained for the long months ahead (the UK enjoyed that responsibility). The white business community in-country earned a small fortune supplying gear ranging from toothpaste to beef.

Many whites were still delusional and still firmly believed that Bishop Muzorewa could win the elections, when he was simply incapable of stopping the war; in fact, as Prime Minister, the war intensified. Under his stewardship, dynamic army raids into Zambia and Mozambique crippled their economies.

The author working in farm security in the Marandellas District during the 1980 elections.

Also, the fact that the white civil service still tightly held onto the economic reins, as well as the police and the armed forces, didn't aid the impression that Muzorewa controlled the country. Additionally, his media performances, unfortunately, came across as weak and indecisive, when compared to the belligerent Mugabe and Nkomo.

If the white intelligence bosses had stepped out of their city offices and talked to the blacks in the tribal areas, they would have found out that rural Africans simply didn't care who won the election as long as the new government absolutely guaranteed the end of the killing – and only Robert Mugabe could do that.

In the murky mist of rumor and speculation during the political transition, an undercurrent swirled among the white troops in the dark Salisbury bars that the army planned to pull off a coup if Mugabe won the election. The gist of the plan lay in the Security Forces utterly flattening the CTs' assembly areas in a surprise attack and seizing power – a very simplistic plan if, indeed, one existed. Looking back, any coup was unrealistic: no country, not even South Africa, could support a coup after a 'democratically' elected government had come to power.

Outside the set timeframes, a dribble of CT gangs and pseudo-CTs wandered the farming areas on the way to the assembly points. They were a nuisance, so firm instructions dealt out by JOC stated that if they were not ensconced at the assembly point, they were legitimate targets. A couple of local-farmer PATU sticks were happy to oblige to get the last legitimate hit in, but others watched anxiously from the sidelines. Who was going to shoot anyone this close to the end? And, of course, miscellaneous bandits slunk about – looking to rob unwary folk. They all had to be dealt with in a diplomatic fashion; the time for the big stick was over.

Soon, concrete realities flew thick and fast. Archenemy Robert Mugabe – the man the white government painted as the Devil Incarnate – flew into the country to an enormous hero's welcome. Vast crowds ecstatically greeted 'Terrorist Number One' as he strode down onto the country's soil. The election process got under way: intimidation throughout the land ran riot; murders of opposition political candidates and their local party supporters accelerated; senior government figures pressured the English Governor, Lord Soames, to abandon the elections; allegations and counter-claims about ZANLA's true numbers in the assembly point camps seesawed; steady reports claimed that *mujibas* and other unemployed youths had turned up with rusted, old SKS and tired PPSH weapons to make up the numbers, while the professional fighters remained in the tribal lands to absolutely ensure the vote went their way; assassination attempts on Mugabe by government agencies were botched; the head of the Central Intelligence Organization, Ken Flower, and the Security Forces' General Peter Walls flew to Mozambique for talks with their government; Josiah Tongogara, the ZANLA commander, died suddenly – and mysteriously – in a road accident in Mozambique; armed RLI troops patrolled the streets of Salisbury to keep the peace – and they represented the final winding down of white aspirations.

Most of this frantic activity bypassed the Mere Estate. I drove the armored Land Rover at night – following the dusty farm roads – and slept and read and listened to the radio news by day. We may as well have been on another planet: farming routines carried on unchanged each day, and not even a national upheaval stopped the cyclic farming practices. One noticeable hiccup concerned the increased number of starving dogs streaming out of the tribal areas hunting for food. The rangy, greyhound-looking animals – emboldened by hunger and, in some cases, rabies – slunk around the housing and I was

Farm workers ready to vote with Colin and Jennifer, 1980.

tasked with shooting and disposing of their bodies. Nearly every day, I was called upon to destroy a loose dog.

In early March 1980, Rusape JOC asked me to carry out an impromptu survey in the Dowa APA to establish the voting aspirations in the upcoming elections. Why not? Dowa was a patchwork of African small-farm holdings that separated the Mere Estate from the Chiduku TTL. With the two ex-RAR soldiers, we sauntered up the main road and stopped to talk with anyone we met. The locals stated bluntly that they'd vote Mugabe, just to stop the fighting, as a Marxist government was better than an endless war. Looking squarely in my eyes, they left no doubt as to their resolve; they were sick of the fighting and absolutely adamant. No one shied away, and all were eager to voice an opinion. I reckon that if Donald Duck could have absolutely guaranteed the end of the killing, he'd have been a hot chance in the election. I handed over the report to the JOC: funny enough, it contradicted the other surveys they had carried out.

Later that month, Robert Mugabe won the election in a convincing landslide. I was not surprised he won, only as to the extent. The result encircled the white community and fed the rampant rumor hurricane. White citizens looked visibly stunned and timid, like alien life had just taken up the reins of power. That night, Mugabe appeared on television looking very much a decent, patient and understanding leader behind his studious glasses – extending a hand of friendship and offering reconciliation. The nervous white community breathed a huge sigh of relief, except those who knew that the man behind the heavy-framed glasses was indeed a Marxist Devil. Mugabe, under the calm exterior, simmered with anger at being cheated out of a military victory, from which he could indiscriminately lash out at the white population. The non-believers packed and departed in big numbers; I was one of them. I sold off a cache of automatic weapons to cash up. The possession of a secret armory to those who remained behind was insurance in the new Zimbabwe. Finally, it was time to pack the bags and go. In early May, I flew out of Salisbury and headed for Auckland.

The war claimed a minimum of 30,000 dead, and hundreds of thousands wounded and maimed. Robert Mugabe began his rule in May 1980 – taking ownership of the white legacy: a stable government; a functioning civil service; an independent judiciary; a national infrastructure in place; and an operating and resilient economy, which was described by President Nyerere of Tanzania as the 'Jewel of Africa'.

The Rhodesians fought a brilliant, but increasingly desperate campaign against an enemy whose numbers grew far too large to possibly contain. The fact that the Security Forces were able to fight the swelling ranks of the enemy to a standstill – and without losing – enabled the politicians to use that strength in their bargaining. The whites lost the reins of political power, but still held economic clout; but for many whites, the change was not positive. From 1976-1980, 48,196 whites from all professions had emigrated – some 20 percent of the European population. From 1980, in the next few years, larger sections of whites reluctantly packed and departed – seeing no buoyant future for their children. Looking back, the Rhodesian leadership failed to see the future first and adapt in time.

The SFA was swiftly disbanded in April 1980 – a month after Mugabe's election win – but the Support Unit is still an active branch of the Zimbabwe Republic Police.

Postscript

In 1980, Phil Smith joined South Africa's 32 Battalion – fighting in Angola. 32 Battalion was a mixture of Angolan Africans formerly aligned with FNLA, with a nucleus of white NCOs and officers; a number of experienced fighters were foreigners. After a couple of years of active service with 32 Battalion, he married and joined the Regular South African Army. After service in South-West Africa (Namibia), he departed the army, but stayed in the fringe element of war. Phil was killed in action with Executive Outcomes in Angola in March 1993. (Executive Outcomes was a private military company founded in South Africa by Eeben Barlow in 1989. Barlow was a former lieutenant colonel in the South African Defence Force.)

Chris Rogers left Zimbabwe in 1980 to join the South African Army, along with many other Rhodesian soldiers. After service in the 44 Parabats, he married and settled into a management role in the private security business. Tragically, Chris was shot dead in an armored car robbery in 1998.

Chris and Janice made arrangements for the disposal of their farm property, sold removable items, departed Rhodesia in May 1980 and then returned to Canada, where Chris continued with the flying bug.

Mick Busby reverted to uniform police in Salisbury. The police offered to pay bonuses to officers that agreed to stay on through the transitional period, which was an offer Mick took up, but he attended a complaint at the Meikles Hotel and arrested Rex Nhongo, who was the senior ZANLA commander. It was alleged that during the patrol car ride back to the police station, Mick mimicked a K-Car commander ("I have terrorists visual.") It was not viewed as politically correct, and Mick returned to London, where he started a private security firm.

Ray Hughes fulfilled his Chibi promise and joined the Rhodesian Air Force Pilot Training Course 33 in September 1978 – passing through the pilot training course and finishing in February 1980. On the demise of Rhodesia, he resigned from the Zimbabwe Air Force and joined the South African Air Force. Ray was killed in a night training flight near Port Elizabeth, South Africa in May 1982.

Billy Pring served with Support Unit and stayed on after Mugabe's election win. He served in the Zimbabwe Republic Police Support Unit until 1983, when he resigned as a lance chief inspector.

André Stapa did not make the SAS selection and turned to pilot training. He finished the battery of tests and was selected for the Rhodesian Air Force's flight training (PTC 34). He finished the course in August 1980, when Robert Mugabe ruled the new Zimbabwe; he was the recipient of the Sword of Honour. He resigned from the Zimbabwe Air Force and joined the South African Air Force. In November 1987, Captain Stapa was lost when his Impala jet failed to pull out of a steep dive (probably shot down) on an operation over Angola and was killed.

THE END

Bibliography

The following books were referred to in order to compare dates and settings:

Caute, D., *Under the Skin* (Evanston IL: Northwest University Press, 1983).

Cilliers, J.K., *Counter Insurgency in Rhodesia* (London: Croom Helm, 1985).

Cole, B., *The Elite. The Story of the Rhodesian SAS* (Transkei: Three Knights, 1984).

Lovett, J., *Contact* (Salisbury: Galaxie Press, 1977).

Moorcroft, P. and McLaughlin, P., *Chimurenga! The War in Rhodesia* (Marshalltown: Sigma Books, 1982).

Ranger, T., *Peasant Consciousness and Guerilla Warfare in Zimbabwe* (Oakland CA: University of California Press, 1985).

Reid-Daly, R. (as told to P. Stiff), *Selous Scouts. Top Secret War* (Alberton: Galago Publishing, 1982).

Stiff, P., *Taming the Landmine* (Alberton: Galago Publishing, 1986).

Wood, Dr J.R.T., *The War Diaries of André Dennison* (Gibraltar: Ashanti Publishing, 1989).